ASSESSING
THE THREAT

ASSESSING
THE THREAT
The Chinese Military and Taiwan's Security

Edited by Michael D. Swaine,
Andrew N. D. Yang, and Evan S. Medeiros
with Oriana Skylar Mastro

CARNEGIE ENDOWMENT
FOR INTERNATIONAL PEACE

WASHINGTON DC ▪ MOSCOW ▪ BEIJING ▪ BEIRUT ▪ BRUSSELS

Carnegie Endowment for International Peace
1779 Massachusetts Avenue, N.W.
Washington, D.C. 20036
202-483-7600, Fax 202-483-1840
www.CarnegieEndowment.org

The Carnegie Endowment for International Peace normally does not take institutional positions on public policy issues; the views and recommendations presented in this publication do not necessarily represent the views of the Carnegie Endowment, its officers, staff, or trustees.

To order, contact:
Hopkins Fulfillment Service
P.O. Box 50370, Baltimore, MD 21211-4370
1-800-537-5487 or 1-410-516-6956
Fax: 1-410-516-6998

Typesetting by Circle Graphics, Inc.

Library of Congress Cataloging-in-Publication Data

Assessing the threat : the Chinese military and Taiwan's security / edited by Michael D. Swaine, Andrew N.D. Yang, and Evan S. Medeiros ; with Oriana Skylar Mastro.
   p. cm.
   Includes bibliographical references and index.
   ISBN-13: 978-0-87003-238-7
   1. China—Military policy—21st century. 2. China. Zhongguo ren min jie fang jun.
3. Taiwan Strait—Strategic aspects. 4. Chinese reunification question, 1949- 5. National security—Taiwan. 6. United States—Military policy—21st century. 7. National security—East Asia. I. Swaine, Michael D. II. Yang, Andrew N. D. III. Medeiros, Evan S.

UA835.A78 2007
355'.033051249—dc22
2007020270

12 11 10 09 08 07   1 2 3 4 5   1st Printing 2007

Contents

Section Three: Threats, Deterrence, and Escalation Control in a Taiwan Contingency

Section Four: Conclusions

Acknowledgments

THIS BOOK WOULD NOT HAVE BEEN POSSIBLE without the diligent and talented efforts of many individuals. We owe a special debt of gratitude to Andrew and Yi Su Yang of the Council of Advanced Policy Studies (CAPS) in Taipei, who organize and fund the annual CAPS-RAND-CEIP conference on the PLA. The Carnegie Endowment's Junior Fellow for 2006–2007, Oriana Skylar Mastro, performed the bulk of the yeoman's work involved in editing and guiding the revision of the original papers. She also contributed greatly to the completion of the introduction and conclusion. Richard Berkowitz of Circle Graphics, Inc. as well as Carrie Mullen and Ilonka Oszvald of Carnegie's publication department facilitated our effort to produce a volume in record time. Evan Medeiros of RAND was instrumental in developing and organizing each of the 2004–2006 PLA conferences and in providing comments on many of the papers selected for inclusion in this volume. Mark Medish, vice president for studies–Russia, China, and Eurasia at the Carnegie Endowment, reviewed the manuscript and also provided invaluable comments. Doris Duangboudda, the China Program assistant, supported us through the publication process and assisted us immensely with proofreading. Betsy Winship of Columbia Publishing Services provided excellent copyediting and Chris Phillips of Circle Graphics, Inc. created the cover design. Lastly, we deeply appreciate the time, effort, and expertise of the authors and the other participants in the 2004, 2005, and 2006 CAPS-RAND-CEIP conferences.

Acronyms

AAA	Anti-aircraft artillery
AAW	Anti-air warfare
ABMI	Asian Bond Market Initiative
AEW	Airborne early warning
AFC	Asian financial crisis
AIDC	Aero Industry Development Center (Taiwan)
AIP	Air independent propulsion
AMRAAM	Advanced medium-range air-to-air missiles
AMS	Academy of Military Science
APEC	Asia-Pacific Economic Forum
APT	ASEAN Plus Three
ARF	ASEAN Regional Forum
ASAT	Anti-satellite
ASCM	Anti-ship cruise missile
ASDF	Air Self-Defense Force (Japan)
ASEAN	Association of Southeast Asian Nations
ASL	Anti-secession law
ASUW	Anti-surface warfare
ASW	Anti-submarine warfare
AWACS	Airborne Warning and Control System
BDA	Battle damage assessments
BVR	Beyond visible range
C2	Command and control

C4I	Command, control, communications, computers, and intelligence
C4ISR	Command, control, communications, computers, intelligence, surveillance, and reconnaissance
CBM	Confidence-building measure
CC&D	Camouflage, concealment, and deception
CCP	Chinese Communist Party
CCPCC	CCP Central Committee
CIS	Commonwealth of Independent States
CMC	Central Military Commission
CMI	Chiang Mai Initiative
CND	Computer network defense
CNE	Computer network exploit
CNO	Computer network operations
CNP	Comprehensive national power
CONUS	Continental United States
CRAF	Civil Reserve Airfleet
CSG	Carrier Strike Group
CSIST	Chung-Shan Institute of Science and Technology (Taiwan)
CTBT	Comprehensive Test Ban Treaty
CVBG	Carrier Battle Group
DCS	Direct commercial sales
DDG	Guided-missile destroyer
DDOS	Distributed denial of service
DoD	Department of Defense (USA)
DPP	Democratic Progressive Party (Taiwan)
DPRK	Democratic People's Republic of Korea
DSP	Defense Support Program
EAEC	East Asian Economic Caucus
EAS	East Asia Summit
ECCM	Electronic counter-countermeasure
ECM	Electronic countermeasures
EEZ	Exclusive Economic Zone
ELINT	Electronic intelligence
EU	European Union
EW	Early warning

FDI	Foreign direct investment
FFG	Guided-missile frigate
FMS	Foreign military sales
FOCAC	Forum of China-Africa Cooperation
FTA	Free Trade Area
FYP	Five-Year Plan, now Five-Year Program
GPD	General Political Department
GPS	Global Positioning System
HARM	High-speed anti-radiation missile
IC	Intelligence community
ICBM	Intercontinental ballistic missile
IDF	Indigenous defensive fighter
IEA	International Energy Agency
IO	Information operations
IRBM	Intermediate-range ballistic missile
IUSS	Integrated underwater surveillance system
IW	Information warfare
JCS	Joint Chiefs of Staff
JDAM	Joint direct attack munition
JMSDF	Japanese Maritime Self-Defense Force
KMT	Kuomintang (Guomindang)
Kt	Knot
LACM	Land-attack cruise missile
LSD	Landing ship dock
LST	Landing ship tank
MAD	Mutual assured destruction
MBT	Main battle tank
MCM	Mine countermeasures
MEADS	Medium Extended Air Defense System
MIB	Military Intelligence Bureau (Taiwan)
MIW	Mine warfare
MMCA	Military Maritime Consultation Agreement
MND	Ministry of National Defense (Taiwan)
MOE	Ministry of Energy (China)
MR	Military region
MRBM	Midrange ballistic missile
MTW	Major Theater War

NAD	Navy Area Defense
NAFTA	North Atlantic Free Trade Agreement
NCO	Noncommissioned officers
NDU	National Defense University (China)
NFU	No first use
NIPRNET	Nonclassified Internet Protocol Router Network
NM	Nautical mile
NPC	National People's Congress (China)
NPR	Nuclear Posture Review
NPT	Nuclear Nonproliferation Treaty
NSC	National Security Council
OECD	Organization for Economic Cooperation and Development
ONI	Office of Naval Intelligence
OODA	Observe, orient, decide, and act
PACAF	Pacific Air Forces
PACOM	Pacific Command
PAP	People's Armed Police
PKO	Peacekeeping operations
PLA	People's Liberation Army
PLAAF	PLA Air Force
PLAN	PLA Navy
PLANAF	PLAN Air Force
POL	Petroleum, oils, and lubricants
PRC	People's Republic of China
PSC	Politburo Standing Committee
PSYOP	Psychological operation
ROC	Republic of China
ROE	Rules of engagement
ROK	Republic of Korea
SAARC	South Asian Association for Regional Cooperation
SAM	Surface-to-air missile
SCO	Shanghai Cooperation Organization
SIGINT	Signals intelligence
SLAMRAAM	Surface-launched advanced medium-range air-to-air missile
SLBM	Submarine-launched ballistic missile

SLOC	Strategic lines of communication
SOA	Speed of advance
SOF	Special operations forces
SRBM	Short-range ballistic missile
TAC	Treaty of Amity and Cooperation (ASEAN)
TAF	Taiwan Air Force
TALSG	Taiwan Affairs Leading Small Group
TDC	Taiwan Defense Command (USA)
TECRO	Taipei Economic Cultural Representative Office
TEL	Transporter-erector-launcher
THAAD	Terminal/Theater High-Altitude Area Defense System
TOW	Tube-launched, optically tracked, wire-guided
TPFDL	Time-phased force deployment list
TRA	Taiwan Relations Act
UNCLOS	United Nations Convention on the Law of the Sea
USAF	United States Air Force
USAFE	United States Air Forces Europe
WIGELC	Wing-in-ground effect landing craft
WMD	Weapons of mass destruction
WTO	World Trade Organization

Preface

THIS VOLUME CONTAINS a selection of updated and revised papers originally presented at the 2004, 2005, and 2006 conferences on the People's Liberation Army (PLA), which were held in Taiwan and co-sponsored by the Carnegie Endowment for International Peace (CEIP), the RAND Corporation, and the Taipei-based Council for Advanced Policy Studies (CAPS). This conference, organized by CAPS each year since 1992, brings together leading American and Taiwan experts (as well as, at times, specialists from across Asia and Europe) to examine in detail different aspects of the Chinese military. The papers presented at the 2004–2006 conferences were particularly relevant to the changing threat environment facing Taiwan. They addressed, respectively, the dangers of military escalation in the Taiwan Strait, the latest advances in PLA capabilities, and China's security relationship with the United States and the Asia-Pacific region. The resulting volume incorporates aspects of all three subjects, divided into four major sections.

Section one, an introductory section, contains two chapters. Michael D. Swaine and Oriana Skylar Mastro summarize the major arguments contained in the succeeding chapters. Alex Liebman provides a unique perspective on the larger regional strategic context for the PLA threat.

Section two contains three chapters that examine a wide range of underexplored topics relating to PLA capabilities and doctrine that are particularly relevant to Taiwan's security. Dean Cheng assesses PLA concepts and actions in the area of joint operations. Lonnie D. Henley looks at Chinese views on war control and escalation management. Roy D. Kamphausen and Justin Liang provide a comprehensive study of PLA power projection.

Section three focuses more directly on the threat to Taiwan and the difficulties in maintaining deterrence and escalation control in the Taiwan Strait that result from existing trends in Chinese military modernization. Kenneth W. Allen and Bernard D. Cole assess the implications for deterrence and escalation of recent advances in PLA air force and naval capabilities, respectively. Brad Roberts discusses how the Chinese and American approaches to nuclear weapons might contribute to instability in a Taiwan crisis. James Mulvenon examines People's Republic of China (PRC) information operations and their potential role in a Taiwan contingency. Andrew N. D. Yang assesses Taiwan's defense modernization and its resulting ability to respond to the Chinese threat to the island. Roger Cliff examines the U.S. regional response to the Chinese military buildup, particularly as it relates to a Taiwan contingency.

Section four, the conclusion, contains two chapters. Alan D. Romberg assesses the drivers for change in the East Asian security environment and their future implications for the PLA. Michael D. Swaine and Oriana Skylar Mastro provide some overarching observations derived from the preceding chapters and other recent sources about the current and likely future characteristics of the PLA threat to Taiwan, the cross-strait military balance, escalation dynamics, and the role of the larger region in a Taiwan crisis.

Each author's personal expertise was essential in making this volume a comprehensive and rigorous analysis of PLA modernization and its implications for Taiwan's security. The authors come from academic, military, and government backgrounds and are all prominent authorities on the topic that they address in this volume. For more information about the authors, please consult the Contributors section at the end of the book.

SECTION ONE

Introduction and Regional Context

1

Introduction

Michael D. Swaine and Oriana Skylar Mastro

TAKEN TOGETHER, the chapters in this volume comprise a unique combination of studies of relevance to Taiwan's changing threat environment
and Asian security. In addition to providing relatively straightforward
assessments of recent major advances in China's air and naval power,
this volume also addresses vital aspects of People's Liberation Army
(PLA) doctrine and capabilities not often (or sufficiently) connected
with the study of Taiwan's security. These include joint operations,
war control, information operations, nuclear capabilities, strategy and
doctrine, and region-wide power projection efforts. Also included
are broader examinations of China's Asian security strategy and the
regional security architecture. In many chapters (particularly in section
three), attention is given to the impact of evolving PLA capabilities and
views on critical aspects of deterrence stability and escalation control,
especially across the Taiwan Strait. The overall result is a more comprehensive and complex picture of the potential Chinese military threat
to Taiwan—and the larger challenge to Asia—than usually appears in
studies of the subject.

The chapter on China's strategy toward Asia by Alex Liebman (chapter 2) provides an important context for the assessment of Chinese
military modernization and the PLA threat to Taiwan. Liebman argues
that Beijing's overarching strategic objective is "to increase its influence
in Asia without provoking the emergence of a countervailing coalition
of states." Its resulting strategy is thus to "deter without provoking,

reassure without appeasing"—a delicate and difficult task because, as Liebman states, "efforts at deterrence make signals of reassurance less credible (and vice versa)." He examines the tactics that China has used to achieve this challenging objective, including efforts to reassure its neighbors through its resolution of border disputes, pledges of noninterference toward weaker states, various economic development initiatives, and growing involvement in multilateral institutions. On the deterrence side of the equation, Liebman recognizes that China has at times employed potentially destabilizing military-political tactics to prevent what it regards as potentially threatening behavior on the part of other countries or Taiwan, such as increasing its military preparation, passing the anti-secession law, and engaging in proactive diplomacy to counter Taiwan independence.

Liebman focuses considerable attention on how China has used multilateral institutions and economic development initiatives to increase its influence in Asia and reassure neighbors in an attempt to offset the negative impact of its efforts to deter Taiwan. Although much has been written on Beijing's increased involvement in multilateral institutions, Liebman offers a different take on the issue; in order to achieve its conflicting goals, China is attempting to use the membership of institutions such as the Association of Southeast Asian Nations (ASEAN) Plus Three, the East Asia Summit (EAS), the Shanghai Cooperation Organization (SCO), the South Asian Association for Regional Cooperation (SAARC), and the Six-Party Talks to balance against stronger states and achieve control over the decisions of the group. As Liebman states, "by being selective in negotiations over the membership of each organization, China can shape the strategic context and prevent unfriendly coalitions from emerging as it gains a say in an ever-widening range of issues within these institutions." He dubs this strategy "hubs and spokes multilateralism" because it creates a set of overlapping institutions in which China is the key duplicated member. However, Liebman acknowledges that the success rate of this "hubs and spokes multilateralism" has been mixed; in most cases, China cannot unilaterally control the membership and cannot prevent other states from forming new organizations in which China is not a member.

Liebman argues that China's approach to economic development is designed largely to support its basic strategic objectives: "grow globally, reassure East Asia." In particular, its approach toward economic regionalism plays a role in its strategy to reassure its neighbors. Liebman reviews the past decade of East Asia economic integration and concludes that, contrary to popular belief, the economic effect of these agreements have been rather limited, while the political gains for China (in terms of convincing its neighbors that China's economic growth is beneficial to them) have been substantial. Moreover, he argues that China's efforts at regional economic integration are designed to reassure its neighbors, not cut off other powers from the region. Hence, given China's interests and goals in the region, China is likely to continue to encourage an East Asia that is open to foreign trade and investment.

Taken as a whole, Liebman shows that Beijing's Asia strategy can operate to constrain significantly Taiwan's political and economic maneuvering room in Asia while facilitating its efforts to deter Taiwan independence through both military and political means.

Section two examines in some detail several aspects of PLA capabilities and doctrine that are often insufficiently examined in standard studies of the Chinese military, despite their implications for Taiwan's security and the larger regional environment. In the first chapter of this section (chapter 3), Dean Cheng examines a central aspect of military strategy: joint operations. While the U.S. military has been conducting joint operations for decades, the concept only began to generate significant attention within the Chinese military in the 1990s, partially as a result of the successful U.S. military campaigns in the first Gulf War and in the former Yugoslavia. The Chinese military leadership realized that it must reorient PLA doctrine and operations to achieve sufficient levels of jointness, especially given the arguably growing likelihood of a Sino-U.S. confrontation over Taiwan. This became especially notable in 1999, when the PLA issued the so-called "Year of Regulations" that encapsulated its new approach to warfare.

By reviewing the evolution of PLA thinking on warfare through the analysis of major Chinese military writings, Cheng shows how the PLA identified, evaluated, and eventually began to adapt the concept of jointness in response to contemporary events. According to Cheng, based on observations of recent wars and trends in modern technology, the Chinese began to appreciate ". . . that joint operations would eclipse single-service operations" in the future of modern warfare. As a result, the PLA developed a quasi-doctrine about joint operations; defining the concept and establishing its essential components, exploring differences from other strategies such as combined arms/services campaigns, and identifying its influence on command and coordination. Cheng argues that the PLA sees great promise in joint operations because they "offer the greatest chance of utilizing synergies among the PLA's services, including their various operating environments. . .and their respective technological strengths. . .to mitigate individual weaknesses."

However, Cheng also points out that, because the PLA's only experience with joint operations to date was the seizure of an offshore island from the Republic of China in 1955 (the Yijiangshan campaign), the Chinese military still has a long way to go until joint operations become an integral part of its military strategy and operations. At the same time, Cheng examines the ways in which the PLA has already begun to move toward joint operations, through changes in its training regimen and in the establishment of joint communications teams, for example. If achieved successfully, this shift toward jointness could have an enormous impact on the prosecution of future Chinese military campaigns, especially actions involving a maritime theater, such as Taiwan. To be effective, any attempt to apply force against Taiwan (and, quite possibly, the United States) would require extensive and detailed coordination between ground, air, and naval forces over a sustained period of time. Cheng's analysis shows that the PLA is serious about moving toward jointness, but faces daunting prospects; how successful the Chinese will be in shifting toward this new war-fighting approach, and how it will affect China's next military campaign, are yet to be seen.

Lonnie D. Henley's chapter (chapter 4) addresses another recent development in Chinese military doctrine that is of great relevance to Taiwan: the integration of the concept of war control. According to Henley, this is a new concept among Chinese security specialists and was discussed in print by military academic specialists for the first time around 2000. War control is "a wide-ranging activity uniting all the elements of comprehensive national power to shape the international environment so as to make war less likely." This includes preventing or containing the escalation of a political crisis into a military conflict, ensuring that China will be in a favorable position and will have the initiative should conflict occur, and, in that case, will be able to control the conflict and ensure that military operations will serve Beijing's larger political objectives.

Henley examines the Chinese concept of war control as it applies to different stages of a crisis or conflict (e.g., efforts to shape the international environment, measures taken to manage a crisis should one occur, and those to be taken during war if crisis management fails). In this analysis, the Chinese identify various military measures that China could take to contain a war, such as military intimidation and deterrence, controlling the overall war objectives and military targets, and controlling the military operational parameters and war-fighting techniques. According to Henley, the Chinese clearly appreciate that it is important to control the pace, rhythm, and intensity of a crisis or conflict as well as the nature of the end of the war and the postconflict environment. He also notes that the Chinese place considerable emphasis on seizing the initiative in war control, but they do not seem to consider the possibility that this emphasis could contribute to unwanted escalation.

Henley argues that one should expect that in the coming years the concept of war control will continue to evolve in Chinese operational doctrine, with particular relevance to a Taiwan contingency. This doctrine already presents some implications for China's actions during a crisis, however. For example, the emphasis on seizing and maintaining the initiative makes it likely that large troop movements, the mobilization of strategic nuclear forces, and other threatening actions will occur in any serious crisis, regardless of whether Beijing actually plans to attack. Moreover, Henley notes that Beijing's approach to war control and crisis management reinforces the Chinese tendency to adopt a rigid stance on issues of principle at the start of crisis; China views this as "an effective tactic for gaining and maintaining control of the situation." Furthermore, if the PLA literature on war control does parallel the thinking of the Chinese leadership, an attack on Taiwan would most likely be designed to also achieve political goals rather than purely military ones, with military targets selected to "maximize the political impact on the enemy's will to fight," for example. Finally, and perhaps most troubling, Henley suggests that if a campaign is going poorly for China, rather than accepting defeat, war control theorists would advocate "bold and unexpected actions to create a more favorable environment for the final political struggle."[1]

The ability of the Chinese military to influence regional security and Taiwan's threat environment in particular extends beyond issues relating to PLA force modernization and operational deployment capabilities. In chapter 5, Roy D. Kamphausen and Justin Liang offer a more comprehensive assessment of how the PLA contributes to the projection of Chinese power and influence in Asia. They argue that the Chinese military is contributing to China's comprehensive national power (CNP) in three ways: by responding to crises, by contributing to deterrence, and by enhancing regional dialogue and understanding.

In analyzing how the PLA projects power by responding to crises, Kamphausen and Liang put forth a much needed analysis on China's role in UN Peacekeeping Operations (PKO). They point out that China's support for UN PKO allows Beijing to add a more significant military component to the pursuit of its foreign policy interests and helps the PLA advance certain capabilities more rapidly. The PLA is also actively involved in deterrence, the act of dissuading others from attaining goals or taking actions detrimental to Chinese interests. In this form of power projection, "military force or presence is present or implied in ways designed to influence the national decision making of other countries." Examples include deterrence of Taiwan, the United States, and to some extent Japan, through air surveillance, submarine patrols, surface missions, amphibious training exercises, and the development of its missile forces.

The PLA also projects power through its self-proclaimed efforts to enhance regional security (e.g., via military-to-military contacts with many of its neighbors and joint/combined military activities such as the 2003 anti-terrorist exercise involving China, Kazakhstan, Kyrgyzstan, Tajikistan, and Russia). In addition, the authors point out that China has numerous military-related facilities or friendly foreign locations (termed "access points") throughout South and Southeast Asia, the South China Sea, and the Pacific Islands. Such base-type arrangements could potentially be accessed for purposes of logistical resupply, maintenance, or relief from operational deployment.

Kamphausen and Liang conclude from their study that there are six major tasks in PLA power projection: (1) observe sovereignty and pay attention to borders; (2) intervene when in China's interests; (3) strengthen support for UN PKO missions outside of Asia; (4) strengthen support for multilateral operations, primarily in Asia, where China can assume a leading role;

(5) conduct small-scale deterrence missions; and (6) enhance naval presence missions. These have many implications for the PLA's future external role, specifically in Taiwan or North Korea scenarios, and for whether China would intervene using military force, even in other countries, when China's interests are at risk.

Taken together, the growing ability of the Chinese military to project power in the ways identified by Kamphausen and Liang will almost certainly enhance Beijing's influence on regional security. However, the authors suggest that it remains to be seen whether such influence will prove positive or negative on balance. They argue that, if deftly wielded, China's power projection activities might actually promote Asian stability by reinforcing more cooperative approaches to regional security. On the negative side, as Beijing increasingly projects military power throughout the Asia-Pacific region, a likely by-product is that Taiwan's sense of isolation and marginalization will grow.

Section three of this volume provides additional in-depth analysis of the PLA, but with a greater emphasis on the implications of PLA modernization for Taiwan's security and, in particular, on the dynamics of crisis stability and escalation control across the strait. It focuses on six specific military issues that arguably could play the greatest role in driving escalation and affecting the outcome of a U.S.-China conflict over Taiwan: the balance of air power, the balance of naval forces, Sino-American nuclear weapons doctrine, Chinese information operations, Taiwan's overall capabilities and defense doctrine, and U.S. force deployments.

In chapter 6, Kenneth W. Allen examines the concepts of deterrence and escalation for the air forces of China, Taiwan, and the United States, specifically in terms of preventing and prosecuting a conflict across the Taiwan Strait. As a basis for his analysis, Allen compares the basic assets of the PLA Air Force (PLAAF), Taiwan Air Force (TAF), and U.S. Air Force (USAF). He emphasizes that each air force is organized differently, so each would bring different assets to bear during a situation of deterrence and/or escalation. Activities that are relevant to deterrence or escalation are: weapon system modernization (in terms of both types and numbers), air force relations between Washington and Taipei, flight activity near the center line of the Taiwan Strait, reconnaissance flights, the forward deployment of air assets to the area, reserve mobilization, an air blockade, and possible air attacks.

Allen first reviews the history of the modernization of the Chinese, Taiwan, and American air forces and their relative capabilities. He points out that estimating the dynamics of air power in a serious crisis over Taiwan is fraught with difficulties. For example, it is difficult to determine how many aircraft each party would actually employ in a crisis. In addition, the state of U.S.-Taiwan air force relations, including the contributions of Taiwan's own defense industry, are a determining factor for how the United States would engage in a Taiwan scenario. Also, there are many potential flashpoints for future air conflict across the Taiwan Strait, including conflicts at the center line.[2] As Allen points out, air activity near the center line has become more and more frequent, with the PLAAF now flying to the boundary routinely. Given the close proximity of Chinese and Taiwanese air forces at this line, the potential for miscommunication and subsequent escalation is very high. Finally, Allen examines the policies and actions of the three air forces and demonstrates how actions seen as a deterrent on one side could be perceived as escalatory by the other. For example, U.S. bomber deployments to Guam and the stationing of cruise missiles there, as well as continued U.S. reconnaissance flights off China's coast, are seen as deterrence by the United States and escalatory by the Chinese; the Chinese see the purchasing of Russian weapons systems as deterrence, whereas the United States and Taiwan may see this as escalatory.

If a conflict does break out as a result of unintended escalation, Allen argues that, if Beijing can achieve air superiority, China will most likely be able to dictate the terms of conflict resolution. However, if the United States starts to bomb the PLAAF's airfields, it will have to move its aircraft farther away from the location of engagement. This means that the PLAAF will not be able to fly enough sorties for a long enough loiter time necessary to maintain air superiority. Whether or not the United States decides to take these measures has much to do with the rules of engagement (ROE). Because of their great relevance to escalation, deterrence, and conflict resolution in a Taiwan contingency, Allen assesses the future ROE of the Chinese and U.S. air forces. Even though these ROE are designed to prevent escalation, Allen explains, "the military doctrines underlying armed forces' operations of both countries can contribute to crisis instability and escalation as much as their force deployments." Only the political authorities in charge of the military forces could counter this impetus, but if the conflict is going poorly, those same leaders "may seek to raise the cost to the adversary by widening the war and attacking targets previously declared off-limits by the ROE." In short, Allen argues, "the blend of capabilities, doctrine, and the dynamic of war produces the uncertainty that even initially prudent ROE may not overcome."

Bernard D. Cole, in chapter 7, also examines the complex relationship between capabilities and perceptions, but in terms of the naval power of China, Taiwan, and the United States. In particular, Cole provides a much needed analysis of the physical geography of the Taiwan theater and explains the challenges that it imposes for naval operations and escalation control in a crisis over Taiwan. High winds, shallow waters, and lack of suitable landing areas are some examples of why it is particularly difficult to conduct traditional amphibious assaults, anti-submarine operations warfare (ASW) operations, and even surface ship operations in the strait. These environmental factors also make it difficult for ships to accurately identify and locate other ships and determine whether they are under attack. In the words of Cole, this "literal and figurative cloudiness would reduce commanders' situational knowledge, increasing the chances of escalation due to the unintended consequences from their decisions." Furthermore, he also points out that the basic geography severely limits the viability of any defense by Taiwan against a seaborne assault supported by air operations.

Given these challenges, Cole assesses and compares the naval and commercial maritime strengths of China, Taiwan, and the United States as they would be understood in escalatory terms. As the PLAN modernizes, it becomes capable of conducting operations further from China's coast. However, this makes communication and logistics more difficult (e.g., because weather conditions worsen as ships get farther and farther from land). This "complicates maintaining effective command and control of those forces, which in turn exacerbates the problem of preventing unintended escalation during tactical operations at sea and in the air." The PLAN and Taiwan Navy are roughly equal in surface combatant capability, but the entry of the United States would tip the balance in favor of Taiwan. However, Cole points out there are both military and political limitations to this "entry." It would also take the United States time to deploy to the Taiwan theater, which would give the Chinese a great advantage. On the other hand, if the United States did enter, "Chinese losses would no doubt draw Beijing to increase its commitments to battle, in terms of both vertical escalation (force size) and horizontal escalation (force capability)." Given these numerous variables, Cole employs a series of maritime scenarios to explore how all the factors would play out in real time; this examination of operational steps demonstrates the variety of escalatory measures that a maritime scenario offers. In short, though the maritime arena offers opportunities to exert pressure, send messages, and "teach lessons," it is also subject to misinterpretation, miscalculation, and unintended consequences.

Conventional capabilities are not the only factors that affect the potential PLA threat to Taiwan and the larger challenge the PLA poses to Asian stability. The nuclear capabilities and doctrines of both China and the United States could have an enormous impact on the dynamics of a crisis over Taiwan. In chapter 8, Brad Roberts analyzes both Chinese and U.S. military preparations in the nuclear realm in order to better determine what role nuclear weapons might play in a Taiwan contingency. According to Roberts, some of the main characteristics of China's nuclear posture have deep historical roots. The so-called "century of humiliation" has given China an intense desire to resist "nuclear bullying." The need to deal with the Cold War Soviet threat has given China an essentially defensive concept of nuclear weapons. The founding fathers of China's nuclear program were committed to creating only the "minimum means of reprisal" and this has left a legacy of a modestly sized retaliatory force. China's deep-seated antipathy to transparency continues to inform the making and articulation of Chinese nuclear policy.

Roberts reviews the ways in which China's nuclear posture has evolved over the last decade—and how the historical roots have given way to new circumstances. The PLA is engaged in a broad-based effort to modernize its doctrinal and operational concepts and this effort touches directly on China's nuclear force, the Second Artillery. But many questions remain about how this attempt on the part of the PLA to get its "intellectual house in order" applies to the role of nuclear weapons: Does China's emphasis in conventional missile doctrine on "seizing the initiative" and attacking the enemy's center of gravity (most likely meaning U.S. bases in the region) influence nuclear operational concepts? How does the PLA's new focus on jointness affect the role of China's nuclear forces in a conflict?

Roberts also highlights the ways in which China's nuclear posture is developing in response to the changing security environment, especially to its evolving strategic relationship with the United States. China wants to ensure the viability of its nuclear force and hence its credibility as a deterrent in the light of changes in the U.S. force posture and especially U.S. deployment of both non-nuclear strike systems and missile defense; both developments seem to strengthen the American capacity for preemption. This has led to debates in China about the credibility of China's no-first-use policy and how to reposture its forces as U.S. capabilities grow. Roberts reports evidence that China has decided not to change its declaratory policy but will make quantitative and qualitative adjustments to its nuclear forces as the U.S. posture evolves. China contends that modernization in these technical and operational realms is consistent with "defensive deterrence." In his discussion of the U.S. Nuclear Posture Review, Roberts notes that China does not play a central role in U.S. military planning like the United States does in Chinese military planning.

Roberts then assesses the prospects for nuclear crisis instability in a confrontation over the Taiwan Strait. He observes that the focus of both sides on how to ensure the credibility of deterrence has obscured their thinking about "failures of deterrence and the challenges of restoring deterrence intrawar or terminating a war gone nuclear on acceptable terms." Indeed, he argues that the potential for instability is significant. Both sides have serious misperceptions about the ways and circumstances under which the other side would employ nuclear weapons in a conflict. Roberts explores four questions that involve such misperceptions on both sides: Who would be the first to escalate? Would that state escalate by nuclear means? Would the further dynamics of escalation be manageable? How might a war with a nuclear dimension be terminated? Roberts concludes that analysts in the United States and China "have very different ideas about the dynamics of nuclear confrontation over Taiwan" and "their analyses proceed from different assumptions about how the other country would act in such a conflict." Even more disconcerting is the fact that both sides are confident in their potentially flawed assessments and in their belief that "strong action will induce the enemy to exercise restraint"—both of which could lead to miscalculations in war. Because "in war, both sides seem to want neither to use nuclear weapons nor rule them out entirely," Roberts concludes that "a conflict over Taiwan could unfold in unpredictable ways in the nuclear dimension, with far-reaching consequences."

In chapter 9, James Mulvenon discusses one additional realm of great relevance to Taiwan in which China's military doctrine is evolving as a result of technological breakthroughs and doctrinal innovation: information operations (IO). According to Mulvenon, misperceptions about this sector persist that seriously affect assessments of capabilities and potential threats for both the United States and China. On the part of the United States, Mulvenon demonstrates that, contrary to the views of some analysts, the ideas on offensive IO promoted by well-known authors such as Shen Weiguang, Zhang Zhaozhong, and Qiao Liang/Wang Xiangsui are in no way representative of the Chinese military's position on the use of IO.

Nonetheless, Mulvenon argues that China does plan on using IO in a Taiwan scenario to affect the will of the Taiwanese people and undermine U.S. intervention. According to Mulvenon, Chinese IO strategists believe that the United States is overly dependent on computer networks, particularly computerized logistics systems, which could potentially be exploited through a network attack. Chinese theorists posit this as an essential part of a comprehensive strategy designed to force Taiwan to capitulate to Beijing that combines network attacks with a coordinated campaign of short-range ballistic missile attacks, as well as "fifth column" and information warfare attacks on Taiwan's critical infrastructure. He adds, however, that "the Chinese tend to overemphasize the U.S. reliance on computers" believing that "the U.S. system cannot function effectively without these computer networks." In reality there is much evidence to suggest that U.S. logistics personnel are currently capable of employing noncomputerized solutions if the network is down, though the logistics system is becoming increasingly automated and therefore more difficult to reconstitute manually.

Another common misconception is that the Chinese government or military has control over patriotic hacker groups within China. Mulvenon assesses this belief and concludes that these hackers are independent actors who are, at most, state tolerated or state encouraged. Finally, and perhaps of greatest relevance to U.S. and Taiwan assessments of the PLA threat, Mulvenon asserts that "China is winning the intelligence war across the strait, raising serious doubts about the purity of Taiwanese intelligence proffered to the United States, the safety of advanced military technologies transferred to the island, and the ability of official Taiwan interlocutors to safeguard shared U.S. secrets about intelligence collection or joint war planning." Such dangers call into question the feasibility and reliability of U.S.-Taiwan intelligence-sharing and defense-planning efforts.

Mulvenon contends that these developments and perceptions relating to information warfare could reduce crisis stability in a variety of ways, stating "the real danger of China's emerging military capabilities is that they may embolden Beijing to make a fundamental miscalculation in a Taiwan scenario and consequently bring about a disastrous outcome for all parties." He argues that, for the sake of deterrence and escalation control, the United States needs to disabuse China of the idea that an attack on U.S. computer networks will dramatically affect the deployment of U.S. naval assets in a Taiwan scenario.

In chapter 10, Andrew N. D. Yang assesses key aspects of Taiwan's defense modernization and how Taiwan's overall capabilities and defense doctrine have evolved in reaction to perceived military threats from mainland China. In the case that China resorts to force to reunify Taiwan with the mainland, he argues that the PLA would have five distinct missions: (1) destroy Taiwan's defense capabilities, (2) cut off its defense links with the United States, (3) eliminate the Taiwanese government and replace it with one compatible with PRC interests, (4) coerce the Taiwanese populace to accept these imposed political arrangements, and (5) minimize PRC casualties throughout the whole process. In order to achieve these goals, China has designed a three-phase strike operation: initially strike Taiwan's critical strategic and military targets, impose a naval blockade followed by devastating air attacks, and conclude with an amphibious landing to seize control of the political center.

While PRC tasks are complex and multidimensional, Yang points out that Taiwan's defense modernization has only one aim: survival. With this goal in mind, Taiwan has modernized its defense structure in order to successfully execute countermeasures to each of the three phases of China's military strategy. For example, in the case of air attacks, the ROC needs to protect its command and control system from being disabled. Because of this, ROC forces have introduced "Project Resolute," a multi-billion dollar effort designed to integrate the command, control, and communication of the three services and strengthen electronic counter-measures (ECM) and counter-countermeasures (ECCM). Furthermore, Yang states that Taiwan would like to improve its air defense capabilities by acquiring the Naval Area Defense (NAD) system from the United States, but the United States has yet to accept this request. To counter the second phase of a PLA operation of a naval blockade, Taiwan's navy has put increasing emphasis on improving its anti-submarine warfare (ASW) capabilities. Lastly, Taiwan's ground forces have undergone major streamlining and restructuring in order to better defend Taiwan against the third phase of PLA operations, an amphibious assault.

Because of the high tension across the strait, Yang states that Taiwan's political leadership has designed crisis management mechanisms to effectively deal with a crisis in ways that avoid miscalculation and unintended escalation. This process includes intelligence gathering and assessments and the convening of the National Security Council with the president in order to "make decisions on all internal and external emergency response recommendations suggested by responsible government departments and on interagency task force operations." Yang demonstrates how this process worked in the 1996 Taiwan Strait crisis. Even though crisis was averted in that instance, Yang argues that there are still clear defense reasons for why Taiwan needs high-speed anti-radiation missiles (HARM) and joint direct attack munitions (JDAM) for its current inventory. Although these weapons are generally seen as offensive in nature, Yang contends that "the primary objective of Taiwanese defense is to deter and suppress PLA's attacks on Taiwan" and that improving its capabilities serves to "send a clear and unmistakable message to Beijing that . . . Taiwan will not initiate a war against Beijing in the first place, but Beijing would encounter a devastating setback should it decide to do so."

Yang concludes by pointing out that Taiwan is building both defensive *and offensive* capabilities because, in the case of a Chinese attack on the island, the "Taiwan military must have the capacity to launch offensive operations to regain control over the Taiwan Strait." In Yang's view, such controversial capabilities ". . . are necessary to frustrate Beijing's wish for a short war and will thus provide an opportunity for the international community to intervene." Yang adds that, unfortunately, Taiwan's defense modernization remains "hampered by the inability of the executive and legislative branches of government to agree on the most appropriate level and type of budget allocations and force structure," which causes some outside observers to conclude that the military balance is shifting in China's favor.

Roger Cliff (chapter 11) concludes section three with an analysis of the relationship between PLA modernization and U.S. force deployments in Asia, while drawing certain implications for a confrontation over Taiwan that will likely prove quite controversial. Cliff examines current capabilities and trends involving the U.S. force structure in the Asia-Pacific region, including U.S. combat forces in Japan, South Korea, Guam, Hawaii, and Alaska, and analyzes their effectiveness against expanding Chinese force levels in the event of a conflict. He observes that the presence of larger numbers of increasingly modern PLA weapons presents a significant and growing challenge to the United States in certain situations. This challenge exists not simply because of the growing capability of such weaponry, but also because Chinese forces would enjoy a distinct advantage over the United States in many regional contingencies (e.g., regarding Taiwan) because Chinese forces would be operating very close to their home base. Cliff notes that such proximity could give them a particularly significant advantage if a Taiwan conflict began with Chinese preemptive or surprise actions. Overall, regarding Taiwan, Cliff observes that Chinese "anti-access" measures would "exacerbate the constraints on U.S. military capability caused by the dearth of air bases near Taiwan and the limited number of U.S. forces forward deployed in the Western Pacific."

Looking toward the future, Cliff believes that the challenges posed by the PLA will only increase over time, assuming that China's military modernization program continues apace. Cliff states that the Chinese defense industry is now beginning to produce weapons systems that are comparable to those in the U.S. inventory. He asserts that, by 2015, the PLA could have, for example, a dozen modern destroyers with air defense capabilities comparable to the U.S. Aegis system, several dozen modern diesel-electric attack submarines, and perhaps a dozen nuclear-powered type 093-class attack submarines. In addition, it is also possible that China will develop the missile technology and C4ISR necessary to hit a moving ship at sea by that time.

On the other hand, Cliff also recognizes that the United States will not be standing still as China's military continues to modernize. Washington intends to increase in its total force the number of Aegis ships in service from seventy to eighty and to commission around six new DDG 1000-class destroyers. The United States plans to decommission about ten Los Angeles-class subs and replace them with Virginia-class ships, which are capable of carrying 30 percent more missiles and torpedoes. The United States also plans to replace about a fourth of its total fighter inventory with more modern systems. U.S. theater ballistic missile defense capabilities will also increase. In addition to upgrading its total force weapons systems, the United States is planning to make significant changes specifically to its force posture in the Asia-Pacific theater, according to Cliff. For example, the United States plans on replacing the *Kitty Hawk* in 2008 with the *George Washington*, a nuclear-powered Nimitz-class carrier that carries 50 percent more fighters and is capable of generating twice as many aircraft sorties per day; also, three additional attack submarines will eventually be based in Guam, raising the number of attack submarines based in Pacific ports to thirty.

Nonetheless, Cliff concludes with the controversial assertion that, despite these planned changes in the U.S. force posture, "the balance of military power in the Western Pacific is shifting in China's favor." This presents particularly dangerous implications for the Taiwan situation. He argues that even with the planned changes ". . . by 2015 China is likely to enjoy a significant quantitative advantage in a conflict with the United States [over Taiwan], particularly in its early stages." Cliff outlines in detail nine adjustments that the United States must make to its force posture in order to reverse the trend, such as carrying through with its current plans for force posture changes, increasing "its capabilities to detect a surprise use of force despite concerted denial and deception efforts by the PLA," and increasing "the readiness levels of air and naval forces in Hawaii and on the west coast of the United States so that they can be surged to the Western Pacific on short notice." The United States also needs to increase the quantity and quality of U.S. air and naval forces in the Western Pacific; strengthen active air defense by, for example, deploying ballistic missile, cruise missile, and manned aircraft defenses; and reduce the vulnerability of U.S. air, naval, and logistics facilities in the region to attacks by covert operatives. The United States should also look into forward-basing even more air and naval forces than planned in the region, possibly in Guam or Singapore, and continuously increase the quality of these naval and air forces over time.

The two chapters that constitute the final section of this volume (section four) examine the possible future evolution of Taiwan's threat environment and the larger regional security environment. In chapter 12, Alan D. Romberg focuses his analysis on the current East Asian security architecture, its possible evolution in the coming years, and its implications for the PLA and Taiwan. Given current regional dynamics, Romberg argues that the term "security architecture" may be an overstatement; instead, he conceptualizes this structure more as "a set of security issues and relationships—some formal, most not—that constitute the totality of the present reality." Romberg states that Chinese military modernization is obviously a major factor that can significantly influence the future Asian security environment and Taiwan in particular. He notes that PLA modernization will continue to be driven in large part by the necessity for Beijing to be prepared to deter, delay, deflect, and, if necessary, defeat the United States in the Taiwan theater.

Romberg identifies three sets of largely political variables that, in his view, will be most important in determining how the Asian security environment evolves over the next fifteen to twenty years and therefore how the putative PLA threat to Taiwan will evolve: (1) the overall situation within Taiwan and in cross-strait relations, (2) U.S.-PRC strategic relations, and (3) Japan's security posture. Romberg considers different possibilities for the future of cross-strait relations that will be play a key role in overall regional security—for example, whether China decides to take a pragmatic approach, reducing military tensions and allowing Taiwan to have a significant level of "international space," and whether the Taiwan leadership continues to push for de jure independence. Also, Romberg argues, "the state of Sino-American relations will be of crucial importance to China's perception of its security needs and its decisions about PLA size and configuration," thereby affecting how China positions itself militarily in the region. The fundamental issue in the Sino-Japanese relationship, Romberg states, "is not history or shrine visits, but the contemporary competition between Japan and China for power and influence"; he explores different scenarios about how both sides deal with this competition and assesses their implications for stability in Northeast Asia.

Romberg identifies four other factors that might not fundamentally alter China's strategic aims, but that could, nonetheless, play an important role in determining the future regional security environment: terrorism, U.S. alliances, economics, and energy developments. For example, given the importance of the U.S.-Japan and U.S.-South Korea alliances to American security and strategic interests, Romberg states that it is likely that U.S. policy will be designed to rectify any weaknesses in them; failure to do so would have enormous consequences. A major act of terrorism could also affect security relations in Northeast Asia, even if the attack occurred elsewhere, as could an economic downturn or cutthroat competition over energy resources.

Romberg posits that "even in the most optimistic scenario, and no matter how smoothly relations are developing across the strait or between Washington and Beijing, PRC leaders will be unwilling to forego a deterrent capability against Taiwan independence and U.S. intervention in a Taiwan contingency." Therefore, he recommends that the United States maintain a hedging strategy, which includes not being complacent about its current technological lead in terms of military hardware. At the same time, *how* the United States approaches China—whether or not hedging is carried out as a "containment" strategy or casts China as a presumed adversary—will be crucial to successfully managing strategic relations. In this respect, he concludes, the future security architecture of East Asia, and how the PLA views and reacts to it, is very much in the hands of the United States; the U.S. government needs to understand this and to adequately factor it into future decisions.

In the concluding chapter, Michael D. Swaine and Oriana Skylar Mastro assess the implications of the analysis presented in sections two and three (along with other more recent scholarly analyses) for our understanding of the evolving PLA threat toward Taiwan and the larger challenge that the PLA poses to the Asian region. They point out that the preceding chapters identify three critical components essential to determining the nature of the future PLA threat to Taiwan: relative PLA capabilities, the escalatory dynamics of a Taiwan crisis, and the impact of the future evolution of the regional security environment. The authors conclude that the balance of power in the Taiwan Strait is not unequivocally shifting in China's favor. However, several features of Taiwan's security environment clearly provide reasons for significant concern. Specifically, the combination of growing Chinese military capabilities in key areas, the high stakes involved for Beijing (and Washington and Taipei), and China's apparent propensity to (a) signal strong resolve in a crisis through both military and diplomatic means, (b) emphasize seizing and maintaining the initiative, and (c) assume that it would possess greater resolve than the United States in a crisis over Taiwan could together increase the likelihood that China's leaders might employ force under extreme circumstances. They add that the views toward military deterrence and crisis management of both Taiwan and the United States could contribute to such a dangerous situation—largely via the continuation of Taiwan's arguably inadequate military response to the growing threat and America's tendency to assume that it will continue to enjoy escalation dominance in a crisis with China, while also prizing military initiative and resolve.

Swaine and Mastro also point out that the larger regional security environment will likely exert an increasing influence over the threat to Taiwan in the years to come in two important yet indirect ways: as a result of both likely enhancements in the U.S.-Japan security alliance and changes in the larger U.S. military posture in Asia, and possible changes in the bilateral relationships that Beijing and Washington enjoy with other countries throughout Asia, including South Korea. They conclude that the former could produce contrasting consequences for Taiwan's security. On the one hand, if properly handled, the strengthening and expansion of the U.S.-Japan security alliance could enhance the ability of the United States to deter a possible Chinese use of force against Taiwan, despite considerable improvements in PLA capabilities. On the other hand, if mismanaged, a stronger alliance could greatly exacerbate overall Sino-American strategic tensions and deepen Chinese fears that Taiwan might seek *de jure* independence with American and/ or Japanese support or acquiescence. Furthermore, should deterrence fail in the Taiwan Strait, an enhanced U.S.-Japan alliance relationship would almost certainly ensure Japan's significant, early involvement in a serious conflict, deepening the adverse consequences that such a conflict would pose for the region.

The impact of Chinese and American bilateral relationships with other regional actors could also vary enormously, depending largely on how Beijing and Washington manage these relationships. If deftly managed, Beijing's relations with Asia could not only further constrain Taiwan's strategic support in the region, but also perhaps limit U.S. options in an escalating crisis or conflict with China over the island. This, of course, would also depend on U.S. behavior. On the other hand, if properly handled, regional relations with both Beijing and Washington could also act as a mutual deterrent, and brake, on possible provocations originating from Beijing, Washington, and Taipei. The authors conclude that it is simply too soon to tell how the regional security environment might eventually evolve to influence Taiwan's security. However, absent a major shift in direction, they believe that most nations in the region will continue to prefer to stay "outside" the issue as much as possible.

The authors also draw several recommendations for future actions that the United States could undertake to reduce the threat of conflict confronting the United States, China, and Taiwan. Most broadly, the United States needs to continue to improve its ability to react swiftly and with sufficient force to deter or shut down a PLA attack—preferably without escalating the confrontation greatly by striking the Chinese mainland early on. This means that U.S. forces must, on the one hand, maintain effective countermeasures against any significant attempt by Beijing to delay U.S. deployments to the vicinity and, on the other hand, sustain an unambiguous ability to interdict Chinese forces without attacking a wide range of targets on Chinese territory. In support of this objective, the United States should strengthen the defenses of its regional bases and military assets against Chinese attack in a variety of ways and forward deploy some additional forces. In addition, Washington should also reduce some of its operational vulnerabilities by strengthening computer network defenses and conduct exercises in which it is forced to process information in different ways, such as deploying forces in the event of a computer network attack.

The authors conclude that Taiwan needs to overcome its domestic political problems and devote more resources to defense. Moreover, Taipei needs to focus such defense efforts on enhancing its capacity to fend off Chinese military coercion (or an outright attack) for at least two weeks without resorting to actions that could dramatically escalate the crisis or conflict, such as preemptive strikes against mainland targets. This should include the strengthening of operational security at key military facilities, as well as the security of Taiwan's entire intelligence and civil infrastructure.

Finally, the authors identify several actions that the United States and China could undertake to reduce the chances of inadvertent escalation in a Taiwan crisis, including efforts to: expand mutual understanding of each side's hostile images and assumptions through a scholarly dialogue and related elite surveys; raise awareness and understanding within both governments of the dangers of Sino-American political-military crises and develop new tools for managing them through "track-two" dialogues and bilateral crisis simulations; enhance crisis communication through the creation of a joint governmental political-military working group designed to develop a set of procedures and mechanisms for improving crisis signaling; and establish clear rules of engagement for naval and air forces that could reduce the propensity for escalation.

NOTES

1. For a detailed examination of Chinese views on crisis management that to some extent confirms (and to some extent departs from) Henley's observations, see Michael D. Swaine, Zhang Tuosheng, and Danielle Cohen, eds., *Managing Sino-American Crisis: Case Studies and Analysis* (Washington, D.C.: Carnegie Endowment, 2006).
2. The "center line" is a boundary that both Taiwan and China have informally respected since the 1950s.

2

China's Asia Policy
Strategy and Tactics

Alex Liebman

CHINA'S DECISION MAKERS face a dilemma. On the one hand, they seek to deter a Taiwanese declaration of independence. This, they believe, not only requires taking firm rhetorical stances against any move toward independence, but also necessitates increased investment in the People's Liberation Army (PLA). Although China is investing in military modernization for a variety of reasons, the most prominent reason is to serve as a deterrent against a Taiwanese declaration of independence. A strong military force will also help to discourage the United States from entering the conflict if the leadership of Taiwan decides to pursue independence in spite of China's actions. In the worst case scenario—direct U.S.–Chinese confrontation over Taiwan—improved military capabilities increase the probability that China will prevail. Largely for these reasons, the People's Republic of China (PRC) has invested in a rapid expansion of its military capabilities, with double-digit percentage increases in military spending every year (except one) for the past decade.

On the other hand, such an increase in military spending works at cross-purposes with perhaps an even more vital long-term Chinese goal: reassuring Asia, and the world, that its rise will be peaceful. China's leaders understand that expectations of its future power are causing great anxiety: How will the PRC use its increasing might? For China, the danger is that this anxiety may be channeled into a region-wide effort to contain the PRC: a system of alliances that exclude China and increasing military cooperation between the United States and Asian states, not only with traditional American allies, Japan and South Korea, but also with states concerned about China's rise (such as Vietnam). For this reason, China has spent a considerable amount of effort trying to reassure its neighbors that its intentions are peaceful. The core dilemma is that increasing military spending to achieve one interest (deterring Taiwan) hurts China's ability to achieve another (assuring a peaceful rise).

The chapters in this volume provide expert accounts of China's improving military capabilities on land, at sea, in the air, and in doctrine and assess the implications of such developments for crisis stability and escalation across the Taiwan Strait. This chapter aims to frame such PLA modernization in the larger context of China's overall goals in the region. Specifically, the chapter focuses on the difficulty for China *in seeking to increase its influence in Asia without provoking the emergence of a countervailing coalition of states.* The first section enumerates several of the measures that China is taking to reassure and to deter. These measures, though, can only have limited effectiveness given the inherent trade-off between these two goals. The second section, therefore, looks at one way that China has tried to square this circle: through increased activity in multilateral organizations. China's strategy, I argue, is to use multilateral institutions to shape the strategic environment in a way that makes countervailing coalitions unlikely to form. I refer to this strategy as "hub and spokes multilateralism."

Finally, China's military modernization cannot be understood without an appreciation of how the PRC provides the economic resources that underpin it. Indeed, China's economic foreign policy creates a dilemma similar to that described above. While Beijing emphasizes its desire for a peaceful international environment in which it can develop, such economic growth is the foundation for future Chinese power and influence, and, as such, tends to make other states anxious about China's rise. How China will use its growing economic clout is a question of common concern, albeit for different reasons, for almost every country in the world.

In the third section, I offer a perspective slightly different from the conventional wisdom. Far from seeking a closed economic region, China is likely to continue promoting an East Asia open to foreign trade and investment. How then does this correlate with China's efforts at regional integration? Analysis shows that such efforts have minimal economic impact; instead, China's support for regional integration is more accurately seen as a political attempt to reassure East Asia than as a move to close the region off to foreign investment and trade.

REASSURANCE AND DETERRENCE

China seeks to maintain the following delicate balance: it wants to increase its influence in Asia and deter the independence of Taiwan without causing an East Asian security spiral—arms races and an alliance system aimed at containing China. This section enumerates key Chinese efforts at reassurance and deterrence.

Reassurance

China is investing considerable resources in reassurance because of the anxiety that its rise might provoke in other powers. Other states expect China's economic, political, and military capabilities to grow. If they also believe, however, that China will use these new capabilities in ways detrimental to their interests, they will take measures against China, notably increasing their own military spending, forming defensive alliances, and taking firm stands on territorial disputes.[1] It is precisely this reaction that China is trying to avoid, and so it must reassure other states that, despite its growing capabilities, its intentions are—and, crucially, will remain—benign.

In 2003, Zheng Bijian, then dean of the Central Party School, issued his "Theory of the Peaceful Rise." While this particular phrase rapidly fell from official favor (replaced by the standard "peaceful development"), the underlying theme and purpose remain. That purpose, reassurance, continues in Chinese statements not to "seek hegemony" and in the policy of "calming, enriching, and befriending neighbors" (ānlín, fùlín, mùlín; 安邻抚邻睦邻), by, among other things, canceling outstanding debts and unilaterally lowering tariffs on imports.[2] Reassurance can take a variety of forms: decreased military spending, increased military transparency, compromise on territorial disputes, and so forth. The key to reassurance is that it must be credible; in the post World War II world, every leader worries about the Hitler model: Clear statements that no further territory was desired ended up being mere scraps of paper. The following text focuses on examples of Chinese reassurance with fairly strong credibility.

BORDER DISPUTE RESOLUTION. With the exception of the disputed border with India, China has resolved all of its outstanding land border territorial disputes. In April 1996, China began talks with Russia, Kazakhstan, and Kyrgyzstan in Shanghai to resolve outstanding boundary disagreements (this mechanism eventually developed into the Shanghai Cooperation Organization). As a result, China signed a series of border treaties with Russia and the Central Asian states starting in 1996 and as recently as 2004. In December 1999, China resolved its border dispute with Vietnam. Even on the still prickly Sino-Indian border, the two governments have signed a principles agreement for an eventual resolution.

The resolution of these land boundaries is important for two reasons. First, as Taylor Fravel points out, these agreements have usually been on terms unfavorable to China (in the majority of cases China has received less than half of the disputed land).[3] Far from using its greater strength to impose unequal or unfair settlements on weaker neighbors, China has instead chosen to make arrangements on terms unfair to itself. While the rationale behind such compromises can be debated—Fravel argues that it was due to domestic regime insecurity—these compromises are convincing as signals of reassurance, because China already has enough muscle to bargain for tougher agreements. Neighboring states can thus reasonably infer that China uses its power in moderate and mutually beneficial ways. Compromise on territorial disputes is perhaps the most vital bellwether of a regime's intentions, because attempts to change the distribution of territory are usually a hallmark of revisionist or aggressive states. Second, China is traditionally a land power, and although it has outstanding maritime disputes, China's land forces will remain relatively more powerful for years to come.[4] For China to compromise in an area of strength in which it has less necessity to offer concessions is reassuring.

PEACEFUL RESOLUTION OF CONFLICTS. The second major step that China has taken toward reassurance has been to radically change its policy on maritime territorial disputes. For most of the 1990s, China took a hard-line stance in the South China Sea. In February 1992 China passed a law outlining its position, which claimed that the Spratley Islands belonged to it and empowered the People's Liberation Army Navy (PLAN) to respond to violations of its territorial waters. Despite the Association of Southeast Asian Nations' (ASEAN) attempt to lower tension by issuing its "Declaration on the South China Sea," Chinese Foreign Minister Qian Qichen's promise not to use force in resolving the conflict in July 1992, and Jiang Zemin's similar pledge in November 1994, the PRC nonetheless decided unilaterally in 1995 to occupy and build a structure on one of the disputed islands, Mischief Reef near the Philippines.[5] While ASEAN was unable to present a unified response to China's action, it did spark reactions in individual ASEAN states, particularly the Philippines, which, after six years of moving toward "autonomous defense," decided that a military relationship with the United States was vital for its protection.[6]

Given such aggressive behavior in the 1990s, China's decision in 2003 to sign the ASEAN Treaty of Amity and Cooperation (TAC) is remarkable. As the first power outside of ASEAN to do so, it shows a fairly clear commitment that China does not intend to bully its smaller neighbors. The signal is relatively credible, because China's reputation would suffer greatly if China were to back out of such an agreement, as other states would question China's intention to carry out other commitments. Why has China so radically changed its stance? While constructivists tend to cite China's participation in international institutions (see below), the crucial reason has been that China saw the adverse reaction resulting from its aggressive behavior and feared a spiral of insecurity in the region. In other words, the PRC realized that these islands are far more valuable to China as a signal of its benign intentions than for the oil and gas that may lie beneath them, especially because those energy resources could be jointly exploited in any case.[7] While China's behavior toward Japan in the dispute over the Diaoyu/Senkaku Islands in the East China Sea has certainly not been as bold diplomatically as that toward Southeast Asia, even there China has approached the issue moderately, most recently offering a proposal for joint development of the Chunxiao oil field in March 2006.[8]

PLEDGES OF NONINTERFERENCE TOWARD WEAKER NEIGHBORS. The third major step that China has taken to reassure its neighbors is strictly to abide by its principles of sovereignty, noninterference, and the peaceful resolution of conflicts. When China invokes such rhetoric at the United Nations or in its relations with the United States, it is easy to consider it mere propaganda. And while it is, of course, in China's interest for states stronger than it to respect these principles, China has upheld them in its own dealings with smaller and weaker states as well (if only to establish a norm that it hopes stronger states will follow in dealing with it). This is reassuring to smaller states that may have political legitimacy problems, including many of China's Central Asian neighbors: Burma, Cambodia, North Korea, and perhaps even Thailand. In light of increasingly aggressive U.S. efforts to spread democracy, these states are likely to find China's stance highly reassuring.[9] To be fair, though, while China has offered support to odious dictators through its principle of noninterference, the PRC has also respected its pledge toward governments that it does not like. For example, China showed restraint in May 2002 when thousands of Kyrgyz protested and blocked roads to prevent the implementation of a new border agreement, and again in June when two of its diplomats were assassinated in the same country. Similarly, after the "Tulip Revolution" in Kyrgyzstan in March 2005, China continued to respect its noninterference pledge.

Deterrence

The need for reassurance is often talked about by those who observe Chinese foreign policy, but China also needs to deter. If reassurance is fundamentally about the future (future capabilities and future intentions), deterrence is about the present. It is difficult to threaten another state with deterrent action to be taken five years hence. Thus, China finds that on the key issues on which it must deter—notably a Taiwanese declaration of independence and U.S. intervention in the event of a Taiwan crisis—it must do so now. It is difficult for China to "leverage" its future power as a deterrent today, and so it must take immediate steps to make efforts at deterrence credibility.

INCREASED MILITARY PREPARATION. The first step that Beijing has taken in strengthening the credibility of its deterrent is to improve its military capabilities. The 2003 official military budget called for a 9.6 percent increase in military spending, the first time in fourteen years that the increase was not in the double digits.[10] China has also become more aggressive in stationing short-range ballistic missiles in Fujian province opposite Taiwan, and has continued to use military exercises to demonstrate its resolve. The most recent PLA exercise directed at Taiwan occurred after Chen Shui-bian's reelection in the summer of 2004, which also featured the U.S. military exercise "Summer Pulse."[11] The other chapters in this volume explain in detail the nature of this military modernization and its impact on a potential crisis with Taiwan.

THE ANTI-SECESSION LAW. China has also adopted some new tactics in its attempt to deter Taiwan. The most original was the passage by the National People's Congress in March 2005 of the national "Anti-Secession Law" (ASL), which obligates the Chinese government legally under Chinese domestic law to intervene in the event that (1) Taiwan declares independence, (2) Taiwan comes under attack by a foreign power, or (3) Taiwan indefinitely postpones reunification talks (this point was made in China's 2000 national defense white paper but was not stressed thereafter until the ASL). The immediate cause of the ASL was increased posturing by Chen Shui-bian toward amending the Taiwanese constitution. In fact, however, the ASL should be seen not only as a response to Chen, but primarily as a response to the United States. Indeed, passage of the ASL was an ingenious move by Beijing. When dealing with the U.S. position on Taiwan, China, since 1979, has had to grapple with the argument that under the Taiwan Relations Act (TRA), the United States is legally obligated under domestic law to provide for Taiwan's defense. The ASL, then, provides a brilliant rejoinder, essentially saying: "You may be obligated under your domestic law to support Taiwan, but we're obligated under *our* domestic law to prevent independence by force." The law is what Thomas Schelling would call an attempt to "tie its hands," thereby increasing the force of its commitment and the strength of its deterrent.

DIPLOMATIC REBUKES AND MILITARY STATEMENTS. China has also expressed annoyance when Southeast Asian leaders have visited Taiwan or met with their leaders. A notable occasion came in July 2005, when China "severely criticized" Singapore for allowing Prime Minister designate Li Hsien Loong

(Li Xianlong) to visit Taiwan.[12] Furthermore, one of Beijing's greatest fears, "nuclear blackmail" over Taiwan,[13] has prompted some Chinese generals to make provocative statements about China's potential use of nuclear weapons.[14] These sorts of statements, while they may make some U.S. policy makers think twice about intervention in the event of a conflict, only cause other states to worry about the sincerity of China's reassurances.

PREVENTING COUNTERVAILING COALITIONS

These efforts at reassurance and deterrence, however, have not allowed China to escape from the fundamental dilemma: Efforts at deterrence make signals of reassurance less credible (and vice versa). As Wang Jisi, the noted head of Beijing University's School of International Studies, put it:

> While many of China's military modernization programs are designed to deter Taiwan from taking adventurous moves toward *de jure* independence, they nonetheless may give rise to unfavorable regional repercussions, and a hardened Chinese posture toward Taiwan would undermine China's assertions of being a benign power seeking harmonious relations with its neighbors.[15]

To counter this problem, Beijing has asserted that its military buildup is aimed only at Taiwan. It is noteworthy that while China passed the ASL directed against Taiwan, it did no such thing in any of its territorial disputes with ASEAN—quite the reverse, China signed ASEAN's TAC. In the next section, I consider another means that China has used to square the circle between reassurance and deterrence.

Hub and Spokes Multilateralism

One way that China has attempted to achieve these conflicting goals—increasing influence while preventing a countervailing backlash—has been the strategic use of international institutions. China's participation in such institutions has increased dramatically throughout the reform era, and substantial attention has been given to this phenomenon. Some scholars argue that China's participation in such institutions is actually changing Chinese preferences through a process of socialization.[16] Others argue that China's goal in such institutions is simply to reassure its neighbors.[17] In an influential piece in *Foreign Affairs*, Taylor Fravel and Evan Medeiros suggest that China's use of multilateralism is part of a "charm offensive."[18] I take a different tack, arguing that by being selective in negotiations over the membership of each organization, China can shape the strategic context and prevent unfriendly coalitions from emerging as it gains a say in an ever-widening range of issues within these institutions.

This approach starts with the observation that China has not sought to participate in all multilateral organizations at all times. Instead, there have been several key mechanisms that China has pushed, and several upon which China has held back. Perhaps more significant, the PRC has sought to control the membership of these institutions. As Michael Yahuda notes, "As ever in regional organizations of this kind, the key is the symbolic significance of who is in and who is out."[19] However, I will argue that in surveying the alphabet soup of multilateral organizations around it, China seeks to control membership in a particular way; the strategy is to create a set of overlapping multilateral institutions in which China is the key duplicated member. In other words, China's goal is to install itself as the hub of a whole group of multilateral organizations. If the United States' bilateral alliances in the Asia-Pacific region are often referred to as "hub and spokes," then we might call China's attempted pattern "hub and spokes multilateralism." In the U.S. system of bilateral alliances, the United States is always the stronger power vis-à-vis its alliance partners. But in bilateral terms, China is not always stronger than the states with which it has relations, notably Japan, Russia, and the United States. For this reason, its criteria for shaping the membership in each multilateral organization is to make sure that, in combination with other friendly states, it can control the decisions of the group against stronger states. At the same time, the PRC does not wish to make its influence in these organizations *too* pronounced, as this might spark a countercoalition. The following text describes the main organizations with which China is working and how China has tried to influence the membership of each.

THE ASEAN PLUS THREE AND EAST ASIA SUMMIT. Such behavior is perhaps clearest in China's attitude toward expanding the ASEAN Plus

Three (APT) mechanism into the East Asia Summit (EAS). (The APT is made up of the ASEAN countries plus "three"—China, Japan, and South Korea). With growing closeness to South Korea and ASEAN increasingly reassured, China feels very comfortable dealing with Japan in the APT—far more comfortable than handling Japan bilaterally. Such an arrangement virtually guarantees that China is at the center of any regional security mechanism, and forces Japan to adapt to the system, or else risk pulling further away from Asia. At the inaugural EAS in December 2005, India, Australia, and New Zealand also participated (Russia was an observer) and signed the Kuala Lumpur Declaration. But China was displeased at the presence of these states and, according to some reports, attempted to marginalize them at the meeting.[20] This makes sense because if Australia and New Zealand (U.S. alliance partners) and India (a country with budding ties to the United States and a close relationship with ASEAN) are allowed to participate, Chinese influence will fall and Japanese influence will rise. So even though China has sought to improve relations with all three of these states, it does not want any of them—nor its great power partner in the Shanghai Cooperation Organization (SCO), Russia—to be a part of it.[21] Instead, it wants regional integration to continue through the APT, not EAS, mechanism.[22]

THE SHANGHAI COOPERATION ORGANIZATION. The SCO consists of six member states: Russia, China, Kazakhstan, Kyrgyzstan, Uzbekistan, and Tajikistan. This is a very manageable coalition for China. With strong Chinese support for the noninterference in the domestic politics of the Central Asian states (see above), China assures that Russia is unable to dominate the region on its own. By excluding the United States, China ensures that the Central Asian members are faced with the joint opposition of Russia and China on issues involving U.S. troops in the region. Recently, several South Asian and Middle Eastern states (notably Pakistan, India, and Iran) have expressed interest in joining the SCO. But China has tread very carefully about allowing any new members, particularly India, as this would serve to dilute China's influence in the organization. Significantly, however, China has also been only lukewarm about admitting its "all-weather" ally Pakistan. In part, this may be because China fears that doing so would leave it no choice but to admit India, but perhaps more importantly, this demonstrates China's fear of establishing *too much* influence within any given institution. If Pakistan were to enter the SCO, it would dramatically tip the balance of power in the organization toward China, causing a likely counterreaction among the other members and perhaps causing the organization to become less relevant, thus reducing Chinese influence.

THE SIX-PARTY TALKS. China's immediate goals in dealing with the Democratic People's Republic of Korea (DPRK) nuclear crisis have been well documented and do not merit excessive attention here. China's immediate goal is to prevent the collapse of North Korea, which would lead to millions of refugees and perhaps also armed gangs forming out of the remnants of the DPRK army trying to get across the Chinese border. In addition, China wants to prevent Japan or South Korea from developing nuclear weapons, as this could set off precisely the sort of chain reaction arms race that China is trying so hard to avoid. If Taiwan developed nuclear weapons, it would gravely complicate any Chinese attempts to retake the island. While Japanese Prime Minister Shinzo Abe's reiteration that Japan will not seek to develop nuclear weapons was undoubtedly welcome in Beijing, as was Secretary of State Condoleezza Rice's statement that the United States will continue to fulfill its obligations to protect Japan (this precludes Japanese need for nuclear weapons), the PRC is still concerned that the North Korean threat will prompt closer Japanese, U.S., and, implicitly, Taiwanese cooperation in theater missile defense. As at the start of the Korean War in 1950, events in Korea always seem to influence China's ability to take the initiative toward Taiwan. For this reason, China will continue to work to prevent the DPRK from sparking a spiral of insecurity which could lead to nuclear arms or missile defense buildups, both of which would only hurt China's relative position.

Indeed, China's stance toward North Korea started to get tougher after North Korea's missile tests on July 4, 2006. While Beijing remained apprehensive about the U.S. proposal for a United Nations Security Council (UNSC) resolution, in late July it did freeze DPRK bank accounts in China worth millions of dollars and in September appointed a new ambassador to North Korea, Liu Xiaoming, who has extensive experience in the United States and whose appointment was seen as a move to increase the pressure on North Korea. Since Pyongyang tested what we can only assume was a nuclear weapon on October 9, 2006, China's stance toward the DPRK has hardened, supporting UNSC resolution 1718 and, at least according to some reports, enforcing some of the sanctions along the 880-mile border that it shares with North Korea. When this book went to press, the success or failure of the February 13, 2007 agreement remained unclear. It is likely, however, that if the DPRK does not give up its nuclear capability, Japan and South Korea will be under increasing pressure to generate their own capacity.[23] China is likely at that point to put substantially more pressure on the DPRK for the reasons outlined above.

The preceding discussion is a straightforward recounting of widely accepted views on China's behavior in the Six-Party Talks. But why is China seeking to *institutionalize* this mechanism, even if the purpose for which it was created (the nuclear crisis) is solved? Indeed, this represents quite a shift for Beijing. While initially hesitant about the Six-Party Talks, preferring instead to convince Washington to deal directly with Pyongyang, China has since suggested that the Six-Party Talks be turned into a regular, institutionalized framework, even if the DPRK nuclear crisis is solved (that, of course, remains a "big if"). It is not hard to see why the framework is so appealing to Beijing. While U.S. and Chinese preferences have aligned relatively closely on the DPRK issue, such would not be the case on other issues that a new, institutionalized Six-Party Talks would deal with, that is, most other Northeast Asian security issues. On such issues—island disputes, Japan's military modernization, and the status of Taiwan—Russia and the DPRK can be expected to line up on China's side, and with South Korea growing increasingly close to China, this is an ideal forum for the PRC to handle the United States and Japan. It would be far better to do so in this manner, at any rate, than in any sort of trilateral way, in which Beijing is clearly at a disadvantage.

THE SOUTH ASIAN ASSOCIATION FOR REGIONAL COOPERATION. It may seem odd to mention a multilateral organization of which China is not a member, the South Asian Association for Regional Cooperation (SAARC), but China has been pushing for membership with the support of Pakistan. At the 2005 SAARC summit in Dhaka, India relented and agreed to give China observer status in the institution, although media reports suggested that India was alarmed by the growing China faction (i.e., Pakistan, Nepal, and Bangladesh).[24] On February 19, 2006, during Pakistani President's Pervez Musharraf's trip to Beijing, he officially expressed support for China's entry into the organization.[25] What is clear from this push is that even though China has sought to keep India out of the EAS and the SCO, China has no objections per se to being in a multilateral institution of which India is a member. The difference is that in the SAARC, China would have a large advantage in strength over India with the support of its alliance partner Pakistan; in the EAS, India would have the advantage because of its relationship with ASEAN and Japan.

OTHER INSTITUTIONS. To be sure, China continues to participate in other multilateral institutions, notably Asia-Pacific Economic Cooperation (APEC) and the ASEAN Regional Forum (ARF), which both have wide membership. APEC, however, discredited by its lack of will and capability in resolving the East Asian financial crisis, is routinely derided as a "talk shop." Meanwhile, the more the United States pulls away from the ARF, the more China seems determined to invigorate it. Indeed, China's hosting of the first session of the ARF Security Policy Conference in November 2004 (even as it sent a low-level delegate to the annual Shangri-la dialogue hosted by the International Institute for Strategic Studies) is seen as a move to marginalize the United States in another multilateral institution.[26]

Patterns in Chinese Multilateralism: The Hub and Spokes

There are a few features of this emerging multilateral order that are worth noting. First, from a geographic point of view, the organizations that China is promoting cover each of China's flanks, with China in the geographic center (see figure 2.1).

Second, China is picking and choosing quite cannily among its different options. Most striking is that while the PRC wants Russia, India, Japan, and the United States to be part of some organizations, it clearly wants to keep them out of others. This can best be seen as a Chinese effort at what is known in American congressional politics as "gerrymandering" or "redistricting." The goal is to create strategic contexts in which China

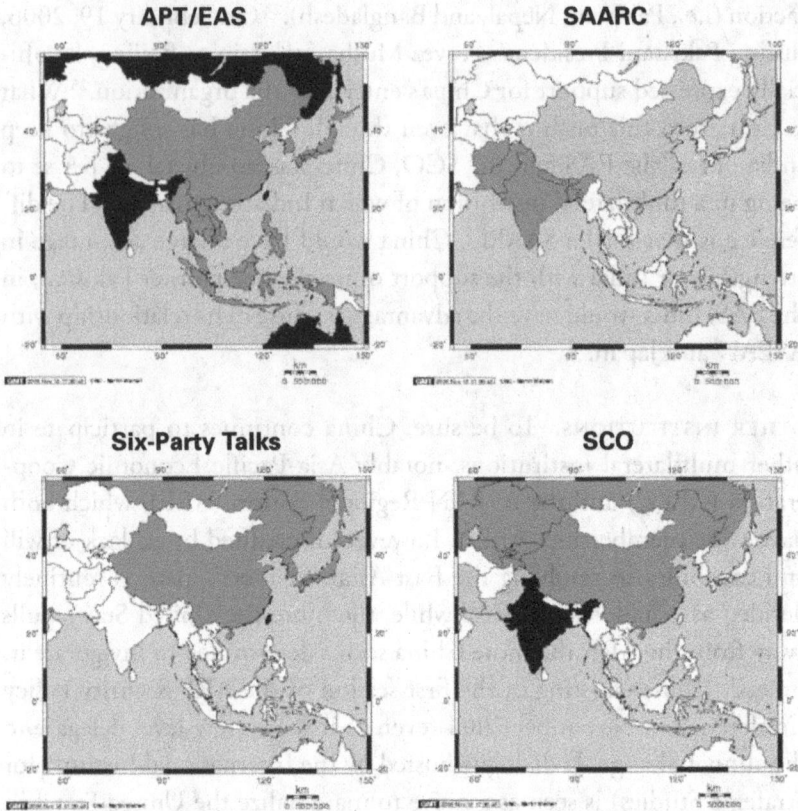

Dark gray: States in the organization. *Black:* States that China wants to exclude. *Light gray:* States that China is willing to consider for membership.

Figure 2.1 Maps of Four Prominent Multilateral Institutions

is at an advantage, but not too much of an advantage, vis-à-vis other states. If China is too weak within an organization, it will lack influence; but if it is too strong, it risks provoking a backlash. As mentioned above, despite Beijing's close friendship with Pakistan, it is still hesitant about supporting Pakistan's entrance into the SCO. In part, this may be because it fears doing so would open the door to India, but another element is that China does not want to scare the existing members into thinking that Beijing is trying to dominate the organization. Just as in a U.S. congressional district both political parties want about 55–60 percent of the electorate, so too does China only want about that much power within each institution (although for different reasons). Furthermore, the PRC wishes to keep potential anti-China coalition partners (such as India, Japan, Australia, Russia, and the United States) away from each other, and therefore not in the same institutions. Finally, Beijing has shown that it prefers such multilateral institutions to bilateral alliances, because it fears that such alliances are more likely to generate countercoalitions. To be sure, bilateral relationships remain vital (Hu Jintao's recent summit visits to India and Pakistan make that clear), but tight bilateral alliances remain somewhat awkward and continue to be eschewed.

In conclusion, Beijing feels that the more it can break down its neighboring states into smaller subgroupings, the more it can create specific strategic environments favorable to it. Specifically, it can prevent the emergence of any coalition designed to contain it, even as it expands its influence. In the future, China is likely to continue to:

1. Encourage the institutionalization of the Six-Party Talks;
2. Keep India out of the SCO and marginalized at the EAS;
3. Try to reduce the EAS to just the APT countries (i.e., not include India, Australia, and New Zealand), or, if that fails, not invest much in the EAS and instead promote the APT as the appropriate mechanism for regional political integration;
4. Push for its own membership in the SAARC; and
5. Stay away from close individual alliances, even with Russia, and downplay the closeness of its alliance with Pakistan.

Has This Policy Been Effective?

China's efforts to "gerrymander" the international environment may not ultimately be successful. First, China cannot unilaterally control the membership; these are, after all, multilateral organizations. This is most evident in China's inability to prevent India, Australia, and New Zealand from participating in the EAS. Second, even if China does largely succeed in controlling the membership, it still cannot avoid the problem that states are free to form other organizations and alliances of which China is not a member. Indeed, Japan and Australia's signing of a security pact in March 2007—even if it falls well short of a mutual defense treaty—is precisely the type of cooperation aimed at hedging against China's rise that the PRC can do little to prevent.[27]

Nonetheless, there are certainly some preliminary examples of Chinese success in these institutions. Perhaps most notable was the call in July 2005 by the SCO for War on Terror Coalition (that is, United States) forces to set a deadline for their departure from the region. This is actually quite a feat for China (and Russia). Central Asian states, sandwiched between two giants (three including India), would typically want to involve more great powers in the region as insurance against overbearing behavior by China or Russia. Their turnaround on military forces is in part the result of increased U.S. efforts to democratize the region, but it is also in no small part the result of China successfully convincing these states that its influence in the region is benign. In this case, the reassurance effort itself helped China expand its influence. As this example shows, the "hub and spokes" multilateralism strategy does seem to lower the probability of countervailing coalitions or at least slow the speed at which they form.

China's strategy in multilateral institutions has also been quite effective in its vital goal of marginalizing Taiwan. In virtually all of the regional organizations of which it is a part, China has successfully prevented Taiwan from participation. Taiwan is not a member of the APT, ARF, EAS, Six-Party Talks, or the SCO. China has more difficulty exercising such control over the membership of global institutions. Taiwan is a member, for example, of the World Trade Organization (WTO). Preventing Taiwan access to these institutions allows China to stop Taiwan from building its international position without getting into diplomatic spats like the one it had with Singapore in June 2005 (see above). In other words, this strategy allows China to marginalize Taiwan without unduly worrying the rest of Asia.

CHINA'S DEVELOPMENT STRATEGY: GROW GLOBALLY, REASSURE EAST ASIA

The PRC has repeated for more than twenty years that it seeks to maintain an international environment conducive to its own economic development. When Deng Xiaoping first put forward the theme of "peace and development" in 1985, it was undoubtedly reassuring; no longer would China engage in ideologically aggressive pursuits as it had during the Mao years. Today, however, the fact that China is pursuing its own development with such great success is no longer a source of reassurance and, instead, has become a source of anxiety. The West worries that unfair Chinese trade and currency practices threaten manufacturing jobs and economic well-being at home. In Asia, particularly in Southeast Asia, there is fear that the huge Chinese economy will cause them to lose competitiveness in exports and divert foreign direct investment (FDI). Even worse, if China does not open its markets to their products, Southeast Asian countries fear the worst of both worlds.

In dealing with these fears, Beijing must balance two objectives. On the one hand, robust economic growth is the foundation of China's future power and influence (as well as of domestic legitimacy) and, therefore, national policy must ensure the ideal circumstances for this growth. At the same time, however, China must be careful that it does not excessively scare its neighbors with the prospect of dealing with an economic juggernaut that dwarfs their own economies. In this context, the PRC has made efforts to promote regional economic integration. But this regional integration has had virtually no effect on international trade and finance flows between the world and East Asia. Indeed, China is unlikely to take any steps to close the region off to such flows because it depends on them for its own development. Far from seeking a "closed off" East Asia, China's basic economic interests imply that it will continue to work for an open region; efforts at regionalization are better seen as an attempt to reassure East Asia than as an attempt to close the region off to outsiders.

East Asian Regional Integration

THE SLOW PROGRESS OF EAST ASIAN POLITICAL INTEGRATION. The most fundamental backbone for economic integration is political integration: unified governmental structures that share a common currency and central banking policy. Although much recent attention has been given to "East Asian integration," this process remains far away from creating an "Asian Union" along European Union lines. Attempts at integration have been driven by ASEAN starting in the early 1990s, and did gain some momentum after the Asian financial crisis (AFC) of 1997–1998. Growing trade cooperation in the Western Hemisphere with the North American Free Trade Agreement (NAFTA) and in the European Union (EU) also prompted Asian leaders to reflect on integration in their own region. As mentioned above, in December 2005, the APT mechanism expanded to hold the first East Asian Summit. But East Asian integration has made little progress, and is unlikely to do so in the short to medium term for numerous reasons.

First, Sino-Japanese relations, the *sine qua non* of any effort at building an "Asian Union," remain far too contentious. In fact, it is Japan and China's jockeying to lead a proto-Asian Union which is impeding progress; compare this to Germany and France putting aside their historical enmity to share joint leadership of the EU.[28] Second, the continued existence of major territorial disputes—over the Spratley Islands in the South China Sea, the Diaoyu/Senkaku Islands in the East China Sea, and Taiwan—is a major impediment. The EU was only able to be formed once major territorial disputes had been settled; imagine such a process if Germany still claimed the Sudetenland or Alsace-Lorraine. Third, the distribution of power in the region remains unsettled, which makes it difficult to institutionalize mechanisms of cooperation. No state wants to agree to anything permanent when it is unclear what the distribution of power will look like in twenty years. This uncertainty is due to the rise of China, but also to questions about Japan's military development, the continued U.S. presence in the region, and the status of the Korean peninsula. Again, this contrasts with the EU, where the distribution of power has been static since after World War II. Finally, there is too much uncertainty about the ability of regimes in the region to survive. It is unclear how long the Communist Party will continue to govern China as a one-party state, and the durability of regimes in Southeast Asia remains highly tentative, especially in Burma, Indonesia, Cambodia, and perhaps even in Thailand. For all of these reasons, political integration faces too much uncertainty and, therefore, despite apparent progress, has largely stalled.

Indeed, the small progress made by holding the EAS cannot camouflage huge differences in perspective between the participants, and even among ASEAN countries themselves. At least two countries in the region maintain bases for U.S. troops (Japan and South Korea), another has close cooperation with the U.S. military (the Philippines), and several other states actively call for a continued U.S. presence in the region (notably Singapore). For this reason, Ian Storey's line that ASEAN countries practice "engagement with insurance" toward China remains accurate.[29] Indeed, China itself is wary about an East Asia without the United States, as was made evident by Beijing's reaction to Secretary of State Rice's reassurances in Tokyo that the United States was still committed to the defense of Japan. Furthermore, many Southeast Asian countries remain distrustful of Vietnam, and it is interesting in this regard that when Wen Jiabao visited Cambodia on April 7, 2006 and offered Cambodia $600 million in loans and grants for development, along with naval patrol ships, most analysts saw this as a sign that China was "balancing" against Vietnam.[30] As Samuel Sharpe points out, ASEAN remains largely unable to take unified stances on a variety of issues, given the often diverging interests of its members.[31] For these reasons, East Asian political integration remains decades away.

ECONOMIC INTEGRATION: LESS THAN MEETS THE EYE. If efforts to establish a union like the EU still have years to go, the more limited goal of creating a free trade area akin to NAFTA appears possible. However, despite apparent successes, economic integration has proceeded far more slowly than media reports indicate, and, crucially, East Asia is not becoming closed off economically to other regions. Especially from the Chinese point of view, economic development remains dependent on a global, not pan-Asian, export strategy.

Proposals for the peaceful economic integration of East Asia date back at least to 1965 to Japanese proposals for a Pacific Free Trade Area (PAFTA).[32] Since then, several other attempts have been made for closer economic cooperation, notably Korea's 1970 calls for an Asian Common Market, and more recently Japan's 1988 proposal for an "Asian Network,"[33] and finally Mahathir Mohammed's calls in 1990 for an East Asian Economic Caucus (EAEC). However, none of these efforts met with any success until after the AFC, at which point the APT mechanism gained momentum. This crisis showed Asian leaders just how connected their economies were, and, some claim, for the first time firmly linked Southeast and Northeast Asia together as "East Asia."[34] The AFC also highlighted the inability or unwillingness of the International Monetary

Fund (IMF), APEC, and the U.S. government to help. It also generated resentment at the West and frustration in Asian countries at their inability to control their own financial destinies.[35]

In the wake of the AFC, several major initiatives emerged which began the process of East Asian economic integration. While the first effort to pool funds to help defend a currency under attack failed (the Asian Monetary Fund, killed by the United States), the Chiang Mai Initiative (CMI) in 2000 represented a step forward in regional financial cooperation. Under the agreement, East Asian states would agree to swap reserves of foreign exchange if their currency was under a short-term, speculative attack by foreign investors. While only $37 billion is currently being used in currency swap arrangements, the APT countries have close to $3 trillion in reserves, so this could potentially be a powerful safety net against hot flows of capital. In addition, the Asian Bond Market Initiative (ABMI) has created an $11 billion bond market to help promote investment within the region. Finally, there has been a flurry of Free Trade Agreements (FTA) since the 1997–1998 crisis.[36] However, a look at both trade and financial data shows that the effect of these agreements has actually been rather limited.

FINANCIAL INTEGRATION. What effect have the CMI and the ABMI had on East Asian financial flows? Skeptics have argued that too little cash has been committed to make a difference,[37] and a quick look at data on financial flows shows that not much has changed. In fact, the United States and the European Union now account for almost 50 percent of total FDI into ASEAN, up from just over 30 percent in 1995. In 1995, 40 percent of all FDI into ASEAN came from the APT countries; in 2005, that number had fallen to 28 percent. China's FDI into ASEAN countries, for all the media coverage of Chinese companies "going global" (*zǒu chū qù;* 走出去), remains miniscule. Perhaps most significant, even though Taiwan has not been a party to any of these finance arrangements (because of successful Chinese political pressure discussed above), it has seen its share of FDI in ASEAN actually *increase* from 3 percent to 5 percent over this period. In this case, it appears that this institutional mechanism has not increased Asia's regional financial integration (see table 2.1).

Table 2.1 Percentage of Total Foreign Direct Investment in ASEAN, 1995 and 2004

Foreign Investor	1995	2004
China	0.05	1
ASEAN	17	11
APT	40	28
USA	15	23
EU	18	25
Taiwan	3	5
Japan	20	12

Source: ASEAN Statistical Yearbook.

TRADE. Trade is observed even more closely than FDI. Asian states have signed sixteen bilateral FTAs.[38] Even more prominent was the pledge between China and ASEAN to create an FTA between them by 2010. In 2004, China and ASEAN signed an agreement to begin reducing tariffs, and this included what were known as "early harvest" provisions to open the Chinese market to ASEAN products faster than vice versa.[39] But all of these agreements have had a minimal to nonexistent effect on actual trade. The percentage of ASEAN's total trade with APT has risen slightly, but this is due entirely to increases in trade with China; Japanese and Korean shares of ASEAN's total trade have actually fallen. Most interesting, again, is the case of Taiwan. Taiwan has been excluded for political reasons from these FTAs, and yet Taiwanese trade with ASEAN actually increased marginally during the 1993–2004 period—unlike that of Japan or Korea, integral members of the APT process. While some authors see Taiwan as being "marginalized" in this new East Asian economic environment,[40] in fact, while Taiwan is hurting politically from being left out, it is not hurting economically (see figure 2.2).

This trend is even clearer in China's trade data. China's trade with every major region of the world, and with the subregional groupings of ASEAN and APT, has remained virtually constant, even with all of the supposed movement toward East Asian integration.[41] While the many authors who refer to the explosion of Chinese trade with ASEAN are not incorrect in doing so, it would be a misinterpretation to think that this implies growing regional integration. Rather, it is simply a by-product of massive—and remarkably even—increases in Chinese trade with every

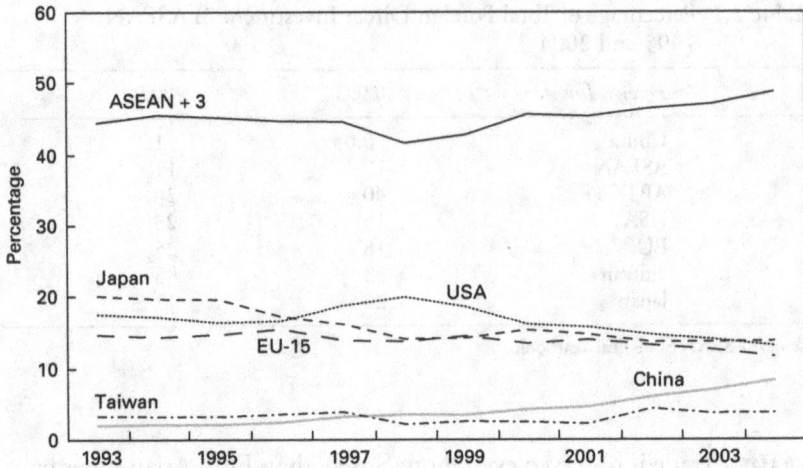

Source: ASEAN Statistical Yearbook.

Figure 2.2 ASEAN's World Trade by Region, 1993–2004

region of the world. Indeed, while some authors suggest that East Asian trade integration has been driven by the failure of the Doha round at the WTO,[42] in fact East Asian integration has barely managed *to keep apace* with the massive increases in world trade since the mid-1990s. In this sense, efforts at East Asian regional integration are best seen as an effort simply to keep up with the accelerating global trade regime, not to replace it (see figure 2.3).

WHAT THIS MEANS FOR CHINA'S ASIA STRATEGY. Several conclusions can be drawn from these data about China's long-term economic strategy and tactics. First, China is unlikely to turn to any type of closed or discriminatory regional system. Although many were worried in 2000 with the signing of the CMI that the world would be divided into three large trading blocs,[43] interregional trade remains vital for China. Some analysts have argued that China is seeking to promote a closed East Asian system,[44] but, in fact, China's trade is truly global, and from a simple interest-based perspective, China will remain a staunch supporter of the global trade system and will resist efforts to turn Asia into any kind of "bloc." It is more likely that Japan or South Korea, which have both seen huge increases in the percentage of their total trade with

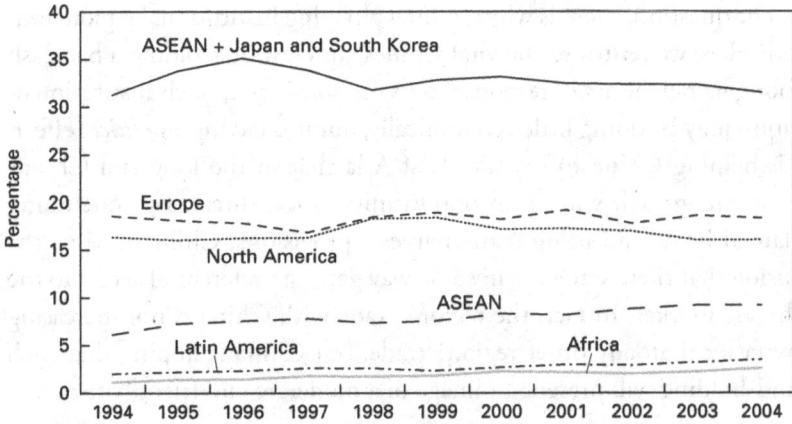

Source: China Statistical Yearbook.

Figure 2.3 China's World Trade by Region, 1994–2004

China, would push for such integration. Finally, it is worth highlight-
ing once again that Taiwan, which is not a part of any of these arrangements, has seen equal if not greater increases in its share of trade with
China and ASEAN. This implies that the institutional infrastructure
currently being built is in many ways not the fundamental cause of
increased trade. The true driver of these increases is the fact that China's
trade with the entire world—and world trade in general—is increasing
at blistering speed.

Indeed, those who interpret the AFC as leading to an inward turn on
the part of Asian leaders may only be partially correct. While it is true
that there was resentment at the West and a desire to take their destiny
into their own hands, the AFC did something else as well: It showed
how dangerous it is to rely on any one region for markets. The danger
is that if that region is hit with turmoil, exports will fall precipitously.
Seeing how quickly the Asian economies could be devastated, an equally
logical reaction would be to make sure that Asian economies remain
open to trade with other regions—indeed, with the whole world—so
that if a similar disaster were to hit again, the effects could be mitigated.
In conclusion, at least in the economic realm, China is not seeking a
"closed" East Asian sphere and is unlikely to do so in the future because
of its interests.

The question, then, is why is China pursuing institutional regionalization? Here we return to the vital Chinese interest of avoiding a backlash among its neighbors in response to its economic rise. Such institutionalization may be doing little economically, but it is having a *political* effect: It is helping China to reassure East Asia that in the long run China's economic growth will be an opportunity, not a threat. By concluding bilateral FTAs and using "early harvest" provisions, China presents the illusion that these states are in some way getting preferential access to the Chinese market. In fact, the region's trade with China is not increasing any faster than any other region's trade, but China is hoping that such hand-holding will present an image of a moderate and friendly rise.

CONCLUSION

Deter without provoking; reassure without appeasing—this is the difficult task that China faces. The PRC's military modernization, laid out in the rest of this volume, is proceeding apace. This chapter argues that it also comes with a substantial cost: provoking concern about China's rise. The PRC seems to be aware of this phenomenon. Beijing has taken concrete steps to reassure its neighbors, even as it continues to build its military and to deter Taiwanese independence. One way in which China has walked this line is to increase its influence through multilateral institutions, which China has managed in such a way as to create strategic contexts in which (1) Taiwan is excluded and (2) countervailing coalitions are unlikely to form. Economically, China has pursued a global development strategy, maintaining an open East Asia to promote its own growth and the foundation of its future power. At the same time, it has supported East Asian financial arrangements, primarily to reassure neighboring states that China's rise will not threaten them economically.

NOTES

1. Michael Yahuda, "The Evolving Asian Order: The Accommodation of Rising Chinese Power," in David L. Shambaugh, ed., *Power Shift: China and Asia's New Dynamic* (Berkeley: University of California Press, 2006), pp. 347–62.

2. Michael A. Glosny, "Heading Toward a Win-Win Future? Recent Developments in China's Policy Towards Southeast Asia," *Asian Security* 2, no. 1 (2006): 24–57.

3. M. Taylor Fravel, "Regime Insecurity and International Cooperation: Explaining China's Compromises in Territorial Disputes," *International Security* 30, no. 2 (2005): 46–47.

4. For more on the land/maritime distinction and its impact on the East Asian balance of power, see Robert S. Ross, "The Geography of the Peace: East Asia in the Twenty-First Century," *International Security* 23, no. 4 (Spring 1999): 81–118.

5. Samuel Sharpe, "An ASEAN Way to Security Cooperation in Southeast Asia?" *Pacific Review* 16, no. 2 (2003): 231–50.

6. Renato Cruz De Castro, "Philippine Defense Policy in the 21st Century: Autonomous Defense or Back to the Alliance?" *Pacific Affairs* 78, no. 3 (2005): 403–22.

7. One small step was taken in that direction in March 2005 when China, the Philippines, and Vietnam agreed jointly to assess the potential for oil and gas exploration under disputed islands.

8. Sakajiri Nobuyoshi, "China Offers Gas Field Proposal," *Asahi Shimbun,* March 7, 2006, http://www.asahi.com/english/Herald-asahi/TKY200603070421.html (last accessed March 29, 2007). For more information on the island dispute and other reasons for Chinese moderation, see Erica Strecker Downs and Phillip C. Saunders, "Legitimacy and the Limits of Nationalism: China and the Diaoyu Islands," *International Security* 23, no. 3 (Winter 1998): 114–46.

9. Most notable was China's demonstration of support for Islam Karimov after Uzbekistan massacred protestors against the regime. See Stephen Blank, "Islam Karimov and the Heirs of Tiananmen," *Eurasia Daily Monitor* 2, no. 115, http://www.jamestown.org/publications_details.php?volume_id=407&issue_id=3365&article_id=2369877 (last accessed March 29, 2007).

10. Keith Crane and others, *Modernizing China's Military: Opportunities and Constraints* (Santa Monica, Calif.: Rand, 2005), pp. 106, xx. As Crane et al. point out, official Chinese military budget estimates do not include foreign weapons procurement and nuclear weapons and strategic rocket programs, among other things.

11. Quansheng Zhao, "Beijing's Dilemma with Taiwan: War or Peace?" *The Pacific Review* 18, no. 2 (2005): 217–42.

12. Ibid., p. 227.

13. Michael McDevitt, "Beijing's Bind," *The Washington Quarterly* 23, no. 3 (2000): 177–86.

14. Stephanie Lieggi, "Going Beyond the Stir: The Strategic Realities of China's No-First-Use Policy," (December, 2005), http://www.nti.org/e_research/e3_70.html (last accessed March 29, 2007).

15. Wang Jisi, *China's Changing Role in Asia* (Washington, DC: The Atlantic Council of the United States, January, 2004), p. 13, http://www.isn.ethz.ch/pubs/ph/details.cfm?q51=wang+jisi&id=10617 (last accessed March 29, 2007).

16. There has been much written by constructivists on Asian multilateral institutions. See, for example, Amitav Acharya and Richard Stubbs, "Theorizing Southeast Asian Relations: An Introduction," *The Pacific Review* 19, no. 2 (2006): 125–34. Alice Ba, "Who's Socializing Whom? Complex Engagement in Sino-ASEAN Relations," *The Pacific Review* 19, no. 2 (2006): 157–79. Alastair Iain Johnston, "Socialization in International Institutions: The ASEAN Way and International Relations Theory," in G. John Ikenberry and Michael Mastanduno, eds., *International Relations Theory and the Asia Pacific* (New York: Columbia University Press, 2003), pp. 107–62.

17. See, for example, Tsuyoshi Kawasaki, "Neither Skepticism nor Romanticism: The ASEAN Regional Forum as a Solution for the Asia-Pacific Assurance Game," *The Pacific Review* 19, no. 2 (2006): 219–37. David M. Lampton, "China's Rise in Asia Need Not Be at America's Expense," in David L. Shambaugh, ed., *Power Shift: China and Asia's New Dynamics* (Berkeley: University of California Press, 2006), p. 314.

18. Evan S. Medeiros and M. Taylor Fravel, "China's New Diplomacy," *Foreign Affairs* 82, no. 6 (Nov./Dec. 2003): 22–35.

19. Yahuda, *The Evolving Asian Order: The Accommodation of Rising Chinese Power*, p. 357.

20. Michael Green, "Executive Decisions: Natural Allies?" *The Indian Express*, March 1, 2006, http://www.indianexpress.com/res/web/pIe/full_story.php?content_id=88748 (last accessed March 29, 2007).

21. China's relations with India have improved rapidly since 2003, with progress made on resolving the border conflict, increased cooperation on energy policy, and, most recently, increased military cooperation after the visit of Indian Defense Minister Pranab Mukherjee with Chinese Defense Minister Cao Gangchuan on May 29, 2006, the latest sign of improving relations.

22. Glosny, "Heading Toward a Win-Win Future? Recent Developments in China's Policy Towards Southeast Asia," p. 46.

23. Henry Sokolski and Andrew J. Grotto, "Is the North Korea Deal Worth Celebrating?" *Council on Foreign Relations Online Debate* (March 16, 2007), http://www.cfr.org/publication/12791/ (last accessed March 28, 2007).

24. C. Raja Mohan, "SAARC Reality Check: China Just Tore up India's Monroe Doctrine," *The Indian Express*, November 14, 2005, http://www.indianexpress.com/res/web/pIe/full_story.php?content_id=81928# (last accessed March 29, 2007).

25. "Pakistan, China Multifaceted Ties Irreversible," *Asian Tribune*, February 17, 2006, www.asiantribune.com/show_news.php?id=17146 (last accessed February 20, 2006).

26. Robert G. Sutter, "China's Regional Strategy and Why It May Not Be Good for America," in David L. Shambaugh, ed., *Power Shift: China and Asia's New Dynamics* (Berkeley: University of California Press, 2006), p. 297.

27. "We're Just Good Friends, Honest," *The Economist,* March 17, 2007, p. 45.

28. Markus Hund, "ASEAN Plus Three: Towards a New Age of Pan-East Asian Regionalism? A Skeptic's Appraisal," *The Pacific Review* 16, no. 3 (2003): 400.

29. Ian James Storey, "Living with the Colossus: How Southeast Asian Countries Cope with China," *Parameters: US Army War College* 29, no. 4 (Winter 1999/2000, 1999): 111.

30. "China Gives Cambodia $600m in Aid," *BBC News,* April 8, 2006, http://news.bbc.co.uk/2/hi/asia-pacific/4890400.stm (last accessed March 29, 2007).

31. Sharpe, "An ASEAN Way to Security Cooperation in Southeast Asia?" pp. 231–50.

32. Peter J. Katzenstein, "Regionalism and Asia," *New Political Economy* 5, no. 3 (November 2000): 357.

33. Richard Stubbs, "ASEAN Plus Three: Emerging East Asian Regionalism?" *Asian Survey* 42, no. 3 (May–June 2002): 441.

34. Takashi Terada, "Constructing an 'East Asian' Concept and Growing Regional Identity: From EAEC to ASEAN+3," *Pacific Review* 16, no. 2 (2003): 251–77.

35. Stubbs, "ASEAN Plus Three: Emerging East Asian Regionalism?" p. 448. Terada, "Constructing an 'East Asian' Concept and Growing Regional Identity: From EAEC to ASEAN+3", pp. 251–77.

36. Christopher M. Dent, "Taiwan and the New Regional Political Economy of East Asia," *The China Quarterly* 182, no. 1 (June 2005): 391–93.

37. Hund, "ASEAN Plus Three: Towards a New Age of Pan-East Asian Regionalism? A Skeptic's Appraisal," p. 407.

38. Dent, "Taiwan and the New Regional Political Economy of East Asia," p. 395.

39. Bruce Vaughn and Wayne Morrison, *China-Southeast Asia Relations: Trends, Issues, and Implications for the United States* (Congressional Research Service: The Library of Congress, April 4, 2006), http://www.fas.org/sgp/crs/row/RL32688.pdf (last accessed March 29, 2007).

40. Dent, "Taiwan and the New Regional Political Economy of East Asia," p. 398.

41. Vaughn and Morrison, *China-Southeast Asia Relations: Trends, Issues, and Implications for the United States*, p. 9.

42. See, for example, Wendy Dobson, "Deeper Integration in East Asia: Regional Institutions and the International Economic System," *The World Economy* 24, no. 8 (2001): 995.

43. Fred Bergsten, "Towards a Tripartite World," *The Economist,* July 15, 2000, p. 23.

44. See, for example, Hund, "ASEAN Plus Three: Towards a New Age of Pan-East Asian Regionalism? A Skeptic's Appraisal," pp. 383–417.

SECTION TWO

People's Liberation Army (PLA) Doctrine and Capabilities

3

The PLA and Joint Operations
Moving from Theory Toward Practice

Dean Cheng

SINCE THE END OF OPERATION DESERT SHIELD/DESERT STORM (1990–1991), the People's Republic of China (PRC) has been engaged in a major effort to restructure and reorient its military forces, the People's Liberation Army (PLA). The speedy prosecution of the first Gulf War indicated to the PLA that its previous views on future warfare were outdated; this conclusion was further supported by the success of the aerial campaign against Serbia in the Bosnia and Kosovo conflicts.

A major part of the Chinese effort to reorient its forces was encapsulated in the so-called Year of Regulations, during which the PLA issued, in 1999, a new set of regulations to govern its future approach to fighting wars. These New Generation Campaign Regulations embody what the PLA has concluded are key lessons and laws (*guīlù*; 规律) regarding "Local Wars Under Modern, High-Tech Conditions."[1]

Prominent among these are new regulations governing "joint operations" (*liánhé zuòzhàn*; 联合作战) or "joint campaigns" (*liánhé zhànyì*; 联合战役). These regulations pave the way for the PLA to undertake a new and significantly different approach to warfare, one which the PLA believes will be the primary form of future conflicts. As one Chinese general has noted, the new military transformation (*xīn jūnshì biàngé*; 新军事变革) will entail a shift to a more joint operational style of warfare.[2] This growing importance of joint operations is reflected in its greater prominence in official PRC publications, including the 2004 and 2006 Chinese white papers on national defense.

This chapter examines these developing views on joint campaigns. It discusses what Chinese authors have indicated are the foremost aspects of this new, primary form of future PLA warfare, including identifying its major characteristics. The chapter briefly explores the major campaign types that are considered "joint." Finally, it lists some of the salient weaknesses that are likely to confront the PLA as the PLA attempts to translate joint operations from theory into reality.

THE EVOLUTION OF PLA THINKING

The PLA's pursuit of joint campaigns is part of a larger reform program that the PLA has been undergoing since the mid-1980s. These efforts were in response to major changes in both the PLA and PRC calculus of the global balance of power.

Most important was the shift to "Peace and Development." Under Deng Xiaoping, the PRC altered its view of the global strategic situation. At the Third Plenum of the 11th Central Committee in 1978, the PRC formally altered its belief that superpower confrontation and the constant risk of imminent war marked the world security situation. Under the new world view, the prospects of world war were considered negligible and China was deemed to face no immediate, major military threats. Consequently, the PRC was no longer compelled to devote its primary energies to preparing for war; instead, its focus shifted to national economic modernization. In this environment, the main threat to the PRC was expected to be more limited conflicts, and thus the PLA prepared for local wars (i.e., those not involving the mass mobilization of the nation and the economy).

By the mid-1980s, however, changes in the technologies of war compelled the modification of the Chinese view of local war, resulting in the formulation "Local Wars Under Modern, High-Tech Conditions." Based on the PLA's observations of the Fourth Middle East War (the 1973 Yom Kippur War), the American war in Vietnam, and the Falklands war, modern technology was seen as exerting a significant influence on the shape of modern warfare. Weapons had greater reach and significantly improved lethality. Equally relevant, surveillance and reconnaissance systems had improved capabilities, making them an essential part of any calculation of force effectiveness. Finally, logistics were a rapidly burgeoning area of concern, as weapons expenditure rates were seen to increase.

By the early 1990s, China's assessment of future wars had shifted again. The continued information technology revolution now not only affected weapons, but also tactics and even strategic outcomes. Modern weapons, as seen in the first Gulf War, shifted the emphasis from the destruction of opponents to paralyzing them, in the course of defeating them. As one key analysis noted, the shape of future wars is likely to entail significant efforts at disrupting the enemy's ability to coordinate its forces, thereby paralyzing the enemy's entire array of combat systems.[3]

Moreover, the new technologies also expanded the operating space, so that land, sea, and air arenas were no longer the complete set of potential battlefields. The same information technologies and improved sensor systems that made modern weapons that much more destructive effectively made information space and outer space key battlegrounds as well. This change was marked in the PRC's 2004 defense white paper, when the formulation "Local Wars Under Modern, High-Tech Conditions" was altered to "Local Wars Under Modern, Informationalized Conditions."

These developments allowed advanced military forces to undertake "noncontact warfare" (*fēi jiēchù zhànzhēng*; 非接触战争) and asymmetrical operations (*fēi duìchèn zuòzhàn*; 非对称作战).[4] The key to such operations rested on the ability to coordinate the various forces and apply one's own strengths against opponents' weaknesses, while ensuring that one's own weaknesses were compensated by other components of the joint operation. The development of ever more capable telecommunications and microelectronics meant that the various participating forces were, in fact, able to operate in a coordinated, integrated fashion.[5] This was enhanced by the development and adoption of common software, standards, and engineering, which have allowed both weapons and command systems to operate as a relatively seamless whole and to behave more like a truly joint organization.[6]

Meanwhile, the pace and destructiveness of modern wars were such that even local wars nonetheless could affect the entire country.[7] Warfare was much more nonlinear in nature, shifting from primarily ground/sea centered, to exploiting all three dimensions; this meant that air power was seen as much more important. At the same time, wars were seen as becoming much more intense, involving round-the-clock operations. This also meant that the sheer material expenditure of warfare was even more substantial, further increasing the importance of logistics and sustainability.

All of these elements were encompassed in the idea of "Local Wars Under Modern, High-Tech Conditions," which became the basis for PLA operational planning in a directive that Jiang Zemin issued to the Chinese Central Military Commission (CMC) in 1993. The "fundamental expression" of "Local Wars Under Modern, High-Tech Conditions," in turn, was joint campaigns.[8]

Based on the observation of trends in recent wars (especially those undertaken by the United States) and modern technology, the expectation was that joint operations would eclipse single-service operations. In the subsequently issued "New Generation Combat Regulations," it was made clear that those regulations governing joint campaigns would take precedence over those for individual service campaigns.[9] By the 2006 defense white paper, the transition was complete, as it was noted, "Taking joint operations as the basic form, the PLA aims to bring the operational strengths of different services and arms into full play."[10]

The PLA's ability to develop a conception of joint operations, however, was hampered by the shortage of homegrown experience with joint operations. Indeed, Chinese writings indicate that the PLA's experience is primarily with combined arms operations, rather than joint campaigns, and even those are predominantly infantry-artillery operations, as will be discussed below. The PLA's experience with joint campaigns is essentially limited to the Yijiangshan campaign of 1955, where a joint PLA task force—incorporating land, sea, and air units—seized the small island of Yijiangshan from Nationalist forces. The PLA considers the Yijiangshan campaign to hold important lessons, despite its small scale.

Given this dearth of domestic experience, the PLA has had instead to rely upon foreign experience. Traditionally, the PLA has looked to the Soviets for inspiration and direction. In the area of joint campaigns, however, that has been less the case. As some PLA authors note, the Soviet Union did not, in fact, have or use the term "joint operation" in its lexicon, relying instead on the term "interservice combined arms operations."[11] In this regard, PLA writers appear to feel that the Soviet experience was primarily with combined arms operations. These tended to focus on the use of a single service, supplemented by other forces. The PRC, by contrast, is apparently much more interested in the development of truly joint (i.e., multiple services on an equal footing) operations.

Consequently, the main foreign model of joint campaigns has been the United States. In particular, the American doctrinal developments in the wake of the Vietnam War were of key interest. The U.S. army's combination of lessons learned from Vietnam and perceived lessons from the "Fourth Middle East War" (the 1973 Yom Kippur War) identified the new circumstances surrounding modern warfare and pushed the United States to adopt the campaign level of war as its cornerstone focus and the "Air-Land Battle" as its expression. In the PLA's view, subsequent U.S. doctrinal developments have built upon these ideas as foundational concepts.

This is not to suggest, however, that Chinese joint operations thinking is a mirror image of that of the United States. Nor does the PLA appear intent upon replicating American concepts of joint operations within its own doctrine. Just as the Chinese will use Soviet terminology, but often with "Chinese characteristics," the same applies to their adoption and adaptation of American concepts of joint operations. It would be most accurate to say that the Chinese version of joint operations builds upon the American experience, using Soviet terminology, to fit Chinese requirements and conditions.

DEFINING JOINT CAMPAIGNS

Given this context, what does the PLA mean when it uses the term "joint?" What are the characteristics of a joint campaign? PLA definitions of joint operations tend to revolve around the following characteristics:

- They involve two or more services.
- These services contribute campaign-level military groupings (*jūntuán*; 军团) to the operation or campaign *jituan* from each of the participating services.
- These forces follow a single, unified campaign plan.
- The plan is formulated, and its execution is overseen, by a single, unified campaign command structure.[12]

This definition suggests four distinct characteristics of joint campaigns. First, joint campaigns are marked by the scale of participation. That is, a campaign is considered joint based on the number of services participating and their respective contributions to the campaign, and *not* on the scale of the campaign itself. Indeed, Chinese writings note that even a very large campaign is still only a service campaign unless there are more than two services participating, and those forces are at least at the *juntuan* level. Otherwise, the campaign is primarily a combined-arms campaign (i.e., single service level), with the non-*juntuan*-level units providing support to the *juntuan*-level formations.

Second, joint campaigns operate under a joint campaign command structure. Joint campaign command structures are superior to the service command structures, even though they may be drawn from the various participating services' and war zone's command structures and personnel. This joint campaign command structure is responsible for planning the campaign and providing command and control once the campaign has begun. This is in sharp contrast to individual service campaigns in which the command structure is comprised of the lead service's command personnel. In service campaigns, other services play a minor role, at best serving to augment the lead service's staff.

Implicit to both the issue of the scale of participation and the command structure is the fundamental equivalence of the participating services. Indeed, it is specifically noted that, in a joint campaign, all the services are considered equal, from a seniority/protocol standpoint, with no service having preeminence over any other. This is a fundamental and major shift in PLA culture. As one article in *Junshi Kexue* has specifically noted, the PLA's historical reliance on the ground forces had resulted in an incorrect view that victory required emphasizing only one service. This perspective, it was noted, was wrong in the context of future joint operations.[13] The primary repository of combat theory and principles lies not solely in the ground forces, but instead among all the services, as well as among nascent elements of the military charged with space combat and information dominance. Joint campaigns presume that ground forces, naval forces, air forces, Second Artillery, and potentially even the militia and People's Armed Police (PAP) formations all can and will make essential contributions to attaining victory.

This is not to suggest, however, that all the services involved in a joint campaign are to be considered equal or interchangeable regardless of the circumstances. Under particular conditions or in pursuit of specific missions, emphasis on one particular service may be more appropriate; that service's forces should therefore take precedence in that instance. However, in the course of the entire campaign, each service relies on the other participating services for support, and, therefore, none are more important than the others in the overall pursuit of the campaign objective.

Finally, the *organization* of the joint campaign is essential. The aim of a joint campaign is to allow the participating forces to mutually reinforce each other and exploit the resulting synergies to help attain overall advantage, thereby achieving the joint campaign objective. The organization and coordination efforts of the joint campaign command structure are instrumental in linking together services' combined arms campaigns towards this end. The cornerstone of Chinese thinking on the operational level of war ("integrated operations and key point strikes") therefore reaches its apotheosis in joint campaigns. It is an effort to integrate various service campaigns and strike at key enemy weaknesses with the overall, comprehensive strength of all the involved forces. Jointness, in this view, is as much an end product of planning and coordination as it is a specific form or style of combat.

DIFFERENCES BETWEEN JOINT AND COMBINED ARMS CAMPAIGNS

For the PLA, joint campaigns are fundamentally different from the services' combined arms campaigns, even when the latter may involve forces from more than one service. Joint campaigns are considered a higher, more complex level of campaign than combined arms campaigns. They involve not only more services, but also more considerations and implications; they differ in scale and scope.

In terms of scale, as noted above, joint campaigns involve two or more services; they involve *juntuan*-level forces (in general) from each participating service and they have a joint command structure, drawn from all the participating services' command staffs. There is no "lead" or "senior" service within the joint campaign (although individual phases or portions may have a specific service's capabilities emphasized). In terms of scope, a combined arms campaign is generally not expected to be nearly as decisive as a joint campaign. Joint campaigns are seen as explicitly having strategic implications; they are expected to have political, economic, and diplomatic ramifications, while requiring the accommodation of political, economic, and diplomatic considerations.[14]

Combined arms campaigns, on the other hand, are more limited in outlook and impact. A combined arms campaign will usually have a "lead" service, which provides the bulk of the forces involved. Thus, an air defense campaign, as an air force combined arms campaign, will draw most of its forces from the air force. Any other participating service's forces in a combined arms campaign will be on a much smaller scale than those of the lead service.

Similarly, the command structure of a combined arms campaign will draw most of its staff from the lead service's command system. Any other participating service would detail lower ranking command elements to the lead service's command structure. Equally important, they would clearly be subordinate to the lead service's personnel and organization. A service campaign, given its more limited scope and scale, is not expected to necessarily have strategic implications.

It is important to note, however, that service-based, or combined arms, campaigns still have a vital role *within* joint campaigns. After a joint campaign plan is established, the component services' activities are developed as service campaigns. Thus, a joint campaign is actually comprised of several combined arms campaigns, undertaken either sequentially or simultaneously.[15] The integrated, overall whole is considered the joint campaign.

The differences are most clearly delineated in comparing joint and combined arms campaigns. Thus, if one compares the characteristics of air campaigns in the joint (counter-air) and service (air defense) contexts, the former are more expansive and include a broader array of considerations and types of combat methods and styles than does the latter. Moreover, they incorporate planning that addresses preventive measures, defensive measures, and countering measures. Thus, key activities undertaken within a counter-air campaign would include:

- *Preventive Measures*:
  - Create an effective early warning and intelligence system; issue air defense warnings at the appropriate time;
  - Utilize various methods to create an aerial defense (including concealment and deception measures); and
  - Organize repair and rescue, to eradicate the effects of aerial attack.

- *Defensive Measures*:
  - Accurately determine the main defensive axes;
  - Combine the use of different defensive methods (including long-range engagement, layered defenses, etc.); and
  - Manage the developing situation.

- *Counterattack Measures*:
  - Pick the right time for counterattacking;
  - Precisely determine the target of the counterattack; and
  - Flexibly apply counterattack tactics.

This is a taxonomy that does not occur in air defense campaigns (i.e., at the service level), and the component activities of each of these measures are not correlated with those seen in air defense campaigns. Instead, defensive air campaigns:

- Firmly grasp the enemy's situation and adjust the campaign elements;
- Counter the enemy's electronic suppression and disrupt their aerial assault;
- Accurately grasp opportunities and counterattack at the right time; and
- Organize for avoidance and reduce the losses from enemy attack.[16]

This difference in the subsumed activities involved in each campaign may be due to the inherently more strategic orientation of the counter-air campaign. Moreover, given the types of activities involved, counter-air campaigns are more likely to require the participation of other services, such as in the formation of layered defenses.[17] Hence, both the greater strategic orientation and the greater number of services (and areas of operation) involved in counter-air campaigns accord with the characteristics of joint campaigns.

COMMAND AND COORDINATION
FOR JOINT CAMPAIGNS

The cornerstone of the ability to undertake joint campaigns is the command and control structure. If a joint campaign is conceptually an orchestrated series of service campaigns, each of which is aimed at contributing to the attainment of the overall campaign goal(s), then the command structure is essential in "conducting" the campaign. It is responsible for resolving issues of timing, phasing, and various other aspects of coordination among the service campaigns. It is this coordination that makes the overall campaign "joint." Not surprisingly, much of the PLA's writings on joint campaigns is therefore focused on the joint campaign command structure and its coordination responsibilities.

Joint Campaign Command Structures

Because no individual service is more important than any other in the context of a joint campaign, the PLA emphasizes that successful joint campaigns require a truly joint command system to undertake operational planning and oversee their execution. According to PLA writings, the joint campaign command structure will vary, based on the scale of the joint campaign.

The largest scale joint campaign, a war zone strategic campaign (*zhànqū zhànlüèxìng zhànyì*; 战区战略性战役), will be built upon a three-tier campaign command structure. It will usually include not only war zone and service command staff, but also, when necessary, senior leadership elements from the central government and the General Staff in its highest tier; "the joint campaign command section is the highest level command structure for campaigns and receives direction from the senior leadership."[18] Its second tier, depending on the type of command structure that is in place, will either be the war zone direction command section or the service campaign command section, drawn from the relevant staff. Finally, the lowest tier of the three-tier joint command structure will be the campaign-level *juntuan* command section, which would be drawn from the leading service's campaign *juntuan* command section. Thus, a three-tier joint command structure will include both high-level command personnel from the central government and the relevant PLA Departments, while still retaining familiar command personnel and relationships, who should be conversant in the unique aspects of the relevant war zones.

A war zone direction (*zhànqū fāngxiàng*; 战区方向) joint campaign command structure on a medium scale has a two-tier campaign command structure. Its members are usually drawn from the war zone and service command staffs. This structure can directly command army, navy, and air force *juntuan* in the course of the campaign. The remaining service staffs are subordinate to the joint campaign command staff. The service staffs are responsible for overseeing their individual *juntuan*'s organization and activities even as they implement the overall joint campaign plan.

A group army-scale (*jítuán jūnjí*; 集团军级) joint campaign, the smallest, will have a single-tier command structure. This will often be centered on the staff of the main service of the campaign, while absorbing relevant personnel from other services. Such a joint command structure appears to be applicable only in very small-scale joint campaigns, where the totality of forces may only amount to a single *juntuan*. It would seem that the difference between a single-tier joint command structure and a combined arms campaign's command structure is marginal, which may be due to the presumed limited scope of a single-level joint command structure's campaign. It should be noted that the Yijiangshan campaign, the PLA's primary combat experience with joint campaigns, is considered to be a case of either a single-tier or, at most, a two-tier command structure.

What is important to note, however, beyond the details of the various tiers of the joint campaign command, is PLA recognition that joint campaign command structures are not "one-size-fits-all." Rather than adopting a "cookie-cutter" approach, the PLA emphasizes that different scales of joint campaigns require different joint campaign command structures.

At the same time, these command structures have similar responsibilities. The joint campaign command staff is in charge of the mission planning, organization, and direction of the subordinate service elements. Mission planning involves setting the campaign objective (with due attention to national requirements); determining campaign methods, preparations, and safeguarding; and the myriad planning tasks associated with each of these tasks. Organization involves laying out coordination efforts among the participating services, preparing the combat support and combat service support forces for their functions ("safeguarding"), including transportation duties, providing specialized training where relevant, and establishing the command centers.

These command centers will actually direct the campaign. It is expected that a joint campaign command will include a combat operations center, an intelligence center, an information center, and a "safeguarding" center—the last being charged with combat support and combat service support-type missions. Other centers that may be established include a combined fire support center and an information warfare center.

In this context, with the participating services talking to each other, the joint campaign command structure is expected to exercise command and control functions over *all* the participating forces, throughout the course of the campaign. This means, in the first place, that the joint campaign command structure is assumed to be the final decision-making body within a campaign. It is presumed to have final and absolute command and control authority (*juéduìde zhǐhuī kòngzhì quán*; 绝对的指挥控制权).[19]

Furthermore, the joint campaign command headquarters is expected to engage in overall assessments of the situation, order forces to respond, determine consequences, and adjust to the new situation as necessary.[20] And it is expected to operate on a flexible, ad hoc basis.[21] It is almost certainly no accident that these functions mirror the classic elements of the "Boyd decision cycle" (i.e., observe, orient, decide, and act—or OODA). At all times, the focus must be on the campaign's objectives, with command activities aimed at achieving the goals by supporting the relevant activities.

Joint Campaign Coordination

The main task of the joint campaign command structure is to implement coordination. This must be exercised over all the participating forces, during the course of the entire campaign and across the breadth of the involved battle space. Campaign coordination is considered essential because the proliferation of new weapons, and the expansion of the joint battlefield to encompass new venues of conflict, make campaign command a much more complex task.

The proliferation of campaign combat power means that there are many more imposing tasks in coordinating different combat tactics (e.g., firepower attacks, missile attacks), across multiple potential battlefields (e.g., sea, space), and eliminates the previous "phased" concept of campaign operations (i.e., an initial defensive phase, followed by a shift to offensive activities). Joint campaign command personnel must be conversant with the strengths and weaknesses of *each* of the participating services, including their attendant weapons and their relative strength in conventional and unconventional approaches to warfare.

Such coordination, it is noted, is possible primarily because of the advances in telecommunications over the past decade. This allows the various services to share a single information network, which in turn allows them to form a single picture of the situation and work toward a common goal.[22]

At present, the PLA continues to emphasize that coordination efforts must focus on the main campaign objective and along the main directions and war zones. That is, there must be *overall* coordination; the joint command structure must, in its coordination plans, focus on the overall objectives and combat missions, and utilize all the available forces toward achieving those ends. Chinese writings repeatedly emphasize that the command structure's foremost responsibility is the application of the right service to the right mission.

To facilitate this, the various participating services are all considered to be on equal footing. The joint command structure, at least in the two- and three-tier cases, is considered to have precedence over purely service-based commands (i.e., it outranks the individual service commands). The joint campaign command structure is responsible for making coordination decisions solely based on what will benefit the overall campaign. It prepares a single, integrated plan, in pursuit of a common set of objectives, which the subordinate participating services are then to execute. Of course, along a specific direction, or on a specific battlefield, one service is likely to be more appropriate or proficient, and in that specific situation, it is to be the lead service. That precedence, however, is likely to change in the course of the overall campaign.

Coordination, according to PLA writings, can therefore be undertaken in three ways: by battle space, phasing, or mission.

BATTLE SPACE. If undertaking joint campaign coordination by *battle space*, each participating service is given specific operational spaces that are its responsibility. It is presumed that such assignments will exploit the relative strengths of each participating service while minimizing their respective weaknesses. This is undertaken after due consideration of overall campaign timing, battle space, and missions; special effort must be accorded to ensuring that the various participating forces do not interfere with one another. Moreover, priority per battle space must be assigned based on the campaign's ends, rather than service interests.

This coordination method is probably the most likely for the PLA, at least in the near term. On the one hand, it takes into account the Chinese assessment that future joint campaigns will almost certainly involve operations across the spectrum of operational spaces. That is, in light of the characteristics of modern, high-tech warfare, joint campaigns mean that future operations will occur across a greatly expanded range of environments, including not only the traditional venues of air, land, and sea, but also outer space, information space, and the electromagnetic spectrum. The campaign command structure must therefore be able to operate within all of these environments.

At the same time, such coordination is also one of the relatively easier means of coordinating among the various services. It involves minimal interfacing between the services and allows each to conduct semi-autonomous operations within their realm of expertise. For forces that have never operationally conducted truly joint operations, coordination by battle space is likely to be relatively easier. At the same time, however, the synergies that might be gained from joint operations are minimized when coordinating by battle space.

PHASING. When undertaking joint campaign coordination by *phasing*, by contrast, it is necessary to first map out the campaign's phases, and then to determine the missions of each of the participating forces for *each* phase. The available strength (*liliàng*; 力量) is then organized to accomplish these key missions, within each phase. It is possible, depending on the phasing, that a given service or force will go from supporting role in one phase to dominant role in another, or vice versa. The most attention must be paid to the transitional period between phases, because this is the most vulnerable period. As PLA authors have noted, if the transition between phases is not properly managed, then the previous phases' coordination efforts are likely to complicate subsequent phases, affecting the ultimate outcome of the entire campaign.

Joint campaign coordination by phasing is more complex than by battle space because the forces are expected to interact more with each other within each phase. Based on the descriptions of such coordination, however, it would appear to be akin to coordinating combined arms campaigns with interservice support (albeit on a higher scale and more complex level of interaction). In many ways, then, joint campaign coordination by phasing is a midway point, gaining greater synergies and benefits, while still accommodating more service-oriented planning.

MISSION. The most complex form of joint campaign coordination is by *mission*. This requires first determining the overall goal of the campaign. Once that is accomplished, then smaller missions necessary to achieve those goals can be determined, and available forces can be assigned to each of those missions. In the process of assigning forces, who is supporting whom needs to be determined as well as which missions need to have priority. The command structure then coordinates the lead and supporting roles of the relevant forces.

As in the U.S. military, this form of coordination is seen by the PLA as the most powerful, because it is, in essence, effects-based planning (i.e., forces are allocated based entirely on whether they are likely to be effective for a given task, without regard for service origination).[23] In this regard, such coordination would represent a fundamental shift in PLA capabilities. The other forms of jointness are described as "bundling" (*bǎngkǔnshì*; 绑困式), wherein the individual services and branches are essentially still autonomous. By contrast, the PLA's ostensible objective is to achieve "melded" jointness (*rónghéshì*; 融合式) in which the various component service and branch forces and activities are essentially integrated and focused together on their mission.[24]

Such coordination, however, is also the most difficult. Mission-oriented jointness would not have neatly defined phases during which one or another service would be in charge. Instead, such jointness would implicitly involve a constant interaction among the participating forces, with a focus on the task at hand. For a military such as the PLA, with a minimal history of acting jointly, this would represent a major and fundamental change in its very corporate culture.

FLEXIBILITY. The level of coordination required for any of these types of joint operations entails extensive planning. But joint campaigns also require flexibility. In particular, they require recognizing when the plan has failed, or must suffer extreme changes in order to achieve the mission ends. In short, one of the key coordination missions is to produce a thorough coordination plan that takes into account likely failures. Toward this end, *Zhanyi Xue* calls for "firm, flexible coordination."[25] Firm flexibility refers to strenuously overcoming all difficulties and obstacles and firmly holding to the coordination plan, but when circumstances change drastically, flexibility implements ad hoc coordination so as to maintain the stability and continuity of the coordination. Whether or not joint combat commanders, based on developments and changes on the battlefield, will be able to implement firm flexible coordination will have an enormous impact on the battle's smooth progress as well as the realization of the preplanned combat goals.

The firmness of coordination is primarily referring to firmly following the coordination plan. Joint combat activities' highly complex nature and prevention/security plans determine that adhering to the coordination plan is the primary means of organizing joint combat coordination. It is also a primary technique by which combat commanders and command structures implement coordination in the course of combat. Therefore, it is necessary to overcome all difficulties and obstacles and not be moved by local sacrifices and friction. It is necessary to constantly seek to revive broken or disrupted coordination, and firmly and thoroughly obey the coordination plan.

The flexibility of coordination refers to being able to respond to changes in battlefield conditions by implementing new coordination plans and efforts. Ad hoc coordination is an essential, important form of joint combat coordination and an essential supplement to precampaign coordination planning. PLA authors recognize that, in joint combat under high-tech conditions, even the most closely planned prebattle coordination plan will not be able to predict the myriad possible changes and eventualities. When the situation undergoes massive change, the original coordination plan may no longer be appropriate to the new battlefield situation. Therefore, based on the changes in the battlefield situation, flexible implementation of ad hoc coordination may be necessary.[26]

This flexible coordination is mainly expressed in two ways. When battlefield situations locally change, one should promptly make the proper adjustments, corrections, and supplements while adhering to the foundation of the original coordination plan. However, when the battlefield situation has undergone a major change, then there must be the prompt development of a new coordinating plan in order to maintain the various combat forces' coordinated activities and ensure that the overall campaign proceeds smoothly.[27]

It is in this latter context that the emphasis on coordination across command levels and between services is most important. Chinese writings suggest that the PLA is seeking to inculcate a new culture of mission-oriented orders and obedience, so that even when the original coordination plans are invalidated by new developments, or otherwise go awry, the PLA will nonetheless continue to focus on achieving its campaign objectives. One article notes that the focus of command efforts should shift from precampaign planning toward midbattle adjusting (*yóu zhànqián jìhuà wéi zhǔ xiàng zhànzhōng tiáokòng wéi zhòng*; 由战前计划 为主 向战中调控为重).[28]

To help achieve this, the various joint campaign command structures are also responsible for facilitating horizontal coordination among the participating service forces on their tier of responsibility. This horizontal cross-coordination is considered to be a special characteristic (*tèzhēng*; 特征) of joint operations.[29]

These command structures are also in charge of creating the preconditions for success for the next lower level, and even the next *two* lower levels, if they are responsible for a main direction or a key transition time or otherwise engaging in vital combat activity. Lower tiers, meanwhile, are expected in their coordination efforts to complete their missions so as to enable higher command's objectives. As *Zhanyi Xue* explicitly states, part of the task of coordination for each command level is not only to direct the activities at their level, but also to understand and facilitate the missions and responsibilities of the next higher *and* lower levels.[30]

The Greatly Expanded Joint Battlefield

Coupled with the expanded range of weapons and capabilities is the increasingly expansive battlefield, which now extends to the electromagnetic spectrum and outer space, as well as encompassing far greater areas of the sea and air. This is due, in no small part, to the concomitant increase in modern technology, especially high technology. It is argued that precision-guided munitions are now commonplace, as are long-range strike platforms and weapons. Therefore, the physical extent of the actual battlefield is much greater. The Gulf War, for example, spread over some 140 million square kilometers.[31] Joint campaign command structures must at least be cognizant of the interplay among land, sea, and air arenas over extended areas.

As important, the PLA, in examining foreign military experiences and the pace of technological change, has concluded that future conflicts will extend beyond the earth-bound realm. Indeed, the authors appear to believe that future warfare will involve space, which will be as vital a battlefield as any on earth, given the growing reliance on space-based sensors for reconnaissance and surveillance, as well as space platforms for data relay, meteorology, and so forth.[32]

These systems represent an increasingly essential role in the command and coordination aspects of joint campaigns. Under present circumstances, space systems primarily provide support functions: reconnaissance, surveillance, data relay, as well as meteorological and earth observation support. It is partly through the application of space systems that weapons are more accurate and far-flung forces can be coordinated. Therefore, in "Local Wars Under Modern, High-Tech (or Informationalized) Conditions," land, sea, and air battlefields all rely much more on information systems, many of which operate in outer space, for support and safeguarding. In particular, given the key support roles that space-based platforms play, PLA authors have noted that securing space dominance is one means of seizing the initiative and preventing opponents from being able to coordinate their forces.

Based on PLA writings, then, it is likely that joint campaigns will involve measures to undertake space-based operations. This aspect has gained particular prominence in the wake of the Chinese anti-satellite (ASAT) test of January 2007. The destruction of a defunct Chinese weather satellite with a kinetic-kill vehicle suggests that the PLA may be intent on developing the ability to destroy space-based assets. However, in the context of joint operations, military operations in space, like joint counter-air campaigns, are likely to entail *fáng* (防), *fǎn* (反), and *kàng* (抗). That is, the PLA is likely to incorporate not only hard-kill methods, but also apply various deceptive measures and stealth techniques to defend against enemy space-based observation.

PLA authors also note the growing importance of the electromagnetic spectrum in military operations. The references to electronic warfare, it should be noted, almost certainly do not refer solely to jamming and electronic countermeasures (ECM) and counter-countermeasures (ECCM), but also to the range of operations in the electromagnetic spectrum, including the entire array of C4ISR.

Furthermore, another likely future arena is the related conflict in "informational space." Sometimes referred to as information warfare, again, the Chinese terminology does not appear to be fully analogous with that of the United States. Chinese references to information warfare include not only computer viruses and network/Internet warfare, but also the importance of stealth, deception, and misleading an opponent. A far more accurate term, then, would be "perception management" or "infospace warfare"—in either case denoting the much broader parameters involved.

The information battle already affects and permeates the joint campaign's various other battlefields and is a key factor in determining the outcome and course of the joint campaign. Joint campaign initiative will be determined by the winner of the infospace war. As one PLA general notes, "Seizing information dominance will become the main activity of joint operations."[33] According to such PLA assessments, in future combat, there will be no campaigns without information campaigns, and information combat will be part of every other combat and campaign activity; for the PLA, information superiority and dominance is a major determinant of the joint campaign battlefield.

In the PLA's conception of future joint campaigns, all three of these new venues are integral to joint operations. Indeed, it appears that they have become recognized as new arenas for combat primarily in the context of joint operations. Whether this is because bureaucratically they had not fallen directly into any specific service's purview, or whether it is because they have an especially great impact on joint campaigns, is unclear.

IMPLICATIONS OF THE PLA'S SHIFT TO JOINTNESS

Organizations do not readily undergo change; military organizations in particular are often very conservative on matters of change. The question therefore arises: Why is the PLA pursuing the transition to a joint campaign-dominated approach to warfare? The answer would seem to involve several levels.

First, given their analyses of recent wars, the PLA appears to have concluded that it is essential to prepare for wars wherein "the nation as a whole will not be placed onto a war footing and would not require the mobilization of the great masses."[34] Instead, the PLA must focus on preparing for limited wars that last for only one campaign, rather than more protracted wars.

Joint campaigns in particular, however, "have an even more prominent strategic consequence than campaigns in general."[35] Since joint campaigns impact and influence not only military considerations, but also the political, economic, and diplomatic arenas, they significantly affect the nation's welfare and the public's safety.[36] The PLA would therefore be derelict not to study and prepare for joint campaigns.

Moreover, joint campaigns are an essential means of creating the synergies that are sought through integrated operations and are instrumental to "Local or Limited Wars Under Modern, High-Tech Conditions." The joint campaign is an essential means of overcoming overall qualitative inferiority by exploiting the interactions among forces and individual service advantages to create local qualitative parity, if not superiority. In this regard, the more integrated the forces (e.g., able to integrate at lower levels, or able to integrate by mission, rather than by battle space), the greater the benefits.

Indeed, in the context of "integrated operations, key point strikes," joint campaigns are especially important. "Key point strikes" involve striking at the enemy's most important vulnerabilities with the greatest effect with one's own forces. It is winning the struggle at the key point that allows the joint campaign to be decisive. Emphasizing the key points of time, space, and objective, the joint campaign allows the PLA to commit its best available forces, regardless of service origin, to the most decisive effect at the most critical junctures in a campaign.

Thus, PLA writings posit that joint campaigns offer the greatest chance of utilizing synergies among the PLA's services, including their various operating environments (land, sea, air) and their respective technological strengths (Su-27s, advanced surface-to-air missiles [SAMs], *Sovremennys*) to mitigate individual weaknesses. The aim is to create a condition of local superiority in both qualitative and possibly even quantitative terms, against generally technologically superior opponents. As one analysis notes, a hallmark of modern warfare is the need to coordinate various weapons systems, in order to "exploit strengths and cover weaknesses" (*qǔcháng, bǔduǎn*; 取长补短) because on the modern battlefield, no single weapon system, branch, or service is likely to be able to dominate.[37] This also allows the PLA to nominally retain its links to Maoist and asymmetric strategy, including the ideas of "nǐ dǎ nǐde, wǒ dǎ wǒde" (你打你的我打我的), and applying PLA strengths against enemy weaknesses.

Conversely, the PLA, looking at recent historical examples of joint warfare (Falklands, Gulf War, etc.) has apparently concluded that single-service campaigns are unlikely to lead to victory. Because of the proliferation of combat styles (*zuòzhàn yàngshì*; 作战样式), no single service is the repository of sufficient skills and capabilities to counter an opponent. Instead, the new face of warfare requires the participation of different services in order to exploit their respective proficiencies. In essence, there are now more sources of strength; wars are no longer ground forces-dominated military situations.[38]

In this revised view, the best means of defeating an enemy air attack, for example, may not be through the use of air defense forces, but may instead draw upon army and air forces assets to conduct missile attacks against staging areas or exploit air defenses arrayed in depth. In order to engage an opponent, especially a technologically more sophisticated opponent, it is therefore necessary to utilize all the available resources at one's disposal. One's opponent is equally likely to do so, making reliance upon a single branch much more dangerous, because it is more subject to "single-point failure." Relying on only one service is more likely to result in the ability to utilize only a limited range of such styles; this allows an opponent to be better positioned to undertake asymmetric operations and exploit more combat space and methods, thereby increasing the opponent's chances of victory.

Moving from Theory to Actual Practice

The PLA has clearly devoted significant time and effort to formulating an approach to joint campaigns suitable for its own requirements. Moreover, as the PLA itself recognizes, it is still in the relatively early stages of jointness. Indeed, one PLA characterization of joint command and control is very illuminating. It is suggested that jointness may be compared to a three-egg model:

• There are three eggs in a bowl—preliminary joint training;
• There are three eggs broken into a bowl—limited joint training;
• There are three eggs broken into a bowl, and then mixed together—all-around joint training.[39]

This analogy neatly captures the sense of both where the PLA is now (it is still in the relatively early stages of preliminary and limited joint training), and where it wants to be, aiming at all-around joint training.

Given its lack of experience with jointness, the PLA is seeking to improve its indigenous foundation. This may be seen in the PLA's characterization of its recent efforts in combating floods and other natural disasters as "quasi-military actions." In response to these major disasters, the PLA sought to apply its new military doctrine to aid and relief efforts. Thus, the 1998 floods reportedly involved "all-round national defense mobilization, deployment of troops . . . [and] *joint command.*"[40]

In the meantime, the PLA apparently hopes to expand upon the experiences of foreign militaries. But whether foreign experiences can be exploited without importing the attendant cultural and experiential aspects to the PLA is open to question. A general reliance on junior officers and noncommissioned officers (NCO), for example, to bear the brunt of the burden for battlefield decision making is essential to much of Air-Land Battle. But that, in turn, builds upon a general willingness to decentralize decision making, not only in the military, but in the culture at large.

Toward this end, the PLA is overhauling its approach to training in order to better prepare its personnel to undertake joint operations. Such training begins with officer education. The PLA's National Defense University is actively educating both mid- and high-ranking officers in "joint command under informationalized conditions" in order to inculcate them with the sense that future campaigns will be joint in nature.[41]

Another aspect of expanding jointness within the PLA has been the increasing emphasis on joint operations in the combat support and service support arenas. Thus, there have been reports on increasingly joint logistics and communications exercises. The Nanjing Military Region (MR), for example, "organized a war-zone joint-combat communications training" event in July 2004 to discuss army, navy, air force, and Second Artillery combat communications requirements.[42] This is only part of the overall effort undertaken throughout the Nanjing MR to transition from *coordinated* joint operations toward *integrated* joint operations (*cóng xiétóngxìng liánhé zuòzhàn xiàng yìtǐhuà liánhé zuòzhàn fāngxiàng fāzhǎn*; 从协同性联合作战向一体化联合作战方向发展). This is, in essence, shifting from "three eggs in a bowl" to "three eggs broken into a bowl" or even "three eggs mixed in a bowl."

This transition is not only at the discussion stage. A June 2004 report, for example, suggests that joint communications teams have already been established and are engaging in exercises. These teams are apparently responsible for safeguarding the communications network for an entire war zone (*zhànqū*; 战区); in this case, the one centered around the Beijing MR.[43]

Along these lines, the PLA's General Staff Department's (GSD) training guidance for 2005 specified that joint and combined arms training were to be top priorities for the year. This included training in "complex electronic warfare environments" and incorporating informationalized conditions into the training regimen.[44]

Whether the PLA will succeed in these efforts remains to be seen. It is unclear, for example, how much institutional resistance has been incurred as service prerogatives are violated. The difficulties in imposing jointness on the American military, despite extensive historical experience with joint operations, are a matter of record, requiring an act of Congress (the 1986 Goldwater-Nichols Defense Reorganization Act) to overcome them.[45] The PLA is likely to entail similar levels of bureaucratic opposition when adopting this new approach. Indeed, as joint campaigns clearly require a downgrading of the relative importance of the land forces and a concomitant increase in the importance of air and naval forces, there are likely to be powerful opponents to such a shift. Some aspects of this opposition have already apparently arisen, with some officers still reflecting an emphasis on ground forces to the exclusion of the other services, while at the same time, other services' officers *overestimating* their home services' importance.[46]

In this regard, very high-level efforts have apparently been focused on overcoming said resistance. For example, one of the new members of the GSD, General Ge Zhenfeng, has reportedly been charged with raising "the effectiveness of the joint command of the three services to cope with the requirement of fighting under conditions of high technology and informationization."[47] Toward this end, he is reportedly expanding the GSD to include more members of the senior leadership of the navy, air force, and Second Artillery. The aim is to break the grip of the ground forces on PLA thinking and instill a sense of jointness at the highest levels in order to complement the lower level efforts at familiarizing the forces and units with joint operations.

The PLA's simultaneous effort to incorporate more advanced technologies and a more expansive sense of battle space into its campaigns complicate even further these systemic factors. The introduction of significant new technologies imposes significant strains on any military; the same applies to the expansion of operational purview. In both cases, there are training, logistics, and deployment considerations.

Impact of Joint Operations on a Taiwan Scenario

The PLA's focus on joint operations has significant implications for a Taiwan scenario. In the broadest sense, from a capabilities-based rather than contingency-based perspective, the inculcation of a more joint approach toward military operations in general within the PLA is expected to lead to a more effective PLA. The fact that joint operations are portrayed as a "basic form of operations" for the PLA, as set forth in the 2006 defense white paper, means that a PLA that is better able to execute joint operations is one that will be more effective in any contingency, including one centered on the Taiwan Strait.

Indeed, many of the types of joint campaigns set out in *Zhanyi Xue* are likely to arise in a Taiwan contingency, but might be of interest under other conditions as well. These include joint air and counter-air campaigns and joint blockade operations (e.g., in the South China Sea). Similarly, joint offensive and defensive ground campaigns would be of use anywhere that conflict arose on China's periphery.

At the same time, from a contingencies-based perspective, increasing proficiency in joint operations means that the PLA will be better poised to undertake operations specifically against Taiwan. In particular, the conduct of amphibious operations requires the ability to operate jointly. As the U.S. military has noted, "an amphibious operation is ordinarily joint in nature and may require extensive air, maritime, land, space, and special operations forces participation."[48]

The seaborne delivery of ground forces against a hostile shore has been characterized as one of the most difficult of military operations.[49] At a minimum, there are problems of simply coordinating the movement of a large number of troops and their subsequent deployment.

> There are organizational and technical challenges, fraught with potential sources of friction in coordinating [sic] and sustaining a wide range of different elements; such as the carriers, land based air, landing craft, helicopters, and the landing force itself. There are the natural hazards of the surf, rocks, and sandbars close to shore. . . .[50]

As important, an amphibious assault entails enormous issues of coordination across services. The coordination of the command and control of the landing forces and the relationship between the landing forces and the naval forces transporting and supporting them is perhaps the most difficult form of joint coordination. A PLA that is incapable of conducting joint operations broadly is one that would likely fail in the difficult task of launching an amphibious attack on Taiwan.

The converse is not necessarily true, however. Simply because the PLA accepts the importance of joint operations, and even if it has trained its forces to undertake joint operations to a high degree of proficiency, does not mean that it could necessarily undertake a successful assault on Taiwan. Unless the PLA finds a prior opportunity to engage in actual joint operations against a live opponent, it would be attempting to implement the most difficult of operations as its *first* joint campaign. It would be employing a doctrine that it has developed in no small part through observation of *foreign experiences* with indigenous forces and command and control structures exhibiting "Chinese characteristics."

Such a situation would be extremely daunting because such an operation would be testing the PLA's success in incorporating a new doctrine, assimilating new weapons, and breeding a new corporate culture, all in the face of enemy resistance. Moreover, as PLA authors have written (as noted above), "Local Wars Under Modern, High-Tech (now "Informationalized") Conditions" are often only one campaign long; thus, success or failure may well be decided in short order, with decisive implications for Beijing's ability to assert sovereignty over Taiwan.

The ability of the PLA to successfully undertake joint operations therefore has potentially enormous repercussions for the PRC. In this regard, the PLA has begun to operationalize its ambitious goals in this area and has made significant strides at the doctrinal level to this end. Nonetheless, in the absence of real combat experience, how well the PLA will be able to actualize these goals in the heat of battle remains a key unknown.

NOTES

This chapter draws from material originally prepared for "Zhanyixue and Joint Operations," in James Mulvenon and David Finkelstein, eds., *China's Revolution in Doctrinal Affairs: Emerging Trends in the Operational Art of the Chinese People's Liberation Army* (Alexandria, Va.: The CNA Corporation, 2005).

1. "Local Wars Under Modern, High-Tech Conditions" is the PLA's description of its concept of future wars. "Local Wars" refers to the idea that these are more limited conflicts, unlike the Mao-era total war; "Modern, High-Tech Conditions" emphasizes that future wars will require high technology and was further modified in 2004 to "Modern, Informationalized Conditions" to reflect the highest importance accorded to information technology and information generally.

2. "PLA Deputy Chief of Staff Xiong Guangjie Discusses the New Military Transformation," September 17, 2003, http://jczs.sina.com.cn (accessed September 17, 2003).

3. Wang Houqing and Zhang Xingye, eds., *The Science of Campaigns* [*Zhanyi Xue*] (Beijing, PRC: National Defense University Publishing House, May 2000), p. 400 (hereafter cited as Wang Houqing and Zhang Xingye, *Zhanyi Xue*).

4. Hong Bin, "Discussing the Six 'Forms' of New Military Transformation," *Jiefangjun Bao*, July 23, 2003 (hereafter cited as Hong Bin, "Discussing the Six 'Forms' . . .").

5. Li Daguang, "Space Dominance: The Basis for Victory in Information War," *Zhongguo Guofang Bao*, January 6, 2004.

6. Li Yingming, Liu Xiaoli, et al., "An Analysis of Integrated Joint Operations," *Jiefangjun Bao*, April 12, 2005.

7. Gao Yubiao, ed., *Joint Campaign Course Materials* [*Lianhe Zhanyi Jiaocheng*] (Beijing, PRC: Academy of Military Science Publishing House, August 2001), p. 45 (hereafter cited as Gao Yubiao, *Lianhe Zhanyi Jiaocheng*).

8. Gao Yubiao, *Lianhe Zhanyi Jiaocheng*, p. 12.

9. Ibid., pp. 12–25.

10. State Council Information Office, "National Defence Policy," *China's National Defence in 2006* (Beijing: Information Office of the State Council, 2006).

11. Gao Yubiao, *Lianhe Zhanyi Jiaocheng*, p. 8.

12. Ibid., pp. 26–27.

13. Zhang Xingye, "The Important Aspects of the Conduct of Joint Campaign," *Zhongguo Junshi Kexue* 2 (2001): 87 (hereafter cited as Zhang Xingye, "The Important Aspects . . .").

14. Xue Xinglin, ed., *Campaign Theory Learning Guide* [*Zhanyi Lilun Xuexi Zhilan*] (Beijing: National Defense University Publishing House, November 2001), p. 191 (hereafter cited as Xue Xinglin, *Zhanyi Lilun Xuexi Zhilan*).

15. Cui Shizeng and Wang Junyi, "Advancing Military Transformation with Chinese Characteristics, Strengthening 'Integrated-Style Joint Operations," *Jiefangjun Bao*, July 7, 2004.

16. Details drawn from Wang Houqing and Zhang Xingye, *Zhanyi Xue*, pp. 320–24 and 407–20.

17. Ibid.

18. Ibid., p. 396.

19. Du Houyin et al., "Implementing the Integration of Campaign Systems," *Jiefangjun Bao*, November 23, 2004.

20. Wang Houqing and Zhang Xingye, *Zhanyi Xue*, p. 399.

21. Du Houyin et al., "Implementing the Integration of Campaign Systems," *Jiefangjun Bao*, November 23, 2004.

22. Ibid.

23. One U.S. Army officer notes, "For full spectrum dominance, we must use joint integrated effects to maximum advantage in military operations: effects-based operations." LTC Batschelet, "Effects-Based Operations for Joint Warfighters," *Field Artillery Journal* (May–June 2003), http://www.army.mil/professionalwriting/volumes/volume1/june_2003/6_03_3.html (accessed April 18, 2007).

24. Du Houyin et al., "Implementing the Integration of Campaign Systems," *Jiefangjun Bao*, November 23, 2004.

25. Wang Houqing and Zhang Xingye, *Zhanyi Xue*, p. 404.

26. Xue Xinglin, *Zhanyi Lilun Xuexi Zhilan*, pp. 180–82

27. Wang Houqing and Zhang Xingye, *Zhanyi Xue*, p. 405.

28. Li Jian and Liu Guichou, "Development and Changes in Integrated Joint Operations Command," *Zhongguo Guofang Bao*, April 21, 2005.

29. Li Yingming, Liu Xiaoli, et al., "An Analysis of Integrated. . . ."

30. Wang Houqing and Zhang Xingye, *Zhanyi Xue*, p. 404.

31. Ibid., p. 400.

32. Ibid., p. 394.

33. MG Zhang Yiyu, "General's Discussion: Informationalized Warfare Will Change Future Battlefields," *Jiefangjun Bao*, March 2, 2005.

34. Yao Yunzhu, "The Evolution of Military Doctrine of the Chinese PLA from 1985 to 1995," *Korea Journal of Defense Analyses* (Winter, 1995): 72.

35. Wang Houqing and Zhang Xingye, *Zhanyi Xue*, p. 389.

36. Ibid., p. 389.

37. Hong Bin, "Discussing the Six 'Forms'. . . ."

38. Zhang Xingye, "The Important Aspects . . . ," p. 88.

39. Yuan Wenxian, "Strengthening Communications and Training in Joint Operations," *Jiefangjun Bao*, April 9, 2002, in FBIS.

40. Emphasis added. Chin Chien-li, "Profile of Communist China's First Deputy Chief of General Staff Ge Zhenfeng," *Chien Shao* (Hong Kong) #171, May 1, 2005, in FBIS-CHI (hereafter cited as Chin Chien-li, "Profile of Communist China's First Deputy Chief").

41. Ling Peixiong and Li Xucheng, "New Efforts at Teaching Joint Operations Command at National Defense University," *Jiefangjun Bao*, June 5, 2005.

42. Sun Xi'an and Wang Xiongli, "PLA Nanjing MR Conducted Tri-Service Communications Exercise in July," *Renmin Qianxian,* July 15, 2004, in FBIS-CHI.

43. Ding Jianjun and Zhang Kunping, "A Certain Technical Unit of the Beijing MR Develops Joint Repair Bases on the 'Battlefield,'" *Jiefangjun Bao*, June 26, 2004.

44. "PLA General Staff Department Issues New All-Army Military Training Work Regulations," *Jiefangjun Bao*, January 15, 2005.

45. For a brief discussion of the difficulties of implementing jointness, see Editor, "Joint Operations: Everyday but Still Remarkable," *Signal Connections* 4, no. 6, http://www.imakenews.com/signal/e_article000771254.cfm?x=b11,0,w (accessed April 18, 2007).

46. Zhang Xingye, "The Important Aspects . . . ," p. 87.

47. Chin Chien-li, "Profile of Communist China's First Deputy Chief."

48. US Joint Chiefs of Staff, *Joint Doctrine for Amphibious Operations*, JP 3-02 (2001), p. 21, http://www.dtic.mil/doctrine/jel/new_pubs/jp3_02.pdf (accessed April 18, 2007).

49. Captain Basil Liddell-Hart, quoted in US Joint Chiefs of Staff, *Joint Doctrine for Amphibious Operations*, JP 3-02 (2001), p. 18, http://www.dtic.mil/doctrine/jel/new_pubs/jp3_02.pdf (accessed April 18, 2007) and Admiral Jay Johnson, "Statement of Admiral Jay Johnson, Chief of Naval Operations Before the Senate Armed Services Committee Concerning Vieques," September 19, 1999.

50. Colonel M.H.H. Evans RM OBE, *Amphibious Operations: The Projection of Sea Power Ashore* (New York: Brassey's, 1990), p. 91.

4

Evolving Chinese Concepts of War Control and Escalation Management

Lonnie D. Henley

War control entails actions by which the director of a war consciously limits and constrains the war's outbreak, development, scale, intensity, and outcome. The objective of war control is to prevent the outbreak of war, or as soon as war cannot be averted, to then control its vertical and horizontal escalation, striving to minimize the war's consequences or to achieve the greatest victory for the smallest price.[1]

Containing war is not only a task in peacetime; the issue exists in wartime as well. In wartime, it generally takes the form of containing enlargement of the scope of the war, restraining escalation of the war's intensity, and so forth. Sometimes it even finds expression in the war aim of "using war to restrain war," particularly by countries with a defensive strategy.[2]

ALTHOUGH ESCALATION CONTROL is a strategic requirement inherent in the Chinese vision of "local wars under high-technology conditions," it generally does not appear as a separate concept in Chinese writings about conventional, non-nuclear conflict. Instead, preventing or containing the escalation of a political crisis into a military conflict, or of a small-scale conflict into a larger war, appears as one aspect of the broader strategic concept of "containing/deterring war" (*èzhì zhànzhēng;* 遏制战争) or "war control" (*zhànzhēng kòngzhì;* 战争控制). The distinction between

85

the two terms is not rigorous in Chinese writings, but "containing" or "deterring war" is used most often to refer to actions taken to prevent a conflict, whereas "war control" is used in a more wide-ranging sense, particularly in military writings. War control employs all elements of comprehensive national power (CNP) to shape the international environment and make war less likely, effectively manage crises and prevent unintended escalation, put China in a favorable position if war does occur, control the course of the conflict once it is underway, ensure that military operations serve political objectives, and above all be sure China retains the political and military initiative and is not forced into a reactive posture with no control over the pace, scale, intensity, or conclusion of the war.

These evolving concepts of how to manage a crisis or conflict expose a large and probably unjustified confidence in China's ability to fine tune its actions and manipulate the opponent's perceptions and reactions, at least among theorists in the People's Liberation Army (PLA) academic institutions. It is less clear whether senior leaders share this confidence. To the extent that "war control" thought does gain traction among military and political leaders, it could have a potentially dangerous influence on China's behavior in a future confrontation with the United States over Taiwan. Without delving into the many potential causes, constraints, and scenarios for a conflict in the Taiwan Strait, suffice it to say that the odds of such a conflict in the next few years are low but certainly not zero, in the view of this observer. In such an event, a better understanding of the mindset and expectations that informed Chinese efforts to manipulate the crisis could significantly improve our chance of gaining the outcome we seek.

This chapter begins with a brief history of the origin and development of war control concepts in Chinese military academic circles, and then lays out the basic concepts and their theoretical justification in Chinese strategic thought. It then examines in more detail the purely military aspects of war control, with emphasis on measures to shape the strategic environment before and during a crisis and to control the pace, intensity, and parameters of the conflict once it begins. After exploring important related concepts, such as the importance in Chinese thought of maintaining the initiative in any confrontation, it then looks more closely at the implications of these modes of thought in a Taiwan Strait conflict.

DEVELOPMENT OF WAR CONTROL THOUGHT

The topic of war control has appeared only recently in Chinese military writings. Major General Peng Guangqian, a leading researcher in the Academy of Military Science (AMS) Department of Strategic Studies, claims to have invented the concept in 1998.[3] War control did not appear in the 1987 AMS edition of *The Science of Military Strategy* or in the 1999 National Defense University (NDU) publication of the same name.[4] There were a few preliminary articles on the concept in 2000, and then the seminal 2001 AMS edition of *The Science of Military Strategy* accorded war control a full chapter equal in weight to war preparation, strategic deterrence, and other major components of the "general laws of war and conduct of war."[5] Not coincidentally, Peng Guangqian, a major proponent of the concept, was editor-in-chief of the 2001 volume.[6]

Since 2001, there have been a number of articles on war control by scholars from AMS, NDU, and other military academic institutions. Dan Xiufa, an AMS researcher on Mao's military thought, noted in 2003 that "there has not been much deep research into Mao Zedong's thought on preventing and containing war," a strong indication that war control is a new concept in Chinese military writing.[7] Dan's work and a 2000 article by researchers from Shijiazhuang Army Command Academy are among the first to mine Mao's writings for insights on the issue; both reached the unsurprising conclusion that Mao was a master of war control despite never mentioning it.[8] Peng Guangqian also invokes the authority of the Chinese military canon, writing in 2006 that Sun Tzu's *Art of War* was an "artistic masterpiece" of war control thought.[9] The most detailed treatment to date is a 2001 NDU doctoral dissertation by Colonel Xiao Tianliang, an assistant professor in the NDU Strategy Teaching and Research Institute.[10]

Outside of PLA military academic literature, phrases related to war control thought have appeared only occasionally in authoritative government statements of recent years, and almost always with an emphasis on preventing conflict rather than modulating the application of military force after the war has begun. President and Central Military Commission (CMC) chairman Hu Jintao enjoined the PLA in March 2006 to ensure it was able to "respond to crises, maintain peace, contain war, and fight and win wars."[11] General Cao Gangchuan, Minister of National Defense and CMC Vice Chairman, used the same words in his July 31, 2006 Army

Day speech, and the December 2006 defense white paper repeated the mantra.[12] As discussed at more length below, it remains an open question whether the theories of war control developed by PLA academic strategists reflect similar modes of thought among the senior political and military leaders who would make the actual decisions on what to do in a crisis.

GENERAL CONCEPT OF WAR CONTROL

> Containment of war includes preventing and delaying the out-break of war, and avoiding escalation of the war once it breaks out. One should point out it stresses the comprehensive employment of military, political, economic, diplomatic, and other means, but certainly does not abandon or neglect the position and role of military means in realizing the strategic objective.[13]

In the Chinese view, war control encompasses several major categories of endeavor, which are discussed below.

Measures Taken to Shape the International Security Environment, Peacefully Resolve Disputes, and Reduce the Threat of War

These measures range from mediation and negotiation of economic and territorial disputes, through "military diplomacy" and confidence-building measures (CBM), to arms control and arms reduction treaties and formal international security mechanisms.[14] China should "adopt various foreign affairs tactics to strive for and unify international forces for peace, isolate and weaken the world's most reactionary and most dangerous war powers, build a fair and rational international strategic structure, and build an international environment to contain war."[15]

Measures Taken to Manage Crises and Prevent or Postpone the Outbreak of War

The overall objective is to contain the crisis, both geographically and in terms of its subject matter and intensity. Allowing a crisis over one issue to spread to include other political, economic, or territorial disputes is a sure way of losing control of the situation. Not only does such horizontal escalation increase the risk of vertical escalation toward higher intensity political and military confrontation, it also increases the risk that the crisis will become internationalized, attracting unwelcome intervention by other interested parties, great powers, and/or international organizations. This would greatly limit China's freedom of action and its ability to control the subsequent development of the conflict to its advantage. In other cases, however, deliberately enlarging the crisis may be the key to China maintaining control and gaining the initiative.[16]

Effective crisis management depends a great deal on the extent to which the crisis has been foreseen and analyzed in advance, as well as the effectiveness of national crisis management structures. Anticipating possible crises, thinking through the likely causes and one's own possible responses before they occur, and having one's resources ready are key to gaining control of a situation and maintaining the initiative.[17] Leadership decision-making processes are at a premium in a fast-developing situation with little hard information.[18]

Good crisis management does not preclude the use of military force. In fact, ostentatious military deployments are a key part of the political and psychological pressure that Chinese leaders would use to gain the initiative and win the contest of wills at the center of any crisis. Xiao Tianliang notes that of the four main approaches to a crisis, the war-mongering approach (*hàozhànxíng;* 好战型) is too likely to incite the other side to extreme action, besides being "unsuited to China's national character," while a soft approach (*ruǎnruòxíng;* 软弱型) could embolden the opponent and lead him to do something rash. The recommended approaches are either military intimidation (*wēishèxíng;* 威慑型) or the bargaining approach (*jiāoyìxíng;* 交易型). Bargaining is often successful, but if one decides on intimidation, the key is to use overweening military power to "cow the opponent into submission" (*shèfú duìfāng;* 慑服对方).[19] (The meaning of *wēishè* 威慑 here clearly is intimidation, not deterrence.) In the extreme, as other authors note, the military approach to crisis management may include "fighting a small war to prevent a large war."[20]

Military writers downplay the distinction between being able to prevent war and being able to win war. Even though the "Military Strategic

Guidelines for the Current Period" emphasize fighting and winning, an AMS strategist argued in 2002 that it remains essential for China's continued economic development that the PLA be able to prevent wars occurring in the first place.[21] Another AMS strategist argued in 2006 that being able to prevent and being able to win wars are indistinguishable, being integral parts of the same capability.[22]

Measures Taken During War to Control the Scale, Pace, Scope, or Intensity of the Conflict Once It Begins

These measures include efforts to prevent escalation, minimize destruction, and shape the course of the war in order to better serve larger political and foreign policy objectives. The main principle underlying Chinese thought on war control is that military operations must be firmly subordinated to the political, diplomatic, and economic objectives that underlie the conflict. This may sometimes require halting military operations short of their intended objectives, or modulating the pace and intensity of operations to create the proper climate for pursuing political ends. Again, this does not always mean lowering the intensity; "sometimes political goals require decisive victory, sometimes creation of an advantageous situation, sometimes just a symbolic attack."[23] This is the case particularly when major issues of territorial sovereignty or national dignity are at stake, there is no hope of avoiding severe harm to China's economic interests, and firm military action is essential. But even in such a case, "an excessive military attack can put us on the defensive politically."[24]

THEORETICAL BASIS FOR WAR CONTROL

Chinese military writers invariably underpin their practical suggestions with an appeal to universal military theory, and those discussing war control are no exception. The central theoretical issues for war control advocates are the evolution of warfare and human society, on the one hand, and the changing international strategic situation on the other. Throughout most of human history, warfare was necessarily unlimited, because the political objectives were so out of proportion to the military means at hand that there was no stopping point short of absolute victory or absolute defeat. From the Stone Age through the end of the Cold War, most conflicts involved existential threats to a country's political system or even the survival of its population. The material means of warfare, meanwhile, did not include subtle or agile control mechanisms or detailed timely knowledge of the battlefield situation sufficient enough to permit the careful modulation of the pace and intensity of the conflict.[25]

The current political and technological situation is seen to be fundamentally different. The advent of "War Under High-Technology Conditions," largely through the application of information technology to the mechanized warfare forces of the late industrial age, creates the novel possibility of grasping and directing even large-scale far-flung military operations in real time.[26] At the same time, the advent of nuclear and other weapons of enormous destructive power make unlimited war far too dangerous to contemplate.[27]

The global strategic situation also has changed such that no major power faces a fundamental threat to its existence. Crises are inevitable and may well escalate into open war, but less is at stake in such a conflict than in past eras. In China's view, the prevailing international trend is toward peace and development, driven by the strategic trifecta of multipolarity, globalization, and "informationization." Furthermore, conflict is much more "transparent" than in the past; it is much more subject to scrutiny by the international community and the general public, again due to the ubiquitous spread of information technology. Finally, of course, nuclear weapons make uncontrolled escalation of a conflict far too dangerous. As a result, China feels that the era of unlimited warfare is over. The material ability to contain war exists and the political imperative is to do so, a major reversal of the situation that prevailed throughout much of human history.[28]

MILITARY MEASURES TO CONTAIN AND CONTROL WAR

What we call "shaping the situation" refers to making full use of the strategic commander's subjective initiative, on the basis of our own military power, through the rational concentration and employment of forces, to create a powerful posture and strong offensive capability that is irresistibly fierce and overpowers the enemy.[29]

As noted above, war control requires a comprehensive application of political, economic, diplomatic, and military capabilities. The military part of this effort encompasses a wide range of techniques and actions to help "shape the strategic situation" (*zàoshì;* 造势).

Military Intimidation and Deterrence

One of the first contributions that the military can make toward controlling a fast-developing crisis is through the existence of a highly visible and capable military force obviously ready to take action. "Preparedness for war and containment of war are a dialectical unity."[30] Overt shows of force and vigorous deployments of troops toward a crisis zone put pressure on the opponent, helping China gain the political initiative and control the development of the crisis. Depending on the situation, this may include the movement of strategic nuclear forces or elite conventional units, or even limited military strikes to "bang the hill to scare the tiger" and make the opponent back down. In other circumstances, visible deployments might need to be limited so the opponent does not overreact, leading to undesired escalation. Even then, however, clandestine movement of forces usually is necessary in case the crisis does turn to conflict, because in modern high-technology local war, the first battle is often decisive.[31] One way or another, the proper posture (and posturing) of China's military force is a central aspect of early crisis management.

Chinese strategists believe that the most important deterrent factor in an age of local wars is not nuclear weapons, even though such weapons are important. The ability to deter encroachment on China's territory or vital interests lies mainly in the nation's overall economic, political, diplomatic, and military strength—its CNP (*zōnghé guójiā lìliang;* 综合国家力量). The military components of China's strategic deterrent include its nuclear missile force, of course, as well as its large and increasingly capable conventional forces. PLA strategists also see the nation's perceived willingness to fight over certain issues of high enough strategic interest—Taiwan, for example—as an important deterrent factor that reduces the likelihood that they will need to do so. Finally, the ability to mobilize and organize huge quantities of manpower, technology, and resources from society at large, under the rubric of "People's War Under

Modern Conditions," "is still the magic weapon for deterring and preventing a large-scale invasion by the enemy."[32]

Control of Overall War Objectives

Unless fundamental national security interests are at stake, military objectives in the conflict should be constrained so as to stay in consonance with political objectives. A review of the history of warfare reveals many examples where military war aims came to outstrip what should have been the guiding political objectives, resulting in uncontrolled escalation of the conflict and complete loss of the political initiative.[33]

Control of Military Targets

Fighting a limited war requires careful balance in the selection of military targets. On the one hand, one must attack vital targets that have a decisive effect on the enemy's military capability and psychological will to continue the fight. On the other hand, the targets attacked must be such that the opponent can endure the loss without being driven to an implacable quest for vengeance and that the international community can tolerate without being moved to large-scale political or military intervention. Failure to strike the right balance can cause unwanted escalation of the conflict or put China on the political defensive and cause it to lose control of the overall situation.[34]

Control of Military Operational Parameters

Having decided on overall war aims and the general nature of the target set, there is still a decision of what "form of warfare" (*zhànzhēng xíngshì*; 战争形式) the military operation should embody. Chinese military theory groups these into the two broad categories of offensive and defensive warfare, each expressed in various "forms of operations" (*zuòzhàn xíngshì*; 作战形式):

- Mobile, positional, or guerrilla warfare;
- Protracted war versus wars of quick decision;

- Wars of annihilation versus wars of attrition versus effects-based operations; and
- Whether the conflict should be high or low intensity, symmetric or asymmetric.

A critical step in Chinese military planning is the "commander's determination" of the situation (*zhǐhuīyuán de juédìng;* 指挥员的决定), which includes deciding the overall military requirements and objectives, designating the primary and secondary "operational directions" (*zuòzhàn fāngxiàng;* 作战方向), and selecting the size and type of military forces to employ. Correct decisions on these operational parameters have a significant effect on the ability to maintain control of the conflict.[35]

Control of Warfare Techniques (*zhànzhēng shǒuduàn;* 战争手段)

Both the increased killing power of modern weapons and the increased transparency of the battlefield due to modern news and information media require strict control on the selection of weapons and tactics. Inflicting excessive damage on the enemy, especially on civilian populations or vital infrastructure, will stir up intense resentment and bring into play political factors that make it much more difficult to maintain control of the situation. This is not to say that extreme measures are not sometimes necessary, merely that they are inherently difficult to control and should be carefully considered. The military commander must not succumb to the temptation to use whatever means is available to achieve the military objective. As always, the warfare techniques employed should serve the overall political objectives of the war.[36]

Control of the Pace, Rhythm, and Intensity of the Conflict

A group of AMS specialists studying U.S.-British operations in Iraq in 2003 concluded that they represented the epitome of "highly-contained warfare." Allied forces tightly controlled the interaction between military operations and the political, economic, and psychological aspects of the situation, and exercised unprecedented control over military targets and the tempo and rhythm of the conflict.[37] Besides its military benefits, careful modulation of the war's pace and intensity also facilitates the larger political struggle. The side that holds the initiative can press the offensive and bring the conflict to a resolution while that advantage still holds; the side that is on the defensive can slow and drag out the conflict while it seeks an opportunity to reverse the situation.[38]

Control of the War's End

Purely military considerations must not be allowed to determine when and how the conflict ends. Throughout most of human history, wars were for national or societal survival, and political war aims could not be achieved without the complete achievement of military objectives. In the era of limited war, however, it is quite possible that political objectives will come within reach before the military operation has played out to its intended end. In such a case, continued conflict could harm rather than serve the national interest; a wise leader will terminate the conflict when it is politically advantageous to do so. PLA analysts assess that China has done this correctly in every conflict since 1949, representing a particular strength of the Chinese strategic perspective.[39]

Properly ending the conflict is not only a matter of timing, but also of closely coordinating military operations with political maneuvers in the final stages of a conflict. It may be necessary to pause the fighting to create space for negotiations, or raise the intensity of the fighting in order to get the opponent to the negotiating table; to spring unexpected "assassin's mace" weapons and throw the opponent off balance at a critical point; or to accelerate efforts to seize key objectives before the situation stabilizes. This is a particularly critical juncture in the struggle to "shape the strategic situation" and seize the initiative. It requires military superiority on the battlefield, possibly entailing rapid commitment of additional elite forces in the final stages of the war, as well as a great degree of flexibility and precise control of military operations. If the war has gone badly for China, it may also require great political agility to gain the best advantage from a bad situation.[40]

Control of the Postconflict Situation

The military's role in war control does not end when the shooting stops. Continued military pressure may be needed to make the enemy abide by the terms of the settlement, including, if necessary, a resumption of military conflict to make the enemy return to the agreement.[41]

IMPORTANCE OF THE INITIATIVE

Mao Zedong incisively pointed out: "War is a competition of subjective capabilities between two military commanders competing for superiority and for the initiative, based on the material foundations of military and financial strength."[42]

Throughout Chinese discussion of how to control war, the emphasis is on seizing the political and military initiative (*zhǔdòng*; 主动) and avoiding situations which would put China in a reactive, passive, and defensive posture (*bèidòng*; 被动). Holding the initiative creates leeway and freedom of action, enabling China to set the agenda. A reactive position limits China's options and makes it impossible for China to maintain control of the situation.

Seizing and holding the initiative requires rapid reaction to an incipient crisis, including immediate deployment of sizeable forces as early as possible. It requires clear, quick, and correct decision making; a strong standing military capability; thorough contingency planning and rapid mobilization of societal resources; a resolute and principled political stance, firmly asserted at the outset and throughout the confrontation; rapid transition to war when events reach that level; and employment of formidable military power at every stage, particularly when settlement talks seem near. Lastly, seizing and holding the initiative especially requires avoiding the internationalization of the problem or outside political and military intervention, especially by hegemonic powers.[43]

It is difficult to overstate how prominent the concept of the initiative is in Chinese writings. To an outside observer, there seems to be a clear risk that such a strong emphasis on gaining the initiative may lead China to overreact to a developing crisis, creating a cycle of reaction and escalation. There is some discussion about the need to avoid crossing some line that could provoke the enemy beyond the point of tolerance (as discussed above), driving him to a quest for vengeance that renders the conflict beyond control. But one finds little consideration of the possibility that what China considers a resolute response to maintain the political initiative, the opponent might misconstrue as alarming preparations for aggressive military action. Chinese military authors seem to be unable to get outside of their own subjective view of China's innocent intentions and righteous principled stance to see China as others might view it. Chinese writers certainly are not alone in this weakness; but it is possible that this strong belief in seizing the initiative as the key to crisis management and war control could itself contribute to unwanted escalation.[44]

CREDIBILITY AND LIMITATIONS OF THE SOURCES

It seems likely that the type of sources consulted for this study—works by faculty members and doctoral candidates at the Academy of Military Science, National Defense University, Shijiazhuang Army Command Academy, and so forth—accurately represents the state of thought among those charged with developing and implementing PLA military doctrine. These writings are not authoritative; they are not of the genre of official regulatory documents and orders (*gāngyào;* 纲要, *jūnshì fǎguī;* 军事法规, *jūnshì guīzhāng;* 军事规章, *tiáolìng;* 条令, *tiáolì;* 条例, etc.) issued by the State Council, Central Military Commission, General Departments, or lower PLA headquarters.[45] Military academic writings of the kind cited here occupy a lower but nonetheless important place in the hierarchy of PLA doctrinal materials.

Judging from the few that have been published openly, authoritative doctrinal regulations provide only general high-level guidance about military operational concepts. Military academic institutions, especially NDU, AMS, and the mid-level Command Academies, are responsible for converting that general guidance into detailed operational doctrine and promulgating it throughout the officer corps. For example, the 2002 *Guide to the Study of Campaign Theory* (*Zhànyì Lǐlùn Xuéxí Zhǐnán;* 战役理论学习指南) from NDU Press seems to be an implementation of the classified 1999 *PLA Outline on Joint Campaigns*

(*Zhōngguó Rénmín Jiěfàngjūn Liánhé Zhànyì Gāngyào;* 中国人民解放军联合战役纲要).[46] There has been a flood of such teaching materials published in the past few years as the PLA implements the new generation of operational doctrine that was developed and codified in the Eighth and Ninth Five-Year Plans (1991–2000).[47]

The articles cited in this study rest on the third rung of the ladder of authoritativeness. They are neither official orders nor regulations, nor are they direct implementing materials used to train officers in the new operational concepts that those orders dictate. Rather, they are the ongoing professional conversation among those who draft the regulations and write the teaching materials, such as the AMS Operational Doctrine and Regulations Research Department, intended for one another as well as for the general audience of PLA officers.[48] As such, they do not represent PLA doctrine, but they embody the state of understanding of a given issue in doctrine-writing circles. This is particularly true, in my view, of the AMS *Science of Military Strategy* and of military science doctoral dissertations such as Xiao Tianliang's work cited here. Dissertations published in NDU's *Military Science Doctoral Dissertation Series* all seem to spend the first three-quarters of the work demonstrating mastery of the current state of knowledge, then add the author's own thoughts and suggestions in the last few chapters. In my view, this makes these dissertations particularly valuable for gauging the PLA's thinking on a given issue at the time they were written.

On a topic such as war control, however, the PLA's perspective is not the only one that matters, and perhaps is not even the most important. PLA officers should be mindful that military operations must support political objectives. But it is the political leaders who will decide what those objectives are and what military posture best advances them. Whether political leaders think of war control in the way that the PLA theorists do is an open question. It is possible that there is a similar body of writings, perhaps from the Central Party School, used to instruct rising political leaders on crisis management and escalation control. If such writings do exist, however, we do not seem to have any window into their content or concepts, at least none evident to this author. In addition, anything used now to train rising midlevel cadres may have only limited relevance to the question of how today's senior leaders, who were not trained in these concepts at the midpoint of their own careers, would behave in a crisis.

We can speculate that rising political leaders are being trained in concepts similar to what military officers are learning, and that the training of all mid-level leaders reflects, at least in general terms, the perspectives of the senior leaders who order such training. But absent any clear evidence to support that speculation, we can only reach the most tentative conclusions.

CONTINUED DEVELOPMENT OF WAR CONTROL THOUGHT

As discussed above, war control seems to have emerged only recently as a topic in Chinese military theory. Since the early 1990s, the PLA has exhibited a fairly standard pattern for developing new operational concepts, best illustrated in the evolution of joint maneuver warfare doctrine from 1990 to 2005. The Eighth Five-Year Plan (FYP), 1990–1995, initiated a period of discussion and experimentation, defining the operational requirements for high-technology warfare and conducting small-scale, decentralized experimentation at a number of units around China. The ninth FYP, 1996–2000, initiated a period of consolidation and codification. This period focused on combining the new techniques into a comprehensive concept of operations and codifying them in a new generation of doctrinal regulations, teaching materials, and training standards, which were published beginning in January 1999. The tenth FYP initiated a period of implementation, focused on education in the military academies and schools and field training for the operational forces to inculcate the new approach to warfare.

The theme of the current eleventh FYP (now renamed a Five-Year Program rather than Plan) is to complete the "first stage" of PLA modernization, fulfilling the target established by Jiang Zemin in 1998.[49] Speaking at the annual expanded meeting of the CMC in December of that year, Jiang established a three-stage program for military modernization, paralleling the dates for three stages of social development established at the 15th Party Congress in 1997.[50] By 2010, the PLA is to "lay a solid foundation" enabling it to fight a war under high-technology conditions. By 2020, it is to "make major progress" in the quality of its weapons and personnel. By 2050, it is to "be capable of winning informationized wars."[51]

The flood of new doctrinal publications, teaching materials, and training standards over the past five years is likely to represent only the first generation of modern Chinese operational doctrine.[52] We can expect the PLA to continue refining and developing its doctrine to incorporate lessons learned from field training and foreign (primarily U.S.) military developments, and the product of additional thinking such as that on war control. The development and codification of operational doctrine is a seminal event in PLA history, a new level of maturity and competence in the complex business of building and developing modern military capabilities.

Considering the concept of war control against this backdrop, its state of development seems to parallel that of joint operations in the early 1990s. War control is under debate and discussion among the same genre of military academics who were central to the development and codification of joint operations doctrine in the late 1990s. Although war control now appears as a separate topic in *The Science of Military Strategy*, it does not appear in campaign-level training materials such as *The Science of Campaigns*, *Guide to the Study of Campaign Theory*, or *Joint Campaigns Textbook*, much less in their tactical-level counterparts, and there has been no hint of a doctrinal regulation on the issue.[53] This implies that the PLA is some years away from the full implementation of these concepts in the operational force, and we can expect further evolution of PLA war control concepts over the coming decade.

IMPACT OF "WAR CONTROL" THINKING ON A TAIWAN STRAIT CRISIS

War control, crisis management, and escalation control occupy a small but fairly well-defined place in recent Chinese strategic thought. Escalation control certainly does not hold as central a place in PLA strategic theory as it did in U.S. thought during the Cold War. As has been discussed, Chinese authors assert that the world is not as dangerous now as it was through most of modern history, and no conflict is likely to escalate to a point where national survival or millions of lives are at stake. The advance of military technology and fundamental changes in the international strategic situation make controlled war both possible and necessary. They do not say it in so many words, but Chinese writers almost seem to think these factors make the world safe for war. There is a danger that this belief in controllable war and in the unparalleled importance of maintaining the initiative could combine to increase rather than decrease the likelihood of escalation.

From the perspective of the United States, and certainly from that of Taiwan, the central question is how war control concepts would affect a crisis over Taiwan. Available Chinese writings do not provide any direct evidence on that question, but a bit of informed speculation is possible.

Before we can proceed, however, a few assumptions are necessary. First, we assume that public writings accurately reflect the state of PLA thought on this subject. It is probable that classified documents such as PLA contingency plans contain more explicit discussions about how to manage an emerging crisis and prevent undesired escalation. Nonetheless, it seems reasonable to assume that public writings reflect at least the general concepts and overall level of interest that the subject receives in Chinese internal documents. (Some Western observers warn that the whole corpus of publicly available PLA writings may be falsified in order to mislead outsiders. Given the vast scale of any such deception campaign, however, and the PLA's clear need to publish for its own consumption, the onus falls on those observers to demonstrate their point).

Second, we assume that the theoretical and doctrinal discussions among midlevel PLA academics reflect to some degree the views of national-level political and military leaders. Some differences are inevitable because of differences in background and experience between mid- and senior-level officials. Given the nature of the Chinese political system, however, it is likely that public writings by PLA academics do not diverge sharply from the views of top leaders, though with large caveats about the role of individual personalities within the leadership collective.

With those assumptions as a foundation, we can draw a few tentative conclusions about the relevance of Chinese concepts of war control to a potential Taiwan Strait conflict or crisis.

First, it is likely that these concepts have only recently become a factor in Chinese planning for a Taiwan contingency. From the available evidence, it appears that serious theoretical consideration of war control among PLA academics began around 1998–2000. Some observers assert that this was roughly the same time Jiang Zemin and the CMC ordered the PLA to begin serious efforts to create capabilities suitable for a potential Taiwan conflict. It seems reasonable to view the interest in escalation control as an offshoot of broader consideration of what a conflict with Taiwan would really entail. If we are right that the PLA is currently working on its first serious, fully developed set of operations plans for a Taiwan contingency, we can expect all aspects of those plans to improve as they are refined and updated over coming years. Like many other aspects of serious operational thought and planning in China, Chinese concepts of war control are still evolving and should become increasingly sophisticated and practical over the coming decade.

Second, large troop movements, mobilization of strategic nuclear forces, and other threatening actions are likely in any serious crisis, regardless of whether Beijing intends to attack. The importance of maintaining the initiative, the perceived value of force movements to create political leverage, and simple military prudence all may impel Chinese leaders to order large deployments early in a crisis, whatever their ultimate objectives. Such movements are one of the few concrete and visible indicators that U.S. and Taiwan decision makers can rely on for warning of attack, but the war control literature suggests that they may provide little insight into China's real intentions.

Third, it is no great revelation to say the Chinese may take a rigid stance on issues of principle at the start of a crisis, but the war control and crisis management literature reinforces this expectation. Throughout the materials studied here, vigorous assertion of China's (invariably) correct and principled stance is presented not just as a political and moral imperative, but also as an effective tactic for gaining control of the situation. It is less clear whether this means that getting China to compromise on the central issue of a crisis would be impossible, or just exceedingly difficult.

Fourth, if the war control literature does parallel the thinking of top Chinese leaders, it is likely that any attack on Taiwan would be carefully designed to achieve political rather than purely military objectives. In particular, war control theorists emphasize the careful selection of targets so as to maximize the political impact on the enemy's will to fight, without arousing such resentment and hatred that the enemy's will is strengthened rather than undermined. There is little indication elsewhere in Chinese writings that they worry about strong resistance from Taiwan, and war control writings do not mention any specific opponent in this context; therefore, it may be a stretch to interpret these passages as indicating such concern. But even if one stops short of that conclusion, it is nonetheless clear that war control advocates advise careful attention to the negative as well as positive political effects (from China's perspective) of striking any particular target.

That said, it is somewhat harder to predict what that would mean in a Taiwan conflict. Would Beijing conclude, for instance, that avoiding widespread civilian casualties is necessary in order to avoid the "Battle of Britain effect," infusing backbone into the Taiwan body politic, or would they see such attacks as contributing to an atmosphere of panic that would foster an early surrender? Furthermore, there is no evidence at this point as to whether PLA targeteers are in any way influenced by war control theory. So in the end, despite offering this as an insight from the war control literature, there is no clear conclusion one can draw so far about how war control thought would affect Chinese target selection.

Fifth, in the immortal words of Yogi Berra, "it ain't over till it's over."[54] Even in what seem to be the final stages of conflict and negotiations for its termination, Chinese leaders will struggle vigorously to hold or regain the initiative, particularly if the war has gone badly for China. Rather than trying to put the best face on defeat, war control theorists would advocate bold and unexpected actions to create a more favorable environment for the final political struggle. And as noted above, a political settlement may not end the fighting if China feels that "postconflict" military strikes are necessary to keep the enemy within the terms of the settlement as China sees them.

These findings from the war control literature are generally consistent with what Swaine, Zhang, and Cohen found in other Chinese statements and writings, concluding that "from the Chinese perspective, a limited use of coercion or force under certain circumstances can prevent a much larger conflict, strengthen the foundations of peace, or achieve narrower Chinese objectives."[55] In general, however, their sources seemed to focus more on the need to "minimize risk and control unwanted escalation," rather than to modulate the level of violence in a calculated effort to shape the crisis to China's benefit.[56]

AREAS FOR FURTHER STUDY

The field of PLA studies has changed enormously in the past ten years, with the flood of valuable Chinese-language materials readily available in PRC bookstores, mail-order catalogs, and online. We have long castigated the Chinese for insufficient "transparency" on military issues, and there do remain important areas where Beijing continues to conceal information that other countries believe a major power should make public in the interests of mutual understanding and stability. The transparency charge is beginning to wear thin, however, in light of the enormous and rapidly growing volume of public information on PLA issues that has not been examined in the English-speaking world. We should all make a vigorous effort to find and read more of these Chinese-language sources and incorporate them into our understanding of PLA modernization efforts.

In the field of war control and escalation management, we need to find more information about Chinese thinking about nuclear escalation and compare it to both U.S. nuclear escalation thought and Chinese war control thought. The writings discussed here made occasional reference to nuclear issues, such as mobilizing nuclear forces for the purpose of political signaling, but they did not directly address nuclear escalation control.

We also need to look for reflections of war control thinking in the statements and writings of the national political and military leadership. We may tentatively conclude that writings on war control by PLA academics are likely to parallel the top leadership's views, but more direct evidence is needed before we can be confident in that conclusion.

CONCLUSION

In sum, then, the literature on war control finds PLA academic theorists arguing that it is possible for China to consciously manipulate the scale, scope, pace, intensity, and duration of any crisis to increase the odds of a successful outcome from China's perspective. Unlike some Western literature on crisis management, it does not automatically assume that it is always preferable to de-escalate a crisis and avoid military conflict. To the contrary, it recommends deliberately escalating the conflict if that strategy seems likely to produce a better outcome. It is unclear whether this mode of thought is as prevalent in the top political and military leadership as among some military scholars, but it may offer useful insights into possible Chinese behavior in a future Taiwan crisis. It suggests that it may be impossible to tell the difference from outward behavior between a determination to take aggressive military action and an effort to gain the political initiative through military posturing and between deliberate escalation and assertive moves intended to limit escalation. It also suggests that rather than accept defeat in the final stages of a Taiwan conflict, we should expect China to try bold, perhaps desperate attacks late in the conflict to shock the opponent and gain a more favorable position at the bargaining table.

The discussion of crisis management, containment, escalation, and war control in Chinese military writings seems to represent a blend of distinctively Chinese modes of thought, practical issues common to all modern militaries, sophisticated assessments of the political and military challenges that China would face in a Taiwan crisis, and naïve optimism about China's ability to control the situation and dictate the course of events. As in all other aspects of Chinese military development, we can expect to see increasing sophistication and realism as PLA theorists explore this relatively new aspect of Chinese strategic thought. The current generation of field-grade officers, the core of PLA planning staffs at every level, is the first in modern Chinese history to have spent their whole military career in an army dedicated to reform and modernization. The only comparable period of military professionalization, in the 1950s, lasted only eight to ten years. In contrast, the current reform period has lasted nearly thirty years, long enough to produce an entire generation of colonels and lieutenant colonels nurtured by reform and succeeding generations of captains and majors who never experienced the bad old PLA. Chinese forces were starting from an extremely low base when today's colonels were lieutenants, and the reform program has suffered fits and starts along the way. The PLA still has a long way to go before it is a fully competent, modern armed force. There is no question, however, that in every field of endeavor—war control included—the PLA will achieve even greater progress in the coming decade than it did in the last.

NOTES

The author is grateful to the U.S. Army War College for publishing an earlier version of this chapter in Andrew Scobell and Larry M. Wortzel, eds., *Shaping China's Security Environment: The Role of the People's Liberation Army* (Carlisle Barracks, PA: US Army Strategic Studies Institute, 2006). All statements of fact, opinion, or analysis expressed are those of the author and do not reflect the official positions or views of the Office of the Director of National Intelligence (ODNI) or any other U.S. Government agency. Nothing in the contents should be construed as asserting or implying U.S. Government authentication of information or ODNI endorsement of the author's views. This material has been reviewed by the ODNI to prevent the disclosure of classified information.

1. Peng Guangqian 彭光谦 and Yao Youzhi 姚有志, eds., *The Science of Military Strategy* 战略学 (English title on cover) (Beijing: Military Science Publishing House, 2001), p. 213. (Cited hereafter as "*SMS 2001.*") Subsequently translated into English: Peng Guangqian and Yao Youzhi, eds., *The Science of Military Strategy* (Beijing: Military Science Publishing House, 2005). Excerpt here retranslated by the author.

2. Yao Youzhi 姚有志 and Zhao Dexi 赵德喜, "The Generalization, Conservation, and Development of Strategy" 战略"的泛化、守恒与发展 (English title in original), *China's Military Science* 中国军事科学, September 30, 2001, pp. 120–27, ODNI Open Source Center (OSC, formerly FBIS) CPP20011126000199.

3. Conversation with the author, Shanghai, September 2006.

4. Gao Rui, ed., *The Science of Strategy* 战略学 (Beijing: Military Science Publishing House, 1987); Wang Wenrong, ed., *The Science of Strategy* 战略学 (Beijing: National Defense University Press, 1999).

5. *SMS 2001,* chapter 8.

6. See, for example, Peng Guangqian 彭光谦, "Three Major Influences of the Worldwide Revolution in Military Affairs on Chinese Advancement" 世界军事变革有三大影响 中国推进三创新, *Outlook Weekly* 瞭望新闻周刊, June 10, 2003, http://www.chinanews.com.cn/n/2003-06-10/26/312572.html (last accessed April 19, 2007).

7. Dan Xiufa 单秀法, "A New Perspective on Deepening Study of Mao Zedong's Military Thought" 深化毛泽东军事思想研究的新视野, http://www.pladaily.com.cn/item/mzd/jn/048.htm (last accessed April 19, 2007). The article is not dated, but it commemorates the 110th anniversary of Mao's birth, putting it probably in 2003. The author's affiliation is not mentioned in this article, but he was identified in 2004 as a researcher in the Mao Zedong Military Thought Research Institute of the Chinese Academy of Military Science (AMS), http://biz.sinobook.com.cn/press/newsdetail.cfm?iCntno=674 (last accessed April 19, 2007), and in the same year as the director of the AMS Warfare Theory and Strategy Research Department, http://jczs.news.sina.com.cn/2004-08-23/1105219944.html (last accessed April 19, 2007). All translations are by this author unless otherwise noted.

8. Yu Shifu 俞世福 and Yin Xinjian 尹新建, "An Initial Exploration of Mao Zedong's Thought on Containing War" 毛泽东遏制战争思想初探, *Military History* 军事历史 (Beijing) 2000, no. 1, http://www.cass.net.cn/zhuanti/y_kmyc/zhuanjia/a00130.htm (last accessed April 19, 2007) (hereafter cited as Yu Shifu and Yin Xinjian). Yu Shifu is a professor at the Shijiazhuang Army Command Academy; see "Stars of the Military Academic World" 軍校群英哨萃 教壇將星生輝, *Liberation Army Daily* 解放军报 September 8, 2000, http://www.pladaily.com.cn/pladaily/20000908/big5/20000908001013_Army.html.

9. Peng Guangqian, "The Historical Declining of Absolute War and Sun Tzu's Thinking of War Control" 绝对战争的历史式微与孙子的战争控制思想 (English title in original), *Journal of Binzhou University* 滨州学院学报 22, no. 5 (2006): 107–12, http://www.wanfangdata.com.cn/qikan/periodical.Articles/bzszxb/bzsz2006/0605/060520.htm (last accessed April 19, 2007).

10. Xiao Tianliang 肖天亮, *On War Control* 战争控制问题研究 (English title on cover). (Beijing: National Defense University Press, 2002) (hereafter cited as Xiao Tianliang).

11. Cao Zhi 曹智 and Li Xuanliang 李宣良, "Hu Jintao Stresses the Need for Rapid Development of National Defense and Armed Forces" 胡錦濤強調推動國防和軍隊建設又快又好地發展, *Xinhua* March 11, 2006, http://www.pladaily.com.cn/site1/big5/database/2006-03/11/content_432416.htm (last accessed April 19, 2007); OSC CPP20060311001006. Retranslated by author.

12. "Ministry of National Defense Holds Magnificent Reception to Warmly Celebrate the 79th Anniversary of the Founding of the PLA; Chen Bingde Presides" 国防部举行盛大招待会热烈庆祝建军79周年 陈炳德出席; *Liberation Army Daily* 解放军报, August 1, 2006, http://www.pladaily.com.cn/site1/database/2006-08/01/content_542314.htm (last accessed April 19, 2007). People's Republic of China, Information Office of the State Council, *China's National Defense in 2006*, December 2006, http://english.people.com.cn/whitepaper/defense2006/defense2006.html (last accessed April 19, 2007). Note: The official English version of this document renders 遏制战争 as "deter war" rather than "contain war."

13. Yuan Zhengling 袁正领, "An Active Defense Strategy to Protect National Interests—Understanding the 'National Defense of China 2002'" 积极防御战略 捍卫国家利益—解读《2002 年中国的国防》, *National Defense* 国防报, December 24, 2002, http://www.pladaily.com/gb/defence/2002/12/24/20021224017143_zhxw.html (last accessed April 19, 2007). English translation by OSC, CPP20021224000044. The article identifies Yuan as a researcher in the Strategy Research Department of AMS. Excerpt here retranslated by the author.

14. *SMS 2001*, chap. 8; Ma Ping 马平, "Foster a Scientific Strategic Outlook" 树立科学的战略观, *Liberation Army Daily* 解放军报 (Beijing), May 1, 2001, p. 3, translated in OSC CPP20010501000034, original text online at http://www.pladaily.

com.cn/gb/pladaily/2001/05/01/20010501001038_gdyl.html (last accessed April 19, 2007); Xiao Tianliang, chap. 4, pp. 96–133.

15. Yu Shifu and Yin Xinjian.

16. Xiao Tianliang, pp. 140–43.

17. Han Jiahe 韩嘉和 and Xiong Chunbao 熊春保, "A Brief Discussion of Military Crisis Control" 浅谈军事危机控制, *China's National Defense* 中国国防报 (Beijing), October 22, 2001, 3, http://www.pladaily.com.cn/gb/defence/2001/10/22/2001102 2017053_zhxw.html (last accessed April 19, 2007). Senior Colonel Han Jiahe is identified elsewhere as a professor at the Nanjing Army Command Academy; see OSC CPP20040218000058. One notes this was published not long after the April, 2001 EP-3 crisis.

18. Xiao Tianliang, p. 147.

19. Ibid., pp. 148–49.

20. Yu Shifu; Dan Xiufa.

21. Yuan Zhengling.

22. Pi Mingyong 皮明勇 and Wang Jianfei 王建飞, "Uphold the Unity of Containing War and Fighting and Winning War" 坚持遏制战争与打赢战争的统一, *Liberation Army Daily* 解放军报 April 6, 2006, http://theory.people.com.cn/ GB/49150/49152/4275658.html (last accessed April 19, 2007). Pi Mingyong is an assistant researcher in the AMS Strategy Department; see http://www.guoxue. com/ddxr/pe_piminyong.htm (last accessed April 19, 2007).

23. Xiao Tianliang, pp. 167, 170.

24. Yuan Zhengling.

25. Yu Jiang 喻江, "War Control: Getting Out of an Exhausting Difficult Situation" 战争控制: 走出力所不及的维谷, *China's National Defense* 中国国防报 (Beijing), March 25, 2004, http://www.pladaily.com.cn/gb/defence/2004/03/25/200403250 17054.html (last accessed April 19, 2007). The author is identified in the article as a researcher at the PLA Academy of Military Science.

26. Ibid.

27. "Reflections and insights on 20th Century Warfare" 20 世纪战争留给我们的思考和示, *Liberation Army Daily* 解放军报 (Beijing), December 25, 2000, OSC CPP20001225000027. This article summarizes a round-table discussion among several PLA strategists; the thought cited was expressed by Professor Xu Yuan 徐焰 of the NDU Strategy Research Office.

28. Han Jiahe and Xiong Chunbao; Xiao Tianliang, p. 164.

29. Xiao Tianliang, p. 171.

30. Feng Changsong 冯长松, "Raise Abilities to Win and Contain Wars" 提高打赢战争和遏制战争的能力, *Liberation Army Daily* 解放军报 (Beijing), August 27, 2003, OSC CPP20030827000124 (hereafter cited as Feng Changsong).

31. Xiao Tianliang, p. 176.

32. Feng Changsong.

33. Yu Jiang.

34. Xiao Tianliang, p. 166.

35. Ibid., p. 184.

36. Yu Jiang; Xiao Tianliang, pp. 180–85.

37. "Chinese Military Specialists Address the Quest for 'High Control' in Modern Warfare 中国军事专家提出现代战争谋求"高控制," *Guangming Daily* 光明日报 April 28, 2004, http://news.xinhuanet.com/mil/2004-04/28/content_1444426. htm (last accessed April 19, 2007).

38. Xiao Tianliang, p. 191; Yu Jiang.

39. Xiao Tianliang, p. 192; Dan Xiufa; Yu Shifu and Yin Xinjian.

40. Xiao Tianliang, pp. 193–98.

41. Ibid., p. 199.

42. Yu Shifu and Yin Xinjian, "An Initial Exploration of Mao Zedong's Thought on Containing War."

43. Xiao Tianliang, pp. 138, 145, 175; Xu Wen 徐文, "The Inspiration of Modern Local War for China's Weapons and Equipment Mobilization Preparation 现代局部战争对我国武器装备动员准备的启示," *Aerospace China* 中国航天 (Beijing) no. 3 (2004), http://www.space.cetin.net.cn/docs/ht0403/ht0403htzc03.htm (last accessed April 19, 2007); Wang Congbiao, "Implement the Strategy of Strengthening the Military Through Science and Technology to Improve the Defensive Combat Capabilities of China's Military—Studying Jiang Zemin's 'On Science and Technology'" 实施科技强军战略:提高我军现代防卫作战能力— —学习江泽民 《论科学技术》 *Liberation Army Daily* 解放军报 February 13, 2001, OSC CPP20010213000086.

44. This point was made in Michael D. Swaine, Zhang Tuosheng, and Danielle Cohen (eds.), *Managing Sino-American Crisis: Case Studies and Analysis* (Washington, D.C.: Carnegie Endowment for International Peace, 2006).

45. For discussion of these types of regulatory documents, see Lonnie Henley, "The Legal and Regulatory Basis for Defense Mobilization in China," paper presented at CNAC/RAND Conference on Mobilization and the PLA, Warrenton, Va., February 2005.

46. The text of the *Outline* has not been published outside PLA classified channels, but its existence is discussed in *Guide to the Study of Campaign Theory* and several other articles. See for instance "CMC Chairman Jiang Zemin Signs Order Implementing Our Army's New Generation of Operational Regulations" 中央军委主席江泽民签署命令我军新一代作战条令颁发, *People's Daily* 人民日报 January 25, 1999, http://www.people.com.cn/item/ldhd/Jiangzm/1999/mingling/ml0003. html (last accessed April 19, 2007).

47. For discussion of the development of this new generation of doctrine, see James Mulvenon and David M. Finkelstein, eds., *China's Revolution in Doctrinal Affairs:*

Emerging Trends in the Operational Art of the Chinese People's Liberation Army (Alexandria, Va.: CNA Corporation, 2005).

48. Bao Guojun and Zhang Xiaoqi, "AMS is the Backbone and Model for Operational Doctrine Research" 军事科学院改进作战理论研究骨干培养模式, *Liberation Army Daily* 解放军报 June 3, 2005, http://www.chinamil.com.cn/site1/ztpd/2005-06/03/content_220696.htm (last accessed April 19, 2007).

49. Cao Zhi 曹智 and Li Xuanliang 李宣良, "Hu Jintao Stresses the Need for Rapid Development of National Defense and Armed Forces" 胡錦濤強調推動國防和軍隊建設又快又好地發展, *Xinhua* March 11, 2006, http://www.pladaily.com.cn/site1/big5/database/2006-03/11/content_432416.htm (last accessed April 19, 2007); OSC CPP20060311001006. Retranslated by author.

50. Pei Fang, "Major Operation to Be Performed on Military Logistic System," *Kuang Chiao Ching* (Hong Kong) March 16, 1999, pp. 50–52, OSC FTS19990402000398

51. PRC, Information Office of the State Council, *China's National Defense 2006*, December 2006, OSC CPP20061229704001; Wen Tao: "China to Speed up Military Transformation with Chinese Characteristics, Push for Informationization of Armed Forces," *Ching Pao* (Hong Kong), June 1, 2003: 40–42, OSC CPP20030609000087.

52. The current publications technically are the second generation of Chinese written doctrine, but all involved concede that the first-generation regulations in the 1950s were a cursory effort of little operational value.

53. *SMS 2001;* Wang Houqing and Zhang Xingye, eds., *The Science of Campaigns* 战役学 (Beijing: National Defense University Press, 2000); Bi Xinglin, ed., *Guide to the Study of Campaign Theory* 战略理论学习指南 (Beijing: National Defense University Press, 2002); Gao Yubiao, ed., *Joint Campaigns Textbook* 联合战役学教程 (Beijing: Military Science Publishing House, 2001); Yang Zhiyuan and Peng Yanmei, eds., *The Science of Tactics* 战术学 (Beijing: Military Science Publishing House, 2002).

54. Pedants who insist there is no proof that Yogi really said these words are missing the point entirely.

55. Michael D. Swaine, "Understanding the Historical Record," in Michael D. Swaine, Tuosheng Zhang, and Danielle Cohen, eds., *Managing Sino-American Crises: Case Studies and Analysis* (Washington, D.C.: Carnegie Endowment for International Peace, 2006), p. 25.

56. Ibid., p. 28.

5

PLA Power Projection
Current Realities and Emerging Trends

Roy D. Kamphausen and Justin Liang

CHINA IS IN THE MIDST of a decades-long pursuit to increase its comprehensive national power (CNP) (*zōnghé guólì;* 综合国力). China's CNP—comprising material power, strength of ideas, and international influence—is derived from gains that China makes in the fields of economics, military affairs, science and technology, and education and resources.[1] These contributions are woven into an interlocking and mutually supporting set of national capabilities that combine to form an intangible strength that allows China to more thoroughly and efficiently achieve its national goals.

But the period of building CNP is a transitional one; vulnerabilities are apparent and other powers may act to disrupt the process or prevent its completion. Consequently, an important aspect of Chinese strategy in the reform and opening up period has included the effort to accumulate greater CNP by focusing on incremental capacity building, conflict avoidance, and the maintenance of stability, while downplaying concerns about China's developing capabilities.[2]

A brief survey of some key contributors to Chinese CNP shows the expected efforts at capacity building, conflict avoidance, and stability. Of note, the appraisal also reveals increased willingness to challenge existing norms. For example, in the economic realm, China's well-documented economic transformation has made perhaps the greatest contribution to the building of its CNP. China has become the world's third largest trading power and its fourth largest economy.[3] The economic tools available to China to increase its CNP include: growing trade; increasing investment—including Chinese outgoing foreign direct investment (FDI); foreign aid; and currency, both valuation and foreign reserves.[4] U.S. efforts to engage China as a "responsible stakeholder" in the international system have largely been focused on this economic domain, seeking to more deeply involve China in the system that has so greatly benefited Beijing's economic development.[5] Nonetheless, there are indications that Beijing may also have goals that, if achieved, might reshape the international economic order in ways more beneficial to China, including efforts to establish new international technical standards that would challenge existing norms and disproportionately benefit Chinese companies.[6]

Similarly, China's political and diplomatic power also contributes to the accretion of Chinese CNP. This power fundamentally derives from China's permanent membership on the United Nations Security Council (UNSC) and from China's status as a nuclear power. Moreover, China is seen as an entrenched member of the international community, with membership in international organizations "approaching about eighty percent of the comparison states."[7] For most of the last decade, China has also demonstrated a robust political energy and influence within Asia. In the Shanghai Cooperation Organization (SCO), China has taken a leadership role: the SCO's Secretary-General is Chinese, the Secretariat sits in Beijing, and, among other indicators, the September 15, 2006 prime ministerial communiqué reads as a testament to China's increasing influence.[8] In Southeast Asia's post-Asian financial crisis environment, not only is Chinese diplomacy proving remarkably adept in bilateral relations, but Beijing is also assuming a strong position in organizations related to the Association of Southeast Asian Nations (ASEAN). These two diplomatic fronts, when combined with apparent Chinese goals for the East Asia Summit (EAS) process, lend a distinct impression that China's newfound enthusiasm to lead multilateral efforts (usually excluding a U.S. presence or contributions) is rooted in a desire to provide policy alternatives to U.S.-led coalition efforts.[9] Yet, these efforts are not heavy-handed; indeed, it is accepted as a truism that "Chinese foreign policy has become far more nimble and engaging than at any other time in the history of the People's Republic."[10]

Even in the intangible realm of ideas, Beijing is harnessing the draw of Chinese culture throughout Asia to actively promote Chinese ends.

Aid, overseas study and scholarship programs, and Chinese language Confucius Centers provide Chinese language instruction and extend the reach of Chinese culture. This "soft power"[11] is much more difficult to quantify but has certainly assisted the People's Republic of China (PRC) in developing the beginnings of an alternative model to what Washington offers, contrasting markedly with China's less-than-stellar past performance in the region.[12]

But how does the military and security domain affect CNP? Is China's People's Liberation Army (PLA) contributing to the growth of overall CNP?

At its most fundamental level, the defense contribution to growing CNP is measured by the pace of China's comprehensive military modernization program, enabled by one and one-half decades of double-digit growth in defense spending. The defense budget increased in 2007 by nearly 18 percent, from 283.8 billion yuan (US$35.3 billion) to 350.92 yuan (US$44.94 billion), making China's declared defense expenditures the largest in Asia and third largest in the world after the United States and Russia.[13] Chinese leaders have asserted that the budget will be used to raise troop wages, train personnel, upgrade the country's defense capacity, and buy fuel in the face of a major rise in oil prices. Meanwhile, other external requirements also drive the growth in defense spending. Defense Minister Cao Gangchuan has said,

> The entire military must eye the historic destiny of China's military in the new century and new era and push forward the main line of a Chinese-style revolution in military affairs. . . . We must unswervingly fulfill our sacred duty to defend state sovereignty, territorial integrity, and security and never tolerate Taiwan independence and never permit Taiwan independence forces under any name or under any circumstances or form to split Taiwan from the motherland.[14]

Growing budgets have allowed China's military modernization program to achieve tangible improvements in military capabilities, and these capabilities will, over time, provide China with both the military power commensurate with its growing global status and with real military options against Taiwan.[15]

However, this effort gives rise to an impression that the PLA remains mired in the capacity-building phase, in which an ever stronger and better resourced defense establishment improves the equipment and systems that mark a "modernized" army, but which essentially provides only a *latent* military contribution to the building of CNP. And this impression is strengthened by those observers of the PLA's modernization process who proceed to "benchmark" the status of PLA modernization programs against Western standards without understanding what the current activities of China's military reveal about Beijing's strategic intent.

The questions then remain: Are there conditions where military modernization does more than simply grow latent power? Is the PLA involved in more than active expressions of Chinese military power? Put differently, is the PLA able to project military power in ways that support China's national goals and render conflict avoidance less necessary? Or, to superimpose the words of former U.S. Secretary of State Madeline Albright into a Chinese context: "What's the point of having this superb military you're always talking about if you can't use it?"[16]

A commonly accepted answer is that the PLA is not pursuing power projection capabilities in any meaningful way, and that the emphasis of the overall modernization effort lies elsewhere. The absence of aircraft carriers, limited number of "blue water" surface combatants, "absence" of overseas bases, incomplete overwater training evolutions, limited in-flight refueling capabilities, and apparent lack of power projection doctrine all serve to demonstrate that there is "scant, if any, evidence of the PLA developing capabilities to project power beyond China's immediate periphery."[17] However, observers who do not test this conclusion risk missing important developments in the study of PLA power projection that have serious implications for U.S. interests.

This chapter argues that China's PLA is currently projecting military power throughout Asia by *responding to crises, contributing to deterrence, and enhancing regional stability* using current capabilities. These abilities are derived from and contribute to the building of Chinese CNP, which in turn serve to increase China's stature in Asia, advance China's foreign policy goals, and even limit U.S. influence in the region. The actions, each of them fully legitimate within the norms of the international system, are sustainable over the long term; understanding the principles that guide them will help observers judge the trajectory of Chinese power projection in the future.

The first section employs the U.S. Department of Defense (DoD) definition of "power projection" as an organizational tool with which to categorize PLA activities. The examples cited demonstrate how PLA power projection is already underway by showing significant activity in each of the DoD categories. The cases chosen illustrate that these developments are predominantly within Asia, but that the methods China employs will increasingly be applied elsewhere, particularly as China's national capabilities grow.

The chapter's second section then discusses a series of trends of ongoing examples of PLA power projection emerging from this study and proposes some ways in which we might see that activity expand in the future. The chapter ends with conclusions and policy implications.

Before beginning, several caveats are in order. First, this chapter focuses on the explicit PLA activities that, as a component of China's overall defense and security policies, actively support the accumulation of CNP. Thus, no time is spent analyzing the growth of China's defense budget,[18] PRC arms sales abroad,[19] production agreements with and/or for foreign governments,[20] or PRC proliferation behavior.[21] Second, this chapter narrowly focuses on the activities of the PLA that can be exclusively carried out by military forces using solely military capabilities. This means that no discussion is devoted to "military diplomacy," including high-level visits or military-to-military exchanges. Whereas the content of these events tends to emphasize defense and security issues, the structure of such activities is identical to other activities performed by parallel government organizations (for example, nearly every bureaucratic organization in China conducts high-level visits). In contrast, this chapter focuses on military activities that are distinct from those of other governmental entities and have no parallels in other government agencies. Finally, the chapter does not attempt to catalogue on a service-by-service basis the advancements in new PLA equipment, although some key systems are highlighted; the fundamental point of this chapter is that the PLA is not just amassing capabilities to be used at some future point, but instead is using current capabilities to project power in the present.

The analysis begins with a definition of power projection.

POWER PROJECTION

What exactly is meant by "power projection?" Earlier, it was shown that the lack of certain high-tech capabilities has signaled to many observers the PLA's perceived inability to project power. As will be shown, this represents an incomplete understanding of the concept of power projection. Even more importantly, this conclusion is inherently risky because activities that fall short of the "power projection" threshold are summarily dismissed as uninteresting or unworthy of study. Yet it is precisely from an accurate understanding of the full range of current PLA power projection activities that one can understand how the PLA might employ its increasingly robust capabilities in the future.

In the classical sense, "power projection" refers primarily to maritime capabilities. Implementing policy and force outside one's own territory was historically believed to be a function of the navy, with sea control as the definitive hallmark of a great power. The empires of England, Spain, Portugal, and France were all built on the foundation of maritime strength and the size, strength, and mobility of their vessels ultimately defined their "power projection" capabilities.

Sea control as the basis for power projection reached its doctrinal heyday during the nineteenth century, when leading wartime strategists such as Alfred Thayer Mahan spearheaded a movement known as "navalism," which advocated the accumulation of state power through the construction and maintenance of a powerful navy. Largely inspired by the military theories of von Clausewitz and Jomini, Mahan's theory—that naval power, economic development, and international relations were inextricably linked and that sea lanes, as avenues for commerce and trade, would become increasingly critical as economic competition intensified—was groundbreaking and prophetic.[22] Indeed, with the growth of international trade in the twenty-first century and the expansion of commerce via critical sea lines of communication, possessing a capable blue water fleet—merchant, military, or both—arguably has never been more important.

Whether the PLA's current power projection goals have a theoretical basis in Mahanian theory is a question that has gained considerable attention lately. A number of scholars have argued that Mahan's proposition of supremacy at sea is shaping, even dictating, China's military aspirations.[23] While it is beyond the scope of this chapter to analyze this argument in scholarly depth, it is worth drawing out a few specific continuities and discontinuities to demonstrate the limitations of a strictly maritime-based power projection definition in the case of the contemporary PLA.

Historically, China's lack of a robust blue water naval capability has restricted its ability to transform economic power into military power, and vice versa. Moreover, memories of Western "treaty port diplomacy" and intervention dating back to the first Opium War (1839–42) continue to inform China's awareness of the maritime component of defense and strategy planning. Mahan's theory, therefore, appears relevant insofar as it foregrounds the interdependence of continental and maritime security, emphasizing the need for naval bases along critical sea lines and for command of key access points (e.g., the Taiwan Strait in China's case). The "three pillars" of commerce, merchant and naval shipping, and naval bases proposed by Mahan[24] resonate strongly with China's growing reliance on seaborne commerce to secure key resources, such as oil.

However, there are a number of factors that limit the utility of this analogy. First, while military buildup itself is important to China, the quantity and concentration of forces—two key metrics for Mahan in determining a country's ability to project power—are no longer as paramount given today's technological advances in military capabilities, such as intelligence gathering. As Harlan Ullman contends about the applicability of Mahanian theory more broadly, the dissipation of geographic borders due to globalization and technology has today made "perceptions, ideologies, and ideas" more important than the "size and number of guns."[25]

Second, a Mahanian vision of maritime power projection assumes that Chinese naval buildup and deployment represent an *offensive* maneuver, designed as a tactical preparation for the physical destruction of an enemy. This proposition, by any account, is a dangerous one, for it fails to consider the alternative that the PLA's current naval activity is not strictly a military power play, but rather part of a broader geopolitical agenda—linked, as this chapter argues, to the development of CNP.

Finally, a change in the international political landscape has redefined the terms upon which such power may be legitimately projected and has brought into question the need for such a large naval force in the first place. Legal issues surrounding maritime territoriality, enforced by the United Nations Convention on the Law of the Sea (UNCLOS) among other institutions, as well as those restricting arms procurement, have made it ever more difficult to amass and project force overseas. Moreover, the norms of today's international system, which are grounded in information flows, transparency, and accountability, have carved out new standards for public diplomacy. For every proposed military maneuver, China can be assured that the rest of the world will be watching, taking note, and responding. Executing maritime strategies now requires far greater precision and tact than in Mahan's era.

Given the constraints noted above, maritime power projection of the sort proposed by Mahan seems inadequate to capture the totality of means, objectives, and rationale of modern-day PLA power projection. Rather than focusing exclusively on the capacity to project power and conjecturing about the threat posed by an offense-oriented PLA force buildup, we should turn attention to the *how*, looking at documented PLA activities to construct a picture of its overall power projection strategy.

The U.S. DoD offers an alternative definition of power projection that can be operationalized in this context. The DoD *Dictionary of Military and Associated Terms* defines power projection as:

> The ability of a nation to apply all or some of its elements of national power—political, economic, informational, or military—to rapidly and effectively deploy and sustain forces in and from multiple dispersed locations to respond to crises, to contribute to deterrence, and to enhance regional stability.[26]

The definition's first part reflects the idea of CNP, in which the ability to project power derives from the component elements of national power. In the definition's second part, the emphasis is on the process of moving and sustaining military forces. As has been shown in the case of the PLA, because of the relative shortage of airlift and sealift capabilities, which enable force deployments, the judgment is often made that the PLA "does not have the capability to project power." This type of analysis again places excessive weight on the *means* of projecting power.

However, the third part of the DoD definition addresses *why* military force is deployed: to respond to crises, contribute to deterrence, and enhance regional stability. On this score, the record of PLA activity is quite full. By cataloguing and categorizing PLA activities in these three ways, one can see Beijing's increasing willingness and capability to project power. Moreover, the number of examples is increasing over time and may mark a transition phase away from the latent capability, conflict avoidance, and status quo maintenance phase of Chinese security strategy.

Responding to Crises

The first way in which the PLA projects power is to use military force to respond to *external crises*. In this category, the nearly exclusive manifestation of this effort is in the form of PLA troop contributions to United Nations Peacekeeping Operations (UN PKO). From Beijing's perspective, UN PKO missions serve several important political functions as China seeks to play a more constructive and active role within the UN. Participating in UN PKO allows China's leaders to show support for multilateral UN efforts, demonstrate responsible leadership, and present opportunities to check U.S. unilateralism.[27] Moreover, supporting UN PKO may also serve to protect Beijing against criticism in those instances when China prevents UN action deemed contrary to China's deep-seated avoidance of interference in other nations' internal affairs.[28] Finally, UN PKO missions allow China to add a more significant military component to the pursuit of China's foreign policy interests.

Support for UN PKO also serves military goals. PLA contributions to UN PKO have come from most of China's seven military regions, thereby distributing the training benefits derived from mobilizing, organizing, and deploying forces overseas. By designating some lead units to provide ongoing support to UN PKO—mostly logistics, medical, and engineering—the PLA can advance certain capabilities more rapidly that will subsequently trickle down to benefit the main force.[29] Finally, PLA doctrine and operational procedures benefit from observing and interacting with foreign militaries.[30]

The following examples demonstrate the points above, as well as the fact that Chinese support for UN PKO has been growing in scale and importance.

- In August 2006, the third rotation to Haiti of 125 Chinese riot police was awarded a commendation by the UN Stabilization Mission in

Haiti prior to returning home from an eight-month UN-led peace-keeping operation in Haiti[31] (Beijing had overcome initial reluctance to send forces in 2004 because of Haiti's diplomatic recognition of Taiwan and Haiti's proximity to the U.S. mainland). In the end, Chinese police performed well, as indicated by the commendation, and a fourth rotation of Chinese police is currently in Haiti.

- In mid-September 2006, China pledged to send 800 more troops to Lebanon under the UN flag, bringing its total force in Lebanon to more than 1,000 soldiers. The new group of soldiers will join an existing PLA contingent comprised of a mine-sweeping company, an engineering company, a logistics company, and an infield hospital based out of an engineering regiment in China's Chengdu Military Region, which has provided PKO support in the past.[32] Premier Wen Jiabao suggested that China's military participation in Lebanon is an expression of China's growing international status.[33]

- On September 27, 2006, Liberia thanked China for its assistance in UN PKO, as more than 500 Chinese officers have participated in UN operations in Liberia.[34]

- In late September 2006, the UN Security Council resolved (UNSCR 1706) to deploy more than 20,000 additional UN peacekeeping troops to Darfur in light of the deteriorating security situation there. China's representative on the UNSC added a proviso that Sudan must first consent to the forces being dispatched, affording Sudan an opportunity to turn down the offer.[35] With Sudan's initial rejection of UN forces, the concern emerged that China might threaten to use its Security Council veto unless the Sudanese government had the right to refuse intervention, perhaps as a reflection of the continuing importance of oil exports from Sudan to China, which represent more than 40 percent of Sudan's total exports.[36] In early April 2007, China boosted military cooperation with Sudan, and then tempered the announcement amid criticism from other UNSC members by urging Sudan to accept the deployment of UN peacekeepers in Darfur.[37]

- In mid-October 2006, China pledged to strengthen its support for UN PKO in Africa. At a briefing at the Forum of China-Africa Cooperation (FOCAC), Xu Jinghu, the head of the Africa Department of the Chinese Foreign Ministry, commented: "China will actively participate in UN peacekeeping operations in Africa to safeguard regional peace and stability." Since 1990, China has participated in a total of twelve UN peacekeeping operations in Africa, involving more than 3,000 Chinese peacekeepers.[38]

The aforementioned examples regarding PLA participation in UN PKO continue the trend of rising Chinese support for multilateral peace-keeping operations over the last two years. As recently as 2004, China was playing a much smaller role in the support of UN PKO. The Chinese 2004 defense white paper asserted that:

China has consistently supported and actively participated in the peace-keeping operations that are consistent with the spirit of the UN Charter.

Since its first dispatch of military observers to the UN peacekeeping operations in 1990, China has sent 3,362 military personnel to 13 UN peacekeeping operations [emphasis added], including 785 military observers, 800 (in two batches) engineering personnel to Cambodia, 654 (in three batches) engineering and medical personnel to Congo (Kinshasa), 1,116 personnel in transportation, engineering and medical units to Liberia, and seven staff officers to the UN Department of Peacekeeping Operations. Since January 2000, China has sent 404 policemen to the peacekeeping operations in six UN peacekeeping task areas including East Timor. In 2004, China has sent 59 policemen to East Timor, Liberia, Afghanistan, Kosovo of Serbia-Herzegovina and Haiti, and a 125-member organic police detachment to Haiti to serve with MINUSTAH at the request of the UN. In the past 14 years, six Chinese servicemen lost their lives and dozens wounded in UN peacekeeping operations.

At present, 845 PLA personnel are working in eight UN peacekeeping task areas. They include 66 military observers, an engineering unit of 175 personnel and a medical unit of 43 personnel in Congo (Kinshasa), an engineering unit of 275 personnel, a transportation unit of 240 personnel and a medical unit of 43 personnel in Liberia, and three staff officers at the UN Department of Peacekeeping Operations.[39]

Since the defense white paper declaration of December 2004, PLA contributions to UN PKO have increased dramatically. According to March 2007 UN statistics, China is the largest contributor to UN PKO among Security Council members, measured in terms of number of troops in the field (1,572), and recently edged out France for the lead in mission participation (12).[40] When the additional deployment of troops to Lebanon (800) occurs, China will have nearly 2,400 soldiers in the field. Moreover, when contrasted with the total number of troops supporting UN PKO cited in China's 2004 defense white paper, *more than forty percent of the total number of PLA troops deployed overseas in support of UN PKO since 1990 is currently in the field.* In the process, China has also shown a willingness to endure limited casualties; only eight PLA personnel have died in UN PKO since 1988.[41]

This growing commitment is also becoming institutionalized as military leaders seek to draft legislation that promulgates mission participation through formal legal channels. In a March 12, 2007 convening of the Chinese National People's Congress (NPC), Zeng Haisheng, a PLA Major General and sister of Vice President Zeng Qinghong, stated that "with increasing involvement of [Chinese] military forces in overseas operations, such as peace-keeping and rescue efforts, it is necessary to enact a law to define the validity of such operations and guarantee the interests of our army men."[42] Such public pronouncements underscore China's interest in letting the world know that its commitment to PKO efforts will be sustained and perhaps given even greater attention in the future.

Why the dramatic shift? Several preliminary answers should be considered. PLA support for UN PKO affords several benefits. China gets the credit for being internationally responsible while obviating the risks that may arise from acting unilaterally. Moreover, PLA operational practice benefits from the demand to deploy in a timely manner that UN PKO requires. But the PLA accrues these benefits without the pressure of assuming singular responsibility for a mission's success.

To be sure, China's contribution to UN PKO is dwarfed by the efforts of nations such as Bangladesh, Pakistan, and others. Among all contributors, China is presently ranked twelfth (out of 115) in total number of forces participating. Moreover, responding to crises in a multilateral way through UN PKO support may seem antithetical to the traditional understanding of power projection activity; indeed, one might argue that these activities are decidedly nonthreatening and ought to be supported by the international community. The point here is not to argue about whether supporting UN PKO is a classic example of power projection, but rather to focus on the "crisis response" routine that the PLA is developing. It may be that the inept PRC response to the Boxing Day tsunami of 2004 served as a catalyst for accelerated crisis response efforts, even if support for UN PKO was only an interim step.

Contributing to Deterrence[43]

A second type of power projection includes the specific activities that demonstrate military contributions to deterrence. These actions are inherently coercive, or counter-coercive; military force or presence is present or implied in ways designed to influence the national decision making of other countries.

In this case, the PLA is also actively involved in that Chinese presence and/or assertion of claims seek to prevent others from accomplishing their goals. These activities usually occur in the areas closest to China (the Taiwan Strait, East China Sea, and South China Sea) and include air surveillance missions, subsurface patrols, and surface missions. These actions are not unique to China; in fact, they are sanctioned by UNCLOS and customary international law, provided they comply with restrictions on activities within territorial seas and airspace.[44] The category also includes domestic military actions that are unambiguously designed to send deterrent messages to Taiwan; the chapter briefly addresses PLA amphibious training against Taiwan and the development and deployment of PRC missile forces.

AIR SURVEILLANCE. The PLA Air Force (PLAAF) and Naval Air Force has or is developing a range of air capabilities with which it can conduct aerial missions, including: Y-8 variants for intelligence collection and airborne battlefield control; indigenous Airborne Early Warning (AEW) systems; domestic fourth-generation F-10 and co-produced Su-27SK; and increasingly advanced fighters, such as Su-30MKK multi-role and Su-MK2 maritime strike aircraft purchased from Russia[45]—all of which are systems that are enabling ever more active reconnaissance activities. According to a report from Japan's Air Self-Defense Force (ASDF), the number of Chinese planes suspected of entering Japanese airspace for surveillance purposes increased eightfold from 2004 to 2005.[46] In

2006, Japanese responses to PRC reconnaissance aircraft have increased to more than a hundred incidents, though numbers seem to have leveled off since Prime Minister Shinzo Abe's recent efforts to thaw Sino-Japanese relations.[47]

Moreover, PLA fighters and other air assets have increasingly crossed the center line of the Taiwan Strait since the mid-1990s, and the Taiwan Air Force has responded in ways that diminish the chances for accidental conflict but may convey that Beijing has greater freedom to operate in the airspace over the Taiwan Strait.[48] Although limited data exist on the precise number of flights that PLAAF jets have made across the center line, the Taiwan Ministry of National Defense (MND) reported in its August 2006 biennial defense review that the number of Chinese fighter planes patrolling the zone has increased dramatically over the past ten years. According to the report, up until 1996 few PLAAF planes breached Taiwan's Exclusive Economic Zone (EEZ). However, in the year of both Taiwan's first direct presidential election and a Chinese missile test off the coast of Taiwan, the number began to climb. By 2000, an estimated 1,200 sorties were reported in the area. In 2001, the number grew to 1,500; in 2005, the number escalated to approximately 1,700.[49] Taiwan's ability to respond is further impacted by the addition of the new S-300PMU2 advanced Russian air defense system, which will enable PRC air defense assets to acquire and target Taiwan aircraft as soon as they take off and reach altitude.[50]

SUBMARINE PATROLS. China's subsurface deterrent actions are potentially even more significant. The stealthy aspects of submarine operations, combined with the cruise missile and ballistic missile capabilities on board China's subs, present current regional and strategic deterrents to those who might act contrary to Beijing's goals. Two recent and well-publicized incidents are illustrative: one in November 2004 and another more recently in October 2006.

From a regional perspective, arguably the most prominent recent example of submarine deterrent action was the November 2004 reported incursion of a Han-class submarine into Japanese territorial waters. In this event, JMSDF detected the submarine east of Taiwan in the southern part of Japan's territorial islands, and then vectored destroyers to the area, resulting in the departure of the submarine and a subsequent expression of regret. Japan was rightly pleased with its own response. But the submarine's other mission objectives (including perhaps undersea surveillance further east of Guam) are unknown, and the submarine commander's apparent familiarity with the channels between islands indicate this type of patrol may be more frequent than is known. Indeed, this was apparently the thirty-fourth such incident in Japan's EEZ in 2004.[51] Moreover, the growth of China's submarine force[52] and the promotion of submarine commanders to more senior positions in the PLA Navy (PLAN) indicate the ascendance of the submarine force, making this type of deterrent activity likely to increase in the future.[53]

Another incident transpired in October 2006, when a Chinese Song-class submarine closed within five miles of the USS Kitty Hawk battle group near Guam, reportedly undetected until the submarine surfaced.[54] The action may result in a reevaluation of the training status of U.S. forces, perhaps precipitating a higher anti-submarine warfare posture in all training events, thereby raising training costs significantly. These developments were not wholly unanticipated, but the PLAN submarine force has demonstrated that it can operate throughout the Asia-Pacific region and is not deterred by the mere presence of U.S. forces.[55]

SURFACE. A third way in which the PLA contributes to deterrence is through surface "presence" missions. The most transparent example of such missions is in the East China Sea, where China and Japan have overlapping claims, made more pressing by the prospect of off-shore oil and natural gas deposits. On September 9, 2005, China deployed five warships to the Chunxiao oil field area: a Sovremenny-class guided-missile destroyer; two Jianghu I-class missile frigates; a replenishment vessel; and a missile observation support ship. Japan regarded this move as a political statement about resource control in the East China Sea.[56] Indeed it was, and the robustness of the Chinese naval force made a comparable Japanese response unappealing lest it appear unduly escalatory. As a result, PLAN actions were clearly a factor in Japanese strategic decision making. Although it is unknown to what degree the PRC deterring presence provided an impetus, after a period of irresolution, for a discussion at the Abe-Hu summit at the November 2006 APEC Forum in Hanoi, Vietnam, on exploration in the East China Sea to accelerate joint development of gas fields there, it is still noteworthy.[57]

AMPHIBIOUS TRAINING EXERCISES. A fourth example of how Chinese forces contribute to deterrence can be found in the amphibious training exercises that the PLA conducts to convey overt deterrent messages to Taiwan. The Pentagon estimates that the PLA has held eleven amphibious exercises with a Taiwan scenario between 1999 and 2005.[58] Most prominent is the series of exercises conducted on Dongshan Island, said to have topographic features similar to the west coast of Taiwan. In annual exercises held from 1996 to 2004, the PLA conducted joint training (all services including Second Artillery) in well-rehearsed and publicized dress rehearsals for an amphibious invasion of Taiwan.[59] The spring 2001 Dongshan exercise contained perhaps the largest number of PLA troops ever assembled for a training event—over 100,000.[60] Exercise goals were said to include the enhancement of joint training; conveyance to Taiwan of the PLA's resolve to handle by force the "Taiwan issue" should Taiwan move toward independence; and reassertion of Beijing's sovereign rights to Taiwan, which brook no foreign interference.[61] Interestingly, the Dongshan series apparently was not conducted in 2005, and overall amphibious training activity in the Nanjing Military Region was not only markedly lower than in the adjacent Guangzhou and Jinan military regions, but also far below the scale of previous years. This led to speculation that Beijing lowered the amount of active military deterrent against Taiwan because of political developments more favorable to Beijing.[62]

MISSILE FORCES. Undoubtedly, the most visible form of PLA deterrent actions is the accelerated development of China's missile forces. The prospect of several hundred missiles raining down on critical targets in Taiwan, or striking other targets in Asia, has already achieved a degree of military deterrent effect in Taipei and complicated security planning elsewhere, including in the United States. The U.S. DoD asserts that, as of late 2005, China has nearly 800 short-range ballistic missiles (SRBM) and approximately 200 launchers; China increases these SRBMs by approximately 100 annually.[63] Moreover, the accuracy of these systems has improved, allowing for precision strikes against a range of targets, including U.S. bases in the Western Pacific, surface ships, and critical infrastructure throughout Taiwan and some of Japan. Perhaps an even greater contributor to deterrence are the approximately fifty Chinese medium-range solid-propellant and road-mobile CSS-5 missiles (with nearly forty launchers), the reach of which extends through much of the Asian continent, depending on selected firing points throughout China.[64]

With the possible exception of the missile force developments, observers could argue that these examples of military contributions to deterrence are reasonable and perhaps even necessary for a country with regional leadership aspirations and capabilities. Many countries climbing to global prominence pursue these types of military deterrent actions when their national psychology and military power permit. While this is true, two considerations warrant the recounting of these events in this section on contributing to deterrence. First, the activities themselves disprove the idea that the PLA's limited power projection systems (transport and long-range war-fighting systems) equate to a lack of power projection ability. Indeed, these cases demonstrate how PLA forces have complicated and even deterred actions on the part of other regional states by introducing the coercive arm of China's increasing CNP.

Second, as China adds to the set of military capabilities that will allow it to contribute to more deterrence, Beijing must reconcile its long-held and principled opposition to U.S. operations intended to achieve the same effect (which are also explicitly permitted by customary international law and convention).[65] U.S. operations, including reconnaissance and hydrographic surveying, in the international airspace and high seas off China's coast are especially galling to China.[66] However, China's national interests will increasingly require it to conduct these same types of operations. Adjusting policy to align Chinese strategic interests, international law, and past rhetoric will prove a challenging process for the Chinese leadership.

Enhancing Regional Stability

From a U.S. perspective, regional stability is enhanced by the presence of U.S. forces within that particular region on a regular basis. This presence is accomplished through deploying forces, usually naval, to a region on a periodic basis; conducting combined exercises with host nation forces; and basing U.S. forces in foreign locations. China also engages in these three types of activities, although this chapter makes no attempt to argue that these specific methods are designed to mimic U.S. actions toward this end.

Moreover, as the following examples demonstrate, whether these activities in fact enhance regional stability is questionable, and largely a matter of perspective. As in any delicate security relationship, a push in one direction often accompanies a pull in the other. Beijing's "presence" deployments in this regard may enhance regional stability from a Chinese point of view, but not from Washington's or Taipei's respective vantage points.

"PRESENCE" DEPLOYMENTS—NAVAL VISITS AND STOPS. For countries in the Asia-Pacific region, the early September 2006 trans-Pacific cruise of the PLAN guided-missile destroyer "Qingdao" (a Luhu-class guided-missile destroyer) and the supply ship "Hongzehu," with stops in Pearl Harbor, San Diego, and British Columbia, as part of a month-long "goodwill tour" of North America, once again demonstrated the reach of China's improving naval capabilities. The trip to the United States was the first by a Chinese naval vessel in six years, but the interval between visits was more a function of bilateral difficulties than a reflection of PLAN deficiencies.[67] (Earlier trips to the United States occurred in 1989, 1997, 2000, and 2003—the last being a visit to Guam with follow-on stops in Brunei and Singapore.)[68]

While the symbolic objectives attained within the context of the complex bilateral U.S.-PRC military relationship are difficult to judge, the fact that these port visits were accomplished successfully confirmed the capability of Chinese naval vessels to establish a naval presence throughout the Pacific. This presence is certainly limited by the number and availability of ships, and further constrained by the requirement for resources to finance such efforts. Nonetheless, the cruise to the United States presented a useful sampling of the PLA's overall set of capabilities to project military power throughout the Asia-Pacific.[69] And as if to emphasize the point, the PLAN ships stopped in the Philippines on their return trip to China.[70]

More recently, in early November 2006, a small Chinese naval formation consisting of the "Shenzhen" missile destroyer and the "Weishanhu" depot ship embarked upon a forty-day tour with visits to Pakistan, India, and Thailand.[71] These latest activities continue recent trends. In the past three years, the PLAN has exercised with counterpart navies in Pakistan (October 2003), India (November 2003), France (March 2004), Great Britain (June 2004), Australia (October 2004),[72] Thailand (December 2005),[73] and Pakistan and India (November 2005).[74]

PLAN ships have also made port calls at the following locations: Gwadar, Pakistan, and Mumbai, India (May 2001, the Luhu-class destroyer "Harbin" and supply ship "Taicang")[75]; Hong Kong, after a visit to Germany, France, the United Kingdom, and Italy (November 2001, the guided-missile destroyer "Shenzhen" and supply ship "Fengcang")[76]; a first ever trip to Vietnam (November 2001, guided-missile frigate "Yulin")[77]; a first ever cruise to the Republic of Korea (May 2002, the missile frigates "Jiaxing" and "Lianyungang")[78]; Singapore (May 2002, the guided-missile destroyer "Qingdao" and the supply ship "Taicang")[79]; and a six-day stopover in Hong Kong to celebrate the 55th anniversary of the PLAN (April 2004, two guided-missile destroyers, four guided-missile frigates, and two submarines).[80] Latest reports indicate that the PLAN will also be making a port visit to Japan in mid-2007, paving the way for future Sino-Japanese naval exchanges as part of an April 2007 agreement between Wen Jiabao and Japanese Prime Minister Shinzo Abe.[81]

JOINT/COMBINED MILITARY EXERCISES. The PLA also increasingly conducts combined military exercises, primarily with SCO partners, which usually focus on countering terrorist actions. This trend began in August 2003 with "Coalition 2003," a combined anti-terrorist exercise involving China, Kazakhstan, Kyrgyzstan, Russia, and Tajikistan.[82] Over the past two years, a handful of similar exercises have followed suit, indicating the scale of involvement and helping to shape our understanding of what the future may entail.

In late September 2006, Chinese and Tajik soldiers conducted a two-day Sino-Tajik military exercise in Kulyab, Tajikistan—a mountain warfare operation code named "Coordination 2006." More than 300 Tajik and 150 Chinese combat troops joined the training. The exercise scenario involved a China-Tajik joint headquarters commanding a combined response to the capture of Chinese and Tajik construction workers on a high-speed road project funded by the Chinese government.[83] Also in late September 2006, members of the SCO observed anti-nuclear terrorism exercises in Yerevan, Armenia, held by the Commonwealth of Independent States (CIS) of Armenia's Anti-Terrorism Center.[84]

In December 2006, Russian Defense Minister Sergei Ivanov visited Beijing to strengthen the strategic partnership between China and Russia. PLA Assistant Chief of General Staff Zhang Qinsheng *suggested there*

*will be eight military cooperatives/exercises in 2007, beginning with a
Russian naval visit and including joint military drills in Russia under the
framework of the SCO.*[85] These plans follow the widely reported Chinese
and Russian combined exercise in August 2005 off China's Shandong
peninsula, entitled "Peace Mission 2005." A total of about 10,000 Chinese and Russian army, navy, and air force personnel participated in that
exercise and displayed a full range of naval, amphibious, and aircraft
capabilities.[86] The scenario featured Sino-Russian military intervention
in a terrorist-related internal conflict in a third country. PRC and Russian forces were invited by the fictional third government to separate the
combatants and prevent wider war.[87]

BASES. Popular impressions notwithstanding, China has a series of
PLA-run facilities or friendly foreign locations throughout Asia, referred
to here as "access points," which provide limited fixed facilities as well
as the capability to provide logistical support to transiting forces. These
points are scattered widely across South and Southeast Asia, the South
China Sea, and the Pacific Islands.

- *South Asia.* China has contributed nearly 80 percent of the construction
  costs for the $1.2 billion dollar modern port at Gwadar, Pakistan; pro-
  vided technical and engineering support for the project; and donated
  most of the financing necessary ($200 million) for the road infra-
  structure between Gwadar and Karachi.[88] Islamabad envisions that
  Gwadar will relieve Pakistan's overdependence on the vulnerable port
  of Karachi, currently handling 90 percent of Pakistan's sea trade.
  From China's perspective, one can imagine a cooperative agreement
  for access to Gwadar. *If* afforded access at Gwadar for naval logistical support, its location just 240 miles from the Strait of Hormuz
  significantly improves Beijing's strategic options.[89] A similar port is
  presently under construction in Sri Lanka, where China has agreed to
  foot 85 percent of the $360 million in construction costs.[90]
- In Burma, China has numerous intelligence collection locations and
  is assisting with the construction of a deep-water port at Sittwe.[91]
  Although the open source record on these locations indicates the
  presence of only a limited number of technicians, they are reasonably
  permanent facilities.

- The PLA has several access points in the South China Sea, in both the Paracel and Spratly Islands. On Woody Island in the Paracels, the PLA reportedly has a 350-meter pier and a 2,600-meter airstrip, fortified defensive positions, and possibly anti-ship missile batteries. On Rocky Island, also in the Paracels, the PLA has a signals intelligence collection station. Meanwhile, in the eastern part of the Spratly Islands, since sparring with the Philippines armed forces in the mid-1990s over Mischief Reef, Beijing has reportedly continued to fortify the facilities with armaments, helicopter landing pads, and communications facilities—now referring to the stations as "sea bastions."[92]
- A final overseas "base" example is that of the satellite tracking station in Kiribati, which PRC technicians closed down in 2004 after new leaders in Tarawa changed Kiribati's official diplomatic recognition to Taiwan.[93]

It is disputable whether a link or "string" exists between these "access points." What is clear is that Beijing has a range of locations that PLA naval and air forces can potentially access for purposes of logistical resupply, maintenance, or even relief from operational deployment. In a potential, if unlikely, conflict with the United States, some of the facilities would still potentially be available for use by PLA forces. Their availability would depend on a range of factors, varying from host nation interest to welcome PLA forces (as in Burma or Pakistan) or in the PLA's determination to defend them (as in the cases of the Spratly and Paracel Islands facilities.)

TRENDS IN PLA POWER PROJECTION AND FUTURE EMPLOYMENTS

The six trends below emerge from the foregoing study of ongoing PLA power projection activities. Understanding these trends presents an opportunity to look forward to how the PLA might project power in the future.

1. *Observe sovereignty and pay attention to borders.* As a matter of long-standing principle, China does not routinely deploy forces into other countries, partly because it seeks to avoid outside interference in its own dealings with Taiwan. Beijing has even shown a willingness to threaten its UNSC

veto to prevent a violation of sovereignty in cases where UN intervention is contemplated and the object of such intervention is itself opposed to the move—the case of Sudan being a recent example. Related to China's concern over sovereignty is Beijing's support for border reinforcement.[94] Security concerns over the preservation of borders remain paramount. In part, the SCO's history began with the demarcation of borders, and the need to defend the heartland from "frontier threats" remains critical to China. Some of the SCO exercises in trans-border regions appear focused on effective cross-coordination across borders such that each sovereign power can more effectively reinforce its own borders. Indeed, China's sole contribution to coalition efforts in Afghanistan (Operation Enduring Freedom) was the closure of its border with Afghanistan.[95]

2. *Intervene when in China's interests.* China will consider involving itself in other countries if its forces are requested by the leaders of that country, as recent PLA exercises with SCO partners demonstrate. Interestingly, the September 2006 Sino-Tajik military exercise demonstrates that the proximate cause for the request for deployment of PLA forces included the capture of Chinese citizens and risk to PRC infrastructure investment, leading to the possibility that Beijing might persuade another capital for permission to intervene militarily if its investments were put at risk.

3. *Strengthen support for UN PKO missions outside of Asia.* China's support and involvement in UN PKO in missions outside of Asia will likely continue to grow. Beijing's October statement about increased support for UN PKO in Africa is the strongest evidence of China's intent on this score. In the early 1990s, the PLA did make a sizeable contribution to UNTAC in Cambodia. However, with the exception of limited police support in East Timor and Afghanistan, China's participation since then has occurred outside of Asia, and this trend is likely to continue.

4. *Strengthen support for multilateral operations, primarily in Asia, where China can assume a leading role.* The amount and quality of PLA activity to date under the rubric of the SCO has presented new options for leadership in an area long avoided by Beijing. This trend also anticipates increasing interaction with China's Southeast Asia neighbors under the rubric of ASEAN.

5. *Conduct small-scale deterrence missions.* Incidents of PLA air, naval surface, and submarine presence throughout Asia have proven effective

in demonstrating the not-so-subtle message that Beijing has increasing military power to back up its claims.

6. *Enhance naval presence missions.* The incidence of small PLA surface groups, often just a guided-missile destroyer and a supply ship or refueler, appearing throughout Asia has helped the PLAN establish itself as a player in the contest to contribute to regional stability.

With these trends in mind, we can anticipate some specific ways in which the PLA might be involved in power projection in the future. Indeed, while smaller scale in size at present, as PLA capabilities increase, these activities have the potential to become much more significant both in scale and regional impact. Over time, even as the actions are intended to enhance regional stability from Beijing's perspective, they may have the altogether other effect of degrading stability, because the activities are perceived as threatening to other countries in the region.

Responding to Crises

By increasing its support of UN PKO, Beijing will demonstrate its accumulation of larger CNP and show its greater ability to project power. In many cases, the deployment of forces will continue trends in areas of strategic interest to China, especially Africa, both strengthening China's role and providing a check on the influence of others in these regions. Moreover, the establishment of PLA units with concentrated peacekeeping capabilities and frequent UN PKO deployments may create a capacity to provide training to regional partners.

There may be other crises to which China might respond, but not under the auspices of the United Nations. Given an absence of global security commitments, these responses are most likely to occur near China, on or near China's territorial borders. The most prominent instance in this second category of crisis response is the North Korean situation. Would China deploy PLA forces to play a role in a North Korea crisis, either to secure China's borders, to help establish domestic order in North Korea, or even to make determinations about future North Korean leadership?

In late October 2006, reports appeared which stated that China had erected barbed wire border fencing near the city of Dandong, in Liaoning

Province, near the border of the Democratic People's Republic of Korea (DPRK).[96] This follows reporting that has appeared at various times since late 2002 that the PLA had either assumed control of the border[97] or deployed more significant forces to the border.[98]

However, on October 10, 2006, while China agreed there should be "punitive action" taken in response to the October 9th North Korean nuclear test in Kilchu, Foreign Ministry spokesman Liu Jianchao stated that military action would be "unimaginable."[99] These seemingly conflicting statements likely reflect some of the internal wrangling between Chinese bureaucracies as to how best to handle North Korea, and the PLA may well be working at cross-purposes with China's diplomatic efforts regarding the DPRK.[100] Nonetheless, one can easily imagine a PLA force deployed to, and perhaps even within, North Korea to secure the border region, thwart large-scale refugee flows, and ensure a buffer zone east of China's own border.

Enhancing Deterrence

In this category of activities, the PLA is most likely to act alone. Naval patrols, both surface and subsurface, in contested areas are likely to continue to increase in number, and aerial surveillance and air presence missions will likely persist in pushing Chinese presence throughout the region.

In the future, the security component of China's Taiwan strategy may include a mix of both deterrence and crisis response activities. This is in part due to a military balance in the cross-strait environment that increasingly favors Beijing. Whereas in 2002–2005, DoD assessments predicted a declining ability for the United States to deter PLA actions within the 2006–2008 time frame, recent public assessments indicate that a "window of opportunity" for PLA action against Taiwan might open between 2008 and 2015.[101] Examples abound as to the ways the PLA might project coercive power toward Taiwan should its contributions to deterrence prove insufficient. These options include naval blockades/sea control, seizure of off-shore islands, incapacitating missile and air strikes, and even a joint assault on the main island—each option affording different strengths and weaknesses.[102] However, the decision to pursue any of these options actually might be in reaction to actions undertaken by Taiwan that may create a crisis from Beijing's perspective, requiring a response.

Enhancing Regional Stability

Sending only one or two ships, consistent with the naval visit pattern of the last five years, will mark Beijing's efforts to demonstrate PLA presence throughout the Asia-Pacific and enhance stability as China sees it. Additionally, the growth of combined training events with nearby countries, especially those in bordering SCO states, is also a trend that will likely continue. In fact, the executive editor of *Shijie Junshi* (*World Military*) has asserted that counterterrorism will continue to be the primary focus of Chinese combined exercises.[103] While counterterrorism is a key component of current interaction between China and SCO states, one wonders whether the increased capabilities that this sharpened focus brings might support other security policy options in the future beyond the counterterrorism cooperation of today, particularly if national interests on China's periphery are threatened.

Of particular interest in this regard, the development of a helicopter capability will bear considerable attention. China's extremely small helicopter force is poised to grow in number, perhaps reflecting more willingness to use the systems and the mobility they bring.[104] In Southeast Asia, Beijing may attempt to build on security policy dialogue progress in the ASEAN Regional Forum to engage in real military cooperation.[105] Of course, U.S. alliance relationships and security partnerships will require Beijing to employ nuanced and nonconfrontational approaches, but the flexibility exhibited elsewhere, and the lessons learned when Beijing has attempted more forceful approaches in the past,[106] make PLA-led efforts in Southeast Asia a real possibility.

With regards to overseas bases, it is anticipated that Chinese-style "access points" will continue to grow in number. In overseas locations where the PRC has helped to fund a commercial infrastructure enterprise, it is conceivable that the efforts will include the implicit ability to bring PLA forces in for resupply and reconstitution. Because the forces will not permanently reside in those locations, Beijing will be able to continue to say that it rejects the use of overseas bases, while retaining the potential benefit of these locations to transiting PLA forces.

The closure of the PRC satellite tracking facility in Tarawa, Kiribati, in its nearly ideal near-equator location, was certainly a blow to Chinese collection capability, both against satellites and potentially for collection against the U.S. missile defense testing facility in the not-so-distant Marshall Islands. Although Kiribati's transfer of recognition to Taiwan made a continuing presence there politically untenable, some have offered that Chinese interest in East Timor, itself near the equator, might become a substitute location in the future.[107]

These three trends—in naval visits, joint exercises focused on counterterrorism, and "access points"—in many ways parallel U.S. efforts to enhance regional stability abroad. But whether such activities truly make progress toward this end is debatable, and, as the following section concludes, contingent upon the ability of China to project power carefully and in ways that do not threaten the interests of its neighbors and their allies.

CONCLUSION AND IMPLICATIONS

This chapter has sought to provide a better understanding of the term "power projection" within a Chinese context. As has been stated, power projection includes three important components. First, the term inherently means that multiple elements of national power make contributions. This comports well in China where the accumulation of CNP is both a process and a national goal, in effect creating a virtuous cycle in which power projection is a product of the elements of national power and, when employed, contributes itself to the development of greater CNP.

The second major aspect of power projection focuses on the coordination and deployment of assets to some location. This aspect, in the PLA context, has garnered the most attention—mostly in the form of an argument that because China *cannot* project power in a traditionally understood way (because of a relative shortage of the assets that facilitate the movement of forces), it *will not* do so. This chapter has shown that this excessive emphasis on the movement of forces and the destructive power they bring is an incomplete understanding of power projection.

Certainly, power projection requires both powerful forces and the ability to move, but they are not the only elements of significance. Therefore, the PLA is not waiting to achieve some threshold of capabilities before beginning to project power; it is doing so within current capabilities, even as its conventional power projection capabilities themselves are increasing.

This chapter has focused its emphasis on the third part of the meaning, which addresses the *how* and *why* of Chinese power projection. The chapter has shown that in this regard, PLA activity is vigorous across all the dimensions identified as power projection: responding to crises, contributing to deterrence, and enhancing regional stability.

The PLA primarily responds to crises through increasingly robust deployments to UN PKO. In the past two years, the number of PLA troops deployed overseas in support of UN PKO has tripled. By establishing domestic structures to support UN PKO, the PLA is increasing capacity for future missions, while potentially laying the groundwork for multilateral training centers to be established in China. Given the sometimes-glacial speed of policy change in the PLA, these changes are truly remarkable. As the PLA increases its capacity to conduct PKO, these will contribute to the growth of China's CNP and will help to achieve Beijing's foreign policy goals.

In the coming years, China may well face crises that threaten its territory, necessitating military responses. The most obvious cases are North Korea and Taiwan. With regard to the former, China has reportedly already conducted actions, including movements of significant numbers of forces that indicate a military component to its plans. Meanwhile, PLA training activity has long demonstrated the full range of actions that a military confrontation with Taiwan might entail.

However, North Korea and Taiwan may also represent less interesting cases, not because the risks are low or the chances of miscalculation few, but because some degree of PLA action has long been anticipated. In this respect, these cases do not help us understand how the PLA might respond to other crises in the future. Yet, they are both nevertheless unique in their own right, as one involves China's only security alliance (North Korea) and the other (Taiwan) is asserted to be sovereign Chinese territory.

The PLA also contributes to deterrence by showing the "steel and electrons" dimensions of Chinese power throughout the region. These

activities include air and sea surveillance missions, long-range submarine patrols, and, most prominently, the deployment of a full range
of Chinese missile systems that on a daily basis communicate to China's
neighbors the increasingly longer (potentially) coercive reach of Beijing.
While ballistic missile systems in particular are directly primarily toward
Taiwan and the United States, the range of these deterrent mechanisms
betray a broader palate of potential adversaries against whom China
might seek to protect itself or interdict, including Japan.

In actuality, however, using these capabilities necessitates costs that
Beijing may be unwilling to bear. Consequently, China is also engaging
in activities that foster regional stability, as judged by Beijing, by showing
the reassuring side of Chinese military power to its neighbors, including
combined military training against common threats, especially terrorism. In this category, Beijing's activities have increased most quickly
and in the most surprising ways. China is becoming more at ease with
"access points" throughout the region where PLA forces may establish
a presence or conduct logistical resupply. Beijing is also conducting a
much larger number of bilateral and multilateral military exercises with
neighboring countries, primarily under the auspices of the SCO, and has
ramped up its public diplomacy to promulgate the PLA's "peaceful" and
"responsible" intentions. Together, these actions have helped acclimatize
the region to a more militarily involved PLA. The exercises have also
revealed China's intent to intervene using military force, even in other
countries, if China's interests are at risk.

The examples also illustrate a number of principles that would govern
Chinese intervention in third countries. From the exercises that the PLA
has conducted, it can be safely concluded that for the immediate future
China would wait to be invited, even in a pro forma way, before becoming involved, and, in these cases, China would most likely seek to conduct combined operations with host nation forces. In so doing, Beijing
would avoid repeating its twin criticisms of U.S. actions, diluting China's
inviolate support for the sovereignty of other nations and being accused
of acting unilaterally. It remains to be seen to what degree a future, much
stronger China might feel compelled to follow this principle.

In light of these trends, China's power projection activities may lead to
two somewhat opposing outcomes. Insofar as China's growing military
power is deftly wielded, Beijing may enhance regional security in ways

conducive to Beijing's interests as its neighbors recognize the stabilizing value of burgeoning Chinese CNP. At the same time, however, China's military power projection is inherently risky, containing the potential to further isolate and marginalize Taiwan, among other neighbors, and to stoke the embers of dissent across the strait. As Beijing increasingly projects military power throughout the Asia-Pacific region, the prospect of cross-strait conflict may increase, potentially contributing to the destabilization of regional relations. And nations beyond Taiwan may themselves feel more insecure as they observe these developments.

Ultimately, the PLA will become an increasingly large contributor to the development of Chinese CNP. In responding to crises, contributing to deterrence, and enhancing regional stability, the PLA's current realities (manifest in UN PKO participation, the expansion of offshore "access points," combined exercises with regional neighbors, and increased military presence worldwide) suggest that Beijing is fully prepared to magnify its military role both regionally and globally. This accrual of military power, brought about by fifteen years of military modernization, will both contribute to the growth of CNP and become an expression of it in ways that, over the longer term, seek to reorder regional understandings of security. In the process of accumulating CNP, the PLA will in turn increase its own ability to project power throughout the Asia-Pacific region and the world.

NOTES

1. Hu Angang and Men Honghua, "The Rising of Modern China: Comprehensive National Power and Grand Strategy" (paper presented at the KIEP international conference on "Rising China and the East Asian Economy," Seoul, South Korea, March 19–20, 2004), p. 2, www.kiep.go.kr/common/board_file_down.asp?74518|1 (last accessed April 9, 2007).

2. Aaron Friedberg, "'Going Out': China's Pursuit of Natural Resources and Implications for the PRC's Grand Strategy," *NBR Analysis* 17, no. 3 (September 2006): 6.

3. Keith Bradsher, "China Reports Another Year of Strong (or Even Better) Growth," *New York Times*, January 26, 2006, p. C5; Wayne Morrison, "China's Economic Conditions," *CRS Report to Congress* (July 12, 2006), p. 2.

4. Philip C. Saunders, "China's Global Activism: Strategy, Drivers and Tools," *Occasional Paper 4*, Institute for National Strategic Studies, National Defense University, October 2006, pp. 11–13 (hereafter cited as Saunders).

5. Robert Zoellick, "Whither China: From Membership to Responsibility?" Remarks to National Committee on U.S.-China Relations, September 21, 2005.

6. Richard P. Suttmeier, Xiangkui Yao, and Alex Zixiang Tan, "Standards of Power? Technology, Institutions, and Politics in the Development of China's National Standards Strategy," *NBR Special Report* (June 2006).

7. Alastair Iain Johnston, "Is China a Status Quo Power," *International Security* 27, no. 4 (Spring 2003): 12.

8. Shanghai Cooperation Organization website, http://www.sectsco.org/news_detail. asp?id=1094&LanguageID=2 (last accessed November 1, 2006).

9. Saunders, p. 28.

10. Evan S. Medeiros and M. Taylor Fravel, "China's New Diplomacy," *Foreign Affairs* 82, no. 6 (November/December 2003): 22–35.

11. Joshua Kurlantzick, "China's Charm: Implications of Chinese Soft Power," *Policy Brief* no. 47 (June 2006): 3, http://www.carnegieendowment.org/files/PB_47_ FINAL.pdf (last accessed April 4, 2007).

12. David Shambaugh, "China Engages Asia: Reshaping the Regional Order," *International Security* 29, no. 3 (Winter 2004/2005): 65 (hereafter cited as Shambaugh).

13. China's defense budget has also approximately tripled within the past decade. See Jeff Lukens, "Commentary: Reassessing the Chinese," *The Post Chronicle*, October 10, 2006, http://www.postchronicle.com/commentary/article_21243601.shtml (last accessed April 2, 2007). China's defense budget has doubled in real terms since 1990. (See NBR's Strategic Asia database, http://www.strategicasia.org, for data that yielded these results.)

14. H. Joseph Herbert, "Top Chinese Diplomat Tells U.S. to 'Shut Up' on Arms Spending," *Agence France-Presse*, August 17, 2006, http://www.commondreams.org/ headlines06/0817-08.htm (last accessed April 9, 2007).

15. Shambaugh, p. 85.

16. Colin Powell, with Joseph Persico, *My American Journey* (New York: Ballantine Books, 1995), p. 576.

17. Shambaugh, p. 86.

18. This is certainly not because it is insignificant. Indeed, the issues of Chinese defense budget growth and overall defense modernization have gained the attention of senior American policy makers. At the "Shangri-La Dialogue" in Singapore, June 4, 2005, Secretary of Defense Rumsfeld famously asked: "Since no nation threatens China, one must wonder: Why this growing investment? Why these continuing large and expanding arms purchases? Why these continuing robust deployments?" See complete transcript of the speech at: http://www.defenselink. mil/transcripts/2005/tr20050604-secdef3002.html (last accessed April 9, 2007). Secretary of State Condoleezza Rice also has questioned the growth in China's defense budget, including during her trip to Australia in March 2006 to discuss the U.S.-Australia-Japan trilateral relationship. "I heard that there's going to be a

14 percent increase in the Chinese defense budget. That's a lot. And China should undertake to be transparent about what that means." See full transcript of text at: http://www.state.gov/secretary/rm/2006/63167.htm (last accessed April 9, 2007). As discussed in the body of the paper, a growing resource pool, represented by larger defense budgets, is necessarily important for the military to make growing contributions to overall CNP, and thus be able to project that power. However, the activity is a function of so much more than military considerations, including leadership decisions about domestic programs that compete for the same resources, and political judgments about how much China wants to draw international attention, as well as opaque bureaucratic infighting.

19. According to statistics from the Stockholm International Peace Research Institute (SIPRI), China has been ranked seventh among nations in arms exports (in dollars exported) worldwide over the past twenty years. In 2005, China exported $129 million worth of conventional weapons; from 2000 to 2005, it sold approximately $1.4 billion worth of arms—about 5 percent of that of the United States. (No figures are yet available for 2006.) See http://www.sipri.org/contents/armstrad/TIV_EXP_TOP20_76-05.pdf/download (last accessed April 3, 2007). A recent report from Amnesty International discussed the lack of transparency in China's arms trade, suggesting that sales of arms could actually be in excess of $1 billion annually. See Amnesty International, "People's Republic of China—Sustaining Conflict and Human Rights Abuses: The Flow of Arms Accelerates," June 11, 2006. http://web.amnesty.org/library/index/engasa170302006 (last accessed April 7, 2007). In response to the Amnesty International report, a spokesperson from the China Arms Control and Disarmament Association responded by saying that "China always abides by related international conventions and imposes rigid self-control in terms of arms export and transfer of military technologies." He added that China adheres to "three principles" in arms trade: enhancing the self-defense capability of import countries; not impairing regional and global peace, security, and stability; and not interfering with other countries' internal affairs. See "Chinese Expert Refutes Amnesty International's Slam on Arms Trade." *Xinhua News*, June 12, 2006, http://in.china-embassy.org/eng/zgbd/t257594.htm (last accessed April 9, 2007).

20. These efforts, while they serve to benefit overall PLA capabilities, are not strictly military activities, and could best be characterized as political security functions. Nonetheless, the scale of the effort is impressive and three recent examples demonstrate the point. In late September 2006, Shanghai's Huangpu shipyard in China debuted a Russian-like Jiangkai-class frigate, a modernized version of the Russian type 054A and the third of its kind for the PLAN. The new frigate has much stronger Russian characteristics than its predecessors. See Yihong Chang, "China Launches Russianised Jiangkai-Class Frigate," *Jane's Defence Weekly*, October 10, 2006, http://www.janes.com/defence/news/jdw/jdw061010_1_n.shtml

(last accessed April 9, 2007). China's Hudong Zhonghua Shipyard is helping to construct frigate ships for Pakistan's navy; the "steel cutting" launch ceremony was attended by Pakistan's Vice Chief of the Naval Staff Vice Admiral Mohammad Haroom. The first F-22P frigate will be delivered to Pakistan in 2009; the second and third in 2010; and the fourth (in Pakistan) in 2013. See "Construction of Frigates Represents a Quantum Leap in Technology: Vice Admiral," *The Pak Tribune*, October 12, 2006, http://www.paktribune.com/news/index. shtml?156876 (last accessed April 9, 2007). And Russia's Siberia-based machine-building enterprise "Zvyozdochka," which is engaged in the repair, modernization, and utilization of surface and underwater vessels—including nuclear submarines—announced it will soon be opening a representative office in China, which has expressed special interest in upgrading its navy ships. See "MP 'Zvyozdochka' to Open Representative Office in China," *Siberian Financial and Economic Information*, October 24, 2006, http://www.engl.fis.ru/news/?nid=17922 (last accessed April 9, 2007).

21. For a full discussion, see Shirley Kan, "China and Proliferation of Weapons of Mass Destruction and Missiles," *CRS Report for Congress* (October 2, 2006).

22. Michael I. Handel, "Corbett, Clausewitz, and Sun Tzu," *Naval War College Review* 53, no. 4 (Fall 2000): 106–23.

23. See, for example, James R. Holmes and Toshi Yoshihara, "The Influence of Mahan upon China's Maritime Strategy," *Comparative Strategy* 24, no. 1 (January–March 2005): 53–71.

24. Alfred Thayer Mahan, *The Influence of Sea Power upon History, 1660–1783* (New York: Dover, 1987), p. 71.

25. Harlan Ullman, "Turning Mahan on His Head," *United States Naval Institute. Proceedings* 132, no. 7 (July 2006): 12.

26. United States Department of Defense's *Dictionary of Military and Associated Terms*, http://www.dtic.mil/doctrine/jel/doddict/data/p/04175.html (last accessed April 9, 2007) (hereafter cited as DoD dictionary).

27. For an excellent summary article about China's recent engagement with the United Nations, see Michael Fullilove, "Angel or Dragon? China and the United Nations," *The National Interest*, no. 85 (September/October 2006): 67–75, http://www. lowyinstitute.org/PublicationGet.asp?i=448 (last accessed April 9, 2007) and "China in Firm Support of UN Peacekeeping Missions," *Xinhua News*, December 13, 2005, http://en.chinabroadcast.cn/2238/2005-12-13/38@287380.htm (last accessed April 7, 2007).

28. "Noninterference in internal affairs," one of the "five principles" of Chinese foreign policy, was first documented by Zhou Enlai in a joint communiqué between India and the People's Republic of China on June 3, 1954 (also called the "Panchsheel Agreement"). The principles are: (1) mutual respect for each other's sovereignty

and territorial integrity; (2) mutual nonaggression; (3) mutual noninterference into each other's internal affairs; (4) equality and mutual benefit; and (5) peaceful coexistence. These principles were originally laid out as part of the negotiations over the boundary issue with Tibet. China's "New Security Concept," which emerged in the late 1990s, is argued to be an updated version of the five principles. See Shambaugh, p. 69.

29. Dennis J. Blasko, *The Chinese Army Today* (New York: Routledge, 2006), pp. 178–81 (hereafter cited as Blasko).

30. *China's National Defense in 2004,* Information Office of the State Council of the People's Republic of China, Beijing, China, December 27, 2004, chap. 2, http://www.china.org.cn/e-white/20041227/index.htm (last accessed April 9, 2007) (hereafter cited as *China's National Defense in 2004*).

31. Chen Feng, "China's 3rd Peacekeeping Police Team to Haiti Returns Home," *Gov. cn,* August 4, 2006, http://www.gov.cn/misc/2006-08/04/content_354789.htm (last accessed April 9, 2007).

32. "China Sets Up Peace-keeping Battalion for Lebanon Mission," *Liberation Army Daily (English) on-line,* March 1, 2006, http://english.chinamil.com.cn/site2/news-channels/2006-03/01/content_421213.htm (last accessed April 9, 2007).

33. See Atul Aneja, "More troops in Lebanon," *The Hindu,* September 21, 2006, http://www.hindu.com/2006/09/21/stories/2006092103631400.htm (last accessed April 2, 2007).

34. "Liberia Thanks China for its Contribution to UN Peacekeeping," *Xinhua News,* September 28, 2006, http://english.people.com.cn/200609/28/eng20060928_306943.html (last accessed April 9, 2007).

35. "Security Council Expands Mandate of UN Mission in Sudan to Include Darfur, Adopting Resolution 1706 by Vote of 12 in Favour, with 3 Abstaining. Invites Consent of Sudanese Government; Authorizes Use of 'All Necessary Means' to Protect United Nations Personnel, Civilians under Threat of Physical Violence," UN Security Council 5519th Meeting, August 31, 2006, http://www.un.org/News/Press/docs/2006/sc8821.doc.htm (last accessed April 9, 2007).

36. See M.S. Ahmed, "Sudan Rejects U.S. and British Attempts to Push UN Troops in Darfur," *Media Monitors Network,* October 24, 2006, http://usa.mediamonitors.net/content/view/full/36983 (last accessed April 9, 2007). Later, after receiving strong criticism from other UN Security Council members, and as a way to mitigate the negative implications of Sudan's rejection of the UN peacekeeping force, China offered to give $1 million in aid to African Union's (AU) Darfur Force after Sudan rejects UN peacekeeping troops in Darfur. See Howard Lesser, "China Contributes $1M to Africa's Darfur Force," *Voice of America News,* October 16, 2006, http://www.voanews.com/english/Africa/2006-10-16-voa4.cfm (last accessed April 7, 2007).

37. "Report: China, Sudan to Boost Military Cooperation," *Associated Press*, April 10, 2007, http://www.iht.com/articles/ap/2007/04/03/asia/AS-GEN-China-Sudan-Military.php (last accessed April 10, 2007).

38. See "China Vows Active Involvement in UN Peacekeeping in Africa," *People's Daily Online*, October 19, 2006, http://english.people.com.cn/200610/19/eng20061019_313208.html (last accessed April 9, 2007).

39. *China's National Defense in 2004*, chap. 9.

40. "Troops" are defined as trained military personnel working in the field; they do not include military observers or police forces. See "UN Peacekeeping: Monthly Summary of Contributors of Military and Civilian Police Personnel," http://www.un.org/Depts/dpko/dpko/contributors/2007/march07_3.pdf (last accessed April 9, 2007). By comparison, the United States had 321 personnel deployed on nine missions (43rd among all participants), as of April 1, 2007.

41. David Lague, "An Increasingly Confident China Lends Clout to UN," *International Herald Tribune*, September 19, 2006, http://www.iht.com/bin/print_ipub.php?file=/articles/2006/09/19/news/china.php (last accessed April 9, 2007).

42. "NPC Proposes Drafting Law on Overseas Military Operations," *Xinhua News*, March 12, 2007, http://news.xinhuanet.com/english/2007-03/12/content_5835951.htm (last accessed April 9, 2007).

43. Deterrence is defined here as the prevention from action by fear of the consequences. Deterrence is a state of mind brought about by the existence of a credible threat of unacceptable counteraction. See DoD dictionary, http://www.dtic.mil/doctrine/jel/doddict/data/d/01667.html (last accessed April 9, 2007).

44. *UN Convention on the Law of the Sea*, http://www.un.org/Depts/los/convention_agreements/texts/unclos/unclos_e.pdf (last accessed October 31, 2006).

45. "Annual Report to Congress: Military Power of the People's Republic of China 2006," Office of the Secretary of Defense, p. 4 (hereafter cited as DoD Report to Congress).

46. See "Info Gathering Boost Eyed for East China Sea," *The Yomiuri Shimbun*, October 24, 2006, http://www.yomiuri.co.jp/dy/national/20061024TDY03001.htm (last accessed November 1, 2006).

47. Robert Wall, "Ready to Rumble?" *Aviation Week: A Defense Technology Blog*, February 21, 2007, http://aviationweek.typepad.com/ares/2007/02/ready_to_rumble.html (last accessed April 9, 2007).

48. Author's conversations with Taiwan Air Force officers, June 2004, Taipei, Taiwan.

49. Rich Chang and Shih Hsiu-Chuan, "MND Confirms Plan to Buy F16s," *Taipei Times*, August 30, 2006, http://www.taiwansecurity.org/TT/2006/TT-300806.htm (last accessed April 9, 2007) and June Tsai, "MND Biennial Report Updates China Threat, Again Requests Passage of Procurement Bill," *Taiwan Journal*, September 7, 2006, http://taiwanjournal.nat.gov.tw/ct.asp?CtNode=122&xItem=23118 (last accessed April 7, 2007).

50. DoD Report to Congress, p. 31.
51. Peter A. Dutton, "International Law and the November 2004 'Han Incident,'" *Asian Security* 2, no. 2 (June 2006): 96 (hereafter cited as Dutton).
52. This includes additional type 093-class SSNs and type 094-class SSBN; increasing production of the indigenous diesel Song-class sub with the ability to launch anti-ship cruise missiles (ASCM) while submerged; Russian *Kilo* subs; and the indigenous, new, and potentially unique Yuan-class submarines.
53. Andrew Erickson, Lyle Goldstein, and William Murray, "'Gate Crashing': Chinese Submarines Test New Waters," *RUSI Chinese Military Update* 2, no. 7 (2006): 1–4.
54. Gordon Fairclough, "Submarine Incident with U.S. Stirs Anxiety about China's Navy," *The Wall Street Journal (on-line)*, November 15, 2006, http://online.wsj.com/article/SB116349775617122583.html?mod=todays_us_page_one (accessed April 7, 2007).
55. Lyle Goldstein and William Murray, "Undersea Dragons: China's Maturing Submarine Force," *International Security* 28, no. 4 (Spring 2004): 191–92.
56. Howard W. French, "China Deploys Ships to Area Japan Claims; Tensions Rise as Fleet of Warships Appears Near Disputed Gas Field Just Days Before Election and a Few Weeks Before Drilling Is to Begin," *New York Times*, September 11, 2005, http://www.sfgate.com/cgi-bin/article.cgi?file=/chronicle/archive/2005/09/11/MNGDGELU7M1.DTL (last accessed April 9, 2007) and "Chinese Warships Make Show of Force at Protested Gas Rig," *Japan Times*, September 10, 2005, http://www.uofaweb.ualberta.ca/chinainstitute/nav03.cfm?nav03=44048&nav02=43872&nav01=43092 (last accessed April 9, 2007).
57. "Abe, Hu to 'Discuss APEC Meet, Gas Fields,'" *The Yomiuri Shimbun*, October 6, 2006, http://www.yomiuri.co.jp/dy/national/20061006TDY01008.htm (last accessed October 31, 2006).
58. DoD Report to Congress, p. 3.
59. For more on the PLA's move toward joint operations, see Dean Cheng's chapter in this volume.
60. Blasko, pp. 151–53.
61. Ibid., p. 154.
62. Research conducted by NBR DC research assistant Luke Armerding from June to September 2006.
63. DoD Report to Congress, pp. 28–29 and 50.
64. Ibid., pp. 26–27 and 50.
65. Dutton, p. 95. Commander Dutton, an international law of the sea specialist, points out that in the aftermath of the November 2004 Han incursion into Japanese waters, China did not demand that Japan relax its restrictive policy on the passage of submarines in the Ishigaki Strait, an international strait in which right of transit passage applies under the Law of the Sea. In so doing, Beijing may have

missed an opportunity to shape interpretations of international law in its favor and may have unintentionally supported a conclusion that the Han was conducting unsanctioned military activities.

66. One of the authors was a member of the U.S. negotiating team on April 18, 2001, at the first U.S.-PRC diplomatic negotiating session upon the release of the U.S. air crew detained on Hainan Island from April 1, 2001 to April 12, 2001. The Chinese side made very clear that the mere presence of U.S. forces within China's exclusive economic zone (EEZ) was a first-order national security concern to Beijing, and PLA's actions and policy statements since continue to demonstrate the PLA's unrelenting desire to force U.S. forces to operate further from China's shores.

67. See "Chinese Navy Visits B.C." *CBC News*, September 25, 2006, http://www.cbc. ca/canada/british-columbia/story/2006/09/25/china-navy.html (last accessed April 9, 2007) and "China Takes Positive Attitude Towards Military Co-Op with U.S." *Xinhua News*, September 15, 2006, http://english.pladaily.com.cn/site2/special-reports/2006-09/15/content_586455.htm (last accessed April 7, 2007). Off of San Diego, the U.S. and PLA Navies participated in a combined search and rescue exercise.

68. After a port call at Pearl Harbor by the training ship Zheng He in 1989, the next PLAN visit to the States was on March 9, 1997, at Pearl Harbor by three Chinese ships: the Harbin, Zhuhai, and Nancang (230, 280, and 280 men crews, respectively). See Robert Benson, "Chinese Navy's Historic Pearl Harbor Visit," *Asia-Pacific Defense Forum* (Fall 1997): 2–12, http://www.pacom.mil/forum/fall_97/ China_r.html (last accessed April 7, 2007). In September 2000, a Luhu guided-missile destroyer ("Qingdao") and an AOR ("Taicang") visited Everett, Washington, and Pearl Harbor, Hawai'i. Charles Smith, "Chinese Navy Visits U.S. Base; Sailors of Both Nations Tour Each Other's Ships," *WorldNet Daily*, November 21, 2006, http://www.worldnetdaily.com/news/article.asp?ARTICLE_ID=20638 (last accessed April 9, 2007). On October 3, 2003, a guided-missile destroyer ("Shenzhen") and supply ship ("Qinghaigu") visited Guam. Ken Wetmore, "Chinese Warships Dock in Guam Harbor," *KUAM* News, October 22, 2003, http:// www.kuam.com/news/7432.aspx (last accessed April 9, 2007) and "Chinese Navy Fleet Back at Port After Overseas Visit," *People's Daily*, November 22, 2003, http:// english.people.com.cn/200311/22/eng20031122_128775.shtml (last accessed April 7, 2007).

69. To be sure, the effort pales in comparison with U.S. Navy operations in the Pacific. Seventh Fleet port calls are so prevalent as to be a terrain feature of the Asia-Pacific.

70. "Chinese Navy Ships Visit Philippines," *Xinhua News*, October 27, 2006, http:// news.xinhuanet.com/english/2006-10/27/content_5256661.htm (last accessed April 9, 2007).

71. See "Naval Fleet Visits Three Asian Nations," *Embassy of the People's Republic of China in India*, November 11, 2006, http://www.chinaembassy.org.in/eng/zgbd/t220462.htm (last accessed April 7, 2007).

72. *China's National Defense in 2004*.

73. "Chinese Naval Fleet Arrives in Thailand for Visit," *People's Daily*, December 9, 2005, http://english.people.com.cn/200512/09/eng20051209_226918.html (last accessed April 9, 2007). The Chinese fleet held a joint military exercise—a marine search and rescue—with the Thai navy, the first time the Chinese navy has conducted joint exercises with the Royal Thai Navy in the Gulf of Thailand.

74. Vijay Sakhuja, "Strategic Shift in Chinese Naval Strategy in Indian Ocean," *Institute of Peace & Conflict Studies, article no. 1899*, December 6, 2005, http://www.ipcs.org/Military_articles2.jsp?action=showView&kValue=1912&keyArticle=1019&status=article&mod=a (last accessed April 2, 2007) and "Chinese Navy's First Joint Exercise Abroad," *People's Daily*, November 15, 2005, http://english.people.com.cn/200511/15/eng20051115_221431.html (last accessed April 7, 2007). The flotilla undertook joint exercises with the Pakistani Navy under the banner "China-Pakistan Friendship 2005," then departed for exercises with India's navy.

75. Atul Aneja, "Chinese Warships Visiting India," *The Hindu*, May 23, 2001, http://www.hindu.com/2001/05/23/stories/0223000c.htm (last accessed April 9, 2007).

76. "PLA Navy Fleet Makes First Port Call to Hong Kong," *People's Daily*, November 10, 2001, http://english.people.com.cn/200111/10/print20011110_84297.html (last accessed April 9, 2007).

77. "PLA Navy Vessel Concludes Visit to Vietnam," *People's Daily*, November 22, 2001, http://english.people.com.cn/200111/22/eng20011122_85116.shtml (last accessed April 9, 2007).

78. "PLA Naval Ships Conclude ROK Visit," *People's Daily*, May 13, 2002, http://english.people.com.cn/200205/13/eng20020513_95594.shtml (last accessed April 9, 2007).

79. "PLA Fleet Arrives in Singapore for Goodwill Visit," *People's Daily*, May 23, 2002, http://english.people.com.cn/200205/23/eng20020523_96336.shtml (last accessed April 9, 2007). The three-day visit was part of a thirty-day goodwill tour that included stops in Egypt, Turkey, Ukraine, Greece, Portugal, Brazil, Ecuador, and Peru, crossing the Pacific, Indian, and Atlantic Oceans.

80. "PLA Navy Task Group Visits Hong Kong," *Xinhua News*, April 30, 2004, http://www.chinadaily.com.cn/english/doc/2004-04/30/content_327786.htm (last accessed April 9, 2007).

81. David Pilling and Mure Dickie, "Japan and China Plan Naval Exchanges," *Financial Times*, April 11, 2007, http://www.ft.com/cms/s/2f004dd6-e7f6-11db-b2c3-000b5df10621.html (last accessed April 11, 2007).

82. *China's National Defense in 2004.*
83. See "Sino-Tajik Exercises Promote Partnership," *China Daily*, September 24, 2006, http://english.people.com.cn/200609/25/eng20060925_306138.html (last accessed April 9, 2007).
84. See "CIS Holds Joint Anti-Nuclear Terrorism Exercise," *Novosti: Russian News & Information Agency*, September 29, 2006, http://en.rian.ru/world/20060929/54372295.html (last accessed April 9, 2007).
85. See "Russian Defence Minister to Visit China," *China Daily*, October 19, 2006, http://english.people.com.cn/200610/19/eng20061019_313248.html (last accessed April 7, 2007).
86. See Richard Halloran, "China's Navy Prompts US Concern," *Taipei Times*, August 27, 2005, p. 8, http://www.taipeitimes.com/News/editorials/archives/2005/08/27/2003269372 (last accessed April 7, 2007). One PLAN expert called the exercises a "notable advance beyond the minor, very basic exercises it has conducted with the French, British, Australian, Pakistani, and Indian navies in recent years. . . . It was initially described by many as preparation for countering U.S. forces in the region. As later and more accurately described, however, it primarily demonstrated that Sino-Russian bilateral relations are strong, especially military-to-military relations and arms sales." See Eric McVadon, "China's Maturing Navy," *Naval War College Review* 59, no. 2 (Spring 2006).
87. DoD Report to Congress, p. 2.
88. Henry Chu, "China's Footprint in Pakistan," *Washington Post*, April 3, 2007, http://www.indianexpress.com/story/27305.html (last accessed April 9, 2007).
89. Christopher J. Pehrson, "String of Pearls: Meeting the Challenge of China's Rising Power Across the Asian Littoral," *Carlisle Papers in Security Strategy* (July 2006), pp. 3–4.
90. B. Muralidhar Reddy, "China to Build Port in Sri Lanka," *The Hindu*, March 13, 2007, http://www.hindu.com/2007/03/13/stories/2007031303211400.htm (last accessed April 9, 2007).
91. Nyi Nyi Lwin, "Economic and Military Cooperation Between China and Burma," *Burma Western News,* September 2006, http://www.narinjara.com/Reports/BReport.ASP (last accessed April 7, 2007). The report discusses four naval bases at Coco Island, Haigyi Island, Mergui, and Thilawa. In addition, Zedetkyikyun Island, Kawthuang, and Victoria Point are reported to be intelligence collection facilities.
92. David G. Wiencek, "South China Sea Flashpoint," *China Brief* 1, no. 2 (July 24, 2001), http://www.jamestown.org/publications_details.php?volume_id=17&issue_id=630&article_id=4558 (last accessed April 9, 2007).
93. Robert Keith-Reid and Samisoni Pareti, "China Stirs the Point of Divided Pacific Loyalties," *Pacific Islands Report*, March 16, 2006, http://archives.pireport.org/archive/2006/march/03%2D16%2Dft.htm (last accessed April 9, 2007).

94. The need to reaffirm China's strategic periphery is consistent with a historical pattern hearkening back to the Qin dynasty (221–207 B.C.), and more prominently since the official establishment of the PRC in 1949. As Michael D. Swaine and Ashley Tellis have noted, this desire for border security historically served three purposes: (1) to eliminate existing or potential threats along the frontiers; (2) to intimidate neighboring states to acknowledge or accept Chinese suzerainty; and (3) to reinforce the personal authority of regime leaders. See Michael D. Swaine and Ashley Tellis, *Interpreting China's Grand Strategy: Past, Present, and Future* (Santa Monica, CA: RAND Corporation, 2000), p. 34.

95. On September 23, 2001, China said it would not let Osama bin Laden enter its territory across the 70-km border it shares with Afghanistan. Chinese Foreign Minister Tang Jiaxuan commented: "I've also made clear our desire and our readiness to further deepen our cooperation with the US, including over anti-terrorism." See "Chinese Border Closed to Osama bin Laden," *China Daily*, September 23, 2001, http://wcm.fmprc.gov.cn/ce/cgny/eng/xw/t31271.htm (last accessed April 7, 2007). This announcement was derided by U.S. defense planners, who interpreted the offer as the most minimal of contributions, especially considering that China borders Afghanistan and has its own concerns about international Islamist terrorists infiltrating into China's western province of Xinjiang. That Beijing had also refused to permit coalition aircraft to overfly China, to establish logistical support locations in western China, to base aircraft in China, or even to conduct search and rescue of coalition pilots in Chinese territory made the offer of border security even less attractive an offer.

96. See Masahiko Takekoshi, "China Erects North Korea Border Fence," *Daily Yomiuri Online*, October 21, 2006, http://www.yomiuri.co.jp/dy/world/20061016TDY02005.htm (last accessed April 9, 2007).

97. The PLA has technically always been in control of China's borders, with the mission of border defense conducted by provincial military districts which have external borders. China's People's Armed Police (PAP) and local Public Security Bureaus manage the flow of personnel.

98. According to Hong Kong's *Sunday Morning Post*, China deployed five divisions of PLA troops (approx. 150,000 men) to Yanbian Korean Autonomous Prefecture in August 2003. (Another Hong Kong-based report cited three divisions and 50,000 total men.) Troops were ostensibly deployed to help stem the flow of Korean refugees into China and to halt the growing violence of the North Korean army, although a Chinese Foreign Ministry spokesman claimed they were deployed to pressure Pyongyang into continuing the Six-Party Talks. See "China Deploys Troops on Border with North Korea," *Taipei Times*, September 15, 2003, http://www.taipeitimes.com/News/world/archives/2003/09/15/2003067928 (last accessed April 9, 2007) and "China Sends Military to North Korean Border," *FoxNews*, September 15, 2003,

http://www.foxnews.com/story/0,2933,97297,00.html (last accessed April 9, 2007). This issue is quite difficult to make judgments about. The movement of operational forces that report to group army headquarters may be simply conducting standard military training, but their uniforms are indistinguishable from the military district troops responsible for border security in normal times. Moreover, the numbers of soldiers is inconsistent with the number of troops in a PLA division.

99. "China Urges UN Action on N. Korea," *BBC News, Asia-Pacific*, October 10, 2006, http://news.bbc.co.uk/2/hi/asia-pacific/6037814.stm (last accessed April 7, 2007).

100. John J. Tkacik, "China's Army Yawns at Pyongyang's Missiles," *Heritage Webmemo #1148*, July 11, 2006, http://www.heritage.org/Research/AsiaandthePacific/wm1148.cfm (last accessed April 9, 2007).

101. "2006 Report to Congress of The U.S.-China Economic and Security Review Commission," pp. 11–12, http://www.uscc.gov/annual_report/2006/executive_summary_06.pdf (last accessed April 9, 2007).

102. Michael D. Swaine and Roy D. Kamphausen, "Military Modernization in Taiwan," in Ashley J. Tellis and Michael Wills, eds., *Strategic Asia 2005–06: Military Modernization in an Era of Uncertainty* (Seattle, WA: The National Bureau of Asian Research, 2005), pp. 414–19.

103. *Xinhua News* (in Chinese), September 25, 2006.

104. Blasko, p. 137.

105. Shambaugh, p. 88.

106. Shambaugh, p. 70.

107. Susan Windybank, "The China Syndrome," *Policy* 21, no. 2 (Winter 2005): 31.

SECTION THREE

Threats, Deterrence, and Escalation Control in a Taiwan Contingency

SECTION THREE

6

Air Force Deterrence and Escalation Calculations for a Taiwan Strait Conflict
China, Taiwan, and the United States

Kenneth W. Allen

Deterrence: The prevention from action by fear of the consequence. Deterrence is a state of mind brought about by the existence of a credible threat of unacceptable counteraction.

Deterrent Options: A course of action, developed on the best economic, diplomatic, political, and military judgment, designed to dissuade an adversary from a current course of action or contemplated operations.

Escalation: A deliberate or unprecedented increase in scope or violence of a conflict.

U.S. Joint Publication 1-02[1]

Deter, Deterrence: Wēishè (威慑)

Escalate, Escalation: Zhúbù Shēngjí (逐步升级)

Chinese Dictionary of Military Terms[2]

THE PURPOSE OF THIS CHAPTER is to address the following key issues: (1) to assess how possible People's Liberation Army Air Force (PLAAF) deployments in a Taiwan crisis might influence the propensity for escalation; and (2) to identify the PLAAF scenarios or individual actions that would, on balance, maximize the chances of avoiding an unwanted use of force or escalation, and those that might have the opposite effect. To

meet these goals, this chapter examines the different deterrence and escalation scenarios leading up to a possible confrontation between China
and Taiwan that involves the PLAAF, Taiwan's Air Force (TAF), and the
United States Air Force (USAF).

This chapter begins with information about the assets available to each
of the three air forces. It then provides some background material about
past and present air activity over the Taiwan Strait. The chapter then
shifts to possible PLAAF deployment and aircraft employment scenarios
to conduct deterrent and escalatory pressure on Taipei and Washington.
Finally, this chapter looks at the positive and negative ways that the
PLAAF might affect conflict termination after a shooting war has begun.
Naval aircraft activities by the United States or China are addressed in
Bernard D. Cole's contribution to this volume (chapter 7).

CAMPAIGN PHASES: DETERRENCE AND ESCALATION

The issue of how China will use the PLAAF for deterrence and escalation
purposes must be viewed in terms of the PLA's four campaign phases. The
PLA's *Science of Campaigns* states that the prosecution of campaigns will
unfold in a sequenced set of four phases: campaign preparation (*zhànyì
zhǔnbèi*; 战役准备), campaign execution (*zhànyì shíshī*; 战役实施),
campaign termination (*zhànyì jiéshù shíjiān*; 战役结束时间), and campaign rest and recuperation (*zhànyì xiūzhěng*; 战役休整).[3]

The campaign preparation phase, which has military, political, economic, and diplomatic components, is a long-term process that occurs
during peacetime and can be considered an integral part of deterrence. For
all practical purposes, China has already implemented this phase against
Taiwan. Each of these four components can also be ratcheted up at any
time to achieve certain goals. During this initial phase, the PLAAF will
pre-position weapon systems, equipment, and personnel in the forward
area. It will also conduct the necessary training to prepare to execute the
campaign operations plan (*zhànyì zuòzhàn jìhuà*; 战役作战计划).

During the campaign preparation phase, the PLAAF can use either
existing aircraft located at forward bases or deploy a certain number
of aircraft to the forward area to fly sorties in the Taiwan Strait. The
number of sorties per day can be adjusted accordingly to the shift from

deterrence to different levels of escalation prior to a shooting conflict. As is discussed below, however, China has to weigh the advantages and disadvantages of escalating the situation, which may allow the United States to become involved diplomatically or begin building up its own military in the area.

During the campaign execution phase, the PLA will implement the campaign operations plan. For the most part, PLA writings indicate that the first part of this plan, which would probably last for several days, is "set in stone" with little flexibility for individual commanders. Part of the reason for this, as PLA writings indicate, is that the PLA expects to have communications disrupted, especially if the U.S. military becomes actively involved in the shooting conflict, and therefore commanders must "follow the plan."

After the initial execution of the campaign plan, the PLAAF's ability to conduct a high sortie generation rate depends on many factors, most important of which is whether they can safely fly out of their forward bases. Specifically, if the United States becomes actively engaged in the conflict and begins attacking PLAAF airfields and air defense assets in the forward area, the PLAAF's sortie generation rate will be severely curtailed.

AIR FORCES AVAILABLE

PLAAF Forces Available

Since 1997, the U.S. Congress has required the Department of Defense (DoD) to provide an annual report on the PLA. The 2006 DoD report states, "The PLAAF and Naval Aviation have 1,525 fighters and 775 bombers. The majority of the aircraft are based in the eastern part of the country. More than 700 aircraft could conduct combat operations against Taiwan without refueling."[4]

According to Taiwan's *National Defense Report* for 2006, "China's Air Force has over 380,000 troops and 3,400 aircraft of various types of which over 700 fighters are deployed within 1,080 km (600 miles) from Taiwan with 150 of them only 450 km (250 miles) away."[5] The International Institute for Strategic Studies' (IISS) *Military Balance* for 2007 states that the PLAAF has 2,643 combat aircraft, including 189 Sukhoi-27/30 and J-11 multi-role aircraft.[6]

According to interviews with Taiwan military officials, since the mid-1990s, the PLAAF has been deploying small units from designated rapid-reaction units from throughout the PLAAF into some of the bases directly opposite Taiwan for six months of familiarization training.[7] In addition to aircraft, the PLAAF has also forward deployed surface-to-air missile (SAM) and anti-aircraft artillery (AAA) units to preselected sites and could do so if necessary preceding or during a conflict.

One example of the PLAAF forward deploying its aircraft was the PLA exercises opposite Taiwan in March 1996. According to some media reports, "A total of 12,000 Air Force and 3,000 Naval Aviation servicemen were involved. More than 280 aircraft were deployed, making 680 sorties, including eighty-two sorties by transports. Over 800 combat aircraft were in combat readiness within 500 nautical miles (nm) or were on alert."[8] Other reports indicate that fewer than a hundred additional aircraft were deployed to thirteen airfields in Fujian Province from other bases, raising the total to only 226 aircraft.

Based on a briefing from the U.S. Office of Naval Intelligence (ONI), the PLA conducted a total of 1,755 sorties during the 1996 exercise. Further press reporting stated that military intelligence had learned that when the PLA carried out its large-scale military exercises near Taiwan in 1996, its second- and third-line fighters were launched from first-line bases.[9] It took about three and one-half hours for them to accomplish the preparation for takeoff, compared to the ten hours they had needed in the past.

As shown in the discrepancy over the number of aircraft and sorties involved, all parties involved in an escalating Taiwan Strait situation could provide the media with selective reporting to increase the threat perception or to defuse a potentially serious crisis among the populace.

Although it may be the conventional wisdom that the PLAAF will forward deploy hundreds of aircraft prior to an offensive attack on Taiwan, PLAAF writings have numerous references throughout to concerns about secrecy and early detection of its plans given U.S. modern intelligence collection capabilities, including satellite and airborne surveillance. PLA writers state, "Major military operations cannot escape from such an intelligence net," and, therefore, conducting frequent movement and a certain amount of dispersal are effective concealment and deception methods.[10] "Forces should integrate the use of feints, camouflage, screening, and dispersion to conceal our command, control, communications, and intelligence systems and to deceive and jam enemy information reconnaissance."[11]

As a result of the need to conduct undetected offensive operations, at least during the early stages of a campaign, yet provide for survivability in a counterattack, the PLAAF has invested time and money into passive camouflage, concealment, and deception (CC&D) measures. Nonaviation units, including SAM, AAA, radar, and communications, have also conducted CC&D and emergency mobile dispersal training. While some of these activities will take place during the preparation phase for an attack, others will not occur until the execution phase.

USAF Forces Available

The primary mission for Pacific Air Forces (PACAF), headquartered at Hickam Air Force Base, Hawaii, is to provide ready air and space power to promote U.S. interests in the Asia-Pacific region during peacetime, crisis, and in war.[12] Since the early 2000s, much of PACAF's attention has focused on Guam, which is the home of the 13th Air Force at Andersen Air Force Base.[13] Although no forces have been permanently assigned there since a B-52 wing was deactivated in 1990, since 2003 a detachment of B-52s has regularly carried out continuous "rotational deployments" and the USAF has invested heavily in the base's infrastructure. For example, during the American buildup to Operation Enduring Freedom in Afghanistan, the base went from having no aircraft (bombers) to seventy-five within forty-eight hours. The USAF will continue to deploy B-52s to Guam on a rotational basis.[14] At present, the number of aircraft is fairly small, but the number could be increased in case of a conflict or the lead-up to a potential conflict. In 2000, Guam also became the first installation outside the continental United States to store long-range air-launched cruise missiles, which are now easily accessible and forward deployed in the event of a future conflict in the region.[15]

From a USAF perspective, these aircraft are in the Pacific region for possible contingencies in multiple areas, not just for a possible Taiwan conflict. If necessary, these aircraft could be augmented by USAF aircraft flying round-trip from the continental United States or deployed to various airfields in the Asia-Pacific Region. Taiwan's Deputy Chief of the General Staff, General Fei Hong-po, stated in May 2004 that "U.S. military deployments to Guam are beneficial to Taiwan."[16]

However, the view from Beijing is different. According to Hong Kong's *Kuang Chiao Ching* (Wide Angle) magazine, which is reputed to have close ties to the PLA, the deployment of USAF aircraft to Guam "clearly indicates the containment psychology of the U.S. military with respect to the daily growth of China's military power. These aircraft deployments, along with other U.S. Navy and Army deployments, will cause Guam to become the most important strategic forward base for the U.S. military to directly threaten the Western Pacific, and especially to deter China."[17]

One of the most significant changes occurred in February 2007, when the USAF conducted the first deployment of twelve F-22/Raptors and 250 personnel from Langley Air Force Base, Virginia, to PACAF's Kadena Airbase on Okinawa as part of a 90- to 120-day air expeditionary force rotation.[18] These aircraft will augment Kadena's existing F-15s. In addition, PACAF will establish its first permanent unit of thirty-six F-22s at Elmendorf Air Force Base, Alaska, in late 2007.[19]

TAF Forces Available

The 2006 DoD report states that TAF has 330 fighters.[20] According to the IISS's *Military Balance* for 2007, TAF has 479 combat aircraft.[21] According to the DoD's 2004 Report to Congress, "Since Taipei cannot match Beijing's ability to field offensive systems, proponents of strikes against the mainland apparently hope that merely presenting credible threats to China's urban population or high-value targets, such as the Three Gorges Dam, will deter Chinese military coercion."[22] As such, some advocates of an offensive capability have encouraged TAF to conduct defensive counterair strikes against PLAAF airfields during a conflict.

BACKGROUND ON FLIGHT ACTIVITY OVER THE STRAIT

Until 1996, TAF basically owned the skies over the Taiwan Strait, but it still observed the center line.[23] Although the PLAAF routinely reacted to TAF flights over the strait, the PLAAF's aircraft flew parallel to the TAF's aircraft but remained above the mainland coast.[24] It was not until 1996 when Beijing reacted to Taiwan's first presidential elections that the PLAAF flew its first flights out over the strait.[25] Even so, the PLAAF did not fly its first flights to the center line until Beijing reacted to President Lee Teng-hui's "two states" comments in July 1999. Today, however, the PLAAF "routinely" flies over the Taiwan Strait and out to the center line. For example, Taiwan's 2006 National Defense Report has a figure showing the number of PLAAF fighter flights in the Taiwan Strait from 1998 (400) through 2005 (1,700).[26] Unfortunately, the figure does not have comparison data for the number of TAF flights in the strait during the same period, which would provide a more accurate picture of the overall flight situation.

Although this activity is now "routine," media coverage takes place only when the PLAAF temporarily increases the number of flights in response to specific activities on Taiwan that concern Beijing. Although the PLAAF conducts routine training flights over the strait, there is no indication that the PLAAF makes decisions independently to increase the number of flights over the strait in reaction to perceived political actions on Taiwan.

Therefore, although Beijing clearly views the number of PLAAF flights during a given period as a tool that can be ratcheted up and down for deterrence, Taipei views this as escalatory but its own response as deterrence. Meanwhile, the USAF is observing activity by both sides as increasing the potential for miscalculation that can lead to escalation. This is of even greater concern because about 340 international flights and 730 domestic flights fly over the Taiwan Strait every day.[27] Given the strict control over military aircraft from the ground, especially by the PLAAF, the more military aircraft that enter the small airspace over the strait, the more difficult it is for the PLA air commander on the ground to control all of them in the midst of all the civil aircraft in the area.

Previous Flight Activity over the Strait

Over the past few years, Beijing and Taipei have traded accusations about each other's fighters approaching and sometimes crossing the center line.

Some of the activity has focused on particular political events in Taiwan, such as comments or activities by Taiwan's Presidents Lee Teng-hui and Chen Shui-bian. Both sides have apparently provided information officially or unofficially to the media to help escalate the situation and gain public support. In Taiwan's case, Taipei hopes to gain U.S. and regional support against China. Beijing, on the other hand, wants to keep pressure on Taipei and let the people on Taiwan know that it has increased the pressure.

In November 1998, the commander of a TAF Mirage-2000 fighter group confirmed that

> since the end of air battles over the Taiwan Strait in 1958, when carrying out patrol duties during ordinary times, our fighters have always kept a distance of 30 nm from the mainland's coast, while the Chinese Communist fighters usually carry out their duties close to their own coast line. If two Communist jet fighters took off, the TAF would dispatch four planes to watch them. Maintaining a tacit agreement on an invisible center line of the strait, neither side has conducted any provocative flights against each other so as to prevent an air battle from breaking out due to misjudgments made by their pilots. In the past, there was a tacit agreement between the two air forces that "we leave when you come, and we come when you leave." Recently, while the TAF was conducting F-16 and Mirage training, Chinese Communist fighters were detected by radar above the Taiwan Strait several times. However, according to the battle control instructions and to avoid sensitive events from happening, fighters from both sides flew on their own routes, moving away from each other. In short, the attempt of Chinese Communist fighters to fly across the center line of the Taiwan Strait has become increasingly obvious. [28]

On July 9, 1999, Taiwan's President Lee Teng-hui made his statement about "state-to-state" relations between Taiwan and mainland China. Shortly thereafter, Taiwan's press reported that PLAAF aircraft began flying numerous sorties over the Taiwan Strait and flew to the center line for the first time. Some of those flights even crossed over the center line several times. On August 3, 1999, *The Washington Post* reported that "a U.S. official said China, which rarely sends planes over the Taiwan Strait, has flown more than 100 sorties with three different types of aircraft, including advanced Sukhoi-27s recently acquired from Russia. Another senior administration official said that Taiwanese aircraft have flown a similar number of times and ventured over the center line of the 100-mile wide strait."[29] According to a Taiwan Ministry of National Defense (MND) spokesman on August 4, 1999, "Following President Lee Teng-hui's comments, about twelve aircraft were detected flying at the same time and more than thirty planes were detected in the air daily."[30]

Although the July-August 1999 activity equates to only a few sorties per day over a three-week period, Beijing achieved its apparent goal of drawing public attention to China's displeasure with Lee's statements. By early August, the number of flights decreased considerably. The most likely reason is that if the number of sorties remained high, it would cease to be reported in the media, so the PLAAF would have to increase the number of sorties to an even higher number to gain attention in the future. Therefore, Beijing can continue to use the PLAAF to ramp up the number of sorties whenever it feels it necessary to get the public's attention. A secondary reason is that the PLAAF does not have the best maintenance capability to sustain a high sortie generation rate for its older-model aircraft, given the small number of hours a single engine can be used before it must be removed and overhauled.

On August 14, 2000, then TAF commander General Chen Chao-min categorically denied a report in China's *PLA Daily* that indigenous defensive fighters (IDF) and F-16 fighters flew over the center line of the Taiwan Strait in July to collect information about a recent amphibious training exercise off China's southeastern coast. According to the news report, Chen thought,

> The report was sheer speculation and absurd. By allowing its official mouthpiece to disseminate such a fabricated report, Beijing apparently wants to mislead mainland people and the international community into believing that Taiwan was provocative. He [Taiwan Air Force Commander Chen] pointed out that the air force leadership has consistently reminded all officers and men to avoid triggering cross-strait tension while performing their official duties. Taiwan's pilots are not likely to fly over the center line by mistake because flight control personnel routinely keep close watch on their operations. The Air Force will under no circumstances take any provocative action if a

mainland Chinese warplane flies over the Taiwan Strait center line. Furthermore, if warplanes conduct long-range training missions, including beyond visual range (BVR) missile test-firing, they conduct such training exercises off Taiwan's eastern coast over the Pacific Ocean.[31]

The next day (August 15, 2000), Taiwan's MND denied a report that mainland Chinese military aircraft flew close to the center line of the Taiwan Strait on the eve of President Chen Shui-bian's first overseas trip to six diplomatic allies—the Dominican Republic, Nicaragua, Costa Rica, the Gambia, Burkina Faso, and Chad.[32] However, unidentified military sources said four mainland Chinese fighters conducted offshore patrol missions on August 12, two of which flew close to the center line of the Taiwan Strait at around 9:53 a.m. TAF then went on heightened alert and kept a close watch on the mainland fighters' flight paths and movements, the sources said, adding that the alert was not lifted until between 10:40 a.m. and 10:50 a.m.

In May 2004, as President Chen Shui-bian was preparing to take office after being elected for his second term, a spokesman for Taiwan's MND dismissed a report in Hong Kong's *Wen Wei Po* newspaper that Taiwan's military jets had entered China's airspace and been turned back by mainland aircraft on patrol.[33] The spokesman said, "It has been our principle that military aircraft do not cross the center line of the Taiwan Strait while engaging in routine missions or drills." *Wen Wei Po* quoted an unnamed Chinese official as saying China would "smash" Taiwan's military jets if they tried to enter Chinese airspace and accused the island of constantly trying to create military incidents.

On August 31, 2004, Taiwan's MND released a report stating that mainland Chinese fighters average nearly a hundred sorties (over the strait) per month, which adversely affects Taiwan's early-warning time.[34] The article did not say when the PLAAF began flying this number of sorties.

The October 22, 2004, *Taipei Times* and *Liberty Times* reported that according to U.S. sources, "The People's Liberation Army (PLA) mobilized 10 groups of various [air force] aircraft, including Su-27s, Su-30s, J-8s, J-10s, and bombers, to conduct over thirty sorties approaching the center line of the Taiwan Strait in late September. The number of sorties exceeded the record set in 1998 for the number of sorties on a single day."[35]

There have been no recent articles from late 2004 through March 2007 concerning PLAAF flight activity over the strait. As noted in Taiwan's 2006 defense report, the number of PLAAF sorties is definitely increasing, but reduced political tension between the United States and China has diminished the political necessity for either side to highlight any particular flight activity.

Reconnaissance Flights

Prior to the 1958 Taiwan Strait conflict, the PLAAF did not have a presence in Fujian Province; as a result, the Nationalists were able to fly at will over portions of the mainland as far north as Tianjin. Following the conflict, the PLAAF moved aircraft into bases opposite Taiwan, which precluded Nationalist combat aircraft from flying over the mainland. From 1959 to 1967, however, the Nationalists flew a hundred U.S. CIA-sponsored high-altitude U-2 reconnaissance flights over the mainland.[36] In November 1963, the PLAAF shot down the first of five U-2s while it was flying over the mainland. The last one was shot down in 1967.

The United States and China have had a long and complex history of U.S. aerial reconnaissance activity over and near Chinese territory.[37] The U.S. Navy and the USAF in particular, working in conjunction with the National Security Agency, have operated aircraft that flew near Chinese territory to collect radar and other electronic signals, to intercept communications, and to sweep up aerial debris from nuclear tests.

Declassified archival material from the first year of the Nixon administration sheds light on Cold War policy on reconnaissance flights near Chinese territory and confirms how risky the policy was.[38] For example, before April 1969, U.S. reconnaissance aircraft could fly as close as twenty miles from the Chinese coast. Moreover, the documents show U.S. policy makers have been reluctant to acknowledge reconnaissance flight activity, much less offer apologies when incidents occur. Ironically, an incident that elicited internal State Department policy review was the landing of a U.S. pilotless reconnaissance aircraft on Hainan Island in February 1970. To retain U.S. freedom of action to fly reconnaissance missions, State Department official Harry Thayer recommended that the United States refrain from any apologies in the event that the Chinese made any formal complaints.

Following the rise in tensions between China and Taiwan in 1995–1996, the U.S. military increased its reconnaissance flights around China's coastal periphery. The issue came to the fore again when a PLA Naval Aviation J-8 collided with a U.S. Navy EP-3 reconnaissance aircraft over the South China Sea in April 2001. At that time, a Chinese military spokesman protested that the United States was sending about 200 reconnaissance flights a year near China's coasts.[39] A Pentagon official responded that the Chinese send up fighter aircraft to intercept about one-third of those flights.

According to one American who was assigned to the U.S. Embassy in Beijing at that time, "The Chinese government views U.S. reconnaissance missions along China's coast as evidence that the United States sees China as an enemy, or at least as something other than a normal, friendly country. In their view, these are the same type of missions the United States might fly against current adversaries such as North Korea and Iraq and previously flew against the Soviet Union."[40] The American also makes the point that Beijing's protests ignore its own lack of military transparency, military threats aimed at Taiwan, and China's own reconnaissance operations in the region.

At the time of the EP-3/J-8 incident, President Bush stated, "Reconnaissance flights are a part of a comprehensive national security strategy that helps maintain peace and stability in our world."[41] In response, China's Foreign Ministry spokesman stated,

> Such flights "constitute a grave threat to China's security" and China has the right to protect its national sovereignty. Therefore, interceptions are "necessary and very reasonable" and in line with international practice. China has constantly opposed U.S. spy flights off China's coast and will continue to lodge serious representations with the United States on the resumption of such flights.[42]

The United States resumed its reconnaissance flights on May 7, 2001. A search of sources since the EP-3 incident found only one article (June 2002) concerning U.S. reconnaissance flights near China or Chinese protests about these flights through March 2007[43]; this is probably because of improvements in U.S.-China relations since 2002, reducing the political need for the Chinese to protest openly, though they may still do so privately.

China maintains the most extensive signals intelligence (SIGINT) capabilities of all the countries in the Asia-Pacific region. Airborne reconnaissance includes photographic and electronics intelligence (ELINT) activities.[44] The principal Chinese airborne ELINT platform is the four-engine turboprop EY-8, an indigenous development of the Soviet An-12s. The system is designed to detect, identify, analyze, and locate land-based or shipborne radar emitters with a high probability of intercept. Although the PLAAF employs these aircraft, no media reports have indicated flights over the Taiwan Strait, around Taiwan, or near U.S. military installations in the region.

CAMPAIGN PREPARATION: FORWARD DEPLOYMENT SCENARIOS

Beijing and Washington have the ability to forward deploy hundreds of aircraft for deterrent or escalation purposes if necessary. Depending on the political situation at the time, these deployments could be either for deterrent, controlled escalation, or war preparation purposes. For example, Beijing could forward deploy its aircraft to deter Taipei from a particular political action, to escalate the situation, or to prepare for an offensive attack—or all three. Washington could also forward deploy its aircraft in response to certain political or military actions taken in Beijing. Either way, one capital may see the other side's activities as escalatory, not deterrent. Because of geographical limits, Taipei does not have many options for forward deploying its aircraft other than moving aircraft from the eastern side of the island to the western side or vice versa.

A Few PLAAF Aircraft

As noted above, Beijing has deployed a small number of aircraft forward rapidly at various times to react to perceived negative political situations on Taiwan. While there, the aircraft have flown sorties over the strait and have then been withdrawn once Beijing believed the "message" was sent.

This type of deployment has its advantages and disadvantages in terms of escalation control. The biggest advantage is that a few aircraft can be deployed fairly rapidly if necessary and can begin flying sorties over the strait immediately from their forward-deployed base. To be effective in influencing public opinion, however, the information has to be available to the media. This type of activity also provides the opportunity for the aircraft unit to practice all of its mobility training in a real-world situation, less real air-to-air engagements and the firing of actual missiles.

The disadvantages of this type of activity are multifold. First, if the information does not reach the public, the "message" may be lost. Second, if the same level of flight activity continues every day, the media and public become desensitized and lose interest, so the number of flights must continually exceed previous levels to draw the public's attention. Third, the PLAAF does not routinely conduct a high number of sorties per pilot in a short period of time, so aircraft maintenance and logistics support are an issue. Fourth, a high number of aircraft and sorties may generate greater concern in Washington, which might then begin to react with its own deployment of aircraft forward. Lastly, this type of activity increases the opportunities for miscalculation and, therefore, the possibility of unintended escalation.

Many PLAAF Aircraft and Surface-to-Air Missiles

As shown during the 1979 conflict with Vietnam, the PLAAF has the ability to deploy several hundred aircraft and several missile battalions forward if necessary.[45] This type of activity also has its advantages and disadvantages.

The main advantage is that a large number of aircraft and SAMs opposite Taiwan can be used as a deterrent and will definitely send a "message" to Taipei and to Washington if necessary. The deployment also helps the PLAAF practice all of the components of a near real-world scenario including mobility, command and control, logistics, and maintenance. Once the aircraft have arrived, a large number of sorties can be flown on a daily basis, while some aircraft undergo maintenance and some pilots are resting. Throughout the activity, the PLAAF will have the opportunity to test its mobility plans and to fix any problems for the next time. One advantage of conducting several large deployments and then sending them home after a reasonable period of time is that this may have the effect of desensitizing Taiwan and the United States to a real deployment intended as a prelude to an actual conflict.

In some respects, the disadvantages may outweigh the advantages. Whereas a few aircraft can be deployed fairly rapidly to address an immediate political situation, the deployment of a large number of aircraft and SAMs may take much longer. While they are deployed, the units may not necessarily be meeting their annual training requirements, which are better met at their home bases. As a result, this could mean that their pilots are "just punching holes in the sky" rather than conducting all of their necessary training subjects. If the aircraft are deployed to a base that normally does not support that particular type of aircraft, the maintenance and logistics support may not be as proficient as at their home base, thus reducing the operational sortie generation rate.

Another disadvantage is that a massive deployment offers Taiwan and the United States the opportunity to collect intelligence information and analyze how the PLAAF would actually deploy and operate during a real conflict, thus providing valuable early warning indicators and countermoves for a real situation.

Finally, the PLAAF has studied how the U.S. military has operated in Iraq, Kosovo, and Afghanistan since the early 1990s. It readily understands that the United States has begun its actual operations by employing cruise missiles and air strikes against the enemy's command and control, radar, and air defense facilities, as well as airfields. As a result, the PLAAF may not actually deploy hundreds of aircraft and supporting SAMs forward in the case of a real conflict. Even if it does deploy them forward at the beginning, it may withdraw them to rear areas when, and if, the U.S. military becomes involved in the shooting war.

CAMPAIGN PREPARATION:
PLAAF FLIGHT ACTIVITY SCENARIOS

There are various scenarios in which China could manipulate PLAAF aircraft flight activity around Taiwan to deter actions by Taipei or to escalate the situation so that it leads to a shooting war.

A Few PLAAF Aircraft and Sorties

As noted above, deployment of a few aircraft opposite Taiwan, which then perform a certain number of sorties over a short period of time, is designed to send a "message" to Taipei, and possibly to Washington. Until now, those aircraft have flown only in the Taiwan Strait and have indeed achieved the media attention that Beijing most likely intended.

In terms of escalation control, this type of flight activity is the easiest for Beijing to plan and ramp up or down over a short period of time. This scenario is also the easiest for Taipei to deal with in terms of its graduated response, knowing that it will probably not escalate to a shooting war.

Many PLAAF Aircraft and Sorties

Beijing could decide to deploy several hundred aircraft opposite Taiwan and fly multiple sorties throughout the day and night over a long period of time. This could easily move from deterrence to escalation where the situation is less manageable. The more aircraft that each side puts in the air over the strait, the greater is the probability of an encounter. The United States could also become involved by deploying more aircraft to the region and possibly demonstrating a show of force by having them fly through the strait.

Although Beijing and Taipei could provide specific guidance to their own operational units about the specific types of activity and the appropriate responses as the number of aircraft increases over the strait, the weakest links are the ground controllers and the pilots themselves. A wrong turn or an inadvertent move misconstrued by the other side could possibly lead to a rapid escalation in terms of more aircraft being launched or a possible shooting event. Furthermore, the longer this type of activity takes place and the more aircraft that fly in the same airspace, the greater is the possibility for escalation.

PLAAF Bomber Flight Activity over Water

On April 6, 2002, a group of PLAAF bombers conducted simulated cruise missile launches over the East China Sea.[46] Based on a review of available material, it appears that this was the first time that PLAAF bombers had flown over the East China Sea. The PLA most likely reported this activity to get the attention of Taipei, Washington, and Tokyo.

To date, the PLAAF has not flown its bombers completely around Taiwan. Should Beijing decide to do this, it could be seen as either a deterrent or escalatory strategy, depending on the perceived activity in Taipei that Beijing is responding to, the number of aircraft involved, and the number of sorties during a given time.

Initially, a single sortie around the island by two aircraft would generate a tremendous amount of media coverage and public concern.[47] If the event took place once a week or once a month, however, it would soon become commonplace and would cease to receive media attention. Therefore, Beijing would have to increase the number of aircraft and/or the number of sorties to gain the attention of the media and public again.

More than likely, the TAF would also scramble its fighters to intercept the bombers and try to escort them as far as possible. This activity would provide information to the PLAAF about the TAF's response capabilities. Like the collision between the U.S. Navy's EP-3 and the PLA Naval Aviation J-8 over the South China Sea in 2001, this type of activity could also inadvertently lead to a possible collision or near collision between PLAAF bombers and TAF fighters.

Should Beijing decide to send a "message" to Washington and Tokyo and receive some real-world training, it could also conduct bomber flights near Okinawa. Depending on where the activity took place, it could elicit intercepts from the Japanese Air Self-Defense Force or U.S. Navy aircraft.

Inadvertent Air Collision over the Strait

Not every scenario leading to war has a long period of political escalation and military mobilization activities. Excluding a predetermined political decision to go to war, one of the potential situations that could act as a catalyst for a conflict to break out is an incident at the center line of the strait that occurs due to an inadvertent situation followed by miscalculations by either or both sides. This could involve two or more combat aircraft pilots transitioning from radar search mode to lock-on mode at a safe distance from each other, an accidental collision of two combat aircraft or a combat aircraft and a civilian aircraft, a collision between a reconnaissance aircraft and a reacting fighter, or actions taken by aircraft from one or both sides while reacting to an incident between two ships near the center line.

The possibility also exists of one aircraft crashing as a result of pilot error or a sudden engine malfunction while in the same area as an aircraft from the other side of the center line. However, the air controllers on the ground from one or both sides may not know this and misinterpret the cause, consequently scrambling more aircraft to deal with what they may consider a provocation.[48]

Given any of the above scenarios where one side's aircraft inadvertently goes down, both sides would most likely immediately begin conducting search and rescue efforts by sending more aircraft and naval ships to the area. Both sides would also probably put all of their relevant aircraft and air defense assets on alert status. Regardless of which side's aircraft went down, both sides would most likely scramble more aircraft to conduct flights in and near the strait in case it was a deliberate provocation and do an immediate recall of any pilots who are away from their bases.

If a PLAAF aircraft is the one that goes down, Beijing could possibly order more aircraft from out of the area to deploy to airfields near the strait and begin flying combat air patrols near and over the strait. If both sides fly to the center line with increasingly larger numbers of aircraft, the possibility of another inadvertent situation would increase.

If a TAF aircraft is the one that goes down, the TAF might be concerned about a missile attack on its airfields. It could respond by either putting more aircraft in the air so they are not destroyed on the ground, or it could begin putting more aircraft in caves and shelters to help protect them.

If there is no hotline between the two sides, or between Beijing and Washington, and neither Taipei nor Beijing takes public responsibility for the event, this activity could be misinterpreted by the other side as a provocation, leading to rapid escalation. This could, in turn, lead to one or both sides scrambling more aircraft and sending them to the area. The more aircraft that one side puts in the area over or near the strait, the more aircraft the other side will scramble to match them. This situation could rapidly get out of control unless both sides communicate with each other to determine the exact cause of the accident and agree to de-escalate the situation.

It might be easier to resolve the situation more quickly if the pilot survives the crash and has the opportunity to explain what happened after being rescued by either side. However, if the pilot does not survive and the wingman does not really know what happened, then the situation might not be resolved as easily.

While logic would state that both sides should pull back and figure out what happened and how to resolve the situation, domestic politics and the political situation across the strait at the time of the incident might not allow cooler heads to prevail. Beijing might see this as the right opportunity to implement its operations plan, especially if the United States is not in a position to come to Taiwan's assistance in a hurry. Meanwhile, if Beijing is building up its forces quickly, Taiwan might want to retaliate with a strike on mainland targets while its forces are still capable. In the end, whichever side lost the aircraft and pilot would be in the best position to de-escalate the situation by backing off, assuming it wants to.

PLAAF Airborne Troop Exercise

It should be kept in mind that China's airborne forces, the 15th Airborne Army, belong to the PLAAF not the ground forces. Therefore, Beijing could decide to task the PLAAF to conduct a major airborne force exercise near Taiwan. The exercise could employ a small or large number of transport aircraft and several regiments out of the force's three divisions.

The number of aircraft and troops involved would send specific signals to Taipei and Washington. The lesson it would expect to teach could also backfire on Beijing if its aircraft and troops did not perform as well as expected. It would also provide Taipei and Washington with an opportunity to analyze how the PLAAF might conduct an actual airborne force operation.

PLAAF Air Blockade Scenario

The PLAAF is the only participant that would conduct an air blockade. Whereas Beijing may see this as a deterrent, it would most likely quickly lead to an escalation of the situation and perhaps even armed conflict among the three sides. In its writings, the PLAAF states that international law and regional politics must be taken into consideration; it is very difficult to maintain blockade stability because of the long time it takes to sustain one and the fact that coordination with all levels in the chain of command is highly complex.

According to the PLAAF,

> An air-blockade campaign is undertaken with the Air Force as the main force, supported by and in cooperation with other forces. It is conducted on aerial battlefields. Its primary purpose is to cut off the enemy's air, land, and sea corridors with the outside, to maximize the enemy's isolation, and to force the enemy to act in accordance with our intent. It is often conducted as part of a combined campaign along with naval and ground blockade operations, but it can be carried out independently.[49]

When conducting air-blockade campaigns, the air force has three primary missions:

- Cut off the enemy's air corridors with the outside, restrict aviation troop activities, and shut the country off from the air.
- In conjunction with the other relevant services, impose a blockade on the enemy's maritime and ground transportation.
- Resist the enemy's ability to counter air-blockade operations.

MOBILIZING RESERVES

All three air forces involved could activate the mobilization of their reserves. In some situations, mobilizing reservists could be used as a deterrent when a situation appears to be escalating. In most cases, however, it would be a clear indicator that the situation is escalating to the point of a shooting war. Because it is expensive to implement, it is difficult to turn on and off every time the political situation heats up. Mobilization could take weeks or months to carry out, depending on the exact aim and how much training the reservists need in advance. Therefore, mobilization is a clear indication of escalation.

CAMPAIGN EXECUTION PHASE:
CONTROLLING ESCALATION

High-level leaders in Beijing will most likely be in complete control of the overall strategic deterrence and escalation components of the campaign preparation phase against Taiwan. They will probably provide general guidance but will most likely not determine the exact number of aircraft to be deployed or the number of sorties to be flown, especially if the number is small. The General Staff Department and PLAAF headquarters will issue orders to implement the existing operations plan and monitor the ongoing situation.

As the political situation escalates, Beijing will most likely provide further general guidance, but will continue to leave the details of the number of aircraft deployed and flights per day to the General Staff Department, PLAAF headquarters, and the Nanjing War Zone commander.

This prewar escalation situation will continue until a shooting war commences and the wartime operations plan is implemented. At that time, leaders in Beijing will continue to provide general guidance, but the Nanjing War Zone commander and PLAAF staff under his command will most likely control the campaign and tactical air situation over and near the Taiwan Strait. This includes the number of aircraft and combat sorties flown per day and determination of specific targets based on the general rules of engagement (ROE) established by the Communist Party Central Committee's Military Commission (CMC).

Once the PLA implements its campaign operations plan, however, the commanders at every level are expected to "follow the plan." The implication from reading PLA writings is that commanders do not have a high degree of flexibility in terms of changing the number of sorties or targets to be struck during the first few days after the operations plan is implemented. After the first few days, the situation will dictate changes to the plan as needed.

If a shooting war begins after all attempts at deterrence have failed, the participants will be involved in an offensive and defensive air campaign that is already determined in the existing operations plan. This can be preemptive or a counterattack after the other side strikes first. Regardless of which comes first, the air conflict will most likely escalate fairly rapidly as the PLAAF implements its operations plan to include deployment of aircraft and ground-based air defense assets as needed.

Any decision by Beijing to escalate the situation by striking U.S. military targets in Japan or Guam would have to be made by the Communist Party's Politburo through the CMC. This would most likely not be a unilateral PLAAF decision. However, the success or failure of any PLAAF strikes on U.S. targets in Japan would directly affect how the United States might decide to escalate its strikes against certain targets on mainland China.

PLAAF's ROLE IN CONFLICT TERMINATION

The PLAAF could have either a positive or negative effect on conflict termination. Specifically, if the PLAAF loses its ability to maintain air superiority over the strait and the battlefield, the terms of conflict termination could be dictated to Beijing. Whether the PLAAF can maintain air superiority is greatly determined by the ROE. The PLAAF needs to operate from airfields safe from U.S. attack, such as the sanctuary it enjoyed north of the Yalu River during the Korean War. If the United States starts to bomb its airfields, SAM sites, radar sites, and the like, the PLAAF will have to move its aircraft farther away from the location of engagement. This means that the PLAAF will not be able to fly enough sorties for a long enough loiter time necessary to maintain air superiority. But if the ROE are such that the United States does not attack PLAAF airfields on the mainland, the PLAAF will have the ability to maintain air superiority over the strait and Taiwan. As a result, Beijing would most likely have the ability to provide the terms of conflict termination most beneficial to China. In this case, the PLAAF could either continue to fly over the strait with force or gradually phase down the number of aircraft and flights in the area.

FUTURE PLAAF CAPABILITIES

Any assessment of the PLAAF concerning its role in a future cross-strait conflict must focus on several factors, including its hardware, training, and ability to sustain operations twenty-four hours a day for a long period of time. It must also be able to protect its own ground-based assets from U.S. missile attacks. Furthermore, one of the keys to the

PLAAF's future success is whether or not the United States becomes actively engaged in the shooting conflict.

The trends are clear that the PLAAF is now flying increasingly more overwater sorties around China's entire coastline every year. Its newer aircraft are also capable of flying during most weather conditions and at night. The PLAAF's aircraft are also conducting more sophisticated air-to-air combat than it did five years ago, to include dissimilar aircraft training, larger numbers of aircraft engaged at the same time in exercises, and increasingly longer mobility deployments to airfields that are not equipped with the same type of aircraft.

It is not clear from open source writings whose pilots are better— those of the TAF or PLAAF. Nor is it clear from these writings whether either side can sustain continuous operations for a long period of time. The TAF is at a clear disadvantage, however, because its runways will be the first targets of the PLA's short-range ballistic missiles and perhaps land-based cruise missiles. It will also have to deal with the PLAAF's long-range SAMs that can reach out across the strait.

Should the United States become involved in the shooting conflict and begin attacking airfields and PLAAF air defense sites in the forward area, the PLAAF will have to adjust its offensive and defensive operations accordingly. If the United States does not become involved in the shooting conflict, then the PLAAF should be able to operate more freely over the strait by rotating more aircraft and pilots in, which will allow it to implement sustained operations for a longer period of time.

RULES OF ENGAGEMENT

Previous PLAAF ROE

During the Korean War, the 1958 Taiwan Strait Crisis, and the 1979 border conflict, the PLAAF received strict ROE from the CMC prior to initiating the campaign.[50] During the Korean War, PLAAF aircraft were not allowed to strike below the 38th parallel for two reasons:

- The CMC was concerned that the United Nations forces would retaliate with strikes against airfields north of the Yalu River, which would essentially destroy the fledgling PLAAF.

- The CMC also limited air combat to "MiG Alley" over North Korea because the aircraft that they had at the time did not have the ability to strike below the 38th parallel and return home without running out of fuel. At that time, no airfields were available for them to land in North Korea.

In the 1958 Taiwan Strait crisis, the CMC established the following three ROE for the PLAAF:

- The air force could not enter the high seas to conduct operations.
- If the Nationalist Air Force did not bomb the mainland, the PLAAF could not bomb Jinmen (Quemoy) or Mazu.
- The PLAAF was not allowed to attack the U.S. military, but could defend against any U.S. aircraft entering Chinese territory.

In the 1979 conflict with Vietnam, Beijing did not allow the PLAAF to conduct air support missions over the border and stated that its aircraft were providing a deterrent, but the CMC was still really concerned about escalating the conflict, which it planned to end after forty-five days.

FUTURE PLAAF AND USAF ROE

Any look at a future air conflict over the Taiwan Strait must include a discussion of ROE for the PLAAF and USAF. Even though each side may establish specific ROE to limit escalation after the conflict begins, these limits may be surpassed rapidly once the first shot is fired. Specifically, the following questions arise concerning actions by either or both sides that could rapidly escalate the situation.

- Are air battles over the Taiwan Strait acceptable to Beijing and Washington? Are USAF strikes only in Fujian Province acceptable to Beijing? Are USAF strikes only in the provinces bounded by the Nanjing Military Region acceptable to Beijing?
- How would Beijing react if the USAF conducted strikes outside the Nanjing Military Region, but still within the Nanjing War Zone? Specifically, a preemptive attack on the three divisions of the PLAAF's

15th Airborne Army and the 13th Air Division's transport aircraft which support the airborne forces—all of these forces are located in the Guangzhou and Jinan Military Regions but may become part of the Nanjing War Zone.

- What USAF actions are acceptable to Beijing before the CMC orders an attack on Kadena and/or Guam? For example, would Beijing accept air combat over the Taiwan Strait, as it did over North Korea's "MIG Alley" in the 1950s, but not accept air strikes against certain mainland targets?
- What U.S. actions would cause China to use its ballistic missiles to attack USAF airbases in Okinawa and Guam to limit USAF actions in the strait? If China does attack these airfields, how would the United States retaliate?
- At what point would Beijing believe regime survival to be at risk and decide to escalate attacks against USAF facilities in the region?
- What mechanisms are available for the USAF and PLAAF to understand what each other's ROE are without having to guess and possibly miscalculate?

CONCLUSIONS

The air power deployed by China and the United States joined with the smaller but still significant TAF to fulfill important deterrent roles in the continuing standoff across the Taiwan Strait. These air forces also contain the risk of undermining crisis stability and escalating a potential military confrontation. A variety of factors can result in these unwanted consequences. Among them, rising political tensions could lead to China increasing its forward deployments and the number of sorties dispatched close to or across the Taiwan Strait center line as a deterrent measure. The TAF would respond in kind by increasing its sorties toward the center line. Under these conditions, a collision in the crowded air space, whether by pilot error or mechanical failure, could undermine crisis stability as Taiwan and China scrambled additional aircraft until certain that the collision was not a deliberate provocation. During a period of increasing cross-strait hostilities, such a response to a collision could well undermine any efforts underway to defuse the tension.

Should rising tensions lead to a military confrontation, the ROE followed by Beijing and Washington could lead to the war's escalation. In the opening phase of a military conflict, will China (as many anticipate) immediately employ its air power and missiles to attack TAF bases in search for air superiority over Taiwan? If it does, will the United States grant China's air bases sanctuary as it did during the Korean War? Similarly, in the event of a military confrontation, will the United States follow the Gulf War model and attack China's forward air and missile bases in order to degrade Beijing's offensive capabilities and achieve air superiority? If U.S. forces implement this strategy, will China respond by attacking U.S. bases on Japanese and American soil, such as Kadena on Okinawa and Anderson in Guam, in order to weaken U.S. air power? If it does, what retaliatory actions will the United States undertake?

These possibilities may seem extreme because the political authorities directing the employment of air power by their respective armed forces are more likely to want to avoid crisis instability and escalation than seek it. Nonetheless, as the above discussion shows, the military doctrines underlying armed forces' operations of both countries can contribute to crisis instability and escalation as much as their force deployments. Since its origin in the 1930s, the PLA's operational doctrine has had at its core the objective of seizing and sustaining the initiative on the battlefield. U.S. operational doctrine has the same military objective—dominance of the battle space. Taiwan's leanings toward offensive capabilities are based more on punishing the mainland than gaining battle space initiative. Even so, the limited offensive operations that Taiwan's air and missile forces are capable of conducting can contribute to crisis instability and escalation. In each case, these offensive doctrines are viewed as the most effective way of achieving favorable war termination conditions. Consequently, the seeds of wartime escalation are present in the military doctrines of the contending armed forces.

Only the political authorities directing the employment of their military forces can minimize the chances of crisis instability and escalation. This could prove difficult. In China's case, the restraint that its leaders placed on the PLAAF during the invasion of Vietnam does not seem to apply in a Taiwan contingency. In 1979, Beijing believed its ground forces were sufficient to achieve China's political objective. In a Taiwan scenario, the PLA's air and missile forces will be the pointed end of the spear in suppressing the island's defenses. As a result, the United States will be under pressure to crush China's air and missile capabilities quickly, which suggests implementation of the Gulf War model. Preventing a military confrontation over Taiwan from spiraling into a wider war will therefore require forceful political leadership on both sides of the conflict to establish ROE designed to diminish the propensity for escalation found in their armed forces' doctrine. It will be difficult for a government that sees the war going badly to sustain these ROE; instead, it may seek to raise the cost to the adversary by widening the war and attacking targets previously declared off-limits by the ROE. Thus, the dynamics of the war can undermine the ROE set by political authorities.

Given the increasing capabilities of air power combined with precision guided munitions and cruise and ballistic missiles, there is considerable uncertainty that a military confrontation over Taiwan involving U.S. military forces will not escalate to a wider war before all parties conclude that terminating the conflict is a wiser course of action than continuing hostilities. The blend of capabilities, doctrine, and the dynamics of war produces the uncertainty that even initially prudent ROE may not overcome.

NOTES

The author thanks Paul Godwin for his contribution to the conclusion.

1. *Joint Publication 1-02: Department of Defense Dictionary of Military and Associated Terms*, April 12, 2001 (as amended through June 9, 2004), pp. 156, 157, and 184, http://www.dtic.mil/doctrine/jel/new_pubs/jp1_02.pdf.

2. Cui Changqi, ed., *A New English-Chinese and Chinese-English Dictionary of Military Terms* (*Xin Bian Han Ying Ying Han Junshi Cidian*; 新编汉英英汉军事词典) (Beijing: National Defense Industry Publishers, October 1999). Neither the PLAAF's 1996 dictionary nor its 2005 encyclopedia have an entry for either term.

3. Wang Houqing and Zhang Xingye, eds., *Science of Campaigns* (*Zhanyi Xue*; 战役学), (Beijing: National Defense University Press, May 2000), p. 78.

4. Department of Defense, "FY06 Report to Congress on PRC Military Power," June 2006, p. 46.

5. *Republic of China: 2006 National Defense Report* (Taipei: Ministry of National Defense, August 2004), p. 62.

6. *The Military Balance: 2007*, International Institute for Strategic Studies (London: Oxford Press, January 2007), p. 350.

7. Interviews in Taiwan in March 2007.

8. Lo Ping, "It Costs China 3 Billion Yuan to Make a Show of Its Military Strength," *Cheng Ming*, Hong Kong, April 15, 1996. Steven Mufson, "China Masses Troops on Coast Near Taiwan," *The Washington Post*, February 14, 1996.

9. "Chinese Exercise Strait 961: 8–25 March 1996," briefing presented by the U.S. Office of Naval Intelligence at a conference on the PRC's military modernization sponsored by the Alexis de Tocqueville Institute, March 11, 1997.

10. Huang Xing and Zuo Quandian, "Holding the Initiative in Our Hands in Conducting Operations, Giving Full Play to Our Own Advantages to Defeat Our Enemy—A Study of the Core Idea of the Operational Doctrine of the People's Liberation Army," *Zhongguo Junshi Kexue* [China Military Science] [in Chinese], November 20, 1996, no. 4: 49–56 (FTS19970619001633, June 19, 1997). Senior Colonel Huang Xing and Senior Colonel Zuo Quandian are research fellows of the Academy of Military Science. Liu Xuejun and Zhang Changliu, "Study of Measures to Counter Unmanned Aerial Vehicles," *Guoji Hangkong* [Flight International], March 1, 1996, (FTS19960301000017, March 1, 1996).

11. Xu Xiangdong, Gu Gang, and Yang Jun: "Mobilize Local Information Warfare Resources to Participate in Anti-Air Raid Combat," *Beijing Guofang*, December 15, 2000: 7–8 (CPP20010207000136, February 7, 2001).

12. http://www.pacaf.af.mil/library/factsheets/index.asp.

13. Adam J. Herbert, "Air Power for a Big Ocean," *Air Force Magazine*, July 2004, Vol 87, no. 7. www.afa.org/magazine/July2004/0704airpower.html.

14. Interview with USAF officers in Guam in September 2004.

15. Patrick Goodenough, "US Has Big Military Plans for Small Pacific Island," CNSNews.com, June, 11 2004.

16. Hsieh Chung-cheng, *Ching-nien Jih-pao*, Taipei, Taiwan, May 20, 2004.

17. Qing Tong, "2002: Focus on Guam," Hong Kong *Kuang Chiao Qing*, October 16, 2002.

18. "Raptors Arrive at Kadena," Langley Air Force Base Story Media. http://www.langley.af.mil/news/story_media.asp?id=123041617. *Defense Industry Daily*, February 17–18, 2007.

19. Bo Joyner, "Ready for the Raptor: Reserve and PACAF Teaming up for the Groundbreaking F-22 Unit in Alaska," *Citizen Airman*, March 14, 2007. http://www.citamn.afrc.af.mil/news/story.asp?id=123044686 (last accessed April 11, 2007).

20. Department of Defense, "FY06 Report to Congress on PRC Military Power," June 2006, p. 46.

21. *The Military Balance: 2007*, International Institute for Strategic Studies (London: Oxford Press, January 2007), p. 374.

22. Department of Defense, "FY04 Report to Congress on PRC Military Power," July 2004.

23. The Chinese term is *haixia zhongxin* (海峡中心), which is usually translated in English as center line, centerline, or middle line. For this chapter, the term center line is used for continuity purposes. The center line was drawn by the United States when it signed the Mutual Defence Treaty with Taiwan in 1954. (www.globalsecurity.org/military/world/taiwan/midline.htm.) An addendum to that treaty marked a buffer zone into which American planes would not intrude. The eastern boundary of this buffer zone is now known as the center line of the Taiwan Strait. Although the three parties, as well as civil aviation authorities, still observe the buffer zone, no one had specified the line's exact course. During November 2002, Taiwan's MND stated, "Taiwan should refrain from taking the initiative to discuss the center line during any negotiations with the mainland about direct transportation links. If mainland China brings up the issue, our negotiators should make every possible effort to avoid substantiating the demarcation." ("Defense Ministry Warns Against Talks on Strait Center Line," Central News Agency, November 11, 2002, www.taipeitimes.com/News/taiwan/archives/2002/11/11/179122). Just two years later, however, Taiwan's new Defense Minister, Lee Jye, attempted to define the exact location of the center line. According to various media reports from Taipei,[24] "On 26 May 2004, Taiwan Defense Minister Lee Jye defined the line during a legislative session in which he threatened to shoot down Chinese military aircraft should they cross the center line of the Taiwan Strait. According to Lee, 'Whenever their aircraft or vessels are approaching the center line, our aircraft and vessels will be standing by. Once they keep going east and enter our 'hunting zone,' we will take care of them.' Unfortunately, his definition of the center line was incorrect, and the ministry later issued a correction, saying the line should run from 26°30' north latitude, 121°23' east longitude to 24°50' north latitude, 119°59' minutes east longitude, to 23°17' north latitude, 117°51' minutes east longitude," (www.taipeitimes.com/News/front/archives/2004/05/27/2003157100/print, www.taipeitimes.com/News/edit/archives/2004/05/28/2003157274). Even though the line has existed for five decades, the PLAAF did not begin flying any distance into the strait until the late 1990s. Today, the PLAAF "routinely" flies out to the center line.

24. Until the late 1990s, the PLAAF did not fly over water anywhere along China's coast. That mission was the responsibility of PLA Naval Aviation. Today, PLAAF aircraft fly over water in each of the PLA Navy's three fleet areas of operation.

25. According to a Taiwan MND spokesman on August 4, 1999, "Following Beijing's 1996 military exercise to threaten Taiwan, Communist Chinese airplanes began flying over the Taiwan Strait." State Department Briefing with James Rubin, *Federal Information Systems Corporation, Federal News Service*, August 3, 1999.

26. *Republic of China: 2006 National Defense Report* (Taipei: Ministry of National Defense, August 2004), p. 49. The figures for each year are as follows: 1998 (400),

1999 (1,100), 2000 (1,200), 2001 (1,500), 2002 (1,300), 2003 (1,200), 2004 (940), and 2005 (1,700).

27. Victor Lai, "PRC Jet Fighters Twice Cross Taiwan Strait Center Line" China News Agency, August 10, 1999, http://www.fas.org/news/taiwan/1999/e-08-10-99-30.htm.

28. "Mainland Fighters Said to Appear Above Taiwan Straits," Taipei *Tzu Li Wan Pao* [in Chinese], November 26, 1998. Lin Chien-hua, "Air Force Watchful for Communist Plane Activities," Taipei *Tzu-Li Wan-Pao*, August 4, 1999.

29. John Pomfret and Steven Mufson, "China, Taiwan Step up Sorties over Strait: As Tension, Flights Rise, U.S. Fears Risk of Clash," *Washington Post*, August 3, 1999.

30. State Department Briefing with James Rubin, *Federal Information Systems Corporation, Federal News Service*, August 3, 1999.

31. "Air Force to Form Mirage Wing Next Year," Central News Agency, August 14, 2000.

32. "PRC Fighters' Movements Normal," Central News Agency, August 15, 2000.

33. "Taiwan Rejects Report Its Military Jets Entered China's Airspace," AFP Taipei, May 25, 2004.

34. Central News Agency, September 1, 2004.

35. The same article written by Nadia Chao appeared in English in the *Taipei Times* and in Chinese in Taiwan's *Liberty Times*. "China Conducted Huge Drills in Strait," *Taipei Times*, October 22, 2004. "Large Group of Communist Aircraft Approach the Center Line," *Liberty Times*, October 22, 2004. The number of sorties in 1998 was not reported.

36. http://area51specialprojects.com/u2_blackcat_taiwan.html.

37. http://www.gwu.edu/~nsarchiv/NSAEBB/NSAEBB41/.

38. http://www.gwu.edu/~nsarchiv/NSAEBB/NSAEBB41/.

39. "US Aircraft Carrier May Be Deployed in South China Sea," *Agence France-Presse*, April 16, 2001. http://www.military.com/Content/MoreContent?file=FL_kittyhawk_041701.

40. John Keefe, *Anatomy of the EP-3 Incident, April 2001*, The CNA Corporation, January 2002.

41. "White House Report: Bush on U.S.-China Relations," April 12, 2001. http://japan.usembassy.gov/e/p/tp-se0112.html.

42. "China Defends Practice of Intercepting U.S. Reconnaissance Flights," *U.S. Star and Stripes*, May 12, 2001, http://ww2.pstripes.osd.mil/01/may01/ed051201b.html (last accessed April 12, 2007). "China Opposes U.S. Spy Flights off Chinese Coast, FM Spokesman," *People's Daily*, http://english.people.com.cn/english/200105/08/eng20010508_69434.html.

43. The *Air Force Magazine* website carried a short article citing the *Washington Times* that two Chinese fighters flew within 150 feet of a U.S. Navy P-3 reconnaissance

aircraft on June 24, 2002. A U.S. spokesperson described the event as nonthreatening. See "Chinese Flying Close Again," http://www.afa.org/magazine/world/0802world.asp#anchortwentyseven (last accessed April 12, 2007).

44. Desmond Ball, "Signals Intelligence in China," *Jane's Intelligence Review*, Vol 7, no. 8, August 1, 1995: 365.

45. Depending on the source, figures vary from 800 to 1,100 aircraft stationed at fifteen air bases in Yunnan, Guangxi, Guangdong, and Hainan, many of which deployed to these areas from elsewhere in China.

46. Liu Zhuanlin and Yang Guoping, "A Bomber Division of the Air Force Successfully Organizes Long-Range Assault Maneuver of an Air Armada," *The PLA Daily*, April 20, 2002, http://www.pladaily.com.cn.

47. The Soviets occasionally sent Tu-16 bombers into the Sea of Japan to conduct simulated missile attacks against land-based radars and air defense targets and Tu-95 bombers/reconnaissance aircraft through the Pacific on the eastern side of Japan. China has yet to conduct this type of air activity near Taiwan or Japan, but has sent oceanographic vessels into Japanese-claimed sea areas.

48. During 1998 and 1999, the TAF lost four F-16s and five crewmembers due to mechanical malfunctions. Lieven Dewitte, "Taiwan Blames F-16 Crash on Engine Failure," *F-16.net* September 9, 1999, http://www.f-16.net/news_article164.html (last accessed April 12, 2007).

49. Wang Houqing and Zhang Xingye, eds., *Science of Campaigns* (*Zhanyi Xue*; 战役学), (Beijing: National Defense University Press, May 2000), chap. 13, pp. 363–66.

50. *China Today: Air Force* (*Dangdai Zhongguo Kongjun*; 当代中国空军), (Beijing: China Social Sciences Press, 1989). Lin Hu, ed., *Kongjun Shi* [History of the Air Force], (Beijing: PLA Press, PLAAF Headquarters Education and Research Office, November 1989).

7

The Military Instrument of Statecraft at Sea
Naval Options in an Escalatory Scenario
Involving Taiwan: 2007–2016

Bernard D. Cole

THE CURRENT SITUATION involving China, Taiwan, and the United States is characterized by three apparently incompatible principles. Each of the three players in this drama has a specific objective: China demands reunification of Taiwan with the mainland, Taiwan wants to continue its current *de facto* independence with *de jure* independence as the eventual goal, and the United States wants to maintain peace and stability in the area.

Taiwan's future is the only potential *casus belli* between the People's Republic of China (PRC, or China) and the United States. Although there are many facets to the situation centering on Taiwan, none draws more attention than the possible use of military force to resolve the issue.

This chapter explores the possibilities of unintentional escalation in a maritime scenario involving conflict over Taiwan's status. A detailed scenario is presented, followed by additional points illustrating some branches and sequels to this scenario; naval platforms and systems, operational choices, and information availability are evaluated as enhancing or suppressing unintended conflict escalation. This analysis also views maritime force capability, physical geography, and the political objectives of China, the United States, and Taiwan.

Escalation may be deliberate, of course, resulting from decisions by policy makers. Such decisions may have unintended or unanticipated consequences, however, which might result in a greater degree or different manner of escalation than the decision maker thought was being selected or risked. Three primary participants form the dynamic in this situation—China, the United States, and Taiwan—which results in a synergistic process that increases the chance of unintentional escalation amidst what Clausewitz calls the "fog of war."

POLITICAL BACKGROUND

A maritime crisis leading to conflict over Taiwan will occur in an intensely political environment. The pivotal issue is Taiwan's political status: it is either a province of China (Beijing's position) or an independent nation (Taipei's position). Only twenty-four nations agree with Taipei—all minor countries in Latin America, Sub-Saharan Africa, and the South Pacific.[1] All of the remaining nations of the world agree with Beijing that "there is but one China, and that Taiwan is part of China," but that simple phrase carries with it gradations of agreement that contribute to the ongoing crisis. Most prominent among these latter nations, of course, is the United States.

Beijing has consistently maintained that the island remains a province of China; strictly speaking, Washington does not disagree, but insists that the island's reunification with the mainland must be peaceful and occur with the agreement of the Taiwanese people. This was most clearly stated by President Bill Clinton in February 2000: "We'll continue to reject the use of force as a means to resolve the Taiwan question. We'll also continue to make absolutely clear that the issues between Beijing and Taiwan must be resolved peacefully and with the assent of the people of Taiwan."[2]

Beijing's refusal to renounce the use of military force frames the dispute. It would be difficult to overemphasize the intensity of Beijing's disappointment at Chen's reelection to Taiwan's presidency in 2004, disappointment deepened by the continuing advocacy for revising Taiwan's constitution. Although American efforts to restrain Chen—headlined by the December 2003 statement of President George W. Bush, with Chinese Premier Wen Jiaobao standing beside him—have been welcomed by Beijing, their effect has to a significant extent been nullified in Chinese eyes by continuing American efforts to increase weapons sales to Taipei, by increased visits to the island by American military officers and civilian officials, and by pro-Taiwan statements emanating from Congress.

These factors have contributed to a deepening sense of frustration in Beijing about reunifying Taiwan with the mainland. Frustration is not a helpful environment in which to make national security policy decisions, or for carefully controlling the application of military force without risking unintentional developments in that application.

China may employ military action against Taiwan for a variety of reasons, from deterrence to coercion to outright subjugation of the island and removal of Chen's government. The People's Liberation Army (PLA), particularly the PLA Navy (PLAN) and the PLA Air Force (PLAAF), is preparing to engage in various levels of activity to carry out the decisions of Beijing's civilian policy makers.

PHYSICAL GEOGRAPHY

The geography of the theater heavily influences policy decisions and military operations. Naval and aerospace power will dominate military action in this area, since Taiwan lies from 90 to 105 nautical miles (NM)[3] from the Chinese mainland. This is well within range of modern missiles and aircraft-launched weapons, but also complicates effective command and control of military forces.

The Taiwan Strait is frequently subject to high winds and seas, tidal ranges up to 15 meters, and complex currents and is susceptible to typhoons during most of the year. Its average water depth is relatively shallow, with a maximum depth of less than 40 fathoms, and marked by shoals. There are very few suitable landing beaches on either of the island's coasts; the east coast is characterized by high cliffs and a steep ocean bottom gradient, while the west coast is marked by wide areas of mud flats.[4]

This geography has serious implications for the conduct of naval operations. First, the lack of suitable landing areas for beaching craft limits the conduct of a traditional amphibious assault. Troops may be ferried ashore via helicopter or air-dropped from fixed-wing transports, but their heavy equipment must be carried in surface craft. U.S. doctrine for conducting an amphibious assault stipulates that the assailant possess a 5:1 advantage in troops over the defender, a ratio difficult for the PLA to establish should Taiwan be forewarned.

Second, the hydrography of the strait is usually not conducive to anti-submarine warfare (ASW) operations. The shallow depth, rapid currents, frequent rough seas, often limited visibility, and the very numerous fishing and merchant craft create a very high level of ambient noise in the strait that severely hampers sonar effectiveness. These conditions also affect submarine operations, but they limit even more ships and aircraft conducting ASW.

Third, the unpleasant weather conditions typical of the strait affect surface ship operations, especially for small landing craft, which are typically flat-bottomed to facilitate beaching for off-loading troops and cargo. One effect is seasickness among assault troops in such craft, which is not serious in the long term, but is a factor. More serious is the difficulty of maintaining formation in bad weather, necessary to ensure a coordinated landing operation. The use of fishing boats or other civilian craft would exacerbate this factor. The advantage of bad weather to an assailant is the increased difficulty for Taiwan patrols trying to detect an assault force, but poor meteorological conditions would also limit the air support so vital to a successful operation; good weather would eliminate that problem and would ease the voyage from the mainland, but would increase its chances of discovery.

Fourth, the strait's narrowness affects both sides. It eases an assault force's problem simply because it has a shorter distance to cover; it also eases the defenders' problem because it places them on interior lines and limits the assaulting force's possible axes of approach.

Fifth, and most significant, the basic geography severely limits the viability of any defense by Taiwan against a seaborne assault supported by air operations. Inhabitants of an island that is 245 miles long by 90 miles wide at its widest point and located no more than 105 NM from the Chinese mainland, whose military is greatly outnumbered in terms of manpower and number of aircraft and submarines, would be able to survive in an all-out war scenario only for a limited period of time.

These factors of geography would also affect U.S. military intervention, which is discussed in detail below. More importantly, the theater's geography, hydrography, and climate all lead to a literal and figurative cloudiness that would reduce commanders' situational knowledge, increasing the chances of escalation due to unintended consequences from their decisions. The basic tactical problem of any commander—where are my forces and where are the opponent's forces—is made more difficult by the lack of good visual range, rough seas, and a confusing acoustic environment.

NAVAL STRENGTH

The geography of a potential Taiwan conflict is not going to change, but the naval forces that the parties may bring to bear will. A comparison of current naval strength among China, Taiwan, and the United States is provided in the Appendix, demonstrating the current and almost certain quantitative superiority of China over Taiwan and the United States over the China.

CHINA'S NAVY

The PLAN is a capable and steadily improving 20th-century maritime force, with an ongoing modernization program bringing it into the 21st century.[5] Increasing naval capabilities allow China to operate at increasing distances from the mainland, but also complicate maintaining effective command and control of those forces, which in turn exacerbates the problem of preventing unintended escalation during tactical operations at sea and in the air. This is particularly significant in the case of the PLAN and PLAAF, which have typically operated under close control of shore-based commanders.

Submarine Force

The PLAN regards its submarine force as its first team, posing the most serious naval threat to foreign forces, especially U.S. aircraft carriers. The PLAN is modernizing its submarine force at a steady pace, replacing old Romeo boats with imported Kilo-class and home-built Song-class submarines. The old nuclear-powered submarines in China's inventory, the five Han class, are nearly obsolete; the first two of their replacement class, the type 093, will probably become operational sometime in 2007. The nuclear-powered type 094 ballistic missile-launching submarine probably will not be operational before 2010, which means that, given the questionable seaworthiness of China's only intercontinental ballistic missile (ICBM) submarine, the Xia, the nation will remain without the sea-based leg in the strategic triad.

By 2016, the PLAN will include twelve Kilo-class, twenty Song-class, and one or two type 93 nuclear-powered boats.[6] This will provide China with a very formidable submarine force, without counting the eighteen Ming class. Especially significant would be PLAN acquisition of submarines equipped with Air Independent Propulsion (AIP) plants. AIP allows a conventionally powered submarine to operate submerged for extraordinary periods of time—perhaps as long as forty days compared to a non-AIP (conventionally powered) boat's duration of four days.[7]

This submarine force includes boats capable of firing cruise missiles (Han and Song classes) and modern torpedoes acquired from Russia, including formidable wake-homers and wire-guided weapons.[8] The presence of subsurface-launched cruise missiles is an especially potent addition. China clearly intends to employ these submarine-launched cruise missiles, possibly as part of a coordinated attack with ballistic missiles to deter and, if necessary, attack U.S. aircraft carriers, which might participate in the defense of Taiwan against Chinese military operations.[9]

Surface Force

China is pursuing ambitious plans for its surface navy. Four Russian Sovremenny-class guided-missile destroyers have been acquired, and at least three new classes of indigenously designed guided-missile destroyers (DDGs) are being launched, some of them equipped with an Aegis-like area-defense air warfare system. This program will significantly improve the PLAN force of modern combatants and, for the first time, provides China's navy with the ability to operate as a self-contained task force able to defend itself across the spectrum of naval warfare.

Additionally, China's newer surface combatants are all being armed with capable guided missiles, improved ASW and anti-air warfare (AAW) systems, and embarked helicopters.[10] Most importantly, the PLAN surface force is continuing to improve integration of its sensor and weapons systems within each ship, among ships in a task group, and in joint operations with the army and especially air force units.

Amphibious Ships

Discussion of China's amphibious lift is rarely enlightening; once one hears "lift for two mechanized divisions," one is faced with the almost unquantifiable issue of using some of China's vast merchant fleet as temporary troop lift for an assault on Taiwan. In fact, China is currently devoting increased resources to building PLAN amphibious ships, while still exploring the use of merchant ships for a massive troop lift across the Taiwan Strait.

These efforts have taken several forms, including mounting artillery pieces on merchant ships for firing against targets ashore; numbers of China's many thousands of fishing boats have been organized into a rough militia for missions including surveillance, early warning, and embarking special operations forces (SOF) for missions against shipping or Taiwanese-held islands.

Although the ubiquitous fishing boats in the Taiwan Strait and surrounding waters are manned by experienced seamen, their use as troop transports is quite problematic because they lack advanced communications and navigation equipment, do not practice formation steaming, and lack a means for landing troops ashore other than at a pier or by running themselves aground—a mission they could perform only once. These drawbacks all increase the possibility of such "unofficial" naval units conducting operations that would cloud events at sea and further complicate command and control; the difficulty in controlling their movements would likely outweigh their operational usefulness.

Civilian-crewed ships have been used as support vessels during operational exercises, including serving as repair ships and supply vessels. Merchant ships may serve as troop and cargo transports for PLAN missions.[11] Using such vessels as assault transports would be difficult for the same reasons cited above for fishing boats.

The PLAN mans three large fuel and ammunitions ships (AOR) capable of replenishing other ships while underway and a large number of repair and other support ships, although their utility in amphibious operations would be secondary. The PLAN's thirty to forty minesweepers would also have an important role in a naval conflict.

Naval Aviation

All PLAN fixed-wing aviation assets are shore-based, with only helicopters deployed from surface ships. The navy's aviation force remains weak in terms of the number of ASW aircraft, surveillance platforms, and air-to-air refueling capability. However, the increasing number of exercises conducted with surface ships and PLAAF units demonstrate the force's emphasis on joint operations and coordinated operations over water. Naval aviation's acquisition of Su-27 and Su-30 fighters will significantly enhance its air-to-air and air-to-surface capabilities.

Two points are likely to affect naval aviation employment. First, the navy's front-line fixed-wing squadrons are likely trained for specific missions, such as anti-surface ship strike or air-to-air superiority. Second, the PLAAF will operationally control naval as well as air force aircraft, certainly those front-line units engaging during a Taiwan scenario. Hence, naval squadrons will not, for the most part, operate under direct PLAN control, but will be employed in a manner similar to the U.S. "single air manager" concept. The employment of air forces over the confined Taiwan Strait theater inherently increases the risk of unintended escalation, as very fast maneuverable aircraft manned by single pilots engage in operations both dangerous and difficult to control by senior authority.

TAIWAN'S NAVY

Taiwan's submarine force consists of just two fully operable boats, 22-year-old, Dutch-built, conventionally powered craft. Two 60-year-old ex-U.S. submarines remain in the inventory, but diving limitations restrict them to training missions. The Taiwan navy certainly wants to modernize and increase this minimal force through acquisition of the eight new submarines "approved" by the United States in 2001.

Taiwan faces two hurdles in obtaining these boats, however: first, the Taiwan Legislative Yuan is reluctant to authorize and appropriate the very large sum of money, perhaps as much as US$8 billion, to procure the submarines. The second hurdle is the difficulty in finding a source to build the boats. American shipbuilders are willing to undertake the job, but their lack of recent (since the early 1950s) experience in constructing conventionally powered submarines and the high cost of creating an assembly line from scratch leads to the very high unit cost cited above.

Surface Force

Taiwan has a more formidable surface fleet. The World War II-era Fletcher- and Gearing-class destroyers obtained from the United States have been replaced by far more modern, capable combatants. By 2010, these will be led by the four ex-U.S. Kidd-class DDGs that joined the navy in 2006. These were the most capable anti-air warfare ships ever built before Aegis went to sea; the Kidds' sensor-weapons suite has special capabilities for long-range targets. Their drawbacks include large crews (almost 400 personnel), deep draft, and missile launchers that have not always been reliable.

The remainder of the Taiwan navy's surface combatant force is composed of twenty-two frigates of the Cheng Kung (Perry), Kang Ding (La Fayette), and Chi Yang (Knox) classes. The first two of these are armed with anti-air missiles; the third was built to conduct open-ocean ASW at long ranges. All three classes are multi-warfare capable, however, and are armed with guns, anti-ship cruise missiles, and helicopters. The Coast Guard, restructured and expanded in 2001, includes over a hundred patrol craft of widely varying capability.

Taiwan's amphibious shipping includes two ex-U.S. LSDs (landing ship dock) and two relatively new ex-U.S. LSTs (landing ship tank). There are also approximately a dozen World War II-era LSTs and several dozen smaller landing craft. The navy mans twelve minesweepers, and appears ready to purchase twelve MH-53 minesweeping helicopters from the United States, which will very significantly increase its mine warfare (MIW) capabilities. Finally, the Taiwan navy deploys one AOR capable of refueling and rearming its ships while underway.

Naval Aviation

Taiwan has no shipboard fixed-wing aircraft, but does deploy twenty-two very capable S-70C ASW helicopters on its frigates. Ashore, Taiwan has twenty-four old S-2T ASW aircraft, which suffer from severe material problems. Taiwan is currently negotiating with the United States for the purchase of twelve P-3C aircraft, which are very capable planes superb at surveillance, ASW, and anti-surface warfare (ASW).

THE U.S. NAVY

The U.S. naval presence in East Asian waters is led by the Seventh Fleet, homeported in Yokosuka, Japan, with a large secondary base at Sasebo, Japan. The Marines who would embark in the fleet's amphibious shipping are based on Okinawa. On an average day, U.S. naval forces in the Japan, Yellow, East, and South China seas include one aircraft carrier, four Aegis cruisers and destroyers, three other destroyers and frigates, and an amphibious squadron, built around a very large (40,000-ton displacement) helicopter carrier, capable of embarking 2,000 Marines. Navy and Marine Corps air groups are also on hand, stationed at fields in Okinawa and metropolitan Japan.[12]

Other fleet units include two minesweepers based in Sasebo and several at-sea replenishment ships able to operate throughout the fleet's area of responsibility. Additionally, three American nuclear-powered attack submarines recently shifted homeports to Guam, where they are much closer to possible employment theaters, including, of course, the Taiwan theater.[13]

Perhaps the most important factor that U.S. military units would bring to a crisis and conflict over Taiwan is the world-leading, state-of-the-art command and control capabilities of American forces. Given their superior command and control architecture, U.S. units and commanders would be less likely than their Chinese and Taiwanese counterparts to make unexpected operational decisions or to draw incorrect conclusions that might result in escalatory steps not otherwise justified. That said, the inadvertent downing of an Iranian airbus in 1988 by USS *Vincennes*, the 1994 encounter between USS *Kitty Hawk* and a Chinese Han-class submarine, and the transit of the Taiwan Strait by USS *Nimitz* in 1995 are but a few instances where even U.S. naval forces found themselves executing unexpected or misunderstood operations open to escalation not justified by national security objectives.

NAVAL FORCE COMPARISON

The PLA was impressed by American military power in the Iraqi wars of 1991 and 2003, and the Afghanistan campaign in 2001–2002. That said, China remains undaunted by possible U.S. intervention in a Taiwan

Strait scenario; the PLA is systematically analyzing lessons learned, closely watching the continuing struggles in Iraq and Afghanistan, and exercising extensively to find the means to achieve Taiwan reunification in the face of U.S. intervention should military means be employed. Hopefully, the PLA is also studying the cases of "friendly fire"—known as "blue on blue" to U.S. forces—and other unexpected encounters that represent or threaten to lead to cases of unintended escalation.[14]

As of 2007, the PLAN and the Taiwan Navy are roughly equal in surface combatant capability, allowing for China's greater numbers against Taiwan's superior technology. In terms of submarine and aviation forces, however, the PLAN is much superior. China's submarine force is beyond compare, both in number and capability—an advantage that will continue to increase.[15]

In the air, the PLAN Air Force (PLANAF) acquisition of Su-27/30 aircraft and the increasing number of joint exercises with the PLAAF will increase China's capability to establish control of the air in a Taiwan scenario. The PLAAF is steadily increasing its capability, joint operational experience, and numbers of modern aircraft; the Taiwan Air Force (TAF) has made only marginal improvements since the completion of the F-16 and Mirage 2000 acquisition programs. The key to comparing air forces, of course, is the airmanship of the pilots; although Taiwan historically has demonstrated advantages in this area, that cannot be assumed in future scenarios.

U.S. Capability

The entry of the United States would of course tilt the balance of military power in Taiwan's favor, but the key word in that supposition is "entry." There are at least three important factors affecting U.S. intervention in a conflict between China and Taiwan.

First is the fact that such a conflict may not be a single campaign, fought to an end accepted by all parties. Instead, Beijing may fight a series of campaigns; if the first ends in continued Taiwan *de facto* independence, China may pull back, regroup, and rearm, and then launch another effort.

How many times will the American people support a Washington decision to intervene in this conflict? Once probably, twice perhaps, but

beyond that, Washington may not be able to justify continued intervention, especially during a continuing "global war on terror." Furthermore,
reiterative Chinese campaigns against Taiwan may differ one from the
other both in scope or character.

These factors are especially potent in terms of escalation. Chinese
losses would no doubt draw Beijing to increase its commitments to battle, in terms of both vertical escalation (force size) and horizontal escalation (force capability). An example of the former would be committing
additional forces from all seven military regions; the latter might lead to
the commitment of nuclear-armed forces to the fight over Taiwan if it is
deemed otherwise unwinnable against U.S. military intervention.

The second and third are two major problems facing the U.S. Navy
following a decision in Washington to come to Taiwan's assistance. First is
the possible lack of ships, aircraft, and precision-guided munitions with
which to intervene. The global war on terrorism has severely impacted
U.S. military resources worldwide, including those in the Pacific theater,
as units from all the services redeploy in normal cycles to the Middle
East and Southwest Asia.

This reduction in available forces is less noticeable with navy units,
since they routinely deploy into and out of the theater, than it is with
army or air force units, which usually are home-based in theater, with
the very extensive shore installations required. A review of operational
schedules for Pacific Fleet units, however, would demonstrate how much
lower in terms of ship-days-in-theater the U.S. naval presence has been
since 2001. Similar periods of reduced U.S. naval presence occurred
during the 1990–1991 buildup and completion of Desert Storm, but
the current focus away from the Pacific has been going on now for more
than three years.

Finally, Seventh Fleet units may face significant tactical difficulties
if ordered into a Taiwan scenario. The time-distance problem is noteworthy, as shown in Table 7.1.

The U.S. Navy of the Cold War era possessed the most effective warfare capabilities in history, especially in the ASW mission. ASW assets
are much less numerous than in 1990. For instance, there are now just
54 P-3C aircraft, down from 108 during the Cold War, and 27 attack
submarines, down from 40 during the Cold War. As for surface combatants, the Pacific Fleet included 154 in 1989, but just 58 today.[17]

Table 7.1 The Time-Distance Factor[a]

From	To	Distance in NM[b]	Time in days at 12 kts[c]	Time in days at 20 kts
West Coast	Hawaii	2,223	8.0	4.6
West Coast	Japan	4,755	16.5	10.0
West Coast	Guam	5,289	18.5	11.0
Hawaii	Japan	3,346	11.5	7.0
Hawaii	Guam	3,303	11.5	7.0
Japan	Guam	1,359	5.0	3.0
Guam	Keelung	1,470	5.0	3.0
East Coast	Singapore	8,364	29.0	17.5
East Coast via Cape of Good Hope	Singapore	12,138	42.0	25.0
East Coast	Guam	6,879	24.0	14.0
East Coast via Cape of Good Hope	Guam	13,561	47.0	28.0

[a]A speed of advance (SOA) of 12 kts allows an aircraft carrier to conduct flight operations as desired; a SOA of 20 kts makes that difficult and also makes it very difficult for escorting ships to keep up with the carrier. Distances are for Great Circle routes, including Panama Canal transit for East Coast ships except as otherwise noted.
[b]1 nautical mile (NM) equals approximately 1.1 statute miles.
[c]1 knot (kt) equals approximately 1.2 mph.

Additionally, the force of civilian-manned ships that monitored the extensive ocean-bottom listening arrays no longer conducts that mission.[18] Today's ships and submarines are more capable than their predecessors—dramatically so, in some cases—but the fact remains that one vessel can only be in one place at one time.

The loss of ASW capability would be particularly important in a Taiwan scenario, should China employ its large submarine force intelligently. If, for instance, Beijing covertly deployed thirty submarines from homeport, and then maintained just twelve of them on station for thirty to sixty days, U.S. naval forces would have to transit the East China Sea with great caution. Locating a dozen or two submarines with possible hostile intent is a difficult task. If Beijing were willing to accept an element of risk, a PLAN submarine or two could even be stationed in the vicinity of the channels into Tokyo Wan, the Sasebo naval magazine complex, or near White Beach, in Okinawa—all locations common to U.S. ship transits.

U.S. MIW assets in-theater are limited to the two Osprey-class minesweepers homeported in Sasebo; the arrival of additional sweeps from Ingleside, Texas would take at least thirty days. The minesweeping helicopters based in Norfolk, Virginia could arrive much more quickly of course, the first two within ten days, but that would require C-5 airlift that is always in high demand and would be even scarcer if a military crisis over Taiwan heated up.

Washington presumably would be tempted into vertical escalatory steps in the face of a determined military engagement by PLA forces against U.S. forces heavily engaged in Southwest Asia. The discussion during the past several years about acquiring new nuclear weapons for tactical employment indicates one such line of thought.

This brief comparison of forces shows China clearly superior to Taiwan in naval strength below, on, and above the ocean's surface by 2016. Given present trends in China and Taiwan, only successful U.S. intervention in a Taiwan contingency would alter this calculus. How might these factors play out in real time?

SCENARIOS[19]

We will consider a single scenario in detail within an escalatory framework, and will then note additional scenario branches and sequels that can flow from any confrontation or decision.

Maritime Scenario

As Chen Shui-bian continues to strengthen Taiwan's status as an independent country, China's leadership decides to make a military demonstration, in conjunction with a demand that Taipei agree to begin unification discussions.

PHASE A (DAY 1). Beijing calls upon Taipei to begin negotiations for reunification. Beijing also announces that all merchant shipping bound for Taiwan must first call at a mainland port (either Wenzhou, Fuzhou, or Xiamen) to obtain clearance, and that the PLAN will deploy its ships, with detachments of legal personnel embarked, to enforce this requirement.

Taipei responds that (a) Beijing must first acknowledge that such talks would be conducted as between two separate states and (b) Taiwan navy combatants are immediately establishing patrol areas extending

24 NM from all ports, to ensure the uninterrupted passage of merchant ships bound for Taiwan. A confrontation soon occurs, as a PLAN Jianghu-class frigate and a Taiwan La Fayette-class frigate close in to within 2 NM of a Taiwan-flagged container ship 35 NM north-northwest of Taiwan, en route to Keelung, Taiwan. The three ships remain in company for three hours during which period they are overflown by TAF Mirage 2000 fighters. Both frigates are in communication with shore-based headquarters; both are cautioned by their headquarters against taking provocative action, but atmospheric conditions and electronic "jamming" leave both frigates in doubt as to their rules of engagement.

After the incident, Beijing warns Taipei that its warship interfered with safe navigation and that future interference would be dealt with strongly, with Taiwan bearing all responsibility for any unfortunate developments. China also issues Notices to Mariners warning against hazardous conditions within that portion of its Exclusive Economic Zone that includes Taiwan, which is claimed as sovereign Chinese territory. This proclamation—if of questionable legality—implies an exclusion zone for all shipping extending 350 NM north, east, and south from Taiwan's coast.[20]

Taiwan responds that Beijing's Notices to Mariners are illegal, states that its navy will continue its patrolling, issues public pronouncements condemning China's "piracy policy," and calls on the United Nations to send observers to Taiwan.

Two flights of mainland-based Su-27 aircraft close to within 15 NM of Taiwan's west coast, crossing the strait center line. They are intercepted by Taiwanese indigenous defense fighters (IDF) aircraft and turn back.

These encounters between tactical operational units on the sea and in the air bear an inherent risk of escalation presumably not desired by Beijing or Taipei: the lower the rank of the participant directly engaged in a military confrontation, the more likely that participant will make a decision with consequences unforeseen and undesired by national authorities. The accidental collision between PLAN fighter and U.S. surveillance aircraft in the spring of 2001 is one such example.

PHASE B (DAY 4). Washington announces that it does not recognize China's Notices to Mariners as legitimate because of the excessive scope of territory covered and the lack of an end date; it urges Beijing not to take belligerent action and Taipei to exert patience. It also announces that the USS *Kitty Hawk*, in port in Yokosuka, Japan, will immediately terminate its planned sixty-day maintenance period and prepare to get underway. Since main engine repairs will require fifteen days to complete, USS *Nimitz*, undergoing predeployment training, will shift that training from Southern California to Hawaii operating areas, in preparation for early deployment to the Persian Gulf.

A Japanese workman onboard the *Kitty Hawk* is accused by an American officer of attempting to sabotage one of the carrier's engines. The worker's union walks off the ship on strike; Washington calls upon the Japanese government to intervene. Although not a case of military escalation per se, this incident has drawn Tokyo directly into the Taiwan crisis, representing an element of political escalation; the military and political elements of national security merge and increase the chances of escalation due to unforeseen developments.

A Guam-based attack submarine is ordered to sea, and the Pacific Commander in Honolulu (PACOM) is directed by the Joint Chiefs of Staff (JCS) to send to Taiwan a liaison team led by the deputy J-5 (a one-star admiral) to assess Taiwan's state of military readiness. Beijing is also requested to receive a visit from the secretary of state to discuss the situation.

PHASE C (DAY 10). U.S. intelligence officials report to Washington that thirty Chinese submarines have left their homeports within the past twenty-four hours; present locations are unknown. JCS orders a second submarine underway from Guam and two P-3C squadrons to deploy from Whidby Island, Washington to Kaneohe, Hawaii, to supplement the two P-3C squadrons already stationed there. One of the Kaneohe-based squadrons is ordered to deploy immediately to Guam—a move that will require ten days to complete.

The two U.S. minesweepers homeported in Sasebo, Japan are ordered to be prepared to get underway for operations within ninety-six hours; one of these ships will be able to comply, but the second one is in dry dock for replacement of its screw and will require ten days to be ready to operate. The U.S. Seventh Fleet commander informally asks his Japanese counterpart if Japanese minesweepers might be tasked with substituting for the inoperative U.S. ship; this request is relayed to Tokyo. The Japanese government protests to the U.S. government, warning it against escalating the crisis in the Taiwan Strait by unjustifiably involving Japan.

Observing U.S. naval movements, President Hu telephones the U.S. president with the message that Beijing is determined to end the unpatriotic and illegal behavior of the Chen clique (he mentions the precedent of Deng Xiaoping informing President Jimmy Carter of the forthcoming invasion of Vietnam in 1979); the United States is very strongly advised not to interfere in this domestic Chinese affair.

More PLAAF aircraft cross the center line of the strait and are intercepted by Taiwanese aircraft before turning back; this has become a daily occurrence, increasingly leading to intemperate exchanges between the pilots. A TAF fighter squadron commander, concerned about his opposing Su-30 pilots' ability to target Taiwan's less capable IDF fighters passively, requests permission for his pilots to activate their fire-control radars "to intimidate" their PLAAF opposites. He is refused, but decides to do so, anyway. Taiwan's military commanders are not aware of this escalatory step taken by a lieutenant-colonel.

PHASE D (DAY 15). A Chinese naval task group composed of a Luhu-class DDG and two Jiangwei-II-class guided-missile frigates (FFGs) operating approximately 60 NM north of Keelung, Taiwan, is observed by a Japanese Maritime Self-Defense Force (JMSDF) P-3C. Taipei learns of this information and announces that it will not be intimidated by military threats. Taiwan's navy begins to shift from its primary base at Tsoying, directly across from Fujian Province, to smaller ports on Taiwan's east coast.[21] This move will require at least fifteen days to complete and will deprive the navy of approximately 65 percent of its logistical supplies until they can be shipped and trucked from Tsoying—a long, slow process. Beijing evaluates this move as an indicator that Taipei intends to inaugurate strikes against mainland targets.

PHASE E (DAY 16). The Chinese task force intercepts a Taiwan-flag container ship apparently en route to Keelung; after firing across the container ship's bow, the PLAN ships force the merchant into Fuzhou. The merchant ship transmits an "SOS" and Taipei accuses Beijing of committing piracy, calling upon the United States for assistance under the Taiwan Relations Act (TRA). Taipei announces that its military forces are being placed at the highest state of readiness. In response, Beijing states that any unidentified ships or aircraft approaching China's coast will be viewed as hostile.

PHASE F (DAY 18). An unknown (but almost certainly Chinese) submarine torpedoes and sinks a Taiwan frigate that had sortied from Keelung. A second frigate in company rescues survivors, but approximately fifty Taiwanese sailors die in the attack.

Taipei announces that its ships will fire upon any unknown underwater contact. Washington immediately protests to Taipei that it has submarines operating in the area. In response, Taipei requests immediate formation of a Naval Coordinating Group in Taipei to coordinate naval operations. Washington does not respond to this request, but does ask the Japanese government to allow full use of its bases for naval and air operations in support of maintaining peace and stability in East Asia.

Taipei's "shoot on sight" order for underwater contacts seriously heightens the chances of attacks on friendly or neutral submarines and on Chinese submarines engaged in innocent operations. The increasingly capable PLAN submarines of the Kilo, Song, and Jin classes are less likely to be detected by Taiwan's ASW forces and even more difficult to identify as Chinese, if they are detected. This increases the opportunities for a Taiwan ship or aircraft commander to misjudge an underwater contact and launch an unjustified attack.

(DAY 19). Beijing announces that Chinese submarines, surface ships, and aircraft are laying minefields near Taiwan's major ports of Keelung and Kaohsiung, and states that any merchant ships desiring to enter these ports must first rendezvous with Chinese pilot vessels to embark a pilot to pass through the minefields. The announcement also notes that minefields are being laid to close the naval ports of Tsoying and Suao. Beijing states that since the minefields are laid within China's territorial waters (i.e., within 12 NM of the Taiwanese ports), they are classified as a measure of shipping control and not an act of war.

Lloyds and other large maritime insurers announce suspension of all coverage for merchant ships en route to any Taiwan port.

Taipei denounces this act of war and announces its minesweeping force will immediately begin clearing these minefields. Washington announces that it is dispatching ten MH-53E minesweeping helicopters to Okinawa via C-5 airlift, with an estimated arrival date for the first two helicopters of day 34; it will take until day 51 for all ten to arrive and achieve operating status. China demands that all foreign military aircraft destined for the province of Taiwan must first obtain clearance from Beijing; failure to do so might be interpreted as an unfriendly act.

(DAY 20). Tokyo tells Washington that bases in Japan may only be used for secondary support purposes: for example, U.S. ships home-ported in Yokosuka and Sasebo may load ammunition and supplies and sail for the Taiwan theater, but direct air support of operations may not use Japanese fields, including those on Okinawa.

Washington announces that the minesweeping helicopters will be flown to Guam instead of Okinawa, which means that to operate around Taiwan, they will require either basing on Taiwan or a carrier (or large helicopter carrier) as a support ship. Congressional cries for the president to invoke the TRA are increasing. The president calls his Chinese counterpart and is told that Beijing is set firmly on a course of reunifying Taiwan; no interference by another country will be tolerated. This warning, directed specifically at the United States, Japan, and the Philippines, is repeated publicly and in diplomatic notes by all Chinese ambassadors.

Beijing repeats its demand to Taipei for talks. Increased readiness of PLA forces in the Nanjing Military Region is announced; only four of the thirty unlocated PLAN submarines have been localized by U.S., Taiwanese, or JMSDF forces. The latter are quietly participating in the ASW effort without official Tokyo sanction.

PHASE G (DAY 21). Taiwanese S-2T aircraft on patrol off the island's northeast coast discover and sink a Chinese Ming-class submarine at snorkeling depth. Taipei makes no public announcement, but informs Washington and Tokyo; the information quickly leaks, but Beijing makes no public response. However, Chinese submarines are instructed to attack all Taiwanese warships and military aircraft when they believe themselves to be threatened. The submarine commanders interpret this as direction to seek out and attack Taiwanese warships and military aircraft.

Kitty Hawk, conducting flight operations in the vicinity of Iwo Jima, detects two unknown submarines. The U.S. Seventh Fleet commander asks his JMSDF counterpart if Japanese submarines are available to patrol areas around the *Kitty Hawk*'s operating area; the Japanese admiral wants to agree to this task, but his inquiry to the Defense Ministry receives an emphatic, negative response.

The USS *Carl Vinson*, operating in the Persian Gulf, is ordered to proceed at maximum speed to the South China Sea; estimated arrival time is day 28, but it will have to make this transit without escorting ships and while conducting minimal flight operations. Washington requests Thailand, Singapore, and the Philippines to permit P-3C and tactical USAF aircraft to operate from their airfields in support of the *Carl Vinson* during its transit from the Persian Gulf. Singapore agrees, but Thailand and the Philippines refuse, fearing involvement in a potential military conflict between two nuclear-armed powers.

During the now daily routine Taiwanese interception of two PLAAF Su-27 aircraft at the center line of the strait, the Taiwanese pilots "lock on" to their opponents with their fire-control radars and the Taiwanese are engaged by the Su-27s; both Taiwanese aircraft are shot down.

A PLAN task group of two Sovremenny-class DDGs and four Jiangwei-class FFGs is observed steaming south, 10 NM off the Fujian coast. Both of Taiwan's operational submarines are at sea, operating in the strait.

Beijing announces the formation in Xiamen of a new Taiwan Provincial Government which will begin reunification talks on day 25; the Taipei Legislative Yuan is invited to send a delegation to participate in these discussions. Beijing calls upon the people of Taiwan to support this legal body. Appeals are also made repeatedly to the Taiwan armed forces to help reunite their country and not to fight their Chinese brothers.

Taipei appeals directly to Congress for U.S. military support; the president announces that the United States will not stand by while Taiwan is reunified with China by military force, but appeals for both sides to begin negotiations. The U.S. Navy and Air Force begin a movement of scarce precision-guided munitions from the Southwest Asian theaters to Guam. Widespread protests against Guam's use as a military base from which to conduct war with China break out in Agana and elsewhere on the island. Guam's delegate to Congress issues an appeal to Chen Shui-bian to negotiate with Beijing, as do European Union and ASEAN representatives.

The government in Taipei believes itself boxed in by China's military superiority and the lack of international support; its military commanders are ordered to prepare a "maximum effort" to attack Chinese military and civilian targets. Beijing learns of this preparation and interprets it as a measure of Taipei's desperation that significantly increases China's belief that immediate, more intensive military operations are required.

PHASE H (DAY 26). Taipei has not sent a delegation to the talks at Xiamen and continues to appeal to the president and Congress for military assistance, cries for help that are widely echoed in Congress.

Strikes of ten M-9/11 missiles each impact the Taiwanese air bases at Hualien, Tainan, and Taoyuan; missiles also strike naval facilities at Tsoying, Kaohsiung, Keelung, and Suao. Beijing had sought to ensure the absence of foreign nationals from these military sites, but the agents watching Hualien failed to report the presence of a ten-member survey team from Lockheed; four members of this team were killed and three were wounded by the Chinese missiles.

Beijing renews its call for a Taiwan delegation to join the reunification talks at Xiamen, which will recommence on day 28. Beijing announces that four of its submarines are missing and accuses Taiwan of attacking the Chinese people.

More Maritime Scenario Parameters

The foregoing scenario assumes an incremental employment of naval and air forces, which yields many opportunities for situational control, as well as for unintended escalation. Each decision by each participant (China, Taiwan, and the United States) at many levels, from second-lieutenant to the president, will evoke decisions by the other participants, some of which will be unanticipated. Additionally, nations not directly involved (Japan, Singapore, the Philippines, South Korea, the European Union states, etc.) will also react to individual and national decisions and actions in ways that are likely to affect the scenario.

A more dramatic scenario would be based on a massive Chinese strike against Taiwan by naval and air forces. Such a campaign would greatly reduce incremental escalation, but would pose an issue of massive escalation: if Washington was surprised by a PLA attack on Taiwan, it might decide that nuclear strikes against China were necessary to save the island. Or Beijing might decide to launch quick, massive military operations against Taiwan to reduce U.S. opportunities for intervention, believing that Washington would not employ nuclear weapons. In either case, an incrementally developing military crisis overall would allow greater control of events by participating national command authorities, although it would also offer many more opportunities for events to be driven by operational commanders in directions they did not understand or with results they could not anticipate.

CONCLUSION

This brief examination of operational steps indicates the variety of escalatory measures afforded by a maritime scenario. First, the time factor is important, but not in the way often described. Naval forces are extremely flexible, but they move relatively slowly, a factor especially applicable in the vast Asian-Pacific theater, as depicted in the time-distance table (Table 7.1).

Second, escalation may easily occur intentionally or unintentionally; an S2T aircraft flying hundreds of miles from home base—even if in radio communication—is a relatively independent actor; the same is true to a degree for a warship's commander prosecuting an unknown underwater contact.

Third, the increasingly capable ships, submarines, and aircraft operated by all participants increases the risk of unintended escalation and unanticipated results from authorized operations. Longer-range, more self-sustainable naval platforms are that much more independent of normal command and control systems.

Fourth, military action over Taiwan's status is usually discussed with China as the instigator; given the distances involved, the problematic nature of even modern command and control capabilities, and the apparent vastly different intensity of determination involved on the part of the participants, actions taken at sea, in the air, or in the council chamber by Taiwan or the United States might also lead to escalation of the crisis.

If China deploys twenty to thirty submarines, some would likely be lost to mechanical failure or personnel error; at what point would Beijing conclude that opposing forces are sinking its submarines? Or, if an aircraft carrier were sunk with the loss of thousands of American sailors' lives, would the U.S. president believe it necessary to retaliate with a nuclear strike? Finally, what one participant intends as "business as usual," the other might well consider "escalatory."[22]

China's increasing realization of the potency of the modernizing PLAN is that of policy makers lacking military experience and with a level of knowledge dependent on information provided by that force. The 2001 EP-3 incident reportedly included a misinformed Chinese leadership, due to (possibly intentionally) erroneous reporting of the situation to Beijing by on-scene PLA commanders.[23] Another aspect of this problem is a lack of full understanding by PLAN personnel as to the capability of the new, technologically advanced but untried ships, submarines, and aircraft both they and their opponents operate.

In other words, while the maritime arena offers many means for exerting pressure, sending messages, and "teaching lessons," it is also at least as subject as other means of statecraft to misinterpretation, miscalculation, and unintended consequences. These factors are exacerbated by China's very poor record since 1950 of correctly estimating the U.S. response to its military initiatives; the 1996 crisis is the most recent major example of Beijing not understanding Washington's response to China's use of military force.

NOTES

The views expressed in this chapter are the author's alone, and may not represent those of the National Defense University or any other agency of the U.S. Government.

1. Belize, Burkina Faso, Costa Rica, Dominican Republic, El Salvador, The Gambia, Guatemala, Haiti, Honduras, Kiribati, Malawi, Marshall Islands, Nauru, Nicaragua, Palau, Panama, Paraguay, Saint Kitts and Nevis, Saint Vincent and the Grenadines, Sao Tome and Principe, Swaziland, Solomon Islands, Tuvalu, and Vatican City.

2. "President Clinton on Resolution with Assent of Taiwan's People (February 24, 2000)," in Shirley A. Kan, *China/Taiwan: Evolution of the 'One China' Policy—Key Statements from Washington, Beijing, and Taipei,* CRS Report for Congress RL30341 (Washington D.C.: USGPO, June 1, 2004), p. 64.

3. Weapons ranges and geographic distances are given in nautical miles (NM), one of which equals approximately 1.15 statute miles.

4. Author's interviews with U.S. Navy Meteorological Service officers, August 1999. Also see Eric McVadon, "PRC Exercises, Doctrine and Tactics Toward Taiwan: The Naval Dimension," in James R. Lilley and Chuck Downs, eds., *Crisis in the*

Taiwan Strait (Washington, D.C.: NDU Press in cooperation with AEI, 1997), pp. 249–78, for a comprehensive discussion of this subject. One fathom equals 6 feet or 1.83 meters.

5. See tables in the Appendix.

6. Ibid. See in particular *Jane's Fighting Ships, 2006–2007* (London: Jane's Information Group, 2006), pp. 115-121.

7. Ibid, p. 118. A good explanation of AIP technology is contained in Richard Scott, "Boosting the Staying Power of the Non-Nuclear Submarine," *Jane's International Defense Review* 32 (November 1999): 41–50. The new tactical submarine is called the Yuan class.

8. *Jane's Fighting Ships, 2005–2006*, p. 118.

9. See especially Rear Admiral Eric A. McVadon, USN (Ret.), "Testimony Before the U.S.-China Economic & Security Review Commission: Recent Trends in China's Military Modernization," September 15, 2005, for an excellent description of possible PLA employment of coordinated ballistic and cruise missile attacks against an aircraft carrier. This possibility is also noted in Tony Capaccio, "Navy Lacks Plan to Defend Against 'Sizzler' Missile," *Bloomberg.com*, March 23, 2007. http://www.bloomberg.com/apps/news?pid=20601087&sid=akO7Y_ORw538&refer=home (last accessed April 9, 2007).

10. *Jane's Fighting ships, 2005–2006*, pp. 122–130.

11. See, for instance, Kuo Nai-jih, "Percentage of Hits of Ship-Carried Artillery of the Communist Troops Reaches 90 Percent," *Lieh-Ho Pao* (Taipei), August 23, 2001, in FBIS-CPP20010823000121; Dai Zhixin, Feng Weihua, and Yang Xiaogang, "Making a Comeback After 'Defeat'—Account of How a Certain Water Transport Group Drills Hard on Support Capabilities Aiming at Actual Battles," *Jiefangjun Bao* (Beijing), February 6, 2002, 2, in FBIS-CPP20020206000059; and "PLA Fujian Military District to Conduct Maritime Logistic Replenishment Drill," *Wenweipo News* (Hong Kong), July 23, 2004, translated by Asian Studies Detachment.

12. http://www.c7f.navy.mil.

13. See Robert Burns, Associated Press report, "Air Force Wants to Put Fighters and Bombers Back on Guam in Pacific" (January 13, 2004).

14. The fall 2004 case of a helicopter shot down in Afghanistan leading to a futile but loss-intense rescue operation by U.S. Special Forces is one example.

15. Even this date assumes that Legislative Yuan appropriation of the required funding could be matched by the emergence of a viable source for new submarines. Alternatives, such as the purchase of existing submarines, are possible, but not likely.

16. Distances are from HO Pub 151, found at http://pollux.nss.nima.mil/pubs/pubs_j_show_sections.html?dpath=DBP&ptid=5&rid=189.

17. These numbers vary by squadron and from year to year, but are accurate to within 10 percent.

18. The bottom-array system (SOSUS) is described at http://www.pmel.noaa.gov/vents/acoustics/sosus.html (last accessed April 9, 2007). Current status of the support ships is at "T-AGOS 1 Stalwart Ocean Surveillance Ship," http://www.globalsecurity.org/military/systems/ship/tagos-1.htm (last accessed April 9, 2007).

19. The actions discussed in the scenario below do not necessarily represent how countries would actually respond, but have been chosen to illustrate some of the issues that could arise in a naval escalation scenario.

20. Bounded, in Beijing's view, only by undisputed Korean, Japanese, Philippine, and Vietnamese territory.

21. The distance from Tsoying to Taitung, for instance, is approximately 117 NM, which would take eight hours to transit at 16 kts.

22. A prime example of this case is the *Kitty Hawk* incident of 1994; the carrier group commander was acting in what he considered to be routine fashion by ordering prosecution of an underwater contact; the Chinese submarine that was the target of this operation interpreted the U.S. actions as hostile, however, as did Beijing.

23. Author's conversations with senior U.S. and PLA officers (2002, 2006).

APPENDIX

Table A.1 PLA Navy

Type	Class	Displacement (in tons)	1985	2007	2010
Destroyers			15	25	31
Type 956	Sovremenny	8,480	—	4	4
Type 52C	Luyang I, II	8,000	—	2	6
Type 52B	Luzhou	8,000	—	1	4
Type 054	Luhai	6,600	—	1	1
Type 052	Luhu	5,700	—	2	2
Type 051	Luda	3,960	11	15	14
Type 07	Anshan	2,040	4	—	—
Frigates			31	42	40
Type 054	Maanshan		—	2	6
Type 059	Jiangwei III	3,000	—	1	2
Type 057	Jiangwei II	2,250	—	4	8
Type 055	Jiangwei	2,250	—	4	4
Type 053	Jianghu	1,925	20	31	20
Type 053K	Jiangdong	1,925	2	—	—
Type 065	Jiangnan	1,400	5	—	—
Type 01	Chengdu	1,510	4	—	—
Guided-Missile Boats			100	83	~65
Type 520T	Houjian	520	—	4	4
Type 343M	Houxin	478	—	14	~36
Type 021	Huangfeng	205	100	65	~25
Submarines			97	68–71	64–67
Type 094	SSBN	8,000	—	1	2
Type 092	Xia SSBN	6,500	1	1	1
Type 093	SSN	6,500	—	2	4
Type 091	Han SSN	5,500	3	4	3
	Kilo	2,325	—	8	12
Type unknown	Wuhan	2,100	—	1	4
Type 039	Song	2,250	—	10–13	17–20
Type 035	Ming	2,100	2	21	21
Type 033	Romeo	1,710	90	20	—
Type 031	Golf SSB	2,700	1	—	—
Amphibious Ships			4	15	29
Type 074	Yuting LST	4,800	—	6	20
Type 072	Yukan LST	4,170	3	7	7
	Yudeng LST	1,850	—	1	1
Type 073	Yudao LCM	1,460	1	1	1

Table A.1 PLA Navy (*Continued*)

Type	Mission	1985	2004	2008
Aircraft		**~680**	**~642**	**~670**
B-6	Bomber	50	30	30
B-5	Bomber	130	80	25
A-5/FH-7	Attack	—	~100	~175
F-7/8II/				
Su-27/30	Fighter	~500	~400	~400
Zhi9/Zhi8/Ka28	ASW/EW/Log Helos	—	32	40

Table A.2 Taiwan Navy

Type	Class	Displacement (in tons)	1985	2007	2010
Destroyers			16	4	4
Tien Tan	Arleigh Burke	9,200	—	—	—
Chi Teh	Kidd	9,500	—	4	4
Chao Yang	Gearing	3,500	14	—	—
Lo Yang	Summer	3,220	2	—	—
Frigates			10	22	22
Cheng Kung	Perry	4,100	—	8	8
Chi Yang	Knox	4,200	—	8	8
Kang Ding	La Fayette	3,500	—	6	6
Tai Yuan	Rudderow	1,950	1	—	—
Tien Shan	Lawrence	2,150	3	—	—
Wen Shan	Crosley	2,150	6	—	—
Fast-Attack Missile Craft			52	64	~35
Jin Chiang		580	—	12	~20
Kuang Hua-VI		200	—	1	~15
Lung Chiang	PSMM MK5	250	2	2	—
Hai Ou	Dvora	47	50	49	—
Submarines			2	4	4
Hai Lung II		2,500	—	—	—
Hai Lung	Zwaardvis	2,600	—	2	2
Hai Shih	GUPPY	2,440	2	2	2
Amphibious Ships			27	20	18
Shiu Hai	Anchorage	13,700	—	1	1
Cheng Cheng	Cabildo	9,375	1	1	—
Chung Ho	Newport	8,792	—	2	2
Chung Hai	LST-1	4,080	22	12	11
Mei Lo	LSM-1	1,095	4	4	4

8

The Nuclear Dimension
How Likely? How Stable?

Brad Roberts

WHAT ROLE MIGHT NUCLEAR WEAPONS PLAY in a Taiwan contingency? The word "contingency" is used advisedly here, to encompass the separate possibilities of political confrontation across the Taiwan Strait under the shadow of military options and of actual military conflict involving the operational engagement of forces. In either case, the answer would seem to depend on factors that are difficult to know for sure before the outbreak of a conflict. What decisions would U.S. and Chinese leaders make in a crisis across the strait? What operational plans would be implemented?

In lieu of answers to such questions, this chapter takes the following approach. It begins with a review of what is known about China's military preparations in the nuclear realm for a Taiwan contingency. These include preparations in both the military technical and doctrinal realms. The chapter provides some historical context necessary to better understand these preparations before turning to a review of U.S. military preparations for such a contingency, because China is not the only factor in determining the role of nuclear weapons in a Taiwan conflict. These summaries of Chinese and U.S. preparations will illustrate a common point: both sides focus on ensuring the effectiveness of deterrence but have devoted far less time and effort to thinking about and preparing for failures of deterrence and the challenges of restoring deterrence intrawar or terminating a war gone nuclear in some acceptable way. Preliminary evidence drawn from informal exchanges among experts suggests that there would likely be some significant challenges associated with managing these processes of nuclear escalation and de-escalation.[1]

CHINA'S MILITARY PREPARATIONS FOR NUCLEAR WAR

China's nuclear forces, strategy, and doctrine all took shape in a period long before the Taiwan problem came to dominate the thinking of military operators and planners in the People's Liberation Army (PLA). This section reviews this historical context in order to better understand how China's military preparations for nuclear war are and are not changing in the present era.

China's nuclear posture has its roots in the "century of humiliation" of China at the hands of imperialist powers; the chaos of the prolonged civil war; the emergence of the new revolutionary state in 1949 and, with it, the desire to consolidate control and power; and the nuclear threats levied by the United States in the 1950s. In Mao's tart phrase in 1964, "we must have this thing if we don't want to be bullied by others."[2] In the minds of the Chinese, the capability exists in order to counter coercion, including those U.S. activities that the United States perceives as deterrence (hence the common Chinese description of its nuclear strategy as counterdeterrence).

A second key factor in influencing the formation of China's nuclear forces, strategy, and doctrine was the original dictum from Mao to expect "early war, major war, nuclear war." In the early decades of China's nuclear program, the Soviet Union (USSR) was the primary military threat to China, in the form of major armored formations backed by nuclear weapons. Accordingly, the PLA planned for such wars fought with the USSR on China's soil and thus conceived of them entirely as defensive operations. They could readily promise not to use nuclear weapons first against others, with the important caveat that this did not preclude first use in China's own territory to defeat a Soviet invasion.

A third key factor was the early commitment to create only the "minimum means of reprisal."[3] China created a posture for the purpose of nuclear defense, not nuclear offense. Because of this, China sees only a credible second-strike capacity without war fighting and counterforce potential as sufficient to this end. In the words of a strategist in China's nuclear technical community, "nuclear weapons cannot be used to fight and win wars."[4] According to a Chinese military strategist, Senior Colonel Yao Yunzhu:

> A defensive posture has always been preferred to an offensive one . . . The renouncement of the first-use option, the willingness to accept vulnerability, the confinement to retaliatory nuclear use, the principle of attacking only after being attacked, the focus on second strike capabilities, and the reservation of nuclear means as the last resort to protect only the most vital national interests, all point to the defensiveness of China's nuclear policy. . . . China's strategists take the concept [of minimum deterrence] as a relative one, defined not only by pure numbers but more importantly by such key criteria as invulnerability of nuclear forces, assurance of retaliation, and credibility of counter attack. When a Chinese document says China intends to possess nuclear weapons only at the minimum or lowest level for the needs of self-defense, it means to have the minimum but assured capabilities of retaliatory second strike.[5]

A fourth factor is the Chinese government's lack of transparency about China's military affairs in general and nuclear capabilities and policies in particular. This lack of transparency has deep roots in Chinese society, not the least of which is the conviction that the onus of transparency falls on the stronger party, so as to allay the fears of the weaker. But there are other sources as well. To cite Yao again: "Concealment, deception and secrecy, all salient ingredients of traditional military strategy, have more to do with China's traditional culture than with its current social system."[6] As a result, China has provided no detailed information about its nuclear forces and only brief statements of policy and strategy in its recent biennial defense white papers.

In sum, the key ideas governing China's nuclear posture were developed in a strategic context with distinct attributes. These include the commitments to "smash bullying," to a no-first-use (NFU) policy, to minimum deterrence, and to a lack of transparency. But obviously the current historical context is different from the prior one. A central analytical question today is how these traditional approaches are being or will be influenced by the transformation of China's strategic posture for the emerging security environment. In order to understand this question, the next section of this chapter explores how the Chinese nuclear force has evolved over the last couple of decades—and why.

BUILDING AND TRANSFORMING THE SECOND ARTILLERY

From modest beginnings in the 1950s, China moved steadily, albeit slowly by the Cold War standards of the United States and Soviet Union, to create a strategic deterrent force. The Second Artillery was formally founded on July 1, 1966 as a counterpart to the PLA's traditional artillery core. Over the next three decades, the Second Artillery developed and fielded a force of missiles of ever-longer range; its first intercontinental-range missile was deployed in the early 1980s. In the early 1990s, the Second Artillery was given the additional assignment of fielding missiles armed with conventional warheads and since then there has been a steady and massive buildup of deployed short-range non-nuclear missiles (to roughly 1,000 at the time of this writing).[7] The development of second- and third-generation replacement systems for medium- and long-range missiles currently in the field has also proceeded, though without the massive deployments.[8] In 2000, then-President Jiang Zemin reportedly gave high-level political endorsement to increased investments for the counterdeterrence force in a July 2000 speech, arguing:

> We must own strategic nuclear weapons of a definite quality and quantity in order to ensure national security. We must guarantee the safety of strategic nuclear bases and prevent against the loss of combat effectiveness from attacks and destruction by hostile powers. We must ensure that our strategic nuclear weapons are at a high degree of war preparedness. When an aggressor launches a nuclear attack against us, we must be able to launch nuclear counter attack and nuclear re-attack against the aggressor. We must pay attention to the global situation of strategic balance and stability and, when there are changes in the situation, adjust our strategic nuclear weapon development strategy in a timely manner.[9]

The cumulative result of these efforts and commitments over a half-century is a force with the following characteristics:

> The doctrine and force structure of China's Second Artillery should be analyzed at three distinct levels, reflecting a multi-faceted force with very different missions: a posture of *credible minimum deterrence* with regard to the continental United States and Russia; a more offensive-oriented posture of *limited deterrence* with regard to China's theater nuclear forces; and an *offensively configured, preemptive, counterforce warfighting posture* or "active defense" or "offensive defense" for the Second Artillery's conventional missile forces [emphasis in original].[10]

Whatever prior interest China might have had in tactical nuclear weapons seems not to have survived that earlier era.[11]

This three-tiered posture reflects the complex strategic environment in which China is positioned. It is important to understand that this strategic strike posture does not encompass everything that fits in China's strategic military "tool kit." Recall the logic of the 2002 Bush administration's *Nuclear Posture Review* (NPR), which characterized the U.S. strategic military "tool kit" as encompassing national capacities to strike with strategic effect, to defend against such a strike, and to outcompete to field new capabilities with any adversary choosing such competition.[12] This so-called New Triad reflects the old way of Chinese thinking. China has developed multiple tools for strategic strike, both nuclear and non-nuclear, kinetic as well as nonkinetic.[13] China has pursued active defenses against shorter-range ballistic missiles (SRBM)[14] and has what may be the world's premier passive defense capability, in the form of a massive civil defense system with tens of thousands of kilometers of tunnels. China has also developed an infrastructure with an eye on posturing for future competition.[15] China's leaders have not and would not describe China's strategic posture in this way and prefer instead to characterize China's strategic force as consisting solely of the long-range nuclear element, just as the United States did for decades. But the different way of thinking about a nation's strategic posture reflected in the 2002 NPR provides useful insights into the multiple dimensions of China's strategic posture.

Two factors have been central to the development of China's current strategic posture. The first is the effort over the last decade by the PLA to get its intellectual house in order. David Finkelstein has described this as an "ongoing revolution in Chinese doctrinal affairs":

> The decade of the 1990s was a period of tremendous change for the Chinese People's Liberation Army. On nearly every front, this massive defense establishment was engaged in a myriad of reforms aimed at making it a more professional force in a corporate and institutional sense as well as a more operationally capable force. These changes affected every facet of the PLA—force structure, equipment, personnel reform, and yet another rectification of the defense research and development establishment, to name just a few. Of particular significance, the 1990s was also a decade of tremendous doctrinal ferment. . . . In 1999, after nearly a decade of study, research, and presumably experimentation in the field, a new and apparently large corpus of officially promulgated doctrinal guidance was issued . . . As a result, it appears the PLA intends to change how it thinks about the conduct of campaign-level operations.[16]

This effort has touched directly on the doctrinal and operational concepts of the Second Artillery. For the first time in 2005 there was a direct characterization of nuclear deterrence:

> [Nuclear deterrence] means the deterrent action and posture of taking nuclear force as a backup power to shock and contain the opponent by threatening to use nuclear weapons or determining to carry out nuclear counterattack. The essence of nuclear deterrence is to warn the opponent in advance [of] the possibility of using nuclear weapons or carrying out nuclear counterattack and the likely grave consequences as a result of taking this action, for the purpose of bringing about the opponent's dreadful mentality by his weighing the advantages against the disadvantages and the gain against the loss, so as to force him to obey the deterrer's volition or to give up his original attempts.[17]

Operational concepts associated with China's wartime use of its strategic forces have also been promulgated and published. These include:

1. "Absorb the first blow, counterattack, and re-attack as necessary." This is the practical translation of NFU into a concept of strategic campaign warfare.
2. "Counterdeterrence." This reflects China's view that there are two versions of deterrence, "one that is defensive and acceptable and one that is offensive and unacceptable." As an operational concept as opposed to a strategic function of the posture, this suggests that specific operations are to be conducted in crisis and war to achieve some additional purposes below.
3. "Key point counterstrikes." This is the use of retaliatory strikes to shock the enemy and degrade its military operations. The stated objectives of such strikes are (1) a heavy psychological shock and (2) a degradation of the enemy's operational military capabilities, explicitly including enemy nuclear forces, command and control, and "war potential."
4. "Demonstrate resolve." This is the use of retaliatory strikes to signal the political will of China to secure its objectives in conflict, including the objective of not acquiescing to coercion by a foreign power.
5. "Maintain control of the overall situation." This is the idea that political leaders will use military means to control the course of a conflict in ways that secure China's political objectives.[18]

The degree to which these operational concepts apply to nuclear missile operations specifically as opposed to missile operations generally is not readily apparent in the available literature. Some Chinese analysts have expressed the view informally that only the first two relate to the Second Artillery's nuclear missions, and the first only insofar as it spans counterattack but not also re-attack (which suggests extended operations and thus war-fighting strategies). On the other hand, the dividing line between conventional and nuclear doctrine is not at all clear to outsiders. Two knowledgeable Chinese authors have argued, "It is very hard to sub-define China's deterrence theory as nuclear or conventional, because the Chinese have always considered the process in a comprehensive strategic framework, of which nuclear weapons are only one component."[19]

The possible convergence of doctrine for conventional and nuclear campaigns raises a number of specific, troubling questions. First, conventional missile doctrine emphasizes the value of seizing the initiative. But seizing the initiative is more ambitious and difficult than "maintaining control." Evidently, seizing the initiative is seen as essential in a high-tech war against an enemy with superior war-fighting capabilities: "once armed conflict is inevitable, no effort should be spared to strive for strategic initiative." This has produced an increased emphasis at the conventional level on preemption as a way to minimize the costs of absorbing the first blow. It would be useful to know how much influence this might have on nuclear operational concepts.

Second, conventional missile doctrine emphasizes the need to attack the enemy's center of gravity. At the conventional level of war, Chinese writings describe the U.S. center of gravity as being its need to deploy forces into bases in the theater and its dependence on the military operational support of allies in East Asia. It would be useful to know whether such targets would be considered possible nuclear targets during a conflict, and under what circumstances.

Third, the PLA's new military doctrine more generally emphasizes the integration of military forces in joint campaigns. In describing the requirements of the strategic offensive, Chinese military writings describe the value of integrating strikes of many kinds to gain the desired psychological and operational effects. It would be useful to know whether Chinese planners conceive of integrating nuclear attack operations with other strategic offensive tools, such as information attack operations, operations by special forces behind enemy lines, and perhaps even space attack operations.

In reviewing these potential nuclear implications of the PLA's efforts to put its intellectual house in order, it is important to note also what is not found in PLA writings that might have been expected. There is no explicit discussion of using nuclear weapons to compensate for conventional weakness, or of using tactical nuclear weapons to deter major conventional aggression. Nor is there explicit writing on the use of nuclear weapons for damage limitation or other "nuclear war-fighting strategies." In the words of Chinese nuclear strategy expert Evan Medeiros, "they do not 'think the unthinkable' or possess the game-theoretic character of U.S. and Soviet writings during the Cold War. The PLA's most detailed, systematic, and technologically sophisticated writings focus on improving the survivability and penetrability of Second Artillery nuclear missile forces."[20]

As argued above, two factors have been central to the development of China's current strategic posture. The first is the PLA effort to get its intellectual house in order, as discussed above. The second is the emergence of the United States as the core challenge in China's nuclear planning environment. This is not to suggest that the United States is the only challenge; indeed, Chinese analysts describe a complex strategic landscape around China's periphery presenting many questions of nuclear stability.[21] But the United States is the most significant challenge by far, not least because, in Chinese eyes, the United States seeks to remake the strategic relationship with China so as to remove its vulnerability to China's counterdeterrence efforts.[22] Here is a representative sampling of Chinese expert reactions to the Bush administration's 2002 NPR:

> Among nuclear powers, the new nuclear strategy would have the greatest impact on China. China is among the seven nations listed as targets of an American nuclear strike. This is a great threat to China's security. The U.S. may use nuclear weapons to defend Taiwan. This will hinder Chinese reunification and thereby threaten Chinese core security. The U.S. has had absolutely military superiority over China. The buildup of the New Triad will further weaken the effectiveness of China's limited nuclear deterrent forces. Finally, the new American nuclear strategy exerts a significant influence on China's security interests.[23]

Similarly, an analyst at the Academy of Military Science raised direct objections about the Bush administration's *National Security Strategy* of 2002:

> The fundamental aim of the US national security strategy is to use the war against terrorism as the means to make full use of the current "period of strategic opportunity" of having no major country whose combined national strength can rival that of the US, and the balance of military forces in the world being seriously unbalanced, to seek the long-lasting and comprehensive political, economic, and military superiority in the new century and ensure and maintain the unipolar world under US hegemony. Actually, the US is seeking absolute superiority rather than absolute security in an effort to establish a balance of the strategic forces throughout the entire world with the US being the axis.[24]

These strongly worded reactions would suggest that China's expert community sees a sharp divide in American strategic thinking and policy demarcated by the publication of the 2002 NPR. This position does not take into account the fact that many Chinese experts see at least as much continuity as change in U.S. strategic thinking and policy in post-Cold War period. They perceive a United States that is much more willing to use force to support its foreign policy objectives than it was during the Cold War, when its room to maneuver was constrained by the Soviet Union. They also perceive antecedents to the new triad capabilities. After all, the U.S. desire for non-nuclear strategic strike options took clear shape in the 1980s. By the mid-1990s, the United States had launched the development of missile defense—first theater and then national. For two decades after the collapse of the Soviet Union, the United States has been remaking its intelligence and surveillance systems. Even the willingness to consider preemption and to talk about it openly at high levels of government has antecedents in the 1990s—and even earlier.[25]

Accordingly, China is concerned with modernizing its strategic posture so as to ensure its continued viability in the face of developments in the U.S. posture. But how (and how quickly) to transform that posture has apparently been a matter of considerable debate. Chinese experts caution that China does not seek an arms race with the United States. In the words of Xia Liping:

> China will not participate in a nuclear arms race with the United States. Firstly, it is unnecessary for China, because China only wants to maintain its minimum capability of retaliatory counterattack. Secondly, China still remembers the lessons of the former Soviet Union. Thirdly, China will be focused on its internal economic development for a long time.[26]

Yao Yunzhu has expressed the core idea somewhat differently: "To prevent the opponent's nuclear use is the only way to neutralize his nuclear superiority."[27]

But China's response to developments in the U.S. strategic posture is more than a simple matter of the number of deployed nuclear weapons. As one Chinese academic, Zhen Huang, has argued:

> Most likely, [China's] program will involve responses to U.S. missile defenses by increasing force levels so as to restore China's minimum deterrence. The problem is, this would still make the Chinese nuclear force

develop into an embryonic limited deterrent at the strategic level . . . For
the purpose of reconstructing minimum deterrence, China is not only
required to keep improving the survivability of its nuclear forces through
measures such as camouflage of deployment sites, development of solid
propellant and acquisition of mobile delivery systems as well as improvements in C4ISR (command, control, communication, computer, intelligence, surveillance, and reconnaissance) capabilities. More critically, it
is required to develop effective means to penetrate U.S. missile defense
structure so as to strike at least some major cities. It is in this connection
that China's nuclear force is likely to move to an initial limited deterrence
capability at the strategic level.[28]

A central question for China's political leaders is whether declaratory
policy must also change to help redress mounting concerns about the
credibility of the NFU pledge.[29] One concern is about the advent of
strategically significant long-range precision strike systems in the U.S.
strategic "tool kit"—strategically significant in the sense that they seem
to promise the possibility of preemption against China. If China is not
able to threaten the United States with a nuclear reply, as the argument goes, the United States might be emboldened to take military
action. Another concern is about the potential for military operations
of a potentially strategic kind against nonmilitary targets. For example,
some Chinese analysts wonder whether it might be necessary to threaten
some substantial retaliation for a military attack on the Three Gorges
dam that would leave millions of people dead and the economy in ruins.
Another concern expressed by some analysts is that China cannot expect
to fight and win across the Taiwan Strait against a U.S. military far superior at the conventional level; therefore, China must cover conventional
weakness with nuclear strength. Some of these views were summed up
in inflammatory public comments made by Chinese General Zhu in
July 2005:

If the Americans draw their missiles and position-guided ammunition on
to the target zone on China's territory, I think we will have to respond with
nuclear weapons. . . . We Chinese will prepare ourselves for the destruction
of all of the cities East of Xian; of course, the Americans will have to be
prepared that hundreds of cities will be destroyed by the Chinese.[30]

Even though Zhu was roundly attacked by some of his PLA counter-parts for making this statement,[31] these public comments brought to a head as a policy matter this long-simmering debate. Apparently senior political leadership felt compelled to review and assess the overall situation, reportedly concluding that any abandonment of NFU would be inconsistent with the "peaceful rise" premise and the main messages of China's foreign policy at the time.[32] As one PLA observer put it, "resorting to first-use . . . would arguably generate misgivings and anxiety in China's neighborhood."[33]

However, a related and highly important parallel message went out on this topic: because problems with the credibility of China's deterrent will not be dealt with by a change in declaratory policy, they must be dealt with in the technical and operational realms, with quantitative and qualitative improvements to Chinese nuclear forces.[34] This suggests that China's nuclear missile forces will be so modernized and transformed as to enable them to absorb a first blow from both U.S. nuclear and non-nuclear strategic strike systems in a way that they can still credibly threaten retaliation. This implies a variety of actions, taken separately or together, including an increase in the number of strike systems, their diversification, and an enhanced capacity to operate in a mobile and dispersed way, and to conduct operations in a way that minimizes China's exposure to preemption. But they must also have a capacity to counterattack and re-attack even after absorbing the first blow and to do so effectively penetrating whatever missile defenses the United States may have put in place. This too implies a variety of actions such as an increase in the number of deliverable warheads, the deployment of penetration aids, and the means to attack and defeat the defenses the Chinese might be trying to penetrate. Bruce Blair has argued that the most important changes likely to be generated in China's military forces due to developments in the U.S. strategic posture are at the conventional, not strategic, level, designed to redress the imbalance of forces that could make escalation seem necessary to either side.[35]

Whatever form the modernization takes, it is defended in China as consistent with "defensive deterrence" and necessary to preserve the status quo ante, meaning the status quo power relationships before the United States sought to improve its strategic "tool kit." As Yao Yunzhu has argued, "China's nuclear modernization is to keep valid its long-standing nuclear policy."[36] As an expert from the Institute for Applied Physics and Mathematics articulates:

> No first use is strategically reasonable because it reflects the confidence of China in its capability to fight conventional warfare and its confidence to deter nuclear attacks with a deterrence-only posture. . . . China should not and need not change its nuclear strategy. A shift to limited deterrence, war-fighting strategy will not happen. The nature of nuclear weapons has not changed, and nor have mainstream views about nuclear deterrence and China's nuclear strategy. A war-fighting strategy would be useless, dangerous, and wasteful.[37]

Western analysts in general put little stock in NFU pledges; they recall the deceit behind propagandistic Soviet pledges and do not believe that a promise of restraint would hold in a crisis in which nuclear use seems necessary for victory or to otherwise secure some vital interest. How much stock should they put in China's NFU pledge today? It seems to remain a significant restraint on the investment pattern in operational forces and the operational doctrine of the Second Artillery, which are ill equipped to strike first and survive the retaliation from any potential nuclear-armed adversary. Would it be honored in crisis? Some Chinese experts are adamant on this point, arguing that NFU encompasses both preemptive use and use in last resort. Others seem to leave the door slightly ajar. In the words of one Senior Colonel, "nuclear weapons, as 'an assassin's mace,' can be used at a time when China's core national security and development interests are fundamentally undermined."[38] He explicitly distinguishes this from a point about retaliation and deterrence and goes on to suggest that "China should further develop nuclear weapons in classified ways to enhance the flexibility of their strategy." A more detailed case with uncertain implications is made by Shanghai academic Shen Dingli:

> For decades, China's nuclear weapons have served core national interests: the nation's independence and survival. Over time, however, the core national interests have changed. China no longer has a survival problem . . . Presently, China's core national interest is national unification . . . It is not viable for China to ignore its core national interests indefinitely. If China's

conventional forces are devastated, and if Taiwan takes the opportunity to declare *de jure* independence, it is inconceivable that China would allow its nuclear weapons to be destroyed by a precision attack with conventional munitions, rather than use them as a true means of deterrence.[39]

In a not-for-attribution discussion of such matters, one well-informed Chinese expert offered the following additional views:

Leaders in both Washington and Beijing could plan a confrontation, should that be avoidable, with tools of conventional means as much as possible. However, China's side also believes that the purpose of its deterrence is to defend China's utmost legitimate national interests: survival of the nation, national unification, and prevention of its economy and society from collapsing due to external threat, etc. Therefore, when Beijing's "red lines" are truly triggered, its use of unconventional means shall be deemed by itself justified, morally and legally. Beijing tends to believe that this is self-plain and applicable to all nations. And even if Beijing were to first use nuclear weapons, if its deterrence fails, the responsibility for the disaster would remain with the one that brings harm to China and refuses to follow the fundamentals of deterrence.[40]

In sum, China's strategy of building and transforming the Second Artillery for emerging national requirements has brought many questions but so far has not dramatically reshaped any of the fundamentals from the earlier era. The commitment to "smash bullying" with a strategic posture that counters coercion remains a central organizing principle for China's nuclear force. Today, nuclear weapons are still described as "a type of political weapon and are valuable primarily for political reasons."[41] NFU and minimum deterrence remain in place, though under some pressure. The lack of transparency remains striking. Although the preceding review of available literature and expert opinion provides some remarkable insights into the ideas underpinning Chinese nuclear policy, it remains at best an indirect reflection. China's lack of openness is in stark contrast to the degree of openness shown by the other nuclear weapon states recognized by the Nuclear Nonproliferation Treaty (NPT). These fundamentals apparently remain valid in the eyes of China's current generation of leaders, despite the many ways in which the world has changed since they first took shape.

In trying to think through questions about the precise status of Chinese thinking, plans, and capabilities, we should recognize the distinction between secrets and mysteries. Some of the answers may be state secrets, knowable if the PRC leadership were to see transparency as in its interest. We should be wary of the publicly traded information that substitutes for such official statements, as it may vary considerably from the underlying reality. It is useful in this regard to recall the findings of the Silberman-Robb Commission on Weapons of Mass Destruction (WMD) intelligence that "we still know disturbingly little" about the WMD capabilities of even countries that have long been studied by U.S. intelligence services.[42] On the other hand, some of the answers to these questions may simply be mysteries unknown even by senior Chinese military and political leaders. Their precise plans for nuclear modernization may not yet be fully formulated or they may remain contingent on future developments of some kind. Furthermore, their operational plans for war cannot fully anticipate the kinds of interests and pressures at play in a crisis over Taiwan that unfolds under a nuclear shadow.

THE U.S. FACTOR

As a potential party to the conflict being explored here, the choices, policies, and forces of the United States would have something to do with the potential for, and character of, nuclear conflict over Taiwan.

Just as China's nuclear policies and forces emerged in a strategic environment different from that of today, so did those of the United States. The U.S. nuclear posture evolved in response to the requirements of containing the Soviet Union and of extended deterrence in Europe and Asia. The search for stability under mutual assured destruction (MAD) led to a highly competitive deployment of large numbers of weapons by the United States and Soviet Union, far beyond what the other nuclear weapon states deemed necessary. In short, the Cold War experience deeply informs U.S. instincts about NFU.

China was not irrelevant to this story, nor was it a central theme. China has been a changing factor in U.S. nuclear war planning.[43] It played a significant role in the decision to create a sea-based leg of the U.S. deterrent. The Clinton administration secured a mutual nontargeting agreement with China in 1998. At roughly the same time, new presidential guidance for U.S. nuclear forces was issued, which reportedly was interpreted by the U.S. military in a way to require bringing China back into nuclear war planning. Reportedly, it had been dropped from such plans during the warming of U.S.-PRC relations in the 1980s.

Like China, the United States has embarked on an effort to modernize and transform its strategic posture for the emerging security environment. The 2002 NPR is the watershed development in this regard, though as argued above, the NPR in some ways captured some essential continuities in U.S. strategic thinking since the end of the Cold War. The NPR reportedly identifies Taiwan as one of seven potential nuclear flashpoints and mentions China by name as a nuclear target.[44] This has caused many experts, both Chinese and American, to conclude that the NPR was "all about China"—a conviction reinforced by the nearly simultaneous appearance of a Quadrennial Defense Review that seemed to identify China as the United States' next peer competitor. One American has argued that "China is prominently featured in the NPR . . . China's strategic forces are increasingly supplanting Russia's arsenal as the primary benchmark for determining the size and capabilities of U.S. forces."[45]

Such interpretations miss the point that the NPR was the first exercise of the Bush administration's new capabilities-based planning effort. This is the effort to plan to develop future capabilities that can be useful in a broad spectrum of contingencies and not just in a narrow set against specific adversaries. It reflects the view that in a strategic environment shaped by uncertainty, the United States cannot know the identities of future adversaries or the nature of conflicts in which it will engage. It is also important to note that the NPR has attracted very little sustained high-level commitment from the Bush administration since it was issued. The leadership of the Defense Department has been seized by other troubles, and the president has not seen it as necessary or prudent to seize the bully pulpit to promote the nuclear transformation agenda envisioned there. The result, therefore, is that the old nuclear stockpile is getting whittled down with time in performance with Treaty of Moscow obligations, but little else has changed.

At present, U.S. nuclear policy remains largely unchanged. Chinese experts tend to interpret it as first use, because U.S. leaders reject NFU and indeed articulate a doctrine of preemption. But a better characterization of U.S. policy is calculated ambiguity. Such an approach is still understood as the best way to influence the deterrence calculus of potential adversaries. Some U.S. observers, however, believe that current U.S. war plans include specific nuclear contingencies over Taiwan.[46]

POTENTIAL FAILURES OF DETERRENCE

The preceding sections have briefly described Chinese and U.S. preparations for potential nuclear conflict over Taiwan. They illustrate the fact that both sides focus on ensuring the effectiveness of deterrence. This suggests that they have devoted less time and effort to thinking about and preparing for failures of deterrence and the challenges of restoring deterrence intrawar or terminating a war gone nuclear. What particular challenges might there be associated with managing the processes of nuclear escalation and de-escalation?

The apparent absence of thinking about how to cope with failures of deterrence and the dynamics of an escalating war over Taiwan may reflect a confidence that such crises can be well managed to contain or otherwise reduce risk. The historical record strongly suggests that this confidence would be misplaced. As a recent study of Sino-American crisis management experience concludes, the two have "a decidedly mixed record in effectively handling political-military crises."[47] Persistent problems include "a strong sense of mutual distrust, continued signaling problems, the tendency to display resolve through decisive action, and a proclivity to fall into the commitment trap. Other complicated features, such as growing popular nationalistic pressures and a more complex decision-making process in China, have emerged."[48] How might these challenges manifest themselves in the nuclear realm?

In the Cold War, answers to analogous questions in the U.S.-Soviet strategic relationships developed over years of dialogue at the official and unofficial levels. That dialogue commenced seriously only after the Cuban missile crisis generated a significant scare. In the present U.S.-China circumstance, such dialogue has been virtually nonexistent.

Nuclear dialogue at the official level and through military-to-military dialogue has gotten almost no traction over the years. There has been more dialogue at the unofficial level, but the sensitivity of the issue has made it difficult to begin and sustain a substantive dialogue among experts. In spite of these limitations, some preliminary conclusions are warranted on the basis of these interactions, in part because Chinese analysts have been forthcoming in not-for-attribution workshops where such matters have been up for discussion. The insights I have gained are collected around four main questions about a potential U.S.-China nuclear conflict over Taiwan[49]:

1. In a China-U.S. military confrontation over Taiwan, where would the burden of escalation fall?
2. Would the state facing the burden choose to escalate by nuclear means?
3. Would the further dynamic of escalation be manageable?
4. How might such a war be terminated?

The insights provide some confirmation that the problems generally evident in U.S.-PRC crisis management experience would be encountered in a nuclear conflict as well.

Where Would the Burden of Escalation Fall?

U.S. experts widely believe that the burden of escalation would fall on China. They perceive an imbalance of military power that favors the United States in both the conventional and strategic dimensions. Accordingly, they see China as doomed to rapid military defeat in any effort to project power across the Taiwan Strait. They expect that Beijing would rapidly come to face a choice between escalation and defeat.

U.S. declaratory policy does, however, acknowledge the possibility that this calculation may prove incorrect. The United States retains the right to use nuclear weapons in the extreme circumstance in which a vital interest is somehow jeopardized by an unexpected defeat of its conventional power projection forces. But in the U.S. expert community, essentially nobody takes as a serious possibility that the United States would use nuclear weapons first.

PRC experts, however, seem to believe that the burden of escalation would fall on the United States. They emphasize a different imbalance—between China's local power and America's global role. They argue that China can pick a moment for war when the United States cannot respond rapidly because of commitments elsewhere. Some believe that it is possible for China to achieve a political and military *fait accompli* in Taiwan that the United States could contemplate reversing only at a very high cost. This is the underlying logic of China's NFU pledge. As one senior PLA officer has argued, "China's objective is to so prepare that it doesn't have to use nuclear weapons because that would be suicide—the U.S. is the one that would have to use or lose."[50] The U.S. China Economic and Security Review Commission has echoed this perception, arguing that "China's leaders believe that the United States, although technologically superior in almost every area of military power, can be defeated, most particularly in a fight over Taiwan in which China controls the timing."[51]

Would the Burdened State Choose to Escalate by Nuclear Means?

American experts are well aware that China has the capacity to escalate a conflict by both nuclear and non-nuclear means. American experts tend to assume that China would have a preference for non-nuclear escalation if faced with the burden of escalation. But what if non-nuclear means fail to cause the United States and/or its East Asian allies to back down from confrontation? Would China then escalate by nuclear means? Among U.S. experts, the common view is that China might well do so, if clearly faced with a choice between losing and escalation in a war against the United States over Taiwan.

Four ideas inform this perception. First, American experts are doubtful that the Chinese Communist Party (CCP) could retain its grip on power if it were to back down from a confrontation with the United States over Taiwan, and thus would be compelled politically to escalate. Second, U.S. experts have heard some Chinese experts express the view that there might be ways for China to employ nuclear weapons that fall beneath the U.S. retaliation threshold (for example, the use of a nuclear device over a carrier battle group to generate electromagnetic pulse).

Third, the United States has been exposed to Chinese doctrine in which the role of actions early in a conflict to shock the enemy and create a decisive military circumstance is prominent. Fourth, China continues to send signals that NFU is not absolute.

In short, U.S. experts are ready to believe that China's interests, as the regime perceives them, may compel it to escalate by nuclear means and thus to set aside the NFU pledge in times of war. U.S. experts hope that the risk of U.S. nuclear retaliation would give Chinese leaders good enough reason not to choose nuclear escalation if faced with this burden. But there is disagreement about whether deterrence would outweigh the cumulative effect of the four factors cited above.

Among Chinese experts, there seem to be some contradictory views. Some believe that the United States would choose to use nuclear weapons first in a situation of escalate-or-lose and find evidence for this position in the U.S. refusal to embrace NFU, the Bush doctrine of preemption and preventive war, and their interpretation of the 2002 NPR as seeking improved nuclear war-fighting capabilities. Other Chinese experts also seem confident that China's capacity to retaliate by nuclear means would induce the United States not to give in to that impulse.

Would Further Dynamics of Escalation be Manageable?

Much analytic work has emphasized the unpredictable nature of nuclear escalation and the likelihood that such wars would spin out of control and result in circumstances in which everyone loses. But some experts have seen nuclear wars as potentially manageable in the sense that they can be fought in a way that secures vital interests and inflicts decisive defeat on the enemy. U.S. experts generally believe that the U.S. ability to manage such a competitive process is superior to that of China. This confidence has two sources. One is the dominance of U.S. strategic forces at any level of nuclear escalation that China might choose. The other is America's success in navigating many crises under the nuclear shadow with the USSR and, more recently, crises with other states under the WMD shadow.[52]

There is an important camp that dissents from this view: the advocates of ballistic missile defense. In their view, crises with nuclear enemies are inherently unmanageable because they require that the United States do the wrong thing or stop short of its goals because it is vulnerable to the threats from "rogues." Thus, they see achievement of a full and effective New Triad of offense, defense, and infrastructure capabilities as the only way to ensure that the United States will be able to weather such crises to its advantage.

A similar confidence seems to inform the thinking of some Chinese analysts about China's ability to cope with the demands of nuclear escalation. The confidence stems not from escalation dominance but escalation uncertainty—that is, from China's ability to impose costs upon the United States at whatever level of escalation the United States chooses, and thus to leave the United States uncertain about what level of pain it might have to bear. No Chinese analyst has argued to me that China could "control" such a war, but some have expressed the view that China could secure its vital interests in a war with the United States that has gone nuclear by manipulating U.S. risk perceptions. There is, however, a Chinese debate about whether the need to secure China's vital interests in such a war requires new technical capabilities to employ China's nuclear forces more effectively in a nuclear conflict (including early warning of attack and more robust command and control).[53]

How Might Such a War Be Terminated?

This is a topic that seems to attract the least attention among experts in either country. Perhaps, as Herman Kahn argued, this is the truly unthinkable part of an unthinkable problem. More likely, however, is that the mutual focus on deterrence, and the apparent confidence that it will work, leaves policy makers convinced that this is a problem not worthy of attention.

Regardless, some views have apparently taken hold. U.S. experts seem generally to believe that a war over Taiwan that has gone nuclear would end only with China conceding defeat—and having paid a heavy price. American experts believe that a war gone nuclear over Taiwan would create vital interests for the United States well beyond the interests in Taiwan that were involved in the opening phase of such a war. A war in which nuclear weapons are used against the United States or its allies would be a war calling into fundamental question the value and credibility of U.S.

security guarantees and its role as a defender of democracy. Any U.S. concession in the face of nuclear threats and attacks would be energetically attacked by those Americans offended by the perception that the United States had appeased a nuclear bully. In addition, a war in which the United States uses nuclear weapons would raise fundamental questions about the purposes of American power and the future global nuclear order. The United States would want to answer such questions in ways that reassure U.S. allies and friends. Hence, in this view, the burden of concession would fall on China.

Among Chinese experts, an opposite view seems to exist. Among those who have talked about this problem, there seems to be a general view that such a war would end only with the United States conceding defeat. The asymmetry of stake and interest between China and the United States in a Taiwan contingency would only be magnified in a war that crosses the nuclear threshold. Therefore, their argument goes, the United States would inevitably concede because its interests are not as vital as those of China. But some Chinese experts have also expressed the view attributed above to American experts: a war gone nuclear would create such a vital interest for the United States that the old logic of asymmetric stakes is no longer valid, leading them to conclude that such a war could be a catastrophe for China.

IMPLICATIONS OF DIFFERENT PERCEPTIONS IN CRISIS

This review of thinking and debate within our expert communities suggests that analysts in the two countries have very different ideas about the dynamics of nuclear confrontation over Taiwan. Their analyses proceed from different assumptions about how the other country would act in such a conflict. Yet these two bodies of thinking seem to have something in common: confidence. Analysts in both countries seem generally confident of their nation's ability to identify and manage nuclear risks in war—despite the abundant lessons of the past cited above.

In my view, there are two problems with this confidence. First, there seems to be no reason to think that this confidence is the result of rigorous testing and debate among analysts whose thinking may differ. Two American academics have coined the term "group think" to describe the effects of the pressure in a group to conform to group values and ideas.[54] The result of "group think" is policy that looks good because there was no permission to probe for flaws and that also feels good because it confirms preexisting beliefs. Is the confidence seemingly reflected in the thinking of Chinese and American experts a result of deep, sustained investigation or merely a result of "group think"? In the U.S.-Soviet experience, the potent effect of "group think" on nuclear strategy did not become clear until their confidence in their crisis management theories was badly shaken by the Cuban missile crisis.

Second, misplaced confidence can lead to miscalculations in war. Given the very different ideas and expectations evident in the survey of thinking above, the ideas of one country, and perhaps both, could be proven wrong in war; this could occur as a result of decisions taken that miscalculate the response of the enemy. The possibility of significant miscalculation may be another part of the nuclear "shadow" in the sense that it reduces the willingness to go to war. But if the possibility is not recognized, it cannot have a restraining effect.

Where does the particular risk of overconfidence and miscalculation lie? It resides in the belief that strong action will induce the enemy to exercise restraint. In a war over Taiwan in which nuclear weapons have been used by one side or both, China and the United States would face essentially the same challenge—to convince the other that the rising costs of war have only strengthened its resolve to secure its interests (as opposed to breaking that resolve). Hence Chinese military doctrine puts significant emphasis on employing re-attacks to demonstrate resolve and maintain overall control and initiative; U.S. military doctrine puts significant emphasis on employing forces in ways that underscore the credibility of U.S. threats. If China and the United States face the same challenge, they face also the same dilemma: Actions taken to demonstrate resolve and credibility may induce not restraint by the enemy but an intensification of conflict. Such intensification would result from a calculus that more decisive actions are necessary to bring an escalating conflict to a rapid conclusion on favorable terms. Each of our actions might be intended to signal "don't escalate further" but might be interpreted by the other as signaling "escalate or lose a vital interest."

It is important to recognize also a potential third source of instability in a U.S.-PRC crisis over Taiwan: Taiwan itself. Taiwan has its own developing capabilities for strategic strike and its own well-documented prior nuclear ambitions. Over the years, leaders in Taipei have hinted at nuclear weapons ambitions. In 1994, Lee Teng-hui, Taiwan's then president, stated that Taiwan had planned to acquire nuclear weapons in the past and suggested further "we should re-study the question from a long-term point of view."[55] The United States reportedly has pressured Taiwan over the years to refrain from seeking to acquire nuclear weapons and the requisite technologies and material.[56] Thus in July 1995, Lee Teng-hui promised not to pursue nuclear weapons.[57] Expert Gerald Segal has described Taiwan's nuclear strategy as one of "nervous and intense ambiguity."[58] In the summer of 1998, Segal reported assertions by Taiwanese officials that "existing weapons-grade materials could be weaponized in three to four months."[59] However, the quantities available must be sharply constrained by the fact that Taiwan possesses neither enrichment nor reprocessing facilities. From Beijing's perspective, any such actions would be a casus belli.

CONCLUSIONS

What role might nuclear weapons play in a Taiwan contingency? In a crisis, both China and the United States might reasonably be expected to attempt to cast a nuclear shadow over a mounting crisis as a way to induce restraint by the other side and reach a resolution short of war. In war, both sides seem to want neither to use nuclear weapons nor to rule them out entirely. This analysis suggests that the most likely route to actual nuclear employment would be through miscalculation and miscommunication. This potentiality greatly underscores the need to so manage the situation between Taiwan, mainland China, and the United States in a way that further reduces the likelihood of war.

NOTES

1. This chapter draws on a small but growing literature from Chinese authors from military and academic institutions that provides insights into Chinese thinking and planning. It is difficult to gauge the veracity of such insights, given the closed

nature of Chinese military planning. Many of the Chinese views presented here were expressed in conferences or in office visits under not-for-attribution ground rules. The resulting compendium of ideas should be taken as well informed but not authoritative. To the extent any judgments or conclusions are represented here, they are those of the author and should not be attributed to any institution with which he is affiliated.

2. "Statement of the Government of the People's Republic of China," October 16, 1964. For more on the genesis of China's nuclear weapons program, see John Wilson Lewis and Xue Litai, *China Builds the Bomb* (Stanford, Calif.: Stanford University Press, 1988).

3. The citation is from the memoirs of Marshall Nie Rongzhen, one of the leaders of China's nuclear weapons program. Cited in Jeffrey G. Lewis, *The Minimum Means of Reprisal: China's Search for Security in the Nuclear Age* (Cambridge, Mass.: MIT Press, 2007), p. 1 (hereafter cited as Lewis, *The Minimum Means of Reprisal*).

4. This view was expressed on a not-for-attribution basis during a visit to the Institute for Applied Physics and Mathematics in Beijing in spring 2005.

5. Yao Yunzhu, "Chinese Nuclear Policy and the Future of Minimum Deterrence," a discussion paper prepared for a U.S.-China Strategic Dialogue, cohosted by the Naval Postgraduate School and Pacific Forum CSIS, Honolulu, Hawaii, August 1–3, 2005. Yao is a senior colonel in the PLA and is director of the Asia-Pacific Office in the Department of World Military Studies of the Academy of Military Science. For an online summary of that dialogue, see http://www.ccc.nps.navy.mil/events/recent/ChinaConferenceAug05_rpt.asp.

6. Zhang Junbo and Yao Yunzhu, "Differences Between Traditional Chinese and Western Military Thinking and Their Philosophical Roots," *Journal of Contemporary China* 5, no. 12 (1996): 221. At the time of writing, Zhang was major general and president of the political academy of the PLA.

7. *Annual Report on the Military Power of the People's Republic of China* (Washington, D.C.: U.S. Department of Defense, 2006), p. 29.

8. This point is brought home in Lewis, *The Minimum Means of Reprisal*, p. 201.

9. "Jiang Zemin Defines Position of China's Strategic Nuclear Weapons," *Hong Kong Tai Yang Pao*, July 17, 2000, FBIS CPP200000727000021.

10. Bates Gill, James Mulvenon, and Mark Stokes, "The Chinese Second Artillery Corps: Transition to Credible Deterrence," in James C. Mulvenon and Andrew N. D. Yang, eds., *The People's Liberation Army as Organization* (Santa Monica, Calif.: RAND Corporation, 2002), pp. 510–86. This characterization of the Chinese missile force is not universally accepted among U.S. analysts of that force. Some see the theater nuclear force as having solely a deterrent function akin to the long-range force and none of the war-fighting function of the conventional missile force.

11. Charles Ferguson, Evan S. Medeiros, and Phillip G. Saunders, "Chinese Tactical Nuclear Weapons," in Alistair Millar and Brian Miller, eds., *Tactical Nuclear Weapons: Emergent Threats in an Evolving Security Environment* (London: Brassey's, 2003), pp. 110–28.

12. The report itself was classified and not released to the public, though a leaked version was posted on various web sites. See Hearings, Senate Armed Services Committee, February 14, 2002; and the briefing on "Findings of the *Nuclear Posture Review*," January 9, 2002, www.defenselink.mil. The third "leg" of this "new triad" remains ill-defined. But the core idea seems to be that the capacity for competition is a strategic capacity, one that should be tailored to dissuade others who might seek such competition by convincing them that they cannot benefit from such competition (by gaining some sort of military advantage) and will only become increasingly disadvantaged in whatever competition that might begin (as, for example, a buildup of nuclear weapons in the hope of gaining supremacy).

13. *Annual Report on the Military Power of the People's Republic of China, 2006.*

14. Brad Roberts, "China and Ballistic Missile Defense: 1955 to 2002 and Beyond," Paper P-3826 (Alexandria, Va.: Institute for Defense Analyses, 2003), pp. 7–8.

15. In the words of Jiang Zemin, "We must pay attention to the global situation of strategic balance and stability and, where there are changes in the situation, adjust our strategic nuclear weapon development strategy in a timely matter." "Jiang Zemin Defines Position of China's Strategic Nuclear Weapons," Hong Kong Tai Yang Pao, July 17, 2000.

16. David M. Finkelstein, "Prologue," in James Mulvenon and David M. Finkelstein, eds., *China's Revolution in Doctrinal Affairs: Emerging Trends in the Operational Art of the Chinese People's Liberation Army* (Alexandria, Va.: CNA Corp., December 2005), pp. xi–xii.

17. Peng Guangqian and Yao Youzhi, eds., *The Science of Military Strategy* (Beijing: Military Science Publishing House, 2005), p. 217.

18. Ibid. See also Michael S. Chase and Evan S. Medeiros, "China's Evolving Nuclear Calculus," and Evan S. Medeiros, "Minding the Gap: Assessing the Trajectory of the PLA's Strategic Missile Forces," a paper prepared for a conference on "Exploring the 'Right Size' for China's Military: PLA Missions, Functions, and Organization," U.S. Army War College, Carlisle, Penn., October 6–8, 2006 (hereafter cited as Medeiros, "Minding the Gap").

19. Zhang and Yao, "Differences Between Traditional Chinese and Western Military Thinking and Their Philosophical Roots," p. 216.

20. Medeiros, "Minding the Gap," p. 9.

21. This argument was presented by a senior PLA official at a conference on U.S.-China Nuclear Dynamics in Beijing in June 2006 and co-organized by the Center for Strategic and International Studies (CSIS), the RAND Corporation, and

the Institute for Defense Analyses (IDA) in partnership with the Foundation for International Strategic Studies, Beijing. A summary of key insights can be found at: http://www.csis.org/media/csis/events/060620_china_nuclear_report.pdf (accessed April 16, 2007).

22. For an elaboration of this argument, see Wang Zhongchun, "Nuclear Challenges and China's Choices," *China Security* (Winter 2007), pp. 52–65.

23. Tian Jingmei, "The Bush Administration's Nuclear Strategy and Its Implications for China's Security," a working paper of the Center for International Security and Cooperation, Stanford University, March 2003. The author is an associated professor at the Institute of Applied Physics and Computational Mathematics in Beijing.

24. Chen Zhou, "US Security Strategy and East Asia," FBIS CPP20021210000027, December 10, 2002.

25. This point is made in a somewhat indirect way by Keir A. Lieber and Daryl G. Press, "U.S. Nuclear Primary and the Future of the Chinese Deterrent," *China Security* (Winter 2007): 66–89.

26. Xia Liping, "China's Nuclear Policy and Nuclear Disarmament," unpublished research paper (Autumn 2002), p. 11. Xia is director and professor of the Center for International Strategic Studies at the Shanghai Institute for International Studies. See also Li Bin, Zhao Baogen, and Liu Zhiwei, "China Will Have to Respond," *Bulletin of Atomic Scientists* 57, no. 6: 25–28.

27. Yao, "Chinese Nuclear Policy and the Future of Minimum Deterrence," p. 6.

28. Zhen Huang, "China's Strategic Nuclear Posture by 2010: Minimum or Limited Deterrence? Likely Impact of U.S. Missile Defense," paper prepared for the 8th ISODARCO-Beijing Seminar on Arms Control, Beijing, China, October 14–18, 2002.

29. The following points are drawn from various conversations with Chinese analysts over many years but most recently at the June 2006 CSIS-RAND-IDA workshop cited above. For further discussion, see also the chapter by James Mulvenon in this volume; Shen Dingli, "Nuclear Deterrence in the 21st Century," *China Security* 1 (Autumn 2005): 10–14 (hereafter cited as Shen Dingli, "Nuclear Deterrence in the 21st Century"); and Sun Xiangli, "China's Nuclear Strategy," *China Security* 1 (Autumn 2005): 23–27.

30. Joseph Kahn, "Chinese General Threatens Use of A-Bombs if U.S. Intrudes," *New York Times*, July 15, 2005, p. A-1.

31. In the words of another PLA general, "General Zhu has raised the wrong theme at the wrong place and at the wrong time. Zhu's problem lies in a failure to see the value of No-First-Use in China's nuclear policy as well as the consequences should China dispense with it." Pan Zhenqiang, "China Insistence on No-First-Use of Nuclear Weapons," *China Security* 1 (Autumn 2005): 5–9. Pan is a retired Major General serving as a professor at the Institute for Strategic Studies of the PLA's National Defense University.

32. These reports were provided in various informal channels, including the Track 1.5 and Track 2 activities noted above.

33. Pan, "China's Insistence on No-First-Use of Nuclear Weapons," p. 7.

34. Again, these messages were reported to the American expert community informally in not-for-attribution workshops.

35. Bruce Blair, "Chinese Nuclear Preemption," *China Security* 1 (Autumn 2005): 12–22.

36. Yao, "Chinese Nuclear Policy and the Future of Minimum Deterrence," p. 8.

37. From a discussion paper prepared for a not-for-attribution workshop in July 2005.

38. Wang Zhongchun, "Nuclear Challenges and China's Choices," p. 61.

39. Shen Dingli, "Nuclear Deterrence in the 21st Century," p. 13.

40. Comment made in 2005.

41. As cited in Wang Wenrong, ed., *Zhanluexue* [The Science of Strategy] (Beijing: Guofang Daxue Chubanshe, 1999), p. 348. This volume is an examination of strategy published by China's National Defense University and should be understood as a teaching text offering indirect insights into official thinking. For a detailed discussion of this and some related Chinese publications on campaign theory, see Michael S. Chase and Evan Medeiros, "China's Evolving Nuclear Calculus: Modernization and Doctrinal Debate," in James Mulvenon and David M. Finkelstein, eds., *China's Revolution in Doctrinal Affairs: Emerging Trends in the Operational Art of the Chinese People's Liberation Army* (Alexandria, Va.: CNA Corp, 2005), pp. 119–58.

42. See *Report to the President of the United States, The Commission on the Intelligence Capabilities of the United States Regarding Weapons of Mass Destruction*, March 31, 2005. The quotation is from the cover letter to the president.

43. The following points are drawn from Hans M. Kristensen, Robert S. Norris, and Matthew McKinzie, *Chinese Nuclear Forces and U.S. Nuclear War Planning* (Washington, D.C.: Natural Resources Defense Council and the Federation of American Scientists, 2006).

44. These oft-reported facts are attributed to versions of the NPR—a classified document—that were leaked and are available on numerous web sites.

45. Lewis, *The Minimum Means of Reprisal*, p. 143.

46. In addition to the previous reference, see also William M. Arkin, "America's New China War Plan," *Washington Post*, May 24, 2006.

47. Michael D. Swaine and Zhang Tuosheng, eds., *Managing Sino-American Crises: Case Studies and Analyses* (Washington, D.C.: Carnegie Endowment, 2006), p. 424.

48. Ibid.

49. The views reported here are as recorded and interpreted by this author. The analysis cannot be defended in a fully systematic manner because circumstances do not make this possible. However, interlocutors on both the Chinese and American sides have included some high-level and well-informed individuals and the insights have been collected from roughly a dozen not-for-attribution workshops since

2000 and in office visits with individuals in many of China's leading institutions on matters of nuclear policy. This suggests that the observations that follow provide at least a logical starting point for further discussion.

50. Comment made in a not-for-attribution workshop in Honolulu in November 2006.

51. *Report to the Congress of the United States, China Security Review Commission, July 2002*, chap. 1.

52. The cases sometimes offered in support of this proposition are the war to evict Iraqi military force from Kuwait and the civil wars in the former Yugoslavia, each of which proceeded in an environment of potential use of chemical and/or biological weapons.

53. For further discussion of degrees of confidence in managing a crisis over Taiwan, see Swaine and Zhang, *Managing Sino-American Crises*, pp. 437–43.

54. L.L. Janis and L. Mann, *Decision Making: A Psychological Analysis of Conflict, Choice, and Commitment* (New York: Free Press, 1977). For purposes of this essay, it is useful to recall the eight main symptoms that they identified: illusion of invulnerability, collective rationalization, illusion of morality, excessive stereotyping, pressure for conformity, self-censorship, illusion of unanimity, and mindguards (self-appointed protectors against adverse information).

55. His comments came in response to the PLA's firing of ballistic missiles across the Taiwan Strait, described at the time by officials in Beijing as a test of new systems but broadly interpreted as aimed at influencing the political debate in Taipei. See Alice Hung, "Taiwan: Taiwan Says It Will Study Need for Nuclear Arsenal," Reuters, July 28, 1995.

56. David Albright and Corey Gay, "Taiwan: Nuclear Nightmare Avoided," *Bulletin of the Atomic Scientists* 54, no. 1 (January/February 1998): 54–60.

57. Cited in Joyce Liu, "Taiwan Won't Make Nuclear Weapons, Says President," Reuters, July 31, 1995. See also Walter Pincus, "Investigators Now Focusing on Lee's Ties to Taiwan," *Washington Post*, December 24, 2000, pp. A-3, 14.

58. Gerald Segal, "Taiwan's Nuclear Card," *Asian Wall Street Journal*, August 4, 1998.

59. As reported in ibid.

9

PRC Information Operations
Myths, Trends, and New Opportunities

James Mulvenon

AN IMPORTANT ELEMENT of the Chinese People's Liberation Army's (PLA) capabilities and doctrine, information operations (IO), is in a period of fascinating dynamism, driven by doctrinal innovation and technological breakthroughs. This chapter does not describe the subject in detail, because many of the key organizational and force structure issues have been given comprehensive treatment in previous works.[1] Instead, this chapter is more topical, addressing current debates. To correct some lingering misperceptions, for instance, the chapter identifies and analyzes three widely held myths in the literature on Chinese IO. The chapter concludes with a discussion of the strategic and operational implications and opportunities presented by the preceding analysis.

THREE MYTHS OF CHINESE INFORMATION OPERATIONS

> **MYTH:** Prolific authors such as Shen Weiguang, Zhang Zhaozhong, Wang Xiangsui, and Qiao Liang are significant players in Chinese IO.

> **REALITY:** Book sales and media profile appear inversely related to influence in the Chinese IO world, and some of the Chinese authors best known in the West are among the least credible sources of insights about military thinking on the subject.

The most widely published Chinese authors on IO are Shen Weiguang, Zhang Zhaozhong, and Qiao Liang/Wang Xiangsui.[2] The profligacy of their published works creates the mistaken impression outside of China that they wield important sway over internal Chinese thinking on the subject.[3] In fact, interviews suggest that these analysts are the least influential on the Chinese IO policy process, except to the extent that their writings play back into the system via leadership reading habits.[4] In terms of content, their books also tend to focus on offensive IO using capabilities at the cutting edge (that in some cases violate either Chinese government policy or the laws of physics), which is in sharp contrast to available *junnei* or *neibu* writings on IO that emphasize the importance of computer network defense and information assurance. Given this variance, one naturally looks to the motivations of the authors, which seem driven primarily by financial gain and personal self-aggrandizement.[5]

Regardless of their impetus, however, the publication of the books themselves does affect external views of China's propensity to use IO. While Shen or Qiao/Wang's books may not have been written for perception management reasons initially, there is some evidence to suggest that Beijing has used the publicity surrounding their books to shape foreign perceptions. For example, admiring interviews with the authors Qiao/Wang appeared in 1999 in *Zhongguo Qingnianbao*[6] and two publications with a long track record of serving as an unofficial channel for government messages—*Ta Kung Pao*[7] and *Liaowang*[8]—despite the fact that the book advocates policies at clear variance with Chinese government policy. A *Washington Post* profile piece on Qiao/Wang by John Pomfret during the same period enhanced the effect.[9] More interesting, the articles appeared at the same time that the two authors were undergoing internal criticism sessions at the Academy of Military Sciences and a Ministry of Foreign Affairs think tank.[10]

Why the discontinuity? For deterrence purposes, it is arguably in Beijing's interests to allow the U.S. security community to think that Beijing has a lower threshold than it actually does for the use of strategic-level IO, while plausibly disavowing the authors, as was done in June 2000 in a critical article again in *Ta Kung Pao*.[11] Indeed, I cannot give a briefing on Chinese IO for military or intelligence community (IC) audiences in the United States without someone asking me about *Unrestricted Warfare* and expressing disbelief that "active duty" military officers could publish material contradicting Chinese policy. They naturally conclude that these books are shadows on the cave wall of China's hidden, global IO policy, not the work of two air force political commissars divorced from the Beijing IO policy community. If Beijing's intent was to inject their memes[12] into the system, then job well done.

MYTH: Before and during a Taiwan scenario, Chinese military hackers will seek to intrude and exploit *classified* U.S. networks.

REALITY: The Chinese military seeks to delay U.S. military intervention by disrupting unclassified networks such as the NIPRNET, while carrying out attacks against Taiwan critical infrastructure.

In the mind of the Chinese leadership, the available evidence suggests that the most important political-military challenge and the most likely flashpoint for Sino-U.S. conflict is Taiwan. In seeking to reunify the island with the mainland, however, it is important to note that the People's Republic of China (PRC) has a political strategy with a military component, not a military strategy with a political component. The PRC would prefer to win without fighting, because Beijing's worst-case outcome is a failed operation that would result in de facto independence for Taiwan. Also, the leadership realizes that attacking Taiwan with kinetic weapons would result in significant international opprobrium and make the native population ungovernable. These assumptions explain why China has generally maintained a "wait and see" attitude toward Taiwan, even though the island elected a president from a party committed to independence. From 2000 until late 2003, China eschewed saber rattling in favor of economic enticement and "united front" cooperation with the Pan-Blue opposition, both of which were believed to be working successfully. In November 2003, in response to perceived provocations by Taiwan President Chen Shui-bian, Beijing once again revived the threat of military force to deter what it saw as further slippage toward independence, which dramatically increased tensions in the United States-China-Taiwan triangle. Yet such threats subsided again after the U.S. intervened vigorously to deter Chen from further actions.

Should the situation deteriorate into direct military conflict, the PLA has been hard at work since 1992, bolstering the hedging options of the leadership, developing advanced campaign doctrines, testing the concepts in increasingly complex training and exercises, and integrating new indigenous and imported weapons systems. At the strategic level, the writings of Chinese military authors suggest that there are two main centers of gravity in a Taiwan scenario. The first of these is the will of the Taiwanese people, which they hope to undermine through exercises, missile attacks, special operations forces (SOF) operations, and other operations that have a psychological operation (PSYOP) focus. Based on intelligence from the 1995–1996 exercises, as well as public opinion polling in Taiwan, China appears to have concluded that the Taiwanese people do not have the stomach for conflict and will therefore sue for peace after only a small amount of suffering.

The second center of gravity is the will and capability of the United States to intervene decisively in a cross-strait conflict. In a strategic sense, China has traditionally believed that its intercontinental ballistic missile (ICBM) inventory, which is capable of striking the continental United States (CONUS), will serve as a deterrent to U.S. intervention, or at least a brake on escalation. Closer to Taiwan, the PLA has been engaged in an active program of equipment modernization, purchasing niche anti-access, area-denial capabilities, such as long-range cruise missiles and sub-marines, to shape the operational calculus of the American carrier battle group commander on station. At the same time, a key lesson learned from analyzing U.S. military operations since Operation Desert Storm was the vulnerability of the U.S. logistics and deployment system.

Center of Gravity Number One: The Will of the People on Taiwan

Chinese strategies to manipulate the national psychology of the populace and leadership on Taiwan involve the full spectrum of IO, including psychological operations, special operations, computer network operations (CNO), and intelligence operations. To this end, Beijing can employ all of the social, economic, political, and military tools of Chinese comprehensive national power (CNP), as well as enlist the assistance of private sector players and sympathetic co-conspirators on Taiwan. The goal of these efforts is to shake the widely perceived psychological fragility of the populace, causing the government to prematurely capitulate to political negotiations with the mainland. In a sense, China seeks to use the immaturity of Taiwanese democracy against itself.

Analysis of both Beijing's strategies in this arena as well as Taipei's ability to resist such methods confirms Taiwan's high-level vulnerability to Chinese soft coercion. The analysis also raises major questions about the island's viability in the opening phase of a PRC coercion campaign, Taiwan's credibility as a keeper of U.S. secrets and source of intelligence information about the mainland, and its expected ability to interoperate successfully with U.S. forces in a crisis.

Taiwan's vulnerabilities in the critical infrastructure protection arena can be divided into two categories: informational and physical. On the information side, Taiwan is a highly information-dependent society with a relatively low level of information or computer security. Significant disruptions in information systems could have major negative effects on the island, particularly in the economic and financial realms, and increase fear and panic among the population. Past Chinese uses of regional media to send psychological operations messages have also enjoyed success in affecting popular morale and public opinion. For example, an Internet rumor in 1999 that a Chinese Su-27 had shot down a Taiwan aircraft caused the Taipei stock market to drop more than 2 percent in less than four hours.

On the physical side of the equation, Taiwan's current capability and readiness level is much lower than one might expect for a state under such a direct level of threat, especially when compared with other "national security states" such as Israel or South Korea. Critical infrastructure protection has been a low priority for the government, and Taiwan is acutely vulnerable to Spetsnaz-like or fifth-column operations, aided significantly by ethnic and linguistic homogeneity and significant cross-border flows, which facilitate entry and access to potential targets. In terms of civilian infrastructure, Taiwan's telecommunications, electric power, and transportation infrastructure are all highly susceptible to sabotage. These weaknesses have been indirectly exposed by periodic natural disasters, such as the September 1999 earthquake and the September 2001 typhoon, when the communications infrastructure effectively collapsed. Taiwan's ports, including Su'ao, Jeelung, and Gaoxiong (the third highest volume container port in the world), are attractive targets. Port charts and ship movements are available on the Internet, and Gaoxiong in particular has two narrow mouths that could easily be blocked with scuttled vessels. Taiwan's highways are a vulnerable bottleneck, particularly given the large number of undefended mountain tunnels and bridges that could be destroyed by SOF units. Finally, the power grid is known to be fragile, marked by numerous single-point failure nodes and no cross-hatching of subgrids to form redundancy. The loss of a single tower in the central mountainous region, due to a landslide, knocked out 90 percent of the grid a couple of years ago, and delays in construction of a fourth nuclear plant have constrained capacity.

SOF and fifth column are also a major threat for disruption of military command and control and decapitation of the national command authority, as well as providing reconnaissance for initial missile and air strikes and battle damage assessments (BDA) for follow-on strikes. Entry into the country for SOF is not a substantial obstacle, thanks to ethnic and linguistic homogeneity and the dramatic increases in the flow of people across the strait. Between 1988 and October 2002, for example, more than 828,000 mainlanders visited the island. Moreover, these special forces could also facilitate control of key civilian and military airfields and ports that could be used as points of entry for invading forces. The lack of operational security at key facilities is particularly inexplicable and appalling. Visits to national political and military command centers reveal them to be relatively unguarded with poor information security practices, including the use of personal cell phones in supposedly secure areas. The Presidential Palace in downtown Taipei, home to the president and his key staff, has no fence line and no security checkpoints. Building information, including the location of the President's office, is openly available on the Internet. Given the poor performance of President Chen's personal security detail during the recent assassination attempt on his life, the possibility of elimination of the top leadership through direct action cannot be discounted.

Finally, there is substantial open source evidence to suggest that China is winning the intelligence war across the strait, raising serious doubts about the purity of Taiwanese intelligence proffered to the United States, the safety of advanced military technologies transferred to the island, and the ability of official Taiwan interlocutors to safeguard shared U.S. secrets about intelligence collection or joint war planning. In the last five years, a steady series of leaked stories have appeared in the Taiwanese and other regional media, describing either the rounding up of Taiwanese agent networks on the mainland or the unmasking of high-ranking Taiwanese agents in the military, with similar successes a rarity on the Taiwan side, despite significant political incentive to publicize such discoveries.[13] Reported examples since only early 2003 include the arrest of the president of the PLA Air Force Command Academy, Major-General Liu Guangzhi, his former deputy, Major-General Li Suolin, and ten of their subordinates[14]; the arrest of twenty-four Taiwanese and nineteen mainlanders in late 2003[15]; the arrest of Chang Hsu-min, age 27, and his 24-year-old girlfriend Yu Shi-ping[16]; the arrest of Xu Jianchi[17]; the arrest of Ma Peiming in February 2003[18]; and the arrest and conviction to life imprisonment of Petty Officer First Class Liu Yueh-lung for passing naval communications codes to the PRC.[19] Farther back, high-profile intelligence losses include the discovery, arrest, and execution of General Logistics Department Lieutenant-General Liu Liankun and Senior Colonel Shao Zhengzhong as a result of Taiwanese government intelligence disclosures about the fact that warheads on Chinese missiles fired near the island in 1996 were unarmed[20]; the arrest and sentencing of Hainan Province Deputy Head Lin Kecheng and nine others in 1999 for providing economic, political, and other kinds of intelligence to the Taiwan Military Intelligence Bureau[21]; and the arrest and imprisonment of a local official in Nanchong, Sichuan named Wang Ping for allegedly also working for the Taiwan Military Intelligence Bureau (MIB).[22] In addition, retired senior Taiwan intelligence officials, including National Security Bureau Personnel Chief Pan Hsi-hsien and at least one former J-2, continue to travel to and often reside in China despite Taiwan regulations barring such movement for three years after retirement.[23] At the same time, Taiwan and international media is regularly filled with leaks about sensitive U.S.-Taiwan military interactions or weapons transfers, sourced to either legislators or standing Taiwan government officials. Examples include disclosures about possible deployment of an integrated underwater surveillance system (IUSS) north and south of the island to detect Chinese submarines,[24] the provision of early warning data on a Chinese missile attack from the Defense Support Program (DSP) satellite constellation,[25] and the alleged signals intelligence (SIGINT) cooperation between the National Security Agency and Taiwan on Yangming Mountain.[26] All of these possible compromises raise serious concerns about future technology and information sharing with Taiwan.

Center of Gravity Number Two: U.S. Military Intervention

STRATEGIES FOR ATTACKING U.S. LOGISTICS. When Chinese strategists contemplate how to affect U.S. deployments, they confront the limitations of their current conventional force, which does not have the range sufficient to interdict U.S. facilities or assets beyond the Japanese home islands. Nuclear options, while theoretically available, are nonetheless far too escalatory to be used so early in the conflict. Theater missile systems, which are possibly moving to a mixture of conventional and nuclear warheads, could be used against Japan or Guam, but uncertainties about the nature of a given warhead might generate responses similar to the nuclear scenario.

According to the predictable cadre of "true believers," both of the centers of gravity identified above can be attacked using CNO. In the first case, the Chinese IO community believes that CNO will play a useful psychological role in undermining the will of the Taiwanese people by attacking infrastructure and economic vitality. In the second case, the Chinese IO community envisions CNO effectively deterring or delaying U.S. intervention, allowing China to cause enough pain to compel Taipei to capitulate before the United States arrives. The remainder of this section outlines how these IO theorists propose to operationalize such a strategy.

GENERAL IO AND COMPUTER NETWORK ATTACK (CNA) ANALYSIS. Before examining this scenario in detail, it is first necessary to provide some background regarding Chinese views of IO in general and CNO in particular. At the strategic level, contemporary writers view IO and CNO as useful supplements to conventional war-fighting capability and powerful asymmetric options for "overcoming the superior with the inferior." According to one PRC author, "CNA is one of the most effective means for a weak military to fight a strong one."[27] Yet another important theme in Chinese writings on CNO is the use of CNA as the spearpoint of deterrence. Emphasizing the potential role of CNA in this type of signaling, a PRC strategist writes "We must send a message to the enemy through computer network attack, forcing the enemy to give up without fighting."[28] CNA is particularly attractive to the PLA because it has a longer range than their conventional power projection assets; this allows the PLA to "reach out and touch" the United

States, even the continental United States. "Thanks to computers," one strategist writes, "long-distance surveillance and accurate, powerful and long-distance attacks are now available to our military."[29] Yet CNA is also believed to enjoy a high degree of "plausible deniability," rendering it a possible tool of strategic denial and deception. As one source notes, "An information war is inexpensive, as the enemy country can receive a paralyzing blow through the Internet, and the party on the receiving end will not be able to tell whether it is a child's prank or an attack from an enemy."[30]

It is important to note that Chinese CNA doctrine focuses on disruption and paralysis, not destruction. Philosophically and historically, the evolving doctrine draws inspiration from Mao Zedong's theory of "protracted war," in which he argued that "we must as far as possible seal up the enemies' eyes and ears, and make them become blind and deaf, and we must as far as possible confuse the minds of their commanders and turn them into madmen, using this to achieve our own victory."[31] In the modem age, one authoritative source states: "computer warfare targets computers—the core of weapons systems and command, control, communications, computers and intelligence (C4I) systems—in order to paralyze the enemy."[32] The goal of this paralyzing attack is to inflict a "mortal blow" though this does not necessarily refer to defeat. Instead, Chinese analysts often speak of using these attacks to deter the enemy or to raise the costs of conflict to an unacceptable level. Specifically, CNA on nonmilitary targets are designed to "shake war resoluteness, destroy war potential and win the upper hand in war," thus undermining the political will of the population to participate in military conflict.[33]

At an operational level, the emerging Chinese CNO strategy has five key features. First, Chinese authors emphasize defense as the top priority and chastise American theorists for their "fetish of the offensive." In interviews, analysts assert their belief that the United States is already carrying out extensive computer network exploit (CNE) activities against Chinese servers. As a result, computer network defense (CND) must be the highest priority in peacetime, and only after that problem is solved can they consider "tactical counteroffensives." Second, CNA is viewed as an unconventional warfare weapon to be used in the opening phase of the conflict, not a battlefield force multiplier that can be employed during every phase of the war. PLA analysts believe that a bolt from the opponent at the beginning of a conflict is necessary, because the enemy may simply unplug the network, denying them access to the target set or patch the relevant vulnerabilities, thus obviating all prior intelligence preparation of the battlefield. Third, CNA is seen as a tool to permit China to fight and win an information campaign, precluding the need for conventional military action. Fourth, China's enemies, in particular the United States, are seen as "information dependent," while China is not. This latter point is an interesting misperception, given that the current Chinese C4I modernization is paradoxically making them more vulnerable to U.S. counter-C4I methods.

Perhaps most significant, CNA is characterized as a preemption weapon to be used under the rubric of the rising Chinese strategy of *xianfa zhiren,* or "gaining mastery before the enemy has struck." Preemption is a core concept of emerging Chinese military doctrine. One author recommends that an effective strategy by which the weaker party can overcome its more powerful enemy is "to take advantage of serious gaps in the deployment of forces by the enemy with a high-tech edge by launching a preemptive strike during the early phase of the war or in the preparations leading to the offensive."[34] Confirming earlier analysis of Chinese views of U.S. operational vulnerabilities in the deployment phase, the reason for striking is that the "enemy is most vulnerable during the early phase of the war."[35] In terms of specific targets, the author asserts that "we should zero in on the hubs and other crucial links in the system that move enemy troops as well as the war-making machine, such as harbors, airports, means of transportation, battlefield installations, and the communications, command and control and information systems."[36] If these targets are not attacked or the attack fails, the "high-tech equipped enemy" will amass troops and deploy hardware swiftly to the war zone, where it will carry out "large-scale air strikes in an attempt to weaken . . . China's combat capability."[37] More recent and authoritative sources expand on this view; "in order to control information power," one source states, "there must also be preemption . . . information offensives mainly rely on distant battle and stealth in order to be effective, and are best used as a surprise . . . Therefore, it is clear that whoever strikes first has the advantage."[38] "The best defense is offense"; according to the authors of *Information Operations,* "we must launch preemptive attacks to disrupt and destroy enemy computer systems."[39]

SPECIFIC TARGETING ANALYSIS OF NETWORK ATTACKS AGAINST LOGISTICS.
There are two macrolevel targets for Chinese CNO: military network information and military information stored on networks. CNA seeks to use the former to degrade the latter. Like U.S. doctrine, Chinese CNA targeting therefore focuses specifically on "enemy command and control (C2) centers," especially "enemy information systems." Of these information systems, PLA writings and interviews suggest that logistics computer systems are a top military target. According to one PLA source, "we must zero in on the . . . crucial links in the system that move enemy troops . . . such as information systems."[40] Another source writes, "we must attack system information accuracy, timeliness of information, and reliability of information."[41] In addition to logistics computer systems, another key military target for Chinese CNA is military reliance on civilian communications systems.

These concepts, combined with the earlier analysis of the PLA view that the main U.S. weakness is the deployment phase, lead PLA IO theorists to conclude that U.S. dependence on computer systems, particularly logistics systems, is a weak link that could potentially be exploited through CNA. Specifically, Chinese authors highlight the U.S. Department of Defense's (DoD) need to use the civilian backbone and unclassified computer networks (e.g., NIPRNET) as an "Achilles heel." There is also recognition of the fact that operations in the Pacific are especially reliant on precisely coordinated transportation, communications, and logistics networks, given the "tyranny of distance" in the theater. PLA strategists believe that a disruptive CNA against these systems or affiliated civilian systems could potentially delay or degrade U.S. force deployment to the region, while allowing the PRC to maintain a degree of plausible deniability.

The Chinese are right to highlight the NIPRNET as an attractive *and* accessible target, unlike its classified counterparts. It is attractive because it contains and transmits critical deployment information in the all-important time-phased force deployment list (TPFDL), which is both valuable for intelligence gathering about U.S. military operations and also a lucrative target for disruptive attacks. In terms of accessibility, it is relatively easy to gather data about the NIPRNET from open sources, although it is more difficult since 9/11. Moreover, the very nature of system is the source of its vulnerabilities; it has to be unclassified and connected to the greater global network, albeit through protected gateways. To migrate all of the NIPRNET to a secure, air-gapped network would likely tax the resources and bandwidth of DoD military networks.

The DoD's classified networks, however, are attractive but less accessible targets for the Chinese. On the one hand, these networks would be an intelligence gold mine, and are therefore a likely Chinese priority CNE target. On the other hand, they are less attractive as a CNA target, thanks to the difficulty of penetrating their high defenses. Any overall Chinese military strategy predicated on a high degree of success in penetrating these networks during crisis or war is a high-risk venture and increases the chances of failure of the overall effort to an unacceptable level. Moreover, internal PRC writings on information warfare show no confidence in the PRC's ability to get inside network-centric warfare aboard deployed ships or other self-contained operational units. Instead, the literature is focused on preventing the units from deploying in the first place, and thereafter breaking the C4I linkages between the ships and their headquarters.

Chinese CNE or CNA operations against logistics networks could have a detrimental impact on U.S. logistics support to operations. PRC CNE activities directed against U.S. military logistics networks could reveal force deployment information, such as the names of ships deployed, readiness status of various units, timing and destination of deployments, and rendezvous schedules. This is especially important for the Chinese in times of crisis, since the PRC in peacetime utilizes U.S. military web sites and newspapers as a principal source for deployment information. An article in October 2001 in the *People's Daily*, for example, explicitly cited U.S. Navy web sites for information about the origins, destination, and purpose of two carrier battle groups exercising in the South China Sea. Since the quantity and quality of deployment information on open web sites has been dramatically reduced after 9/11, the intelligence benefits (necessity?) of exploiting the NIPRNET have become even more paramount.[42] CNA could also delay resupply to the theater by misdirecting stores, fuel, and munitions, and corrupting or deleting inventory files, thereby hindering mission capability.

The advantages to this strategy are numerous: it is available to the PLA in the near term; it does not require the PLA to be able to attack/invade Taiwan with air/sea assets; it has a reasonable level of deniability, provided that the attack is sophisticated enough to prevent tracing; and it exploits perceived U.S. casualty aversion, over-attention to force protection, the tyranny of distance in the Pacific, and U.S. dependence on information systems. In short, it could achieve the desired operational and psychological effects: deterrence of U.S. response or degrading of deployments.

Assessment: Is the Scenario Realistic?

Chinese IO theorists assert that CNA against unclassified computer systems or affiliated civilian systems, combined with a coordinated campaign of short-range ballistic missile attacks, "fifth column," and IO attacks against Taiwanese critical infrastructure, could quickly force Taiwan to capitulate to Beijing. This strategy exploits serious vulnerabilities, particularly with regard to Taiwanese critical infrastructure and U.S. military reliance on the NIPRNET, but is also partially predicated on a set of misunderstandings, misperceptions, and exaggerations of both U.S. logistics operations and the efficacy of PLA IO. This final section assesses the balance of these perceptions and misperceptions, concluding with an evaluation of the cost–benefit calculus for the PLA in undertaking such an effort.

CHINESE STRATEGIES AGAINST U.S. LOGISTICS SYSTEMS AND OPERATIONS. The Chinese are correct to point to the NIPRNET as a potential vulnerability, but would such an attack actually produce the desired effect? First, there is the issue of the "ready" carrier battle group at Yokusuka, which is only a few days steam away from Taiwan. Though extended resupply might be degraded, the group's arrival time would not be heavily affected by attacks on the NIPRNET; this would indicate a failure of one of the primary strategic goals of the attacks. In response, PLA analysts point to times in the last several years when there was no ready carrier in the Pacific because it was "gapped" in the Mediterranean or in the Persian Gulf. More recently, PLA analysts took note of the DoD's formal revision of its strategy from two major theater wars (MTWs) to one MTW. In both cases, they could envision scenarios in which U.S. forces would require seven or more days to arrive at the Taiwan theater, potentially providing China with a "window of opportunity" to carry out rapid coercive operations against Taiwan.

Second, there is the issue of Chinese characterizations of the U.S. logistics system itself. The Chinese tend to overemphasize the U.S. reliance on computers. The writings of some Chinese strategists indicate that they believe the U.S. system cannot function effectively without these computer networks. Moreover, PRC strategists generally underestimate the capacity of the system to use paper, pencil, fax, and phone, if necessary. In fact, interviews with current U.S. logistics personnel suggest that downtime on these systems is a regular occurrence, forcing them to periodically employ noncomputerized solutions. At the same time, there is also evidence that U.S. logistics systems are moving toward increasing automation, which would increase the potential impact of an attack against the NIPRNET.

Third, Chinese analysis seems predicated on questionable assumptions about American casualty aversion, particularly the notion that U.S. forces would not deploy to a Taiwan contingency until all of its assets were in place. If logistics delays meant that some part of the force protection package would not be available, they assume, then U.S. forces would wait until the whole force protection package had arrived before intervening in the conflict. This is a debatable assumption, particularly given the precedence of the two carrier strike groups' (CSG) deployment in 1996 and Washington's considerable interest in maintaining peace and stability in the strait.

COULD THE CHINESE ACTUALLY DO IT? In terms of courses of action, interviews and classified writings reveal interest in the full spectrum of CNA tools, including hacking, viruses, physical attack, insider sabotage, and electromagnetic attack. One of the most difficult challenges of this type of analysis is measuring China's actual CNA capability. In rough terms, a CNA capability requires four things, three of which are easy to obtain and one that is harder. The easy three are a computer, an Internet connection, and hacker tools, thousands of which can be downloaded from enthusiast sites around the globe. The more difficult piece of the puzzle to acquire is the operator himself, the computer hacker. Although individuals of this ilk are abundant in China's urban centers, they are also correctly perceived to be a social group unlikely to relish military or governmental service.

An additional issue related to measuring capability involves the assessment of a group or country's ability to generate new attack tools or exploits. Outside analysts, many of whom are programmers themselves, tend to reify countries like Russia that abound with highly talented programmers, and look down upon countries or individuals that simply use off-the-shelf "script kiddie"[43] tools such as distributed denial of service (DDOS) programs. DDOS is admittedly a blunt instrument, but a fixation on finding more sophisticated attacks, which reflects the widely held but logically tenuous assumption that state sponsorship correlates with sophistication, may be counterproductive. Instead, analysts should employ a simple "means-ends" test. In the Chinese case, DDOS, despite its relatively simplicity, looks like the right tool for the right mission. From the Chinese point of view, for example, hammering the NIPRNET and forcing it to be taken down for repairs would be considered an operational success, because it could potentially delay or degrade U.S. logistics deployments to Taiwan.

In conclusion, therefore, a strategy to disrupt U.S. logistics systems with CNA seems well matched to U.S. vulnerabilities and Chinese capabilities, though the final operational impact of the effort may be undermined by important Chinese misperceptions about the political will of the United States and the nature of its logistics operations.

MYTH: Patriotic hacker groups are actually under government or military control.

REALITY: Patriotic hackers should not be treated as government actors, but as semi-autonomous nationalists that are both useful to the regime during crises but also feared as uncontrollable provocateurs.

As demonstrated by the "hacker wars" that followed former Taiwan President Lee Teng-hui's announcement of "special state-to-state relations," the U.S. bombing of the Chinese Embassy in Yugoslavia, and the EP-3 crisis, patriotic hacking appears to have become a permanent feature of Chinese foreign and security policy crises in recent years. On the one hand, the emergence of this trend presents the PRC military and political leadership with serious command and control problems. Specifically, uncontrolled hacking by irregulars against the U.S. and Taiwan systems could potentially undermine a PRC political-military coercive diplomacy strategy vis-à-vis Taiwan and the United States during a crisis. Unlike traditional military instruments such as missiles, many of the levers of CNO by "unofficial means" are beyond the control of the Chinese government. This could negate the intended impact of strategic pausing and other political signals during a crisis. Yet, at the same time, patriotic hacking offers several new opportunities for the PRC. First, it increases plausible deniability for official Chinese CNA/CNE. Second, it has the potential to create a large, if unsophisticated, set of operators who could engage in disruption activities against U.S. and Taiwan networks. One classified PLA document obtained by Taiwan intelligence emphasizes the use of the "unofficial power of IW" and highlights the role of nonstate actors in achieving state coercion goals.

For these reasons, some Western analysts have been tempted to assert that the patriotic hackers are "controlled" by Beijing. Among the arguments marshaled to support this thesis is the fact that consistently harsh punishments are meted out to individuals in China who commit relatively minor computer crimes, while patriotic hackers appear to suffer no sanction for their brazen contravention of Chinese law. Other analysts begin from the specious premise that since the Chinese government "owns" the Internet in China, patriotic hackers must work for the state. Still others correctly point to the fact that a number of these groups, such as Xfocus and NSFocus, appear to be morphing into "white-hat" hackers (i.e., becoming professional information security professionals), often developing relationships with companies associated with the Ministry of Public Security or with the ministry itself. Yet interviews with hackers and officials strongly suggest that the groups truly are independent actors, more correctly labeled "state-tolerated" or "state-encouraged." They are tolerated because they are "useful idiots" for the regime, but they are also careful not to pursue domestic hacking activities that might threaten "internal stability" and thereby activate the repression apparatus. Indeed, most of the groups have issued constitutions or other organizing documents that specifically prohibit members from attacking Chinese web sites or networks.

Because patriotic hacker groups are not controlled by the state, Beijing is worried about the possible effect of their behavior in a crisis with the United States and/or Taiwan. Analysis of several "hacker wars" over the last two years suggests an evolving mechanism for shaping the activities of "patriotic hackers." In August 1999, after the conclusion of the cross-strait hacker skirmish that erupted in the wake of Taiwan President Li Teng-hui's declaration that the island's relationship to the mainland was a "state-to-state relationship," a *Liberation Army Daily* article lauded the patriotic hackers and encouraged other hackers to join in during the next crisis with Taiwan. In April 2001, *Guangzhou Daily* reprinted without attribution a *Wired* article on the impending outbreak of a "hacker war" between Chinese and American hackers, which many hackers saw as a sign of government backing. A media-generated hacker war thereafter ensued, with Chinese and American hackers defacing hundreds, if not thousands, of web sites. In May 2001, however, an authoritative *People's Daily* article rebuked both Western and Chinese hackers, calling activities by both sides "illegal." This signaled to the hackers that the state had withdrawn its sanction of their activities and hacker activity quickly tapered off in response to the warning.

A year later, patriotic hacker chat rooms were filled with discussion and planning for a "first anniversary" hacker war. In late April 2002, on the eve of the proposed conflict, *People's Daily* published another unsigned editorial on the subject, decrying the loose talk about a hacker war and warning of serious consequences. Participants in the hacker chat rooms quickly recognized the signal, and the plans for a new hacker war were abandoned. In neither case could this dynamic be called control, but instead reflects the population's keen sensitivity to the subtle messages in government propaganda, which continues to successfully create a Leninist climate of self-deterrence and self-censorship that is more powerful than active state repression. As some groups move into "white-hat" positions, however, the relationship might actually transition from a ruler-ruled dynamic to a partnership motivated by reasons ranging from nationalism to naked self-interest.

CONCLUSIONS AND IMPLICATIONS

The United States faces a more powerful, confident, and capable China than at any point in previous history. Beijing's military modernization program, after years of desultory development, has enjoyed almost a decade of focused, successful advances, aimed principally at providing the civilian leadership with credible options against both Taiwan and U.S. military forces in a contingency involving the island. While the topic of Chinese IO is riddled with myths and deliberate attempts at perception management, it is important to note that the PLA has also seriously pursued operational capabilities in electronic warfare and CNO, as well as its traditional strengths in psychological operations and deception.

These Chinese military developments have important implications for the cross-strait military balance and possible U.S. military intervention in a Taiwan contingency. Chinese writings about attacking unclassified U.S. military logistics networks, possibly manifest in reported China-origin intrusions into NIPRNET systems, represent a significant threat to the ability of the U.S. military to project maximum power in a fast-moving Taiwan contingency. While senior U.S. military and civilian leaders increasingly appreciate the problem, the structural requirement to use unclassified communications backbone for power projection limit effective countermeasures, though the succeeding paragraph offers some ideas for damage mitigation. The potential Chinese capabilities displayed in these intrusions, combined with other unconventional capabilities and Taiwan's appalling lack of attention to its vulnerabilities, also present a significant threat to Taiwan's critical infrastructure. This is especially the case given that the island possesses a highly informationalized society and economy, and successful prosecution of these attacks, whether by governmental actors or the so-called "patriotic hackers," could play a decisive role in achieving the PRC's goal of undermining popular will and forcing the Taipei's political leadership to capitulate to Beijing's coercion.

Chinese IO developments also potentially alter the deterrence and escalation control dynamics in a Taiwan scenario. The threat of CNO against the NIPRNET is designed in part to deter the United States from militarily intervening on behalf of Taiwan. While Beijing's growing capabilities do complicate the ability of U.S. forces to enter the fray, Beijing's confidence in its ability to produce successful deterrence may be based on dangerous misperceptions about U.S. casualty aversion, will to fight, and commitment to Taiwan. As a result, the real danger of China's emerging military capabilities is that they may embolden Beijing to make a fundamental miscalculation in a Taiwan scenario and consequently bring about a disastrous outcome for all parties.

However, one must also try to explore the possible opportunities, both strategic and operational, that the Chinese military trends outlined in this chapter present. In the information operations realm, relevant personnel must work to disabuse the Beijing authority of the idea that it can conduct CNA against the NIPRNET and hope to dramatically affect the deployment of U.S. naval assets to the Taiwan theater. One effective response would be a highly publicized naval exercise in the Pacific in which the participating naval assets were intentionally denied access to NIPRNET logistics systems and were forced to process the information in different ways, but nonetheless completed their mission.

NOTES

1. For a recent discussion of Chinese information warfare writings, see Timothy Thomas, "Chinese and American Network Warfare," *Joint Forces Quarterly* (August 2005): 76–83.
2. Shen Weiguang is the most prolific author, penning more than five books, including: *2010 Information Disaster: A Developing Country's Survival Strategy* [*2010 Xinxi Zaihai: Fazhanguojia Shengcun Zhanlue*] (Beijing: Xinhua, 2005); *On the Chinese RMA* [*Lun Zhongguo Junshi Geming*] (Beijing: Xinhua Chubanshe, 2004); *On New War* [*Xin Zhangzheng Lun*] (Zhejiang: Zhejiang Daxue Chubanshe, 2000); *Future World War* [*Fulai Shijie Zhanzheng*] (Zhejiang: Zhejiang Daxue Chubanshe, 2000); *Information War* [*Xinxizhan*] (Zhejiang: Zhejiang Daxue Chubanshe, 2000). Zhang Zhaozhong's publications include: *Network Warfare* [*Wangluo Zhanzheng*] (Beijing: Jiefangjun Wenyi Chubanshe, 2001); *China Allows Warfare to Get Away* [*Zhongguo Rangzhan Zoukai*] (Beijing: Dangdai Zhongguo Chubanshe, 2001); *Who Makes War?* [*Shuizai Zhizao Zhanzheng?*] (Beijing: Dangdai Zhongguo Chubanshe, 2001); *Who is Able to Win a War?* [*Shei Neng Daying Xia Yiyang Zhanzheng*] (Beijing: Zhongguo Qingnian Chubanshe, 1999); *How Far Away Is War?* [*Zhanzheng Likai Women Youduoyuan*] (Beijing, Jiefangjun Chubanshe, 1999).
3. A typical example, which incorrectly claims that Shen is "a writer who appears to be at the forefront of PRC IW theorists," is Charles B. Everett, Moss Dewindt, and Shane McDade's "The Silicon Spear: An Assessment of Information Based Warfare (IBW) and U.S. National Security." See http://www.ndu.edu/inss/siws/ch2.html.
4. Qiao Liang and Wang Xiangsui's 1999 book, *Unrestricted Warfare*, is the most salient example. On its face, the book looks credible. The authors were senior colonels in the Chinese Air Force, and a military publishing house published the book. Closer examination, however, reveals important details that undermine the

authoritativeness of the text. While Qiao and Wang were active-duty officers, they worked at the Air Force Political Academy, which is not involved in any aspect of IO except that of psychological operations. Before co-authoring *Unrestricted Warfare*, Qiao Liang wrote techno thrillers for the Air Force, including a 1995 fictional work entitled *The Gate of Armageddon* [*Mori Zhimen*]. See http://product.dangdang. com/product.aspx?product_id=58435 (last accessed April 18, 2007). Moreover, *Unrestricted Warfare* was published by the PLA Arts and Literature Press, not one of the publishing houses associated with important doctrinal documents.

5. Qiao Liang, Wang Xiangsui, and Shen Weiguang are frequent commentators on Chinese television and print media. Wang has converted his notoriety into a professorship at the Beijing University of Aeronautics and Astronautics (BUAA).

6. Sha Lin, "Two Senior Colonels and 'No-Limit Warfare'," *Zhongguo Qingnian Bao*, June 28, 1999, p. 5.

7. Ma Ling interview, *Ta Kung Pao*, September 19, 1999, B3.

8. "Unrestricted War—New Concept of War Presented by Non-Military Experts," *Liaowang*, no.11 (March 13, 2000): 55–56.

9. John Pomfret, "China Ponders New Rules of 'Unrestricted Warfare'," *Washington Post*, August 8, 1999, A01.

10. Interviews in Beijing, 1999–2000.

11. Kao Chieh-chien, "What Limits Has 'Unrestricted Warfare' Exceeded—Also Discussing the Phenomenon Where 'Readers and Experts Stick to Their Own Views,'" *Ta Kung Pao*, June 21, 2000.

12. A meme is a piece of cultural information that is transmitted verbally or through repeated action from one mind to another.

13. Among the rare examples, which perversely strengthen the case for significant counterintelligence concerns on Taiwan, are three military officers (Major Pai Chin-yang, Tseng Chao-wen, and Chen Sui-chiung) arrested for spying, and two individuals (Huang Cheng-an and his girlfriend) arrested for transferring technology from the Chungshan Institute for Science and Technology to the mainland. See William Foreman, "Taiwan Arrests Military Officer on Spy Charges—The Third Such Case in Month," *Associated Press*, December 3, 2003; and "Taiwan Detains Woman over Alleged Spying," *South China Morning Post*, January 30, 2004. An earlier case also involved Yeh Yu-chen and Chen Shih-liang and technology from the Chungshan Institute. See "Taiwan Attempts Damage-Control After Alleged Chinese Spy Ring," *Agence France-Presse*, August 7, 2003.

14. "Top PLA Officers Accused of Spying for Taiwan," *Straits Times*, April 16, 2004; "Beijing Arrests Military Officers on Spy Charges," *China Post*, April 17, 2004.

15. The timing and propaganda exploitation of the arrests, which coincided with the Taiwan presidential campaign, suggest that the Chinese already had the individuals under surveillance and chose to arrest them for maximum political effect. See

Philip Pan, "China Arrests 43 Alleged Spies; Move Increases Effort to Undermine Taiwanese President," *Washington Post*, December 24, 2003; "Chinese Mainland Smashes Taiwan Spy Ring," *Xinhua*, December 24, 2003; "Espionage, Corruption Cases in China, Dec 03–Feb 04," *BBC Monitoring International Reports*, February 14, 2004; Joe McDonald, "China Parades Accused Taiwanese Spies in Front of Cameras amid Tensions with Island," *Associated Press*, January 16, 2004; and "Taiwan Spies Visited by Families," *Xinhua*, January 20, 2004.

16. "China Detains Two More Taiwanese Suspected of Espionage," *Agence France-Presse*, February 13, 2004, cites Chinese state media.

17. *Chongqing Ribao*, August 8, 2003, p. 1.

18. *Agence France-Presse*, September 2, 2003, p. 1.

19. Brian Hsu, "Taiwan Naval Officer Gets Life for Espionage," *Taipei Times*, December 18, 2002.

20. John Pomfret, "Taiwanese Mistake Led to 3 Spies' Executions," *Washington Post*, February 20, 2000.

21. *People's Daily* article in August 1999, cited in Pomfret, "Taiwanese Mistake."

22. Sichuan television report in October 1999, cited in Pomfret, "Taiwanese Mistake."

23. "Former Taiwan Spy Chief Denies Leaking Secrets During His Four Years in China," *Taiwan News*, April 14, 2004.

24. Michael Gordon, "Secret U.S. Study Concludes Taiwan Needs New Arms," *New York Times*, April 1, 2001.

25. "US to Share Early-Warning Missile Data with Taiwan," *Agence France-Presse*, October 8, 2002.

26. Wendell Minnick, "Taiwan-USA Link Up on SIGINT," *Jane's Defence Review*, p. 23, January 2001; Wendell Minnick, "Spook Mountain: How US Spies on China," *Asia Times Online*, March 6, 2003; and Wendell Minnick, "Challenge to Update Taiwan's SIGINT," *Jane's Intelligence Review*, February 1, 2004.

27. Wang Houqing, Zhang Xingye, et al., *The Science of Campaigns* (Beijing: National Defense University Press, 2000) pp. 173–74.

28. Nu Li, Li Jiangzhou, and Xu Dehui, "Strategies in Information Operations: A Preliminary Discussion," *Military Science*, April 2000.

29. *The Science of Campaigns*, p. 170.

30. Wei Jincheng, "New Form of People's War," *Jiefangjun bao*, June 25, 1996, p. 6.

31. Mao Zedong, "On Protracted War" (May 1938), in *Selected Works of Mao Zedong*, vol. II (Beijing: Foreign Languages Press, 1961), paragraph 83.

32. Lu Daohai, *Information Operations* (Beijing: PLA Arts and Literature Press, 1999), *neibu faxing*, p. 288.

33. *Information Operations*, p. 296.

34. Lu Linzhi, "Preemptive Strikes Crucial in Limited High-Tech Wars," *Jiefangjun bao*, February 14, 1996.

35. Ibid.
36. Ibid.
37. Ibid.
38. *The Science of Campaigns,* pp. 178–79.
39. *Information Operations,* p. 324.
40. Lu Linzhi, "Preemptive Strikes Crucial in Limited High-Tech Wars."
41. *Information Operations,* p. 293.
42. The Department of Defense's revised website administration guidance, http://www.defenselink.mil/webmasters/policy/dod_web_policy_12071998_with_amendments_and_corrections.html (accessed April 17, 2007), specifically prohibits the following: "3.5.3.2. Reference to unclassified information that would reveal sensitive movements of military assets or the location of units, installations, or personnel where uncertainty regarding location is an element of a military plan or program."
43. "Script kiddie" refers to a person who is not technologically savvy who learns about a specific weakness that someone else has discovered, then searches the Internet for sites to exploit that suffer from that weakness.

10

Taiwan's Defense Preparation Against the Chinese Military Threat

Andrew N. D. Yang

HOW TO DEFEND TAIWAN against possible military attacks by China is a pivotal issue for the 23 million people who live on the island and a daunting task for the armed forces of Taiwan. China possesses an ever-increasing capability to accelerate the modernization of high-technology weapon systems, adopt new strategies and tactics, and conduct a series of exercises aimed at paralyzing Taiwan's key economic, political, and military installations. Short of the unlikely possibility of an all-out assault on the island, China's aim in a conflict would be to put Taiwan's key interests in grave danger in order to compel Taiwan to resolve the cross-strait dispute on China's political terms. Taiwan's political and military leaders have been engaged in a process of upgrading defensive capabilities in the last few decades to reassure both the domestic and international community that Taiwan not only possesses the determination, but also the capabilities to deter and defeat any future Chinese military coercion or attack.

To provide a better understanding of how Taiwan's defense capabilities can effectively deter and defeat Chinese military threats, this chapter examines several key aspects of Taiwanese defense modernization in the context of several possible types of military pressure or attacks by China. The first aspect is to look into Taiwanese defense upgrades in recent years designed to cope with several types of Chinese attacks, largely involving precision bombardment over the island. Specifically, this analysis focuses on Taiwan's ability to deter long-range precision air strikes, a naval blockade, and amphibious landing and special forces attacks. The second section of this chapter explores institutional improvements in Taiwan's military crisis management and its implications for Taiwan's ability to avoid all-out cross-strait conflict. This part of the analysis concentrates on Taiwan's policy guidelines and institutional mechanisms intended to de-escalate tension in a crisis situation.

REASONS FOR POTENTIAL PRC USE OF MILITARY FORCE AGAINST TAIWAN

The question of whether the People's Republic of China (PRC) intends to use military means to achieve its political objective of "unifying Taiwan" is contingent on its perception of political developments in Taiwan over the issue of sovereignty. Since the establishment of the PRC in 1949, the Beijing government has upheld the policy of unifying Taiwan, which is considered an integral part of Chinese sovereignty, either by peaceful means or by the use of force, if necessary. The dispute over the political control of Taiwan between the Republic of China (ROC) government in Taipei and the PRC's government in Beijing has resulted in military conflicts over offshore islands close to the China mainland between 1954 and 1958, and also resulted in a military crisis in the Taiwan Strait in 1996 when Taiwan was conducting its first direct presidential election since 1950. The potential military conflict between the two sides of the Taiwan Strait is directly linked to the dispute over Taiwan's sovereignty. Beijing has offered Taiwan the peaceful unification formula of "one country, two systems," a model that would enable Taiwan to maintain its current autonomous status and all aspects of governmental functions while accepting Beijing as the central government of all of China after unification; however, Taiwan insists that it is already an independent sovereign state and its future should therefore be decided by its citizens rather than by Beijing. Taiwan is willing to engage in peaceful dialogue or negotiation to solve the sovereignty dispute and future political integration with the mainland on an equal footing, but insists that any resolution of these political disputes should occur without the acceptance of any preconditions regarding the status of Taiwan and should receive the Taiwanese people's assent.

Beijing's ever-increasing military buildup designed to deter Taiwan independence in the last decade demonstrates that Beijing perceives Taiwan's insistence over sovereignty as stalling the unification process and is alarmed by Taiwan's refusal to compromise under the "one country, two systems" unification formula. Beijing stated its intention to use force to deter independence in the 2005 PRC national defense report and has emphasized the use of "nonpeaceful means" to solve the political dispute in the March 2005 Anti-Secession Law.

In short, Beijing has clearly indicated that it is prepared to use military means to solve the sovereignty issue, if necessary, although it claims to prefer a peaceful resolution of the problem. The maximalist objectives of China's armed forces, the People's Liberation Army (PLA), in an all-out future war against Taiwan are fivefold:

- Eliminate Taiwan independence political forces and uphold the territorial integrity of China;
- Replace the Taiwanese government with one compatible with PRC interests;
- Eliminate Taiwanese defense capabilities and cut off its defense links with the United States;
- Restore order by persuading or coercing the population to accept the imposed political arrangements; and
- Minimize PRC war casualties.

The PLA may face considerable difficulties in executing all five of these aims. Replacing a democratically elected government could trigger a mass uprising in Taiwan, unless the PRC directly commits massive amounts of forces and represses the popular resistance quickly, but this would risk increasing the casualty rate on the island and strong international intervention. However, without ensuring territorial integrity, other aims would be imperilled. This is a war-planning problem that the PRC must solve.

The complexity of the PRC's war tasks contrast dramatically with Taiwan's single objective: survival. For a government in Taiwan that chooses to declare outright independence, mere survival equates to victory. As for the PRC, simply destroying a regime that favors independence does not guarantee success. Instead, the PRC must achieve all its military tasks; it needs to exert sufficient destructive power on the Taiwanese armed forces and its command and control systems in order to neutralize the military and destroy the political will of the population. Therefore, the PRC's strategy must have two key elements: the rapid isolation and destruction of Taiwan's government and the subsequent rapid introduction of a credible replacement government. Preventing or deterring the United States from effectively assisting Taiwan is, of course, a precondition of success for the PRC.

If the first objective is achieved without the second, then territorial integrity cannot be guaranteed. Any outcome in which regime change is not rapidly executed endangers the PRC's war mission, as does any outcome in which regime destruction does not set the stage for the rapid achievement of the PRC's other goals. Therefore, the PRC's aims must be built on the confidence that the Taiwanese government can be rapidly eliminated and replaced successfully, and that the Taiwanese armed forces will not resist effectively—all of which require the ability to stave off timely U.S. intervention as well.

PERCEIVED MODES OF CHINESE ATTACKS

The kind of military threat that Beijing may pose against Taiwan will be guided by its effort to establish capabilities for winning a local war under high-tech conditions. Under this military strategic principle, the PLA will focus upon the enhancement of its preemptive strike and "quick strike" capabilities, and on improving tactics, combat skills, and technology in order to achieve air superiority and control of sea in the Taiwan Strait.

In order to achieve these goals, the Chinese have designed three phases of Chinese strike operations:

Phase 1: A sudden, overwhelming attack on critical strategic and military targets using air power and special forces designed to force a rapid conclusion to the war;

Phase 2: An effective naval blockade of major ports, to be followed by an extended air campaign designed to cripple Taiwan economically and militarily;

Phase 3: An amphibious landing to facilitate a multi-divisional armored and mechanized attack on the political center.[1]

The following analysis represents the most likely ways in which military conflict between the two sides of the Taiwan Strait might happen. Other scenarios can be constructed and there are numerous possible variations within the basic scenario. The three phases of combat operation outlined in this chapter can in fact take place in sequence or simultaneously. It depends on the assessment of offensive/defensive capabilities by those concerned and what political objectives are set for the forces. Taiwan's defense modernization is specifically designed to counter each one of these phases.

Phase 1: Air Attacks[2]

To launch a sudden, overwhelming air strike over Taiwan, the PLA needs to achieve the capabilities to conduct precision strikes over critical Taiwanese military and strategic targets such as command, control, and communication centers; radar and early warning stations; air force bases; air defense systems; key railway and road links; critical power supply systems; and oil and ordinance depots. Furthermore, China must disrupt the Taiwanese command and control system early in the campaign and do so effectively in order to reduce the Taiwanese leadership's ability to organize and direct a coherent resistance. The PLA has devoted significant time and effort to developing weapon systems for this purpose, either indigenously or by acquiring them from abroad, including long-range precision-strike weapon systems such as short-range ballistic missiles (SRBMs) and land-attack cruise missiles (LACMs).

Currently the PLA has deployed more than 700 DF-15 and DF-11 SRBMs in coastal provinces facing Taiwan. According to U.S. estimates, these missiles are increasing in number and lethality against key Taiwanese installations. Furthermore, the PLA has successfully developed various types of LACMs—which will most likely become operational by late 2007—that could be used to conduct "decapitation" operations. To enhance the effectiveness of air strikes over Taiwan, the PLA Air Force (PLAAF) has acquired advanced fighter aircraft such as the SU-27, SU-30 MMK, J-10, and FB-7A as platforms to facilitate missile strikes and to win air superiority in the Taiwan Strait.

TAIWANESE COUNTERMEASURES TO AIR ATTACKS. Taiwan's main task during any type of PLA attack is to protect its command and control system from being disabled by air strikes. To accomplish this task, the ROC armed forces' countermeasures are based on two elements. The first is to strengthen the protection of the critical command, control, and communication centers. The other is to modernize and improve its air defense system.

To achieve the first objective, the ROC armed forces have launched the multi-billion-dollar "Project Resolute" to integrate the command, control, and communication systems of the three services; to enhance the electronic countermeasures (ECM) and electronic counter-countermeasure (ECCM) ability of its overall command, computers, control, communication, and intelligence, surveillance, and reconnaissance system (C4ISR); and to harden the infrastructure that protects those command and control assets. This effort at overall consolidation and improvement is not only designed to permit those assets to survive precision air strikes, but also to enhance their capability to survive electromagnetic strikes and cyber warfare.[3] Project Resolute also covers the integration of long-range early warning radars (due to be installed in late 2007), the air force's Internet strengthening (qiáng wǎng; 强网) effort, the navy's Da Chen surveillance radar system, and the E2-T Airborne Warning and Control System (AWACS), so as to provide a well-integrated, multi-service, early warning capability in meeting missile strikes. The improvement of C4ISR and air defense capabilities has been integrated into the Ministry of National Defense's (MND) "10-year (2000–2010) consolidation and improvement plan"[4] and is subject to further improvements and upgrades depending on the requirements of Taiwan's expanding air defense program. For example, the consolidation of C4ISR capabilities could lead to the incorporation or integration of the China Defense (huáwèi; 华卫) II photo reconnaissance satellite built by Taiwan's National Science Research Council, to permit the down-linking of real-time images of PLA missile battery activities so as to enhance the reliability of intelligence analysis.[5]

To further improve Taiwan's air defense capability, a new missile defense command has been established directly under the supervision of the General Staff Department (GSP) since early 2004.[6] The missile defense command directs ground missile batteries made up of mainly the

U.S. Hawk system, locally developed Tien Kong I and II systems, three batteries of Patriot PAC2-plus systems acquired in 1997 (which will likely be upgraded to the level of PAC-3), six new batteries of Patriot PAC-3 systems (currently awaiting budget approval), several naval air defense systems provided by four Kidd-class destroyers purchased in 2003 (to become operational in late 2007), and other air defense systems currently under Air Force Command. The new missile defense command is meant to cut across the chain of command so as to provide a more timely and adequate response to a possible air strike across the strait.

To further enhance Taiwan's counter-air-strike capability, the local Chung-Shan Institute of Science and Technology (CSIST), a defense research and development institute, is also in the process of upgrading the Tien Kong II missile to the Tien Kong III anti-missile system. Tien Kong III was successfully test fired in 2001–2002 and will probably be ready for operational deployment in the near future.

However, Taiwan still lacks an effective missile defense system that can reliably intercept the PRC's SRBMs; even the future PAC-3 systems will be inadequate to defend against a PRC missile attack. To fill this gap, the MND is trying to acquire the Naval Area Defense (NAD) system based on the Aegis-equipped Arleigh Burke-class destroyers. Although the United States has not accepted this request, it has offered four Kidd-class destroyers equipped with Standard II air defense systems. Once delivered and deployed, the Kidd-class destroyers will provide much more effective air defense for the ROC Navy. Nevertheless, the ROC will continue to try to secure the Aegis system because all of its other existing or pending air defense systems are less effective in defending against China's SRBM strikes.[7]

In terms of protecting its valuable advanced fighter aircraft from PRC air strikes, the ROC Air Force has strengthened the protection of air force bases in the western coastal region. New hangars and tunnels which can withstand precision bombing have been constructed. In addition, two relatively recent air force bases with hardened underground shelters were constructed in eastern Taiwan in the early 1990s. Surrounded and protected by mountains, these bases can shelter at least one-third of the fighter aircraft currently in service. If and when required, the air force's Mirage 2000-5 interceptors and F-16 multi-role fighters can be deployed in these well-protected bases to fight for air superiority.[8]

In order to fend off PRC preemptive air strikes, the ROC armed forces are currently working closely with the U.S. military to enhance their C4ISR. Project Resolute II will combine the existing *Da Chen* surveillance radar system, Internet strengthening, and Project Resolute I elements into an integrated command and control system that is designed to provide fast and direct links between the high command and basic combat units, thus ensuring rapid responses in a changing war situation.[9] ECM and ECCM devices will protect this joint operation command and control system, thereby enhancing Taiwan's capabilities against electromagnetic attacks.

CHALLENGES THAT FACE THE PLAAF IN CONDUCTING AIR STRIKES. The challenge to the PRC's air force is whether it can rule the sky over Taiwan. To achieve this, the PLAAF must effectively destroy most of Taiwan's key air defense assets, command and control centers, and most of its air force bases. In order to do so, defense planners in Beijing must gain the element of surprise, which requires the PLA to compromise the Taiwanese advanced early warning and surveillance systems, C4ISR, and communication networks. In addition, China has to undermine successfully the more sophisticated and advanced U.S. surveillance and intelligence-gathering systems and cut off communication and intelligence links between U.S. and ROC armed forces. Without achieving these objectives, the effects of a PLA air strike will be limited.

To the Taiwanese, the challenge in the event of a full-scale attack will be to preserve its scarce and valuable air defense assets as well as sustain its command, control, and joint operation networks while countering massive air strikes. Equally important, the Taiwan leadership must maintain confidence and order in Taiwan during these SRBM bombardments. The resilience of the general public and their determination to not allow China's tactics to affect their morale are also critical to any effort by Taiwan's military forces to conduct effective counterattacks and regain air superiority.

Phase 2: Naval Blockade

Chinese military writings indicate that immediately after initial air strikes the most logical next step would be a naval blockade, in part because it would allow the PLA to prepare the ground for PLA amphibious and airborne operations. A blockade also serves the purpose of cutting off outside assistance by closing Taiwan's oceanic lines of communication and supplies.

A PRC blockade would be conducted mainly by submarines, which would be used to lay mines at crucial waterways near Taiwanese harbors such as Kaohsiung, Keelung, Suao, and the Tsoying naval base. The PLA navy's (PLAN) approximately forty Kilo-, Song-, and Ming-class diesel-electric submarines, which are equipped with mines and missiles, would be deployed for such tasks.

TAIWANESE COUNTERBLOCKADE AND ANTI-SUBMARINE WARFARE CAPABILITY. Since 1992, the ROC Navy has put increasing emphasis on anti-submarine warfare (ASW) as a way to counter and deter a blockade. Several billion dollars worth of ASW weapon systems and platforms have been purchased from the United States. They include twenty-eight S-70C (M) anti-submarine helicopters, eight Knox-class frigates, and four minesweepers. To further enhance the ROC Navy's ASW capability, the Bush administration further approved the sale of a large quantity of naval systems and platforms in April 2001, including eight diesel-electric submarines, twelve P-3C Orion ASW aircraft, four Kidd-class destroyers, and eight CH-53 minesweeping helicopters. If entirely acquired, as intended, during the period 2012–2015, these newly approved ASW systems will form the backbone of ROC Navy's ASW capability over the next ten to twenty years.[10] Deployed with previously acquired ASW systems, these new weapons will greatly enhance Taiwan's ASW capability not only in the vicinity of waterways to key harbors, but also in the general region of the Taiwan Strait. Furthermore, despite the fact that U.S. shipyards no longer build diesel-electric submarines, the Bush administration is committed to helping Taiwan procure eight such modern submarines, possibly from allies in Europe, though this is a remote possibility, especially before 2015, given delays in the Taiwanese budgeting process.

To China, a successful blockade of Taiwan would require preempting or foiling any Taiwanese counteroffensive and/or an amphibious attack against its naval bases. For these purposes, Chinese submarines alone would not be adequate; China also needs to maintain air superiority to back up the blockade in order to neutralize Taiwan's ability to counterattack and cut off Taiwan's badly needed supply of materials and other essentials from abroad.

Taiwan's objective, on the other hand, is to preempt or destroy a PRC blockade attack; consequently, Taiwan would have to either destroy the PLA bases used to conduct the blockade by launching amphibious attacks on them or destroy the PLA invasion fleet in the strait. To be able to do either or both effectively, according to the MND, the Taiwanese would need to use submarines as the main instrument to neutralize a PLA blockade.

Phase 3: Amphibious and Airborne Operations

Before launching amphibious and airborne operations, the Chinese would need to successfully completely the first two phases of initial air strikes and the naval blockade, as well as seize the necessary ports for amphibious landings. Furthermore, these operations would only be launched on the assumption that Taiwan's capability to resist had already been severely degraded.

The first and second stages described above have in fact been constructed on the basis of two key hypotheses. First, the ROC's direct command and control capability would be shattered by air attacks, and, once this has happened, Taiwan's forces would be unable and/or unwilling to resist effectively. Second, an amphibious assault would be carried out with hovercraft and wing-in-ground effect landing craft (WIGELC), which could ferry 10,000–15,000 marines and special operation forces and their hardware to Taiwan's beaches and ports. An airborne operation would most probably involve the PLA's 15th Airborne Corps dropping, in the first instance, three regiments of airborne troops from their newly acquired Russian-made IL-76 Candid transports to attack one of the Taiwanese air force bases in western Taiwan.[11] The objective of the initial amphibious and airborne operations would be to secure suitable landing sites to enable a large number of ground forces and heavy equipment to be deployed. Once this objective has been attained, a decisive ground attack would follow.

TAIWANESE COUNTERATTACK. In assessing Taiwan's ability to counterattack in such circumstances, one needs to work on the assumption that its command and control system survived the initial air attacks, its ground forces have managed to remain in combat formation, their mobility remains largely undamaged, and the Taiwanese people remain loyal to the existing political leadership on the island. However, it is assumed that most of Taiwan's air defense system would be compromised, and its marine corps unable to launch counter-amphibious attacks as a result of an effective PLA blockade. In other words, Taiwan's command and control system would need to function well enough to direct surviving ground forces to counterattack quickly against the small PLA landing forces on the ground in order to defeat an amphibious and airborne assault.

Taiwan's ground forces have undergone major streamlining and restructuring recently. As a result, its first-line land force has been reorganized into twenty composite brigades equipped and trained to conduct two-dimensional operations. Each brigade constitutes 5,000–8,000 soldiers and is equipped with good transportation and communication gears, its own logistic support network, air defense systems such as the Stingers shoulder-launched missiles, artilleries, armor units, and mobile radar systems. It is also supported by OH-58D survey helicopters, AH-1W Cobra assault helicopters, and AH-64D Apache Longbow attack helicopters. All of them are equipped with tube-launched, optically tracked, wire-guided (TOW) and Hellfire anti-tank missiles. Each brigade is a formidable and effective unit against a lightly armed landing force on the ground. Taiwan's ability to counterattack on the ground is also enhanced by the deployment of CH-47 heavy-lift helicopters, which should enable the rapid deployment and reinforcement of individual brigades. A command and control system that quickly recovers from previous attacks and effectively directs remaining air defense and air force assets to support ground counterattacks are key to defeating PLA landing forces and driving them offshore.

DETERRING THREATS WITH EFFECTIVE CRISIS MANAGEMENT MECHANISMS

When assessing PLA military maneuvers, exercises, and activities across the Taiwan Strait, it is important to identify exactly whether these military postures would lead to tension escalation, potential crisis, or a real crisis. Equally important is the activation of Taiwan's emergency reaction mechanisms to cope with potential threats and report to the commander-in-chief, the president, in order to ensure an effective response to the situation. If faced with a potential military escalation, the MND will activate emergency reaction mechanisms in accordance with the "Regulations of Coping with Surprise Situation in the Period of Regular Combat Readiness" and immediately proceed with military crisis and threat assessments to identify trends of crisis development. The minister of national defense and general chief of staff then immediately report to the president through the chain of command. The president, after receiving a situation assessment report and recommendations on crisis management options, either directly orders the defense minister to implement measures to deal with the situation or calls an emergency convening of the Taiwanese National Security Council (NSC) in order to reach more comprehensive decisions in coping with the potential military threats (see Figure 10.1).

In the process of identifying the nature of a threat, intelligence gathering and intelligence assessment are vital to deciding the appropriate emergency response mechanism. The ROC's military intelligence operations possess the capability to detect nearly all air, sea, and ground PLA military activities including signals intelligence (SIGINT) to a range of 250 NM inside China's southwest coastal provinces. For example, during the March 1996 PLA missile exercises near Taiwan, with the assistance of SIGINT, former President Lee immediately ordered the upgrade of the level of combat readiness, which included a twenty-four-hour stand-by combat alert of the armed forces and the issuance of live ammunition to ground forces stationed at offshore islands, including Penghu, Kinmoy, and Matzu.

President Lee also immediately called an emergency conference of the NSC in order to make decisions on all internal and external emergency response recommendations suggested by responsible government departments and regarding interagency task force operations. The emergency response actions were carried out without declaring a national emergency in accordance with the National Emergency Act. There was a brief period of panic in the Taiwanese financial market, which resulted in a stock market crash of over 1,000 points. The foreign currency exchange was confronted with excessive demand but was eventually stabilized via an emergency supply of hard currencies. During the crisis, the military stayed on full alert and kept very close eyes on the PLAAF activities in the coastal region. At the same time, preventive diplomacy also took

Clear indication of a possible attack on Taiwan

⇩

MND conveys an emergency operation conference report to the secretary general of the NSC, advising the president to hold an emergency conference at the NSC

⇩

NSC Conference

MND briefs the NSC regarding possible hostile operations, enemy strengths and weaknesses, existing ROC war-fighting capabilities, and the implementation of efforts to enhance ROC war-fighting capabilities

⇩

NSC discusses issues such as the probability of ending the war, the international response, the people's will, the effect of national mobilization, the likely end result of the conflict, etc.

⇩

Presidential Decision Making

| negotiation (end war) | stalling (no decision) | engage in war |

Primarily relies upon political and diplomatic negotiations; combat readiness is a secondary backup

a. Recommend issuing Martial Law and declare national emergency, activate mobilization system;
b. Activate joint operation command center to direct war;
c. Coordinate with other government task forces to support combat operation; and
d. Mobilize population to support war campaign.

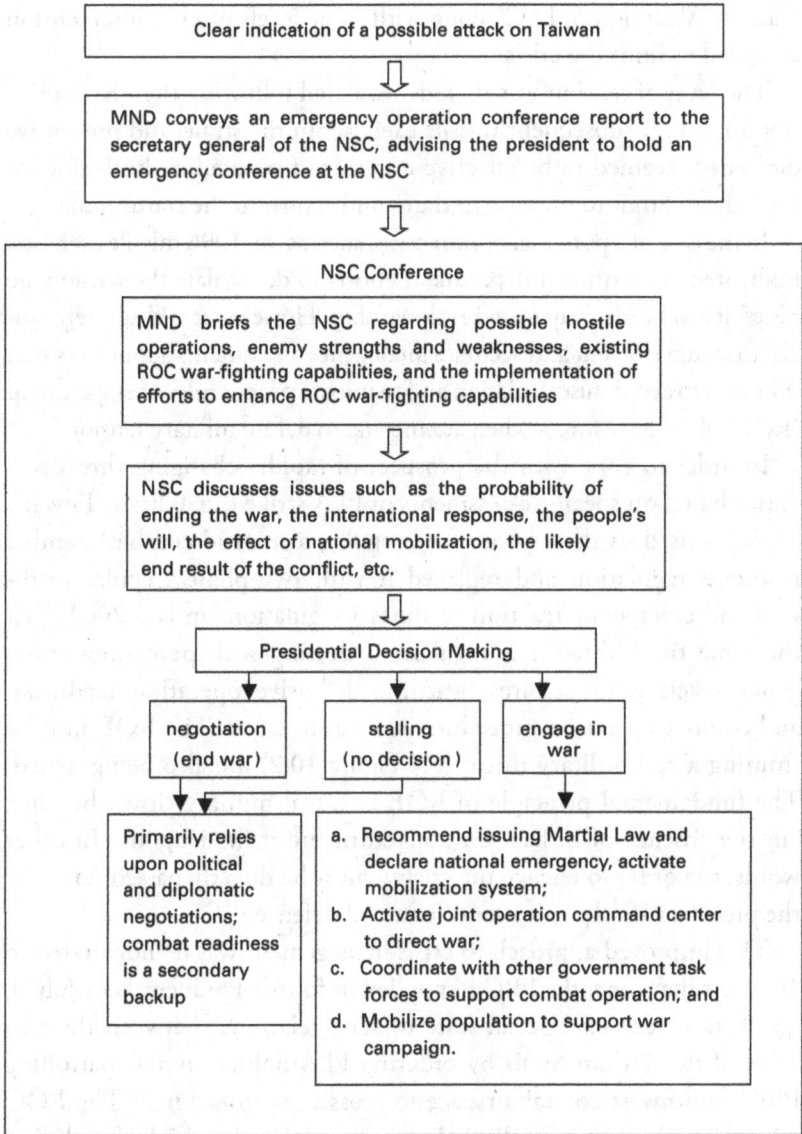

NSC, National Security Council; MND, Ministry of National Defense.
Source: The Ministry of National Defense, Taiwan, R.O.C., 2006.

Figure 10.1 Decision-Making Process of the ROC's Defensive Operation

place in Washington, D.C. along with some levels of U.S. intervention intended to limit the crisis.

The level of tension was then de-escalated following the PRC's decision to call off subsequent missile exercises in the strait, and preventive diplomacy seemed to be effective in terms of persuading both sides of the Taiwan Strait to exercise restraint and return to the status quo.

In the case of a potential or near crisis, such as the 1996 missile exercises, multilateral government department efforts to de-escalate the tension are necessary to break away from brinkmanship. However, it is absolutely crucial to secure efficient and accurate intelligence assessments about the situation so as to avoid miscalculation and to initiate proper rules of engagement (ROE) of military forces when attempting to defuse military tension.

In order to cope with the prospect of rapidly changing threat scenarios based on specific assessments of PLA strike capabilities, Taiwan's MND revised its three-phase (i.e., regular, alert, and combat) combat readiness regulation and replaced it with two-phase (regular readiness and emergency reaction readiness) regulations in late 2003.[12] At the same time, three new regulations dealing with peacetime emergency reaction procedures, wartime defensive operation readiness, and combat operation procedures were also issued. The ROE in confronting a real military threat (see Figure 10.2) are also being issued. The fundamental principle of ROE in a real military threat became: "in the absence of orders, do not return fire if fired upon." In other words, the order to engage the enemy must be directly passed down by the president via the minister of national defense.[13]

This improved approach to crisis management was demonstrated in 1999. At that time, the PRC responded to former President Lee's July 9, 1999 statement of "special state to state relations" between the two sides of the Taiwan Strait by ordering PLA fighter aircraft patrolling PRC's southwest coastal airspace to cross the center line.[14] The ROC Air Force fighter jets patrolling the area were placed on high alert during the crisis. To manage such a potentially volatile and sensitive situation requires very precise intelligence assessments about provocative or hostile maneuvers and the provision to the pilots of precise ROE. Had it not been for the issuance of the fundamental ROE of "in the absence of orders, do not return fire if fired upon," a serious incident and perhaps rapid escalation could have occurred between pilots from both sides.

Engagement Requirements
a. Fight with resolve. b. Extend maximum restraint, refrain from starting a war. c. Be patient, always look at the big picture.

Engagement Principles
a. Do not provoke. b. Do not escalate. c. De-escalate hostility.

Advise Principles
a. Do not intimidate. b. Do not retreat. c. Do not show weakness.

War Preparation Method
Actively prepare for war with maximum concealment from the enemy.

Policy Guidance
In the absence of orders, do not return fire if fired upon.

Guidelines of Rules of Engagement

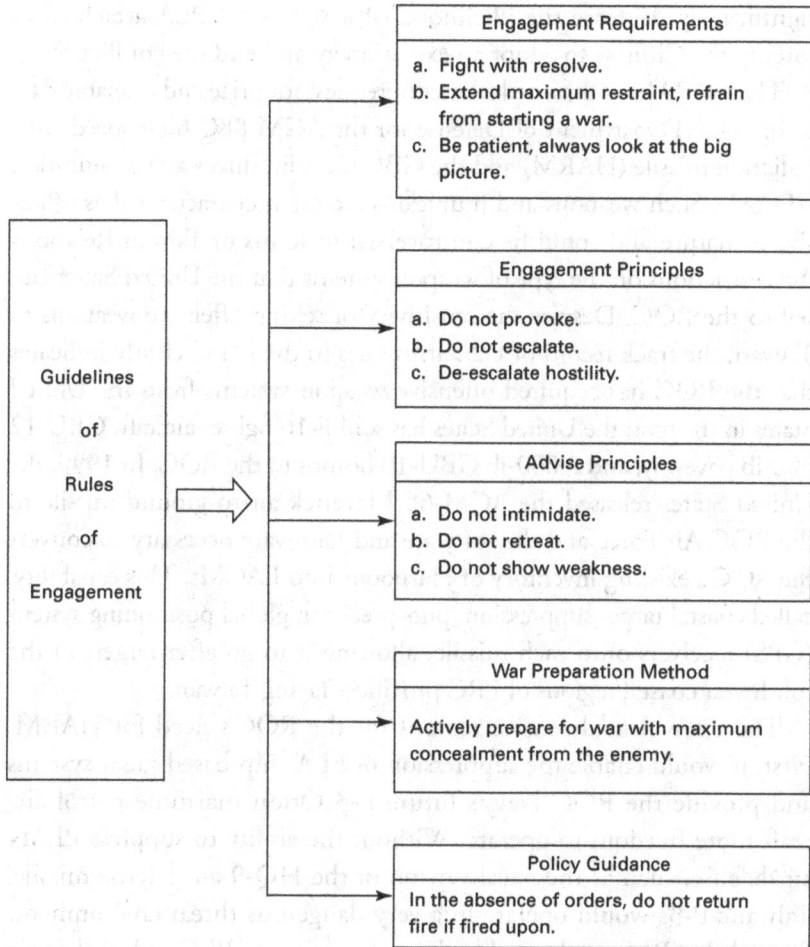

Source: The Ministry of National Defense, Taiwan, R.O.C., 2006.

Figure 10.2 Rules of Engagement (ROE)

USE OF OFFENSIVE COUNTERMEASURES

While continuously enhancing its defense capabilities and war-fighting/war prevention crisis management mechanisms, Taiwan is also putting some efforts into developing offensive countermeasures in an attempt to destroy or degrade PLA war-fighting facilities on the mainland. This is primarily intended to enhance deterrence and, if deterrence fails, to significantly decrease the likelihood of a successful PLA attack, thus forcing the Chinese to adopt an exit strategy and end the conflict.[15]

The MND has submitted a letter of request for price and available data to the U.S. Department of Defense for the AGM-88C high-speed anti-radiation missile (HARM) and the GBU-31 joint direct attack munition (JDAM). Such weapons and munitions are often characterized as offensive in nature and could be controversial in terms of Taiwan Relations Act restrictions on the type of weapon systems that the United States can sell to the ROC. Despite the sensitivity of selling offensive weapons to Taiwan, the track record of U.S. arms sales to the island clearly indicates that the ROC has acquired offensive weapon systems from the United States in the past; the United States has sold F-16 fighter aircraft, GBU-12 500-lb paveway, and 2,000-lb GBU-10 bombs to the ROC. In 1999, the United States released the AGM-65 Maverick air-to-ground missile to the ROC Air Force and the software and hardware necessary to convert the ROC's existing inventory of Harpoons into LACMs. This capability, called coastal target suppression, puts precision global positioning system (GPS) receivers onto each missile, allowing it to go after targets in the southwest coastal regions of PRC provinces facing Taiwan.

There are clear defensive reasons for the ROC's need for HARM. First, it would enable the suppression of PLA ship-based radar systems and provide the ROC Navy's future P-3 Orion maritime patrol aircraft more freedom to operate. Without the ability to suppress PLAN air defense, such as the naval version of the HQ-9 air defense missile, Taiwan's P-3s would operate in a very dangerous threat environment. Second, HARM would enable the suppression of PRC radars that are supporting air strikes against Taiwan. PLAAF and PLAN air operations are highly centralized and dependent on ground air command and control for coordination and direction of complex strike missions. This air control depends upon radar relays for situational awareness. By disrupting the air controller's source of information, it can disrupt the PLA's ability to conduct strikes against Taiwan.

Third, suppression of PLA air defenses would be necessary to enable the ROC to conduct strike operations against key installations of PLA SRBM batteries with minimal losses. Key installations would include command and control centers and logistical support stations. Going after SRBM's support systems is far more cost-effective and would achieve better effects than going after missile launchers. In addition, HARM would enable the suppression of surface-to-air missile systems operating along the PRC's southeast coast. For example, during Taiwan's annual military exercise, Han Guang 18 in 2002, the ROC Air Force, after surviving simulated PLA missile and air strikes, attempted to conduct a major air campaign against key targets on the PRC's coast, employing about 90 percent of its surviving F-16 fleet. They lost 70 percent of these F-16s to PLA air defenses due to an inability to suppress enemy air defense capabilities via such means as HARM, land-attack cruise missiles, and airborne SIGINT platforms that could provide operating parameters of radars operating along the coast.

ROC's interest in JDAM is twofold. First, ROC would reduce the risk of collateral damage by using precision-guided bombs. JDAM kits would enable the bombs to hit their target instead of hitting innocent people and facilities. Second, using smart bombs would mean that the ROC Air Force would only have to make one mission over a specific target, hence reducing the risks.

Other domestic efforts to enhance Taiwan's offensive countermeasures against PRC's strikes are also in progress. The CSIST is in the process of upgrading the Shung-Fong II anti-ship missile to the Shung-Fong 2E LACM and Shung-Fong III supersonic anti-ship and anti-land missile systems.[16] Their objective is to suppress and retaliate against the PLA's key coastal installations, command and control centers, and SRBM systems with long-range precision-guidance munitions, and reduce the risk of air strike operations. Shung-Fong 2E LACM and Shung-Fong III supersonic anti-ship and anti-land missiles would probably have a range exceeding 300 km, and would be launched by air, sea, and land platforms. At the same time, the National Science Research Council also confirmed that it is collaborating with CSIST in the research and development of medium-range ballistic missiles (exceeding 1,000 km) which will enhance the ROC's offensive operations against key PLA targets inside China.[17]

CONCLUDING REMARKS

It is abundantly clear that preventing outright military confrontation in the Taiwan Strait is in the best interest of not only China and Taiwan but also the entire Asia-Pacific region. The primary objective of Taiwan's military is to deter and/or suppress any possible PLA attacks. Taipei's defense strategy is designed to send a clear and unmistakable message to Beijing that the people and the armed forces in Taiwan are determined to confront PLA military pressure or attacks with whatever means available. Taiwan's defense policies and war-fighting doctrine are also designed to send a message that Taipei will not initiate a war against Beijing, but that Beijing would encounter a devastating setback should it decide to do so.

In order to achieve these goals, Taiwan's defense modernization puts an increasing emphasis on building both defensive and *offensive* capabilities, as discussed above. This derives from the belief that, assuming Taipei's military assets largely survive an all-out PLA attack, the Taiwan military must have the capacity to launch offensive operations to regain control over the Taiwan Strait. Such capabilities are necessary to frustrate Beijing's wish for a short war and will thus provide an opportunity for the international community to intervene.

In deterring the type of possible PLA attacks listed above, the ROC armed forces and NSC are continuing to make improvements in a variety of military areas. Many of these advances have come about as a result of the annual "Han Guang Exercise" held since 2001. This war game is designed to improve Taipei's existing crisis management procedures when confronted with various possible PLA attacks. The exercise has helped enormously in strengthening political-military coordination and intramilitary operability.

Despite these advances, Taiwan's defense construction and military modernization remain hampered by the inability of the executive and legislative branches of government to agree on the most appropriate level and type of budget allocations and force structure. Without a clear agreement, observers in the United States and elsewhere will continue to fear the emergence of a significant military imbalance across the Taiwan Strait. Moreover, such a perception might eventually encourage China to use force to achieve its political objectives.

NOTES

1. These are projected PLA attack scenarios against Taiwan, presented as a possible sequence in *National Defense Report 2006*, Ministry of National Defense (July 2006), pp. 134–35.

2. This air attack scenario was made after taking into account the advanced technology and weapon systems that China had developed and acquired from Russia and other countries, the lessons the PLA reportedly gained from the U.S. air campaigns in Kosovo and in the Gulf War, as well as new air war tactics developed by the PLA Air Force (PLAAF). According to the intelligence department of the ROC's Ministry of National Defense (MNO), the PLAAF conducted a major exercise of an attack air group (AG) in its full order of battle and supported by a support air group (SG) for the first time in July 2002. The AG was composed of frontline fighters, and attacked the mock enemy at intervals of 180–300 seconds in cooperation with the SG. The SG was a composite group made up of reconnaissance, air defense suppression, electronic gaming, and AWACS units, and it carried out its missions at intervals of 120 seconds. According to an intelligence officer of the MND, the PLA has already completed precise location surveys of the five military airfields and four air-defense missile bases in Taiwan's western coastal areas and had fed precise positioning data for these military facilities into its fighter-borne computers. ETToday.com, September 14, 2002, http://www.ettoday.com/2002/09/14/303-135/331.htm.

3. See Part 2: National Security and Defence Policy, chap. 4: "National Defence Policy and Military Strategy" in Ministry of National Defence *National Defence Report 2006, Rep. of China* (Taipei, 2006), pp. 92–93.

4. See former Defense Minister Tang Yao-ming's report at the Legislative Yuan, *Legislative Gazette* 91, no. 62 (2) (November 2, 2002): 198–203.

5. According to the National Science Research Council, the Hwa Wei Satellite project is conducted by the Office of Space and Satellite Programs NSRC and began in 1996. Meant mainly for scientific research purposes, the Hwa Wei II Satellite focuses on agriculture survey and remote sensing of the earth. However, the dual-use image technology can be used for military purposes. The satellite was launched in late 2003. See "The Report on C4ISR Capability and Evaluation of National Military Science and Technology Policies," Technology and Information Committee, Legislative Yuan, in *Legislative Gazette* 88, no. 28 (May 29, 1999), pp. 182–83.

6. Missile Defense Command was established on April 1, 2004, part of the restructuring and consolidation reform conducted by the MND in accordance with the new Defense Law. See *Legislative Gazette* 93, no. 30 (June 6, 2004), p. 278.

7. On August 17, 2002, Premier Yiu Xi-kung announced that the ROC government will spend 700 billion Taiwan dollars from 2006 to 2016 on defense acquisition; priority goes to acquiring Aegis platforms. See *Freedom Daily* (August 18, 2002), p. 4.

8. The ROC Air Force constructed a new Chia Shang Air Force Base in Hwalian, eastern Taiwan in the early 1990s. It is surrounded by high mountains and faces the eastern Pacific Ocean. The geographic conditions make it difficult to be attacked

by air from forces based on mainland China. This author made a visit to Chia Shang Base in 1998, and saw huge underground hangars inside the mountain.

9. See *China Times* (August 12, 2002), p. 1.

10. *Legislative Gazette* 96, no. 17 (March 17, 2006), p. 135.

11. Mei Ling, "PLA's Amphibious Landing Capability Development," *Studies on Chinese Communism* 35, no. 4 (April 15, 2001), pp. 55–64.

12. *National Defense Report, 2006,* July 2006.

13. *Legislative Gazette* 93, no. 32 (June 16, 2004), p. 131.

14. Legally speaking, the center line no longer exists after the United States cut off its diplomatic relations with ROC in January 1979, and terminated the U.S.-ROC defense treaty by the end of 1980. Both Beijing and Taipei never formally agreed on the center line; it has since become a tacit understanding to avoid misunderstanding and miscalculation.

15. The MND is very prudent about developing an offensive capability. Officially, the military insists that the objective of defense modernization is not to develop an offensive capability per se, but rather to augment Taiwan's defensive capacity by acquiring the capability to launch offensive strikes against targets in the mainland, designed to deter follow-up attacks.

16. See *Minshen News* (July 3, 2005), p. 1. According to the report, CSIST has successfully tested fired Shung-Fong 2E LACM with a range of up to 500 km.

17. Mr. Wu Mao-Qun, chairperson of the National Science Research Council, admitted during a Q & A at the Legislative Yuan subcommittee meeting October 11, 2004 that the Council is currently evaluating the feasibility of developing medium-range missiles, and is collaborating with CSIST in missile development. See *China Times* (October 13, 2004), p. 4.

11

The Implications of Chinese Military Modernization for U.S. Force Posture in a Taiwan Conflict

Roger Cliff

U.S. FORCE POSTURE in the Asia-Pacific region may soon be inadequate to deter a Chinese use of force against Taiwan. China is in the process of rapidly modernizing its military capabilities, and its military doctrine emphasizes surprise and rapid operations. If China were to succeed in achieving surprise against the United States, the capabilities that China is likely to possess within the next ten years will be sufficient to overwhelm those U.S. forces that would initially be available unless a fundamental readjustment of U.S. force posture in the Asia-Pacific region is implemented.[1]

CURRENT U.S. FORCE POSTURE IN THE ASIA-PACIFIC

In the Asia-Pacific region, the United States maintains combat forces in Japan, South Korea, Guam, Hawaii, and Alaska (as well as on the west coast of the contiguous United States). Naval, air, and marine forces currently based in Japan are substantial. The U.S. Navy's Seventh Fleet is headquartered at Yokosuka on Tokyo Bay. U.S. Navy ships based in Japan include the fleet aircraft carrier USS *Kitty Hawk,* an amphibious assault carrier, and eight Aegis cruisers and destroyers. In addition to the *Kitty Hawk's* air wing, U.S. air forces in Japan include the 15th Air Force Wing at Kadena Air Base on Okinawa, the 35th Fighter Wing at Misawa Air Base in northern Japan, and Marine Aircraft Group 12 based at

Iwakuni in southwestern Japan. In total, these forces comprise 150 land-based or carrier-based F-15, F/A-18, and F-16 fighter aircraft. Ground forces consist primarily of the III Marine Expeditionary Force, which includes the 31st Marine Expeditionary Unit, capable of conducting amphibious assaults. A total of about 18,000 U.S. Marine Corps personnel are based in Japan.[2]

The United States also maintains significant air and ground forces in South Korea. These include the headquarters of the 8th Army and elements of the heavy 2nd Infantry Division (including the division headquarters and a heavy brigade combat team), with over a hundred M-1 tanks and a total of 21,000 personnel. U.S. air forces in South Korea include the 51st Fighter Wing at Osan Air Base and the 8th Fighter Wing at Kunsan Air Base, with a total of about sixty F-16 fighter aircraft and twenty-four A-10/OA-10 close air support aircraft.[3]

The United States also maintains significant and growing forces on the U.S. territory of Guam, in the Western Pacific. Two nuclear attack submarines are currently based in Guam and B-52, B-1, and B-2 bombers frequently deploy temporarily to Andersen Air Force Base.[4]

U.S. military forces based in Hawaii include the light 25th Infantry Division and other U.S. army units totaling 17,000 personnel, nine Aegis cruisers and destroyers, seventeen nuclear attack submarines, and twenty-four Hawaii Air National Guard F-15s. U.S. military forces based in Alaska include the 172nd Stryker Brigade Combat Team, the 3rd Air Force Wing, and the 354th Fighter Wing. Approximately seventy F-15 and F-16 fighter aircraft are based in Alaska (the portion of the continental United States closest to East Asia), along with a dozen A-10/OA-10 close air support aircraft.[5]

In addition to the above forces, additional U.S. naval forces frequently transit into or through the western part of the Pacific Ocean.

CURRENT CHALLENGES POSED BY THE PLA

Despite massive downsizing in recent years, the People's Liberation Army (PLA) is still the world's largest military in terms of the number of active-duty personnel. Its ground forces comprise roughly 1.4 million personnel and the equivalent of about fifty maneuver divisions. These forces field nearly 8,000 main battle tanks (MBTs) and over 15,000 artillery pieces. China's naval forces comprise about twenty-five destroyers, forty-five frigates, and sixty attack submarines; its air forces comprise over 3,000 combat aircraft.[6]

Much of the equipment of China's military forces, however, is obsolete by modern standards. Over 5,000 of China's MBTs, for example, are based on the Soviet T-54, which entered service in the 1950s. Most of the remainder of China's MBTs are still a generation behind the U.S. M1, which first became operational in 1983.[7] Only about a hundred of China's MBTs are comparable in capability to the M1. Similarly, most of China's surface naval combatants mount no surface-to-air missiles and thus are essentially defenseless against attack by modern naval weapon systems. Most ships that do have surface-to-air missiles, moreover, have relatively short-range systems. As of early 2007, only two Chinese ships had long-range air defense capabilities comparable to those of U.S. Aegis ships, which first entered service in 1983.[8] Finally, most of China's fighter and ground-attack aircraft are based on the Soviet MiG-19 and MiG-21, which first entered service in the 1950s. China currently fields only about 300 "fourth-generation" fighters (comparable to the U.S. F-15 and F-16, which entered service in the 1970s), and only about 100 of China's fighters can carry active-radar air-to-air missiles, whereas all U.S. fighters can. The limitations of the PLA's weapons, moreover, are paralleled by weaknesses in its intelligence, surveillance, reconnaissance, logistics, and other support systems, and in the PLA's doctrine, organization, training, personnel, and leadership.

Despite these limitations, however, even today the PLA could present significant challenges to the United States in certain contingencies. The most obvious reason for this is geography. Taiwan, for example, is only 90 miles from the Chinese mainland at its closest point and only 250 miles from the mainland from its most distant point. China could base hundreds of aircraft within striking range of Taiwan and has at least 800 conventional ballistic missiles capable of reaching any location on the island. The nearest U.S. combat aircraft, by contrast, are the fifty-four F-15s at Kadena Air Base on Okinawa, 400 miles away. The continental United States, where the bulk of U.S. combat forces are, is 6,000 miles away. Additional fighters could be deployed to Okinawa in relatively short order (roughly another 120 land-based fighters are normally stationed in mainland Japan and Korea), but at most only approximately 200 could effectively operate from there. The next-nearest U.S. air base is Iwakuni Marine Corps Air Station, which is almost twice as far from Taiwan as Okinawa. Thus, in a conflict over Taiwan, China could actually enjoy numerical superiority in fourth-generation fighter aircraft operating from nearby bases close to Taiwan, at least initially.[9] Over two or three weeks, however, the United States would be able to bring several aircraft carriers to the vicinity of Taiwan, which would tip the balance of fourth-generation fighter aircraft in favor of the United States.

Similarly, although the U.S. Navy comprises a dozen aircraft carriers, over seventy Aegis cruisers and destroyers, and over fifty attack submarines, as noted above, only one aircraft carrier, eight Aegis cruisers and destroyers, and two attack submarines are currently based in the Western Pacific. Ships departing from Hawaii would need at least a week to arrive in waters off of Taiwan and ships departing from the west coast of the United States would need at least ten days. Thus, for the first week of a conflict over Taiwan, although its naval forces would be qualitatively inferior to those of the United States and Taiwan, China could enjoy a numerical advantage of almost 2:1 in major surface combatants (cruisers, destroyers, and frigates) and as much as 15:1 in submarines. Although China does not have an aircraft carrier, land-based aircraft would be nearly as effective as carrier-based aircraft in naval combat in the waters around Taiwan. Also, China possesses roughly 150 aircraft capable of launching anti-ship cruise missiles, as compared to the thirty-six naval strike aircraft carried by the *Kitty Hawk*.[10]

There are a number of "anti-access" measures that China could take, moreover, that would exacerbate the constraints on the U.S. military capability caused by the dearth of air bases near Taiwan and the limited number of U.S. forces forward-deployed in the Western Pacific. As noted above, China has at least 800 conventional ballistic missiles and in the future some of these will be capable of reaching targets not just in Taiwan, but also on Okinawa and mainland Japan. Depending on the effectiveness of the Patriot PAC-3 batteries currently being deployed to Okinawa,[11] ballistic missiles with runway-penetrating submunition warheads could be used to attack the airstrips there while ballistic missiles with a larger number of smaller submunitions could be used to attack the PAC-3 batteries themselves. If successful, these attacks would render the runways temporarily unusable, trapping any aircraft on the ground and leaving them vulnerable to follow-up attacks. Follow-up attacks could consist of additional ballistic missiles with submunitions, which would be highly effective in destroying unprotected aircraft, and attacks by cruise missiles and manned aircraft with precision-guided munitions, which could be used to destroy critical air base facilities as well as aircraft in hardened shelters.[12]

The emphasis on preemption and surprise in Chinese military doctrine also serves to facilitate China's geographic advantage in a conflict with the United States over Taiwan.[13] If a Chinese use of force against Taiwan occurred at the end of a prolonged crisis between Beijing and Taipei, the United States would have ample time to deploy additional aircraft carriers, surface combatants, and submarines to the waters near Taiwan, and additional missile defense forces, fighters, and support aircraft to air bases in the Western Pacific. Although only about 200 fighters could effectively operate from Okinawa, with support from aerial refueling aircraft, additional fighters could operate from airfields in mainland Japan, Guam, and possibly South Korea. The greater distances from Taiwan of those bases would reduce the average effectiveness of the fighters operating from them; however, several hundred additional land-based fighters could be made available that way, decisively tipping the military balance in favor of the United States and Taiwan.[14]

If, on the other hand, a Chinese use of force on Taiwan was launched with little or no prior indication, it is possible that for the first few days of the conflict the only U.S. forces involved would be a limited number of land-based aircraft. (If China chose to attack U.S. bases in Japan, air bases on Okinawa could be unusable for the first few days of the conflict; some aircraft stationed at more-distant U.S. air bases, however—such as those at Iwakuni, Misawa, or South Korea—which might not be targeted by Chinese attacks, as well as the *Kitty Hawk's* air wing, might be able to participate, depending on the number of aerial refueling aircraft initially available.) After the first few days, growing numbers of land-based aircraft would become available and the *Kitty Hawk* and its associated surface combatants, along with a number of attack submarines (the two based in Guam plus whatever other submarines were operating in the Western Pacific at the time the conflict began) would arrive in the Taiwan theater. Missile attacks on Okinawa might force U.S. land-based aircraft to operate from more distant airfields and, as noted above, even with the entire Seventh Fleet present, China would enjoy a significant numerical advantage in naval strike aircraft and surface and subsurface naval combatants. After about a week, additional surface combatants and submarines would arrive from Hawaii but, unless another aircraft carrier had already been underway in the Pacific (or eastern Indian Ocean) at the time the conflict began, at least ten days would elapse before additional aircraft carriers could arrive from the west coast of the United States.

This situation has implications for both deterrence and escalation control. First, it implies that the U.S. ability to deter a Chinese use of force against Taiwan is not just a function of the relative balance of military capabilities, but also of Beijing's combined beliefs about both its ability to achieve surprise against the United States and how long Taiwan would hold out in the face of Chinese attacks. The more China's leaders believe in their ability to achieve surprise against the United States and think resistance in Taiwan would quickly collapse,[15] the more likely they are to judge that a use of force against Taiwan would be successful; this also means it would be more difficult for the United States to deter China.

Second, the advantage China could potentially gain from a successful preemptive attack means that a conflict between China, Taiwan, and the United States could rapidly escalate. If there were no military advantages to China of preemption and surprise in a Taiwan conflict, Beijing would likely prefer to implement a campaign of gradually increasing coercion against the island, beginning with a verbal ultimatum, followed by symbolic missile firings and other shows of force, then gradually increasing air and missile strikes against military and economic targets in Taiwan, and finally, if necessary, a large-scale amphibious assault. China would likely avoid attacking U.S. forces initially in the hopes that the United States would not intervene in the conflict. If the United States were to intervene but confined its actions to defending Taiwan's air space, shipping lanes, and so forth, and refrained from attacking targets on mainland China, then China would likely similarly refrain, at least initially, from attacking U.S. air bases and other facilities in the Western Pacific. This graduated course of events would maximize Beijing's chances of achieving its military objectives at a minimum cost, but would also give the United States and Taiwan significant time to find some sort of negotiated solution to the conflict before it escalates to a full-scale war.

Such gradual escalation, however, would have major military disadvantages for China. Verbal ultimatums and missile firings would provide the

United States with ample time and pretext to deploy additional aircraft carrier strike groups, fighter aircraft, missile defense forces, and so on to the Western Pacific without interference from Chinese anti-access measures. When actual hostilities begin, these forces would be ready to provide a vigorous defense of Taiwan and initially would be able to do so without concern for the safety of their own bases. If China subsequently decided to attack those bases, it would by that time have lost the advantage of surprise and those bases could have in place robust defenses against missile, aircraft, and covert operative attack.

Preceding a use of force against Taiwan with a preemptive attack on U.S. forces in the Western Pacific, by contrast, would have huge military advantages for China. U.S. forces would be in a peacetime readiness state and thus particularly vulnerable to attack. Furthermore, damage to airfields and ports that were only weakly defended when attacked would slow the deployment of additional forces. The effect of such preemptive attacks, however, would be to significantly raise the stakes for the United States, causing the conflict to skip several levels of escalation from the very beginning. Having already suffered significant losses, there would be little possibility that the United States would seek to limit the magnitude of forces committed to the conflict. Moreover, it would be unlikely that the United States would refrain from attacking targets on Chinese territory if U.S. bases and territories were themselves subject to attack. Finally, assuming that some of those U.S. bases were on Japanese territory, Japan would likely now be a belligerent as well. Thus, given its continued vulnerabilities (marked, for example, by limited missile defenses, lack of aircraft shelters, etc.), current U.S. force posture in the Western Pacific creates significant risk for the rapid escalation of a conflict over Taiwan, especially if the PLA believes that it can achieve a successful outcome through a preemptive attack, and that it cannot achieve a successful outcome without a preemptive surprise attack.

FUTURE CHALLENGES POSED BY THE PLA

The challenge that the PLA presents for U.S. force posture in the Asia-Pacific will only increase in the future. China's rapidly growing economy will make increasing levels of resources available for defense spending;

China's defense industries have already begun to produce weapon systems that in many cases are comparable in capability to those that currently dominate the U.S. inventory.[16] By 2015, China will have the capability and resources to build approximately a dozen modern destroyers with air defense capabilities comparable to the U.S. Aegis system and several dozen modern frigates. China will also have the resources to build dozens of modern diesel-electric attack submarines along with a dozen nuclear-powered type 093-class attack submarines. China will have the resources to acquire hundreds of additional fourth-generation fighters (Russian-designed Su-27s and Su-30s along with indigenously designed J-10s), all of which would carry active-radar air-to-air missiles, along with a hundred or so JH-7 supersonic fighter-bombers capable of carrying anti-ship cruise missiles and a similar number of H-6 medium bombers capable of carrying anti-ship or land-attack cruise missiles (LACMs). China will also have the resources to acquire several hundred long-range Russian S-300 series or indigenous HQ-9 surface-to-air missiles (which are comparable in capability to the U.S. Patriot system), and a thousand or so more conventional ballistic missiles capable of reaching Taiwan or more distant targets. It is also possible that by 2015 China will have developed missiles, along with the required surveillance, reconnaissance, command, and control systems, capable of hitting a moving ship at sea.[17] The capabilities of China's other intelligence, surveillance, and reconnaissance systems will likely increase in parallel with the capabilities of its weapons platforms, and the PLA's doctrine, organization, training, logistics, personnel, and leadership will likely improve as well.

While China is fielding systems that are largely comparable in capability to those currently in the U.S. inventory, the U.S. military will be fielding the next generation of weapon systems. The pace of U.S. modernization, however, will not be as rapid as that of the PLA. Between now and 2015, the United States plans to increase the total number of Aegis ships in service in the U.S. Navy from about seventy to eighty, and to commission half a dozen or so new DDG 1000-class destroyers [formerly known as the DD(X) class], which will have superior air defense and anti-submarine capabilities to the Aegis cruisers and destroyers.[18] The U.S. Navy also plans to replace most of the approximately twenty frigates it currently operates with a comparable number of Littoral Combat Ships, which will have greater speed and reduced radar, acoustic, magnetic, and infrared signatures. The overall size of the U.S. inventory of nuclear attack submarines will remain approximately constant at fifty, but approximately ten Virginia-class attack submarines are planned to be commissioned by 2015, replacing an equal number of older Los Angeles-class ships (there were only two Virginia-class submarines in service in the U.S. inventory as of early 2007). The Virginia class is quieter and capable of carrying 30 percent more missiles and torpedoes than the Los Angeles class. The U.S. Navy will also have completed the conversion of four Ohio-class nuclear ballistic missile submarines into guided missile submarines, each capable of carrying 154 Tomahawk LACMs. Finally, the remaining two conventionally powered aircraft carriers in the U.S. inventory as well as the oldest nuclear-powered carrier, the *Enterprise*, will have been retired and replaced with a larger Nimitz-class nuclear-powered ship and the first of the new CVN-21 class, which will be capable of sustaining a significantly higher tempo of operations than the Nimitz class. Thus, the overall capabilities of U.S. naval combatants will increase measurably by 2015, but the U.S. Navy will not experience the wholesale transformation that China's navy will likely see.[19]

Between now and 2015, the United States also plans to field significant numbers of next-generation aircraft. In 2015, the overall U.S. combat aircraft inventory (U.S. Air Force, U.S. Navy, and U.S. Marine Corps) will include about 180 F-22 air superiority fighters, which are significantly more capable than any other aircraft currently in the U.S. or Chinese inventories; 450 F-35 joint strike fighters, which will have dramatically improved signature reduction compared to fourth-generation fighters; and 450 F/A-18 E/F/G Super Hornets, which are sometimes described as "fourth-and-a-half generation" fighters. However, the remaining 2,100 fighter aircraft planned for the U.S. inventory in 2015 will be existing fourth-generation aircraft and the U.S. Air Force plans to operate the same 140 long-range heavy bombers as it does today. Thus, roughly one-quarter of the U.S. fighter inventory will have been replaced with more-modern systems by 2015 (about twenty F-22s and 250 Super Hornets were already in service as of early 2007),[20] but the remainder of the fighter force and all of the bomber force will consist of aircraft already in service today.[21] In contrast, as much as half of China's current inventory of obsolete second-generation and third-generation fighters could be replaced by modern fourth-generation fighters by 2015.

U.S. theater ballistic missile defense capabilities will also increase significantly between now and 2015. The total U.S. inventory of theater ballistic missile defense forces in early 2007 consisted of about 500 PAC-3 missiles and a lesser number (fewer than sixty) of ship-launched SM-3 Aegis ballistic missile defense interceptors. By 2015, however, the United States plans to field 900 PAC-3 missiles; 700 missile segment enhancement missiles, which will have a greater effective range, be more agile, and be less susceptible to countermeasures than the PAC-3 missile; 600 Terminal High-Altitude Area Defense System (THAAD) missiles, which will have a significantly larger engagement envelope than the PAC-3 or missile segment enhancement missiles; at least eighteen Aegis cruisers and destroyers with the SM-3 ballistic missile defense interceptor as well as at least a hundred SM-2 Block IV missiles, capable of intercepting short-range ballistic missiles (SRBMs) in their terminal phase, on three Aegis cruisers; and an uncertain number of airborne laser aircraft.[22] This compares with the 2,000 or so conventional ballistic missiles China may have by 2015.

Significant changes to U.S. force posture in the Asia-Pacific are also planned. First, in 2008, the *Kitty Hawk,* a conventionally powered ship, will be retired and replaced by the *George Washington,* a nuclear-powered Nimitz-class carrier.[23] The *George Washington* carries 50 percent more fighters (fifty-four vs. thirty-six) and is capable of generating twice as many aircraft sorties per day (and thus has roughly twice the combat power as the *Kitty Hawk*). In addition, as a result of an October 2005 agreement between the United States and Japan, several other changes to U.S. force posture in Japan will occur. Among them, the capabilities to support U.S. contingency operations of Japanese Air Self-Defense Force bases at Nyutabara and Tsuiki on the southern Japanese island of Kyushu will be strengthened and the headquarters of the III Marine Expeditionary Force and approximately 8,000 Marine personnel will be relocated from Okinawa to Guam and other locations by 2014.[24]

The United States also plans on making changes to its force posture in the Asia-Pacific outside of Japan. Three additional attack submarines, for a total of five, will eventually be based in Guam, and overall the number of attack submarines based in Pacific ports, including the west coast of the United States, will increase from about twenty-five to over thirty. Similarly, the number of aircraft carriers based in Pacific ports will increase from five to six.[25]

Even with the above changes to U.S. capabilities and force posture, however, the threat that the PLA presents to U.S. force posture in the Asia-Pacific will likely increase between now and 2015. Even if the U.S. F-15s based in Japan are all replaced by F-22s, and the U.S. F-16s, F/A-18s, and A-10/OA-10s based in Japan and Korea are all replaced by F-35s, the United States will have a total of only about fifty F-22s and fewer than 250 F-35s (including the *George Washington's* air wing) based in Japan and Korea. As noted above, however, by 2015 China could have well over a thousand Su-27, Su-30, and J-10 fourth-generation fighters. Although the F-22 is significantly superior in performance to the Su-27/Su-30, and the F-35 significantly superior in performance to the J-10, China could enjoy a several-to-one numerical advantage in fighter aircraft in the initial stages of a conflict with the United States. The ability of U.S. aircraft to operate from bases in Japan or Korea, moreover, could be compromised by the hundreds of conventional ballistic missiles capable of reaching targets in Japan that China is likely to possess by 2015.

Similarly, even if the six Aegis destroyers currently based in Japan are replaced by DDG 1000-class destroyers, and the two Los Angeles-class submarines currently based in Guam are replaced by five more-capable Seawolf-class or Virginia-class submarines as noted above, by 2015 China could have a dozen or more modern destroyers, several dozen modern diesel-electric submarines, and up to a dozen modern nuclear attack submarines. Thus, China could still enjoy a 2:1 numeric advantage in modern (Aegis or better) cruisers and destroyers and a several-to-one advantage in modern submarines during the initial stages of a conflict with the United States and Taiwan. The *George Washington's* air wing will have about sixty naval strike aircraft, while China, in addition to having the capability to hit a moving ship at sea with a ballistic missile, could have as many as several hundred Su-30 and JH-7 (land-based) naval strike aircraft by 2015. Because the combat radiuses of the Su-30 and JH-7 are about 1,000 miles,[26] China could enjoy as much as a 10:1 numeric advantage in naval strike aircraft over waters within 1,000 miles of China's coast for as long as the first ten days of a conflict, until additional carriers could arrive from the west coast of the United States.

The growing disparity between China's forces and U.S. forces forward-deployed in the Western Pacific will undoubtedly increase the difficulty of deterring a Chinese use of force against Taiwan, as China's advantage in initially deployed forces will lessen the degree of surprise it would need to defeat the United States and thus increase its leadership's propensity to believe that a use of force against Taiwan could be successful. This same reality, however, will likely reduce somewhat China's incentives for a preemptive attack on U.S. bases and facilities in the Western Pacific; China's growing military capabilities relative to the those of the United States will diminish its dependence on such an attack to achieve victory. The military advantages of a preemptive attack will remain large, however, and thus the risk of such a highly escalatory action will remain high.

IMPLICATIONS FOR U.S. FORCE POSTURE

The current and future challenges posed by the PLA have a number of implications for U.S. force posture in the Asia-Pacific region. The most prominent of these is the importance of intelligence and early warning. The overall capabilities of the U.S. military will surpass those of China for the foreseeable future. China's ability to enjoy local superiority in the Western Pacific in the early stages of a conflict with the United States, therefore, is largely a function of the fact that the United States normally has relatively few of its forces forward-deployed in the region. Ships can reach waters off of Taiwan from Hawaii in about seven days, however, and from the west coast of the United States in approximately ten days. The U.S. Air Force can redeploy the equivalent of about one fighter squadron a day. Thus, if the United States had at least ten days' warning of a Chinese attack, it could increase the number of aircraft carriers in the Western Pacific from one to at least three, for a total of about 180 naval strike aircraft; increase the number of Aegis cruisers and destroyers from eight to about twenty five; increase the number of attack submarines from two to about twenty; and increase the number of land-based fighters from about 175 to at least 400.[27]

Even given the number of modern destroyers, submarines, fighters, and naval strike aircraft China is likely to have by 2015, simply having a ten-day advance warning of an attack would thus allow the United States to largely neutralize China's numerical superiority in a conflict. The United States could potentially have more modern destroyers and cruisers in the area than China, and China's numerical advantage in submarines would be reduced from several times as many to perhaps twice as many as the United States (and only a minority of China's submarines would be nuclear powered, while the U.S. submarines could include as many as a dozen Seawolf- and Virginia-class boats, which are significantly quieter and more capable than any submarines China is likely to operate by 2015). China's advantage in fighters would also be reduced from several times as many to perhaps twice as many as the United States (hardly an advantage at all given that by 2015 most of those U.S. fighters would be fifth-generation F-22s and F-35s, while China's would likely all be fourth-generation Su-27s, Su-30s, and J-10s). The advantage in naval strike aircraft would be reduced by a less dramatic amount, but most U.S. naval strike aircraft in the region would be fifth-generation F-35s, whereas China's naval strike aircraft would likely be fourth-generation Su-30s and third-generation JH-7s.

Decreasing China's ability to surprise the United States would also have positive implications for deterrence and escalation. If recognized by China's military, it would reduce Beijing's confidence in being able to defeat the United States, and thus increase U.S. ability to deter China. It would also reduce the likely effectiveness of a preemptive attack against the United States, and thus reduce the likelihood of such an escalatory action.

Given the emphasis on surprise and preemption in PLA doctrine, however, it is quite possible that Beijing would go to extreme lengths to avoid providing any indication of its intention to launch an attack. Although preparations for an effective attack would have to begin well in advance of any military action and could not be completely concealed, they might not be easily detected or recognized. U.S. intelligence and early warning capabilities, therefore, must be capable of detecting preparations for a possible attack despite concerted denial and deception efforts. This implies not only robust technical (imagery, signals, etc.) and human collection means, but also an analytic capability to recognize the indications of a possible attack hidden among a significant amount of routine military and economic activities.

A related implication is that, despite the inevitable desire of diplomats to avoid escalating or complicating a situation, the United States should be biased in favor of dispatching air and naval forces to the Western Pacific from Hawaii and the West Coast, even when indications of a possible conflict are weak or ambiguous. Given that the United States might need to surge these forces to the Western Pacific on extremely short notice in the event of an actual conflict, routinely deploying them in response to what may turn out to be a false alarm would, through frequent practice, increase the U.S. capability to respond rapidly if China actually used force. Such deployments could be done without publicity or under other pretexts, and put in the context of a new rapid-reaction philosophy, to avoid arousing excessive attention or causing alarm when they occur. Such actions might run the risk of escalating relatively minor incidents that had little chance of precipitating an actual war, but would have the advantage of increasing the U.S. ability to deter a Chinese use of force and decreasing China's incentives for launching a preemptive attack. Moreover, as such deployments became commonplace, their escalatory effects would likely diminish over time.

At the same time, the United States should also investigate prospects for forward-basing additional air and naval forces. In the near term, basing additional air forces in Japan may be difficult, as the existing forces already cause considerable complaints about noise and the danger of a potential accident. The attitude of the Japanese public could change, however, if concerns about China's military buildup increase or if an incident were to occur that would significantly worsen tensions between Japan and China. In the meantime, the United States should base at least one fighter wing and aerial refueling aircraft at Andersen Air Force Base in Guam, which under current and future plans has no permanently stationed combat air forces. Although Guam is relatively far from Taiwan (about 1,700 miles), Andersen has a number of advantages. First, it is a very large facility easily capable of accommodating a large number of aircraft (during the Vietnam War, a hundred B-52s were based at Andersen). Second, although far from Taiwan, Guam is even farther from mainland China, meaning that it is more difficult for the Chinese to attack with missiles and aircraft. Furthermore, Guam is U.S. territory and so far the population there has not objected to the increasing military presence in recent years. With aerial refueling, fighters taking off from Guam could conduct combat operations in the area of Taiwan almost as effectively as aircraft based in Japan. Thus, basing one or more fighter wings at Guam would significantly increase the number of tactical aircraft available for immediate employment in a Taiwan contingency.

The United States should also investigate prospects for basing an aircraft carrier strike group in Guam or Singapore. A second forward-deployed carrier would double the number of naval strike aircraft available in the early stages of a conflict with China and the strike group's half a dozen or so surface combatants would be a valuable addition to the nine surface combatants currently based in Japan (eight Aegis ships plus a frigate). As noted above, an aircraft carrier departing from the west coast of the United States would need at least ten days to reach the Taiwan theater; an aircraft carrier departing from Guam could arrive off of Taiwan in two days. The intervening week could be crucial to the outcome of a conflict over Taiwan. As an alternative to Guam, if space could be found for the strike group and its air wing, and it were politically feasible, Singapore would also be a desirable location to base an aircraft carrier strike group. A carrier departing from Singapore could arrive off of Taiwan within three days. Singapore would also be convenient location from which to send a carrier to the Persian Gulf or Arabian Sea, and the strike group could also be used to protect the strategic Straits of Malacca if needed.

Finally, as noted above, currently only two attack submarines are based in Guam, although the U.S. Navy plans to increase this number to five. In view of the number of modern submarines China is likely to have in the future, five is probably the minimum number of attack submarines that should be based in the Western Pacific. The feasibility of basing additional submarines in Guam should be investigated. Alternatively, now that the Japanese taboo against nuclear-powered naval vessels has apparently been broken with the 2005 agreement to allow the *George Washington* to replace the *Kitty Hawk* in 2008, the possibility of basing attack submarines in Japan should be investigated.

In addition to increasing the quantity of air and naval forces in the Western Pacific, the United States should also ensure that their quality increases over time. Barring a dramatic change in the political and economic situation in Russia, no country other than China has the potential to pose both a large-scale and high-tech military threat to the United States. Consequently, the United States should focus most or all of its most advanced military assets in the Asia-Pacific theater. Specifically, when sufficient numbers of F-22s become operational, they should replace the F-15s currently based in the Asia-Pacific.[28] When sufficient numbers of the Marine Corps version of the F-35 become available, they should replace the F-18s and AV-8s at Iwakuni Air Station; when sufficient numbers of the Navy version of the F-35 become available, they should replace the

F-18s of the *George Washington's* air wing; and when sufficient numbers of the Air Force version of the F-35 become available, they should replace the F-16s and A-10/OA-10s at Misawa, Osan, and Kunsan Air Bases.

Most Seawolf-class and Virginia-class submarines should be based in the Pacific, with as many as possible forward-based in Guam or Japan. As Littoral Combat Ships and DDG 1000-class destroyers are commissioned, they should be based first in the Western Pacific. When the first CVN-21-class carrier is commissioned, it too should be based in the Pacific. Most of the eighteen Aegis cruisers and destroyers with the SM-3 ballistic missile defense interceptors as well as all three Aegis cruisers with SM-2 Block IV missiles capable of intercepting SRBMs in their terminal phase should be based in the Pacific.

Increasing the quantity and quality of U.S. air and naval forces in the Western Pacific will strengthen the U.S. ability to deter a Chinese use of force against Taiwan. At the same time, however, it will also increase China's incentives for launching an escalatory preemptive surprise attack against those forces. Consequently, the United States should simultaneously take steps to reduce the vulnerability of U.S. air, naval, and logistics facilities in the region. One such measure consists of strengthening passive defenses at air bases and associated facilities. Runways should be reinforced, to reduce the damage cause by ballistic missiles with runway-penetrating submunitions, and capabilities to rapidly repair damaged runways should be increased. As many hardened aircraft shelters as possible should be constructed at U.S. air bases in the Western Pacific, and underground aviation fuel tanks and dispensing systems should be constructed.

In addition to strengthening passive defenses, active air defenses should be deployed near air bases and other critical facilities in the Western Pacific. As noted above, the United States and Japan recently agreed to deploy three to four Patriot PAC-3 batteries to Okinawa. Three Patriot batteries could have a total of as many as 300 interceptor missiles, depending on the size of the battery and the number of reloads per launcher. In the near term, this will provide a significant capability to defend airfields in Okinawa against ballistic missile attack, although the performance of the PAC-3 system against Chinese ballistic missiles is unproven. As the number and capability of China's ballistic missiles increases, however, the number and capability of U.S. ballistic missile defenses will need to increase as well.

Additional PAC-3 batteries may need to be deployed to Okinawa as well as near U.S. air and naval bases in mainland Japan. When the missile segment enhancement missile begins to become available around 2010,[29] it should replace, or be added to, the PAC-3 missiles in Japan, with Okinawa having first priority. When the first THAAD battery becomes available around 2009,[30] it should be deployed to Okinawa as well, with subsequent batteries deployed near U.S. air and naval bases in mainland Japan and, if China develops a conventional ballistic missile capable of reaching Guam, on that island as well. It should be noted that, given the Chinese emphasis on preemption and surprise, such missile defenses must be deployed in peacetime, *before* a crisis occurs or hostilities commence. Not only would several days be required to relocate missile defense systems from the continental United States to locations in the Western Pacific, but also if they are not in place to prevent China's initial attacks on U.S. airfields, the attacks may render those airfields unusable by the large cargo aircraft required to transport the missile defense systems needed to protect them.

In addition to deploying ballistic missile defenses, the United States also should deploy defenses against cruise missiles and manned aircraft. Ballistic missiles have the capability to temporarily prevent flight operations at air bases but, particularly at bases with hardened aircraft shelters and buried fuel tanks, the primary utility of doing so is to render the air bases and other nearby facilities vulnerable to attack by more accurate weapons such as cruise missiles and aircraft with precision-guided munitions. When configured for nonballistic threats, the PAC-3 system is highly effective against medium- and high-altitude aircraft. For defense against cruise missiles and low-altitude aircraft, the most effective current systems are the Avenger short-range surface-to-air missile system and the Phalanx gun-based close-in weapon system. By 2009, however, the surface-launched advanced medium-range air-to-air missile (SLAMRAAM) system, which will be more effective than both the PAC-3 and Avenger in defending against cruise missiles and low-altitude aircraft, will begin to enter service.[31] Again, the first SLAMRAAM units should be deployed to Okinawa with subsequent units deployed to U.S. air and naval facilities in mainland Japan and Guam. Finally, around 2015, the Medium Extended Air Defense System (MEADS), which will further increase capabilities against cruise missiles and low-altitude aircraft, will begin to enter service.[32] As with SLAMRAAM, the first

MEADS units should be deployed to Okinawa with subsequent units deployed to U.S. air and naval facilities in mainland Japan and Guam.

A third measure that the United States can take to reduce the vulnerability of U.S. air, naval, and logistics facilities in the region is to strengthen its defenses against attacks by covert operatives. Because such attacks would generally originate from locations outside of U.S. bases, the United States should ensure that local security forces (primarily those in Japan and Guam) are prepared to prevent and respond to such attacks and mechanisms are in place to ensure smooth coordination between U.S. base security forces and local security forces. In addition, the United States should install automatic anti-sniper systems at its air bases and other critical facilities, increase perimeter security, and block critical areas from view.

China's incentives for an escalatory preemptive attack can be further reduced and U.S. ability to deter China from using force against Taiwan can be further increased by maintaining U.S. forces in the Western Pacific at a heightened state of alert, ready to immediately go to a wartime footing even when indications of a possible conflict are weak or ambiguous. In particular, because ships are most vulnerable (to aircraft, submarines, mines, and even ballistic missiles) when in or leaving port, U.S. Navy ships should put to sea as soon as any hint, however ambiguous, of a possible Chinese use of force is detected, and until they can put to sea they should activate their air and missile defenses. Similarly, land-based air defenses should also be activated as soon as any hint of a possible Chinese use of force is detected. Finally, U.S. air forces in Japan and South Korea should be prepared to redeploy to and operate out of airfields, including Japanese Air Self-Defense Force airfields, other than their home bases.

CONCLUSION

The balance of military power in the Western Pacific is shifting in China's favor. By 2015, China is likely to enjoy a significant quantitative advantage in a conflict with the United States, particularly in its early stages, if the U.S. force posture in the Asia-Pacific region does not change. The U.S. ability to deter a conflict, which could be highly escalatory, will correspondingly diminish. To prevent this from happening, and to reduce the advantage to China of an escalatory preemptive attack, the United States should make several adjustments to it force posture.

1. The United States must follow through with currently planned enhancements to U.S. force posture in the region, including replacing the Yokosuka-based *Kitty Hawk* with a Nimitz-class aircraft carrier, basing five nuclear attack submarines in Guam, and increasing the number of attack submarines and aircraft carriers based in Pacific ports.
2. The United States must improve its capabilities to detect a surprise use of force despite concerted PLA denial and deception efforts.
3. It must increase the readiness levels of air and naval forces in Hawaii and on the west coast of the United States so that they can be surged to the Western Pacific on short notice.
4. The United States should further increase the number of tactical aircraft, aircraft carriers, surface combatants, and submarines based in the Western Pacific beyond those currently planned.
5. It must ensure that its most capable new weapon systems are deployed first to the Pacific theater as they are fielded.
6. The United States should strengthen passive defenses at air bases and other key facilities in the Western Pacific.
7. The United States should deploy active air defenses near these facilities.
8. The United States should strengthen the defenses of air, naval, and logistics facilities in the region against attack by covert operatives.
9. All U.S. forces in the Western Pacific should be maintained at a heightened state of alert, ready to go to a wartime footing on short notice.

The rapid growth in PLA capabilities, coupled with the challenges created by geography, are eroding U.S. ability to deter a conflict over Taiwan. To prevent this from happening, and to reduce the risk of escalation should deterrence fail, the United States must begin to take steps now to strengthen its force posture in the region.

NOTES

Michael Dalesio of RAND provided invaluable research assistance in the preparation of this chapter. The views expressed here are solely my own and should not be construed to represent the views of the RAND Corporation or any of its sponsors.

1. The level of readiness and overall resistance capacity of Taiwan's armed forces and society are obviously important variables affecting any assessment of the likely dangers confronting U.S. force posture regarding a potential Taiwan conflict. This study does not examine how such variables might influence the analysis presented herein.

2. "Ships in the Seventh Fleet," Commander, Seventh Fleet web site, http://www.c7f.navy.mil/Pages/shippage.htm (last accessed November 24, 2006); "Facts," Kadena Air Base web site, http://www.kadena.af.mil/facts.htm (last accessed November 24, 2006); Misawa Air Base web site, http://www.misawa.af.mil/ (last accessed November 24, 2006); Marine Aircraft Group 12 web site, www.1maw.usmc.mil/index.asp?unit='MARG-12' (last accessed April 9, 2007); "Marine Links," III Marine Expeditionary Force web site, http://www.iiimef.usmc.mil/marinelinks.htm (last accessed November 24, 2006); International Institute for Strategic Studies, *The Military Balance 2006* (London: Oxford University Press, 2006), p. 42.

3. Web site of United States Forces Korea command, http://www.usfk.mil/USFK/index.html (last accessed November 4, 2006); the 8th United States Army, Korea, http://8tharmy.korea.army.mil/ (last accessed November 4, 2006); web site of the U.S. Army 2nd Infantry Division, http://www-2id.korea.army.mil/units/ (last accessed November 4, 2006); "Osan Air Base," GlobalSecurity.org web site, http://www.globalsecurity.org/military/facility/osan.htm (last accessed November 24, 2006); "Kunsan Air Base," Global Security.org web site, http://www.globalsecurity.org/military/facility/kunsan.htm (last accessed November 24, 2006); International Institute for Strategic Studies, *The Military Balance 2006*, p. 42.

4. "Ships in the Seventh Fleet," Commander, Seventh Fleet web site; "Andersen AFB," GlobalSecurity.org, http://www.globalsecurity.org/military/facility/andersen.htm (last accessed November 24, 2006).

5. "Garrison Hawaii," U.S. Army Garrison Hawaii web site, http://www.25idl.army.mil/usaghi/sites/about/facts.asp (last accessed November 24, 2006); "Ships, Submarines, and Aircraft," Commander Navy Region Hawaii web site, http://www.hawaii.navy.mil/ (last accessed November 24, 2006); "Units," Elmendorf Air Force Base web site, http://www.elmendorf.af.mil/units/ (last accessed November 24, 2006); Eielson Air Force Base web site, http://www.eielson.af.mil/ (last accessed November 24, 2006).

6. International Institute for Strategic Studies, *The Military Balance 2007* (London: Oxford University Press, 2007), pp. 346–50.

7. Timothy L. Laur and Steven L. Llanso, *Encyclopedia of Modern U.S. Military Weapons* (New York: Berkley Books, 1995), p. 227.

8. "Cruisers – CG," United States Navy Fact File (online at http://www.navy.mil/navydata/fact_display.asp?cid=4200&tid=800&ct=4 (last accessed November 29, 2006); "Luyang II (type 052C) class (DDGHM)," *Jane's Fighting Ships*, January 29, 2007.

9. This excludes Taiwan's approximately 200 F-16 and Mirage 2,000 fighters, although the effectiveness of these aircraft in the face of Chinese ballistic missile attacks on their airfields is questionable.

10. International Institute for Strategic Studies, *The Military Balance 2006*, 32, 267–8, 293.

11. See Chisaki Watanabe, "Japan, U.S. Announce Plan to Deploy Patriots in Okinawa," Associated Press, June 20, 2006 and "U.S. to Deploy Intercept Missiles in Japan," Associated Press, June 26, 2006. As of March 2007, twenty-four PAC-3 missiles had reportedly been deployed to Kadena Air Base. "PAC-3 (ERINT)," *Jane's Strategic Weapon Systems*, March 19, 2007.

12. See Roger Cliff et al., *Entering the Dragon's Lair: Chinese Antiaccess Strategies and Their Implications for the United States* (Santa Monica, Calif.: RAND Corporation, 2007), for a more extensive discussion of potential Chinese anti-access measures.

13. Cliff et al., *Entering the Dragon's Lair*, pp. 28–34.

14. The availability of additional U.S. air and naval forces for a Taiwan contingency is not significantly affected by current U.S. military operations in Iraq and Afghanistan, as those operations primarily involve U.S. ground forces. The occurrence of other major conflicts involving U.S. forces, such as a Korean contingency, however, could slow down the rate at which additional forces could be made available for the defense of Taiwan.

15. A belief that resistance in Taiwan would quickly collapse could come from either an assessment on Beijing's part that the Taiwanese people lack the fortitude to support a war with mainland China, or from a belief that Taiwan's military could quickly be defeated.

16. See Keith Crane et al., *Modernizing China's Military: Opportunities and Constraints* (Santa Monica, Calif.: RAND Corporation, 2005) and Evan S. Medeiros et al., *A New Direction for China's Defense Industry* (Santa Monica, Calif.: RAND Corporation, 2005) for details, including estimates of Chinese acquisition budgets through 2025. The statements about possible future Chinese force structure that follow present a force mix of new weapons systems that might be achievable based on aggregate resources available by 2015, as calculated in Crane et al. and Medeiros et al. These new forces are based on the assumption that the cost to China of acquiring different weapon systems will be comparable to the acquisition costs of similar U.S. systems, as documented in Under Secretary of Defense (AT&L), *Selected Acquisition Reports* (electronic database), Washington, D.C.: U.S. Department of Defense, various years from 1964 to 2005.

17. Yihong Chang, "Is China Building a Carrier?" *Jane's Defense Weekly*, August 17, 2005; Ted Parson, "China Develops Anti-Ship Missile," *Jane's Defense Weekly*, January 25, 2006.

18. In this chapter, official U.S. force development plans are taken at face value. Force development plans are likely to change between now and 2015, but there is no cur-

rent evidence suggesting how they might change and, in the aggregate, any changes are likely to be relatively small, barring a major fiscal crisis for the U.S. government or a fundamental transformation of U.S. defense strategy.

19. Congressional Budget Office, *Long-Term Implications of Current Defense Plans: Detailed Update for Fiscal Year 2005*, September 2004, pp. 17–18 (online at http://www.cbo.gov/showdoc.cfm?index=5864&sequence=0 (last accessed September 30, 2005); U.S. Navy, *Vision/Presence/Power: 2005 Guide to U.S. Navy Programs*, http://www.navy.mil/palib/policy/vision/vis05/top-v05.html (last accessed October 5, 2005), pp. 64, 75–76, 78–82, 108, 115, 121–22; Jane's Information Group, "Virginia Class (SSN)," *Jane's Fighting Ships*, August 3, 2005; Jane's Information Group, "Los Angeles Class (SSN)," *Jane's Fighting Ships*, May 2, 2006; Jane's Information Group, "Ohio Class (SSGN)," *Jane's Fighting Ships*, May 2, 2006.

20. International Institute for Strategic Studies, *The Military Balance 2007*, pp. 33, 36.

21. Congressional Budget Office, *Long-Term Implications of Current Defense Plans: Detailed Update for Fiscal Year 2005*, pp. 20, 26, 27; International Institute for Strategic Studies, *The Military Balance 2006*, pp. 34–40.

22. Under Secretary of Defense (AT&L), Selected Acquisition Reports (electronic database), Washington, D.C.: U.S. Department of Defense, 2000–2005; Lorenzo Cortes, "Surface Warfare Chief Identifies Primary Anti-Access Threats," *Defense Daily*, July 9, 2004, p. 2; "Aegis Ballistic Missile Defense," Missile Defense Agency Fact Sheet, http://mda.mil (last accessed July 2006); Department of Defense, *Program Acquisition Costs by Weapon System* (Washington, D.C., February 2005), p. 63, online at http://www.defenselink.mil/pubs/pdfs/QDR20060203.pdf (last accessed September 26, 2006); U.S. Army, *2005 Army Modernization Plan*, February 2005, D-46–49, -50–52, online at http://www.army.mil/features/MOD-Plan/2005/ (last accessed September 20, 2005); Jane's Information Group, "Lockheed Martin Missiles & Fire Control Theater High-Altitude Area Defense (THAAD) Missile System," *Jane's Land-Based Air Defense*, August 11, 2006; Duncan Lennox, "Terminal High-Altitude Area Defense," *Jane's Strategic Weapon Systems*, February 21, 2005; U.S. Department of the Army, Missile Procurement, Army, Department of the Army Procurement Programs, Committee Staff Procurement Backup Book, Fiscal Year (FY) 2007 President's Budget, http://www.asafm.army.mil/budget/fybm/FY07/pforms/missiles.pdf (last accessed September 18, 2006); "Navy to Field Terminal Phase, Sea-Based Missile Defense Capability," *Inside the Navy*, June 5, 2006.

23. "USS *George Washington* to Replace USS *Kitty Hawk* as U.S. Navy's Forward Deployed Carrier," U.S. Department of Defense News Release, online at http://www.defenselink.mil/releases/2005/nr20051202-5177.html (last accessed November 28, 2006).

24. "U.S.-Japan Alliance: Transformation and Realignment for the Future," http://www.state.gov/documents/organization/55886.pdf (last accessed November 22, 2006); Donna Miles, "Pace Visits Guam to Assess Infrastructure Growth Plans," American Forces Information Service News Articles, June 2, 2006, online at http://www.defenselink.mil/news/Jun2006/20060602_5311.html (last accessed December 1, 2006).

25. Tony Capaccio, "Pentagon to Shift Navy Forces to Counter Rising China," Bloomberg.com, January 25, 2006; Miles, "Pace Visits Guam to Assess Infrastructure Growth Plans"; Richard Halloran, "Submarines Focus on Terrorism," *Honolulu Advertiser*, November 26, 2006; Bill Gertz and Rowan Scarborough, "Inside the Ring," *Washington Times*, May 20, 2006.

26. "Sukoi Su-30 (Su-27PU)," *Jane's All the World's Aircraft*, December 19, 2005; "XAC JH-7," *Jane's All the World's Aircraft*, June 16, 2006.

27. There are four aircraft carriers, twenty-seven Aegis cruisers and destroyers, and twenty-four attack submarines based in Hawaii and on the west coast of the United States. I assume that roughly two-thirds of these ships would be able to immediately set out for the Western Pacific. See, "Aircraft Carriers – CV, CVN," United States Navy Fact File, online at http://www.navy.mil/navydata/fact_display.asp?cid=4200&tid=200&ct=4 (last accessed November 29, 2006); "Cruisers – CG," United States Navy Fact File; "Destroyers – DDG," United States Navy Fact File, online at http://www.navy.mil/navydata/fact_display.asp?cid=4200&tid=900&ct=4 (last accessed November 29, 2006); and "Attack Submarines – SSN," United States Navy Fact File, online at http://www.navy.mil/navydata/fact_display.asp?cid=4100&tid=100&ct=4 (last accessed November 29, 2006).

28. This is apparently already occurring to some degree. Elmendorf Air Force Base in Alaska has begun taking delivery of the first of thirty-six F-22s and it is planned that F-22s will also be assigned to Hickam Air Force Base in Hawaii. Deborah Van-Nierop, "PACAF Unveils First F-22," U.S. Pacific Air Forces web site, August 3, 2006, http://www.pacaf.af.mil/news/story_print.asp?id=123024586 (last accessed April 14, 2007).

29. U.S. Army, *2005 Army Modernization Plan*, February 2005, D-47.

30. Ibid., D-49.

31. Ibid.

32. Ibid., D-47–48.

SECTION FOUR

Conclusions

12

Future East Asian Security Architecture
Implications for the PLA

Alan D. Romberg

"SECURITY ARCHITECTURE" is too grand a term for what currently exists in East Asia and what is likely to exist in the foreseeable future. What we have, rather, is a set of security issues and relationships—some formal, most not—that constitute the totality of the present reality, with little prospect that this will change significantly.[1] Therefore, although this chapter may occasionally lapse into the use of the term "architecture," there is in fact no discernable structure to guide our analysis.

This chapter makes reference to Chinese security concerns in Central, South, Southwest, and Southeast Asia, but the focus is on Northeast Asia, because the main drivers for the People's Liberation Army (PLA) increasingly lie in that region. Over the course of the next fifteen to twenty years, questions relating to terrorism and other transnational issues could arise in other quadrants around China's periphery. For example, Tibet in the post-Dalai Lama era could give rise to some particularly delicate conditions drawing PLA attention. Uighur separatism is likely to continue to be a focus of military responsibility as well. Moreover, at some point China may well feel the need to consider what would necessarily be an expensive strategic lines of communication (SLOC) protection force in Southeast and South Asia, especially for growing energy imports. But the fundamental fact remains that, as they are now, the issues that relate to China's core national security interests will be far more concentrated in Northeast Asia than elsewhere.

The state of Sino-American relations will be of crucial importance to China's perception of its security needs and its decisions about PLA size and configuration. If relations with the United States are strained or characterized by continuing or even deepening mutual strategic suspicion, the PLA will be tasked with countering any U.S. developments from around China's periphery that hint of containment. But the nature of cross-Taiwan Strait relations, and the possible U.S. role, will remain a primary driving force for the PLA. Moreover, China will seek to exercise increasing control over approaches to the mainland from the Pacific. Even if Sino-American relations are more relaxed, Beijing will continue to hedge against the ongoing U.S. buildup in the Pacific, just as Washington will hedge against the uncertainty of China's future strategic decisions. Thus for now, and for the foreseeable future, the PLA's emphasis will be on continuing air and naval modernization that have greater relevance to the situation to China's east than areas at other points of the compass.

CURRENT SITUATION

Today, the issues that drive the security policies of the principal security players in East Asia—and particularly Northeast Asia—are in the realm of what one might call "traditional" national security. For China, the overwhelming focus is on Taiwan. That does not mean that the focus is only on sizing and shaping the PLA to deal with Taipei's military; rather, and far more important, it means being prepared to deter, delay, deflect, and, if necessary, defeat the United States in the Taiwan theater. Even more specifically, it means two things: (1) developing the capabilities to act with sufficient speed and effect to "win"—whatever that may mean under the circumstances—before the United States can intervene with more than token forces; and (2) developing asymmetric capabilities to counter the United States in recognition of the fact that force-on-force match-ups may not be to China's advantage over any conceivable time frame.

In assessing U.S. goals, more than a few analysts in the People's Republic of China (PRC) view the United States as determined to prevent the mainland's unification with Taiwan. They see U.S. efforts dedicated to maintaining the status quo, with no war and no peace, in which the island stands as both a physical obstacle to China's access to the Pacific and a potential base of operations against the mainland.

These concerns come against a more generalized background of the "hundred years of humiliation" and an underlying "never again" mentality that informs PLA priorities, budgets, and strategies. Still, at this time at least, it is hard to conjure up a scenario that would pit the PLA against another major power, including the United States, in all-out conflict other than one relating to Taiwan. So, while one has to presume that a significant proportion of the efforts and resources devoted to military modernization have a general national security purpose, they *also* (in general) must be useful in a Taiwan scenario.

As a result, the prevailing strategic condition in Sino-American relations is schizophrenic. Both countries seek constructive relations as a fundamental national goal, not just for the short run but for the medium and long term, as well. This means not only diplomatic and economic engagement, but specifically a lively military exchange at various levels, going beyond academic institutions to operational forces and senior military and civilian defense leaders. At the same time, each side is preparing for war against the other both as a deterrent and as a means of securing "victory"—or avoiding defeat—should conflict prove unavoidable.

In this context, although Sino-Japanese relations have been improving since fall 2006, they remain tentative, at best. [2] The U.S.-Japan alliance is the cornerstone of the American security presence in the region and of the ability of the United States to project power in fact and in perception. It is decidedly a mixed blessing in China's view.

Beijing has long seen the value of the alliance to itself in the sense that the U.S. strategic assurance means Japan does not need to consider seriously developing either extensive conventional offensive capabilities or nuclear weapons. [3] Its implicit contribution to stability on the Korean Peninsula is also valuable to the PRC.

But China is not convinced of the limits of American ambitions for Japan and for the alliance, and many strategic planners in China consider the alliance an American instrument to enlist Japan in U.S. hegemonic plans, including the containment of China. On the other hand, they also worry that Japan will use the alliance to enlist the United States in Tokyo's "assertive" policies as it moves toward the status of a "normal" country. Japan's deepening role as an alliance partner, not just in terms of logistical support but potentially as a more active participant in a Taiwan contingency as well, is of great concern to PLA military planners.

Indeed, beyond the underlying competition with China for power and influence in the region, and beyond competing claims over resources and Exclusive Economic Zone (EEZ) limits that are the most obvious sources of potential bilateral conflict, Japan's ultimate ambitions toward Taiwan remain perhaps the most important short- and medium-term concern for Beijing. Whether Prime Minister Abe's apparent new emphasis on good relations with the PRC—including his reaffirmation of Japan's "one China" policy—will prove reassuring to China is an open question. But it is likely that, even with agreement on a new "strategic" relationship and plans for robust military exchanges, the PLA will continue to plan for the worst. Thus, the PLA will want to have the capacity to deter and, if necessary, defeat Japan in a Taiwan scenario (at least one area of Chinese military modernization is specifically designed with Japan in mind—medium-range missiles).

The approach to the Korean Peninsula of both China and the PLA is far more relaxed than in years past. Bilateral relations with South Korea (ROK) are prospering along a variety of tracks—political, economic, cultural, and even security. And while in some technical, legal sense the PRC-North Korea (DPRK) alliance remains in effect, in every way it can without openly renouncing that alliance, Beijing has made clear that it regards North Korea's security like that of any other country. That is, it feels no special commitment to come to Pyongyang's aid with military forces. It is not hard to draw up a list of reasons why this is so.

One issue, of course, is what might happen if the DPRK simply collapsed. Would U.S. forces end up north of the 38th parallel? Would the currently shrinking U.S. force presence on the peninsula be reversed? Would Washington be willing to provide some guarantees to Beijing—perhaps ahead of time—about ultimate disposition of U.S. forces for the longer term, even if some movement northward were to take place in the immediate wake of a DPRK collapse?

Whether stemming from DPRK collapse or not, the PLA must assess what a future "unified" Korea would look like, and what the security alignment vis-à-vis the United States would be. Especially if a more conservative South Korean government comes to power in spring 2008, as seems likely, and if the recent tensions in U.S.-ROK relations—including alliance relations—are reversed, what will the consequences be for China?

All around the PRC's periphery, it is clear that Beijing is wasting no time in seeking to develop relationships that will help ensure that the United

States would have fewer opportunities to launch attacks on China, should it come to that. The success of this approach is seen in ROK President Roh Moo Hyun's announced proscription on the deployment of U.S. forces in Korea into combat in the region without prior Korean approval. Similar restrictions would appear to exist elsewhere and, indeed, it is hard to imagine a scenario in which any nation in Southeast, South, Southwest, or Central Asia would consent to the American use of its bases for such purposes. Whether the PLA is currently working to establish real basing arrangements for itself in some of these countries (for example, in Burma or Pakistan) is a hotly debated issue. But what cannot be debated is that, in terms of military diplomacy, China's approach is highly activist and successful. Moreover, although China's "military power" is currently more a matter of perception than reality for countries in the region, in bureaucratic parlance, that is good enough for government work. Even if Beijing is not seen as posing a direct military threat to the region, the perception of a strong and strengthening China serves to encourage the nations on China's periphery to remain on good terms with Beijing even as they also seek some balancing presence from the United States (and perhaps Japan) across the spectrum of national power—economic, political, and military.

China's attitude toward and relationship with Russia is extremely complicated but not terribly threatening to anyone, except perhaps in terms of the firepower the Russians are all too ready to sell to the PLA, which could be used against American or other forces in a Taiwan contingency. The joint exercises held so far between China and Russia do not appear to be precursors to joint military operations in any foreseeable real-world scenario.

DRIVERS FOR CHANGE

What will influence this picture over time? One of the most important drivers will be the success of the PLA in modernizing its forces in ways that enhance China's influence and power. For the purposes of this discussion, we assume that almost regardless of what happens to China's economy and its foreign relations, modernization will continue apace and China will not only continue to acquire an impressive array of weapons systems, but also an increasing capability to use them effectively.[4]

There is some debate about how effectively the PLA can integrate the plethora of new systems it is acquiring into its military strategy and doctrine. Whatever the facts in that regard, even though the United States should remain well ahead in most weapons categories, the "problem" is not simply a capabilities match-up; the issue is whether each side develops reliable capacities, including asymmetric ones, to cope successfully with the strengths of the other side. In a metaphor of traditional naval battles, one might say that the task of each side will be to "cross the 'T'" of the other side's forces.

Over the next fifteen to twenty years, three issues will be the most important in determining how security relations play out and, therefore, how the PLA will seek to position itself: Taiwan, U.S.-PRC "strategic" relations, and Japan. This is not to dismiss other factors, such as the course of economic change for China, the United States, and the world; major terrorist incidents; the collapse of Pakistan; widespread conflict in the Middle East; or the potentially disruptive effect of developments on the Korean Peninsula. Although this chapter addresses some of these contingencies, none of these would fundamentally alter China's strategic aims. For example, in the event of a crisis on the Korean Peninsula, all of the governments concerned should be able to cope in ways that do not threaten the basic national security interests of the others. It might involve the PLA developing some capacity to help stabilize the situation on the DPRK-PRC border, perhaps even including some limited cross-border intervention. However, absent a total breakdown in Sino-American relations *and* PRC-ROK relations, not only is it hard to envisage a massive PLA intervention deep inside Korea, but also there is no significant prospect of U.S. forces being deployed in northern Korea on a long-term basis or in a way that China would perceive as overly threatening. (On the other hand, China might not share that view and it would be useful to consider how to convey it credibly to Beijing.)

The weakening of the U.S. alliance system is also something to take into account and ought to be a matter of considerable concern to Washington policy makers. In most respects, Washington and Tokyo would claim that the alliance is stronger than ever and the prospect is for even closer and stronger ties in the years ahead. But while recent public opinion polls in Japan have shown substantial and growing support for the alliance, there is greater tension and fragility to that relationship than is obvious—or healthy; looking out over the next couple of decades, both countries will need to be alert to the implications of this situation and to rectify it as best they can.

The U.S.-ROK alliance is under even greater strain. Efforts have been made to patch up some of the damage done over the past several years, including through high-level meetings.[5]

Although the implications of the failure to rectify the weaknesses in U.S.-ROK and U.S.-Japan ties could be substantial, this analysis proceeds on the assumption that, because of the essential importance of the alliance to both nations and the obvious desire of both governments and both publics to maintain it, issues in the U.S.-Japan alliance will be self-rectifying; one hopes this will prove to be the case with South Korea, as well.

As suggested earlier, one cannot rule out developments in Central, South, Southeast, or Southwest Asia that could cause Beijing to react in some substantive fashion, including perhaps the redeployment of some military assets closer to those regions. But a scenario in which the PLA might feel that its priority must be shifted to those areas in any significant manner is highly unlikely.

The chapter now turns to discuss briefly the possible range of developments in the three principal areas already identified, to address a couple of the "lesser" contingencies, and then to talk about the creation of a "regional security structure."

Taiwan

Assuming that Beijing continues along its current generally accommodating course with Taiwan, and carries it the logical next steps forward, no matter whether a Democratic Progressive Party (DPP) or Kuomintang (KMT) government takes power in 2008 in Taipei, and in the years thereafter, the impulse on the island toward independence, though deeply felt, will remain in check. This is not to say that sentiment in favor of unification will grow substantially, but rumbling dissatisfaction with Taiwan's current ambiguous status could attenuate, even if a meaningful minority continues to hold strong views in favor of pushing for *de jure* separatism.

In this scenario, differences over the ultimate resolution of Taiwan's relationship with the mainland would be more or less set aside in favor of pragmatic cross-strait ties, reduced military tensions, and some significant level of "international space" for Taiwan (even if there is no concession in the area of sovereignty). One cannot expect that, even under these benign circumstances, all dimensions of the military face-off across the strait would disappear. After all, what leader in Beijing could afford to "assume" that there would not be another turn of sentiment on the island toward pushing for independence and that it was therefore safe to give up all aspects of deterrence against that possibility? But the quality of cross-strait relations would change. Moreover, if the administration in Taipei were to embrace some version of "one China," confidence-building measures (CBMs) could be developed, as specified in the "authorized statement" of the State Council Taiwan Affairs Office in May 2004, and the "state of hostility" between the two sides could even be formally ended, as provided for in the "Jiang Zemin 8-point proposal" of 1995. But creating confidence that such an agreement would not collapse with the next change of administration in Taipei would not be easily generated, which would make especially this last step very difficult.

Although some in the United States (and in Japan) might be nervous about the implications of such an evolution, it would be hard (and self-defeating) for either government to oppose such a change. These developments would neither come close to effecting unification (which will not take place for a very long time) nor change the fact that Beijing would not be in control of Taiwan's policies.

Although one would hope that mutual steps would lead to a reduction in the military component of cross-strait relations, in response to the PRC's determination to preserve a deterrent against Taiwan independence, Taiwan would still need to maintain a hedge against a malign change in the mainland's policies. Thus, while some of the grander designs for glitzy arms purchases would most likely be scrapped (as they should be), the United States would still press Taipei to adopt adequate defense budgets. Moreover, the United States would maintain an adequate capability of its own to cope with any threat to Taiwan, not only because this is required by the 1979 Taiwan Relations Act (TRA), but also because, from a strategic perspective, it would be prudent to do so. All of that said, however, a reduction in tensions would clearly serve the overall U.S. strategic national interest.

Even if the cross-strait relationship did not evolve beyond this level, Japan would still be nervous about the long-term implications for its own supply lines, especially to the Middle East, and about China's ability to establish a regular military presence in a wider region of the Western Pacific. Nonetheless, overall stabilization of cross-strait relations and reduction of military tensions between Taiwan and the mainland would also tend to stabilize the strategic picture of both Japan and the United States.

As noted above, a requirement for such improvement in cross-strait relations is that Beijing maintain and extend its current approach to Taiwan, agreeing to set aside issues of unification and to take a number of steps to meet Taiwan's aspirations while reducing its sense of threat. Given current trends, one might speculate that this is not only possible but likely. The problem is that straight-line projections are notoriously hazardous. Moreover, there is some risk that Beijing will underestimate the importance of its peaceful handling of the Taiwan question to the United States.

There is a tendency on the mainland to assume that, while Taiwan is a "core" issue for the PRC, it is of lesser, perhaps even marginal, importance to U.S. security. Because of this, China believes it could take some risks without fear of precipitating a Sino-American war.[6] Viewed from an American perspective, this considerably understates U.S. interests in Taiwan itself.[7] Moreover, it ignores the larger implications of a potential PRC use of force, whether in the Taiwan Strait or elsewhere, that Washington sees for its security interests in the region.[8] Thus, any PRC assumption about a second-order U.S. interest in Taiwan's security could lead to a tragic miscalculation; it was precisely this concern about misperception that led the United States to deploy two aircraft carrier battle groups to the Taiwan area in the spring of 1996.

Setting aside purposeful military confrontation, if there were either economic disruptions or political chaos in mainland China, would that lead, as some postulate, to an attempt by the leadership in Beijing to divert attention and perhaps even stimulate the economy or political unity by adopting a harder line against Taiwan?

The answer is unclear, especially because the personalities of future leaders in the PRC will obviously play a central role in what sorts of decisions are made. That is one reason to maintain a hedge and work continuously on the underlying political relationship to shore up the mutual commitment to resolve issues peacefully. Even so, it is hard to come up with a scenario in which it makes sense for Beijing to seek remedy for domestic woes through overseas adventure, including over Taiwan.[9] Such a course would require the total overthrow of a carefully constructed foreign and security policy that is designed, first and foremost, to provide a benign external environment. Even if the domestic situation that external environment is meant to foster encounters difficulties, as it almost assuredly will at some point, the underlying logic will not change. In this analyst's judgment, it would take something of a revolution on the mainland to drive China to reverse its policies and risk all it has achieved by undertaking an overtly aggressive foreign policy.

If Taiwan politics were once again to produce leaders who wanted to push the envelope on *de jure* independence—meaning primarily via constitutional change but also perhaps through blatant assertions of sovereignty in other ways that Beijing could not ignore—then things could change. But it seems that the broad outlines of a *modus vivendi*, at least in this respect, are emerging and the frequently reaffirmed insistence of the people of Taiwan that their leaders not needlessly or recklessly rock the boat is firmly grounded. To repeat, if Beijing can rise to the occasion to give the people of Taiwan a deeper sense of satisfaction that their interests are being met, their needs satisfied, and their achievements respected, it is reasonable to assume that Taiwan can and will become a more stable element in the regional security architecture.

The PLA will not lose interest in modernizing and significantly upgrading its capabilities, including, as noted, with respect to deterring any resurgent Taiwan independence sentiment.[10] Furthermore, its perceived position of military inferiority to the United States will be a sufficient motivator to ensure that substantial PLA defense budgets are adopted for the indefinite future. This will include upgrading not only hardware, especially in the form of air and naval platforms and missile capabilities, but also information technologies and exotic capabilities in terms of electronic and space warfare, in addition to increased investment in training and retaining qualified personnel.

Still, the transformation of the Taiwan situation could pose some significant "guns versus butter" choices for the leadership. If the stabilizing trends in cross-strait relations outlined above were to continue, and if China were to experience an internal crisis that would change the nature of the debate in Beijing, the only factor that would significantly heighten tensions over Taiwan (and hence the level of PLA concern) would be a serious deterioration in Sino-American relations.

U.S.-PRC Strategic Relations

While the substantial transformation of the Taiwan issue would have a major impact on the choices of both China and the United States, the actual difference that the new situation would make in terms of policy would depend, as stated, on the overall state of U.S.-PRC relations. That said, it is currently difficult to untangle the Taiwan issue from the overall relationship. After all, a good deal of the mutual strategic suspicion that exists between the United States and the PRC is tied to perceptions of the other side's goals in Taiwan. Many in China believe the United States wants to use to Taiwan to hem in China's naval forces and even to use the island, eventually, as a base of military operations against the mainland. In turn, many in the United States see the PLA coveting Taiwan as a base for their own outward reach with a "blue water" navy and, at a minimum, as a strategic buffer against pressure from the east. In these circumstances, how can the Taiwan situation really be transformed unless the strategic suspicion is reduced? Conversely, how can the strategic suspicion be reduced unless the Taiwan situation is transformed?

Approaching this issue from a Washington perspective, it is hard to sustain the case that some PRC analysts make that the United States intends to hold Taiwan separate from the mainland in order to hem in the PRC or keep it focused on an issue that drains its energies from other areas. Even if unification were a realistic prospect in any foreseeable future, the United States still would not seek to obstruct it, although the debate in the United States over this question could well be more animated.

But unification is not a realistic prospect in any foreseeable future, and thus the issue needs to be posed differently. Would a reduction in tensions across the strait, a lessening of the possibility of war over Taiwan (however slim it may be now), and the substantial elimination of "the Taiwan question" as a burr under the saddle of Sino-American relations be in the U.S. national interest? Or would it threaten to lull the United States into complacency about both the Taiwan situation itself and Beijing's larger ambitions, causing Washington to lower its guard and invite challenges to its influence and interests?[11]

To this writer, the answer is indisputable; it is clearly the former, positive response, not the latter, doomsday approach. But, having said that, one must still ask what the prospects are that Beijing and Washington can move to a relationship that is at least more trusting and more cooperative, if not a full partnership approaching an alliance.

First of all, reducing mutual concerns over Taiwan is a *sine qua non* for the long-term improvement of the overall relationship and reduction of mutual strategic suspicion. As already noted, it is hard to imagine another issue that holds the possibility of real war between China and the United States. In addition, it is hard to think of how the need to prepare for war in an active and focused way can be reduced if the Taiwan issue is not placed in a more stable and predictable context.

A great deal has actually been achieved since 2003–2004 in creating some mutual confidence that one side will not take steps, and is not pursuing near-term goals, that challenge the other's fundamental interests with respect to Taiwan. Although Beijing was determined even before the George W. Bush administration took office in 2001 to avoid confrontation on any issue including, if possible, Taiwan, the president's negative attitude toward the PRC and his rather assertively expressed support for Taiwan's security created doubts in Chinese minds about President Bush's ultimate intentions.

Especially in the wake of the EP-3 incident in April 2001, the president showed extreme reluctance to embrace publicly the fundamental principles on Taiwan that have been crucial to U.S.-PRC relations since the 1970s. Even though he had openly supported the U.S. "one China" policy during the 2000 presidential campaign, and he grudgingly referred to it during his February 2002 visit to Beijing, it was not until Jiang Zemin visited President Bush's ranch in Crawford, Texas in October 2002, a full twenty-one months after taking office, that President Bush was willing to publicly endorse the entire "mantra" of the "one China" policy and adhere to the three U.S.-PRC joint communiqués (as well as the TRA).

He did so, it is important to note, not simply in the context of China's cooperation on post-9/11 issues, though that was obviously crucial, but also in the wake of President Chen Shui-bian's articulation of *yibian, yiguo*

("one country on each side") and his implicit threat to move to independence ("go down Taiwan's own road"). A little over a year later—when
Chen was not only pushing for referenda that the United States found
problematic in terms of cross-strait issues, but even raised the idea of a
"brand new" constitution to be approved directly by the people, bypass-
ing the normal amendment procedures—President Bush was moved to
chastise Chen Shui-bian with PRC Premier Wen Jiabao at his side at the
White House.[12]

Then and through much of 2004, even after Chen's May 2004 inaugural address when he pulled back from some of his more problematic
proposals, Beijing questioned the American will and ability to rein in
the Taiwan president. Over time, however, the PRC leadership gained
greater trust in Bush and his intention to oppose Taiwan moves toward
independence. The PRC's narrowing of its own focus from promotion
of unification to blocking independence also helped.[13] The net result of
all of this was that Washington and Beijing came to see each other as
working to move the situation away from confrontation, and possibly
war, over Taiwan.

This has not completely relieved the mutual strategic suspicion that
exists. In addition to their bottom-line adherence to differing perspectives on Taiwan, the robust PLA modernization program, on the
one hand, and active U.S. reinforcement of Pacific forces as well as
diplomacy and military deployments around China's periphery, on the
other, keep that mutual suspicion alive and well.[14] The "strategic" (or
"senior" in U.S. parlance) dialogue developed in 2005 (a reprise of
an effort almost a decade earlier under President William J. Clinton)
held the prospect of beginning to get at this issue. But the departure
of Deputy Secretary of State Robert Zoellick from the administration
cast its prospects into doubt. The "strategic economic dialogue" created
under the aegis of Treasury Secretary Henry M. Paulson and Vice Premier Wu Yi can make an important contribution to a sense of mutual
confidence, and it should not be denigrated. Indeed, in some respects
it is the most important current bilateral conversation. But it cannot
substitute for the political/security dialogue that former U.S. Deputy
Secretary of State Robert B. Zoellick began with Senior Vice Foreign
Minister Dai Bingguo. Whether his belatedly appointed replacement,
John D. Negroponte, will have the interest, or time, over the remaining

months of the Bush administration to resume the conversation with the same focus and determination that Zoellick brought to it remains to be seen.

If the positive scenario outlined here for Taiwan and cross-strait relations becomes reality, it will open the door to a more broadly based reduction in tensions between Washington and Beijing. Furthermore, if this is reinforced by greater overall mutual strategic trust, while it will not bring peace and harmony to the world or even to Northeast Asia, it will have a major effect on the region's "security architecture."

As noted earlier, the PLA will continue to modernize its forces—especially air, naval, and missile forces—as a natural aspect of China's growing power, giving China a basis for protecting its national security and other interests and for projecting its political power in the region and beyond. The United States will also continue to develop its military capabilities, including in highly sophisticated areas of weaponry. But just as the PLA will need to take care not to give the impression of an outsized ambition, the United States will need to carefully ensure that its defense policies and plans affecting China are thought through beyond their short-term value to include also their long-term effect. Thus, assuming the United States gets beyond the nonsensical Rumsfeldian "What do they need all that capability for? Who is their enemy?" line, it will be important to have greater transparency on both sides about national security policy, military doctrine, capabilities, and plans.

Japan

Ask any mainland Chinese analyst or official what "other" factor could spoil such a positive evolution in the regional strategic picture, and the likely one-word response is: Japan. The Chinese understand the fundamental importance of constructive Sino-Japanese relations to the future of the region and, hence, to China's own well-being.[15] And, at least for now, there is a noteworthy effort being made by both Japan and China to deal constructively with history issues and the modalities of bilateral interaction that have plagued bilateral ties for the past several years. Prime Minister Abe's trip to China in October 2006, within two weeks of assuming office, and Premier Wen's return visit in April 2007 are certainly welcomed developments. Yet, the historical overlay and the instinct among both sides to seek to manipulate the situation complicate the relationship. Furthermore, the preliminary steps taken to date are far from immune to setbacks. It will require considerable political will to move beyond atmospherics to substance.

More important yet, the fundamental issue is not history or shrine visits, but the contemporary competition between Japan and China for power and influence. There has been a remarkable rise in Japanese concern about China's growing strength across the political, economic, and military spectrum and a change in Japan's underlying attitudes toward the foundations of the relationship. No longer does the "friendship paradigm" govern Japan's approach to China or the underlying adherence to "permanent penitence" obtain.[16] Moreover, lingering Chinese apprehension about a resurgence of Japanese militarism, especially if ("when," some Chinese would say) Tokyo's alliance with the United States frays, has not been allayed.

Yet, for all of the focus on constitutional revision in Japan and becoming a "normal" nation, it is highly unlikely that the Japanese will reverse their strong aversion to militarism. Under Prime Minister Abe, and no doubt under the rising younger generation of leaders who will follow, Japan will adopt a more assertively nationalistic stance to protect and advance its interests. But assertiveness and nationalism do not equate to aggressiveness, and abandoning passivism does not equate to abandoning pacifism. That said, under two sets of conditions, Japan's security orientation could change, with significant implications for China and the PLA.

First and of greatest importance, if the U.S.-Japan alliance were to weaken or lose credibility, especially with regard to extended nuclear deterrence, Japan would face a wrenching choice. It could simply adjust to a situation in which its security depended much more on strengthening political relations with China and accommodate to China's dominance. Or, it could choose to strike out on its own with a major shift in policy in the direction of obtaining offensive, and possibly even nuclear, weapons capabilities.

Second, if China was, for whatever reason, to become more assertive in confronting Japan, Tokyo might also go further along the path of "normalization" than seems likely at present. This could be the case even if the U.S. alliance were intact (and certainly if it were not), with Japan opting for a far more active defense role. If China, for example, opted to mount direct challenges over disputed ocean areas and islands, dispatch more submarines and other naval vessels into the Japanese EEZ or even territorial waters, or openly threatened Japan over Tokyo's possible involvement in a Taiwan contingency, this could force Japan to decide on a more robust approach. Perhaps in recognition of the fact that its actions affect Japan's choices, China has made changes to its behavior; even before the current warming trend after Abe's rise to prime minister, there were far fewer Chinese challenges to Japan's air and sea space in 2006 than in previous years.[17]

Although Taiwan may be the most fraught issue politically, perhaps the trickiest issue currently is competition for resources in the ocean areas lying between Japan and China. Many experts believe the quantity of oil and gas resources, while not trivial, is not enormous. Especially for Japan, one hears that the issue is more related to questions of sovereignty and, from Tokyo's perspective, compelling Beijing to observe international norms. In a way, this is actually more disturbing than it is reassuring; emotions can run high in such circumstances. Recent recommitment by both sides to approach these issues cooperatively is encouraging, but one has yet to see a workable model for "sharing resources" even if sovereignty-related claims can be shelved for now.

Avoiding negative scenarios depends primarily on commonsense decisions in Washington, Tokyo, and Beijing. Given the fundamental interests of all parties, the odds that such decisions will be forthcoming are high—if not consistently, then at least as the predominant trend. Thus, one ought not to anticipate Japan "breaking out" as an independent military force of great concern to China.

That said, even if Beijing analysts and policy makers agree that the odds of a remilitarized Japan are low, they will keep a weather eye on those possibilities and, although the lead time for detecting any such major changes would likely be substantial, they will want to have both the contingency plans and surge capabilities to cope with any unexpected developments. This will argue for continued modernization of their missile force—moving apace toward road-mobile, solid-fuel models—and the development of air and naval capabilities to deter or confront Japan.

OTHER ISSUES

There are also other factors that could affect the national security decisions of the major players in the East Asia/Pacific region and their future relations.

Terrorism

A major act of terrorism in any number of places could shake things up in Northeast Asia, even if the attack did not take place there. For example, another assault on the United States could, depending on its presumed source, either cement U.S.-PRC relations further (if cooperation dramatically increased, including the continuation of U.S. pressure on Taiwan to avoid provocations) or drive a wedge (if the weapon's source was suspected to be North Korea, for example).

An attack within China itself could also cement relations further, if the United States showed itself to be more open to backing a PRC crackdown on domestic elements that might have been involved. The 2002 labeling of the East Turkestan Islamic Movement as a terrorist organization upset many foreigners, including Turkish-American groups, who were worried about the repression of Uighurs. But for all the political pain it caused the Bush administration, in fact it was not viewed as terribly significant in Beijing. Whether a major terrorist incident in China would produce a more meaningful American reaction, generating more positive assumptions about U.S. intentions, would have to be seen. But if so, there would likely be a price paid at home and elsewhere in terms of perceptions of U.S. human rights policy.

U.S. Alliances

The key role the U.S.-Japan alliance plays, and will continue to play, in the Northeast Asian security architecture is discussed above. On balance, assuming the alliance remains healthy and that the Taiwan situation remains calm, the net impact of the alliance should be positive for maintaining regional equilibrium and should not create any major driving issues for the PLA. If the alliance becomes troubled, however, all bets are off.

The U.S.-ROK alliance is a somewhat different matter. It too contributes to regional stability and, as long as it is not seen as threatening to China, will be viewed in Beijing as contributing to the maintenance of peace and stability on the peninsula (thus in China's interest). But it is not at all clear that the PRC currently holds such a benign view of the alliance nor is it clear that the United States and China are engaged in a sufficiently candid level of dialogue through which they can provide each other with mutual assurances about what might happen in a North Korean collapse contingency. This could be fixed, but it will take some effort on both sides.

The less predictable scenario is one in which the North is believed to be transferring nuclear weapons-related material, equipment, or expertise. As President Bush made clear in his statement in reaction to the DPRK nuclear test in early October 2006, any such transfer would likely generate a forceful American response. In this analyst's view, that includes the possibility of a military strike on those facilities that could be identified with the DPRK's nuclear program. Strikes on other targets may also be seen as part of a "justified" response.

It is possible in this scenario that not all nuclear-related targets would be eliminated and the DPRK could retaliate in some fashion. Thus, the risks of U.S. strikes on selected targets in the DPRK would be very high. Even if this course of action was based on highly credible evidence, accompanied by statements about both the limits of the purpose and extent of the strikes and the open-ended nature of further strikes should the North retaliate, the effects on Sino-American relations could be serious if China saw the net result to be a degradation of its security.

U.S.-ROK relations would definitely suffer in this scenario and Beijing would be expected to make common cause with Seoul in a way that could seriously, perhaps fatally, weaken the alliance over time (if the strike had not already done so). This would not necessarily affect PLA planning or deployments in a significant way. The United States is already reducing its presence in South Korea. While Chinese concerns about possible basing of U.S. strike aircraft in South Korea would be reduced by the weakening of the alliance, announced ROK limitations on the American use of South Korean bases has most likely already made the alliance a relatively peripheral aspect of PLA planning.

As mentioned earlier, a North Korean collapse scenario would send tremors through Zhongnanhai and could lead to certain PLA deployments, including those across the DPRK border to defend China's interests from within the DPRK. However, as discussed above, well-managed responses by all concerned should be able to contain reactions to avoid confrontation.

Economy and Energy

An economic nosedive, not just in China but globally (especially in the United States), could have enormous implications for security relations in the region and hence for all the militaries concerned, including the PLA. Under these circumstances, it would be incumbent upon all to exercise restraint and communicate clearly. That said, it is in everyone's mutual interest to resist the most extreme beggar-thy-neighbor types of reactions and, unless particular countries were at loggerheads for other reasons, to focus on cooperative rather than competitive measures.

Still, the PLA will probably not take an extraordinary budgetary hit anytime soon. Beijing would continue to place a high priority on signaling that it is not vulnerable, even at a time of economic distress, and that no party—especially the United States, Japan, or Taiwan—should seek to take advantage.

Energy demand will also be a long-term issue that has the potential for cutthroat competition, on the one hand, and for cooperation in times of emergency, on the other. Whether over the next ten or fifteen years China can be brought into an integrated relationship with the International Energy Agency (IEA) remains to be seen. Membership seems unlikely, since the IEA is made up of only Organization for Economic Cooperation and Development (OECD) member countries. But there has already been considerable contact; an October 2006 workshop in Beijing produced a brief statement that highlighted the fact that "the Chinese government places great importance on its exchanges and cooperation with the IEA in the energy field, particularly regarding oil security and oil reserves."[18]

SLOC protection is, of course, another matter. But over the period under consideration, it seems likely that the PLA will only be able to produce between token and minimal protection and will still depend heavily on U.S. forces for this purpose. Should bilateral relations turn sour, Beijing would no doubt accelerate not only the provision of some naval forces for this purpose, but perhaps even the current development of alternative land transportation routes for oil.

ALTERNATIVE SECURITY FUTURES IN NORTHEAST ASIA

Putting all of this together, at one extreme one could posit a hostile U.S-PRC relationship with Washington perceived as supporting indefinite separate status for Taiwan (perhaps even going beyond that to press for far greater international standing, though perhaps short of full sovereignty) and generating continued pressure on China for its human rights and legal deficiencies. U.S. alliances, especially with Japan, could be increasingly geared to confronting China not just over a cross-strait contingency but with regard to any effort by Beijing to expand its military reach. In addition, a global economic downturn could drive governments to abandon all pretense of international cooperation, even at a high cost, and focus on satisfying protectionist sentiments, however self-defeating that might be in the long run. Finally, a terrorist attack could be seen as stemming from faulty policies of the party attacked—for example, a PRC crackdown on Uighurs that generated cross-border terrorist activity—leading to mutual recriminations rather than mutual support.

A rather happier scenario, at the other extreme, is one in which the Taiwan issue, although perhaps not permanently resolved, is in a state of equilibrium with both sides satisfied with a vibrant status quo; tensions in Sino-American relations—and mutual strategic suspicions—have largely abated (importantly though not solely as a result of the evolved Taiwan situation); Japanese relations with China are thriving even though aspects of national competition still exist; the Korean Peninsula has sorted itself out one way or another with the DPRK no longer seen as a threat; and the American alliance system is intact alongside a growing emphasis on cooperative security relations through multilateral mechanisms, with a rich pattern of cooperation having emerged across the board on counter-terrorism, energy management, and deepening, more balanced trade and investment relations.

Of course, the reality will rest somewhere in between. However, the nature of international relations, including the increasing institutionalization of various global economic, political, and security-related regimes, will push the reality more in the direction of the optimistic scenario than the gloomier one. National loyalties, even national*ism*, will not go away; indeed such phenomena may grow. But this is not necessarily inconsistent with a realization that determined "one-upping" of others is not the optimal approach. Unless others are seen as determined and capable of harming one's own interests, cooperation rather than confrontation should be adopted as the wiser course.

IMPLICATIONS FOR THE PLA

As noted earlier, the PLA will continue to modernize in terms of both equipment and technology. In addition, the PLA will continue to command a significant portion of the budget on the general grounds of protecting and promoting China's national interest, even if a particular focus (e.g., Taiwan) no longer requires the same priority level of attention.

But even in the most optimistic scenario, and no matter how smoothly relations are developing across the strait or between Washington and Beijing, PRC leaders will be unwilling to forego a deterrent capability against Taiwan independence and U.S. intervention in a Taiwan contingency. While China will not allow itself to get into a debilitating and ultimately unwinnable tit-for-tat arms race with the United States, Beijing will want to continue to develop capabilities to thwart any U.S. instinct to use pressure tactics, however remote that might seem in an era of better relations.

An end-of-hostilities agreement with Taipei would lead to some significant refocusing of PLA priorities and redeployments. Not only would shorter-range missiles be pulled back, they would likely be reduced in number. If trends continued to be positive over time, the recent emphasis on landing craft would also likely ease.

However, electronic and information warfare techniques would still be honed, a wide variety of increasingly capable surface ships and submarines would continue to be introduced into the fleet, faster and more versatile aircraft would be acquired, and medium- and long-range missiles of different varieties would continue to have an important place in the arsenal. Moreover, the PLA would in any case accelerate its vigorous military-to-military activity, in a ceremonial and exercise mode in order to bolster overall relations with others as well as create space for shoring up China's specific security interests.

The variations from different scenarios could be significant, but lead times will be great enough for China to adapt and for others to react in turn. In the meantime, however, given current trends, one should anticipate neither a sharp acceleration nor a sharp decline in current activities. There may be discontinuities as technological advances permit them, and the United States should not be complacent about its current lead in any area. However, the U.S. military and the PLA should take into account how any individual step or cluster of steps will appear on the other side of the Pacific and what contribution they make to perceptions of enmity versus cooperation.

In principle, hedging is not a containment strategy, but a prudent approach to future uncertainties, even though China's current behavior is, as one observer notes, "decidedly more risk averse than that of the United States."[19] That said, the way hedging is carried out can have a major impact on the PRC's own responses.

In other words, much of what the future will look like, and how the PLA will view and react to it, is in U.S. hands; that should be an important factor in any decisions Washington takes.

NOTES

1. Jonathan Pollack puts it this way: "Any characterization of an 'Asian security order' . . . is a major oversimplification . . . [and] expectations of a cooperative security order seem equally premature." "The Transformation of the Asian Security Order" in David Shambaugh, ed., *Power Shift: China and Asia's New Dynamics* (Berkeley, Calif.: University of California Press, 2006), pp. 331–2.

2. The complex Chinese attitudes toward the alliance, including its relationship to Taiwan, are analyzed by Thomas J. Christensen "China, the U.S.-Japan Alliance, and the Security Dilemma in East Asia," *International Security*, 23, no. 4 (Spring 1999): 49–80. Alastair Iain Johnston also addresses that relationship in a broader regional context in "China's International Relations: The Political and Security Dimensions," in Samuel S. Kim, ed., *The International Relations of Northeast Asia* (Lanham, Md.: Rowman & Littlefield, 2004), p. 78ff.

3. Discussing this point in an even broader East Asia context, two Chinese scholars note that "China realizes that the U.S. presence in the region is useful to some extent, and that the U.S. security umbrella makes regional states more comfortable in dealing with China." Zhang Yunling and Tang Shiping, "China's Regional Strategy" in Shambaugh, *op. cit.,* p. 53.

4. Michael D. Swaine observes, "One of the primary goals of modern Chinese nationalism has been for the Chinese state to develop a sufficient level of military power to deter future aggression by other states, to support China's long-standing desire to achieve national wealth and power, and to attain international recognition and respect as a great nation." Swaine discusses in some detail the likely capabilities that the PRC will seek to develop in terms of its overarching national security objectives. "China's Regional Military Posture" in Shambaugh, *op. cit.,* pp. 266–72.

5. One effort to mend fences was the Bush-Roh Moo Hyun summit in November 2005, which produced a joint statement full of upbeat sentences ("Joint Declaration on the R.O.K. –U.S. Alliance and Peace on the Korean Peninsula," Office of the Press Secretary, White House, November 17, 2005. Available online at http://www.state.gov/p/eap/rls/ot/57075.htm). The lack of a common vision about the alliance's longer-term purposes on the peninsula and in the region, however, represents an underlying vulnerability.

6. Wang Jisi and Xu Hui, "Pattern of Sino-American Crises: A Chinese Perspective," in Michael D. Swaine and Zhang Tuosheng, eds., *Managing Sino-American Crises* (Washington, D.C.: Carnegie Endowment for International Peace, 2006), p. 139.

7. Michael D. Swaine, "Trouble in Taiwan," *Foreign Affairs* 83(2), March-April 2004, available at http://www.foreignaffairs.org/20040301faessay83205/michael-d-swaine/trouble-in-taiwan.html.

8. Michael A. McDevitt lays out in depth the U.S. defense perspective on China's growing power. See Michael A. McDevitt, "The China Factor in Future U.S. Defense Planning" in Jonathan D. Pollack, ed., *Strategic Surprise? U.S.-China Relations in the Early Twenty-first Century* (Newport, R.I.: Naval War College Press, 2004), pp. 149–57.

9. In discussing the specific question of the connection between threats to internal security and external behavior, M. Taylor Fravel presents a persuasive argument that, at least in China's case, but likely well beyond China as well, internal insecurity leads to cooperation and delay over external disputes, perhaps even compromise, not confrontation. As he puts it, internal problems create incentives for "diversionary peace" rather than diversionary war. Fravel makes the point that compromise on certain core sovereignty issues (e.g., Taiwan) is unlikely, however. See M. Taylor Fravel, "Regime Insecurity and International Cooperation: Explaining China's Compromises in Territorial Dispute," *International Security,* 30, no. 2 (Fall 2005): 46–83.

10. David Shambaugh discusses specific PLA's requirements regarding Taiwan in "China's Military Modernization" in Ashley J. Tellis and Michael Wills, eds., *Strategic Asia 2005-06: Military Modernization in an Era of Uncertainty* (Seattle, Wash.: The National Bureau of Asian Research, 2005), pp. 68–69.

11. Of course, if Sino-American relations were in very bad shape, one could conceive of proposals to block unification. But even at a time of great U.S.-PRC enmity in the 1950s, Dean Acheson had the wisdom not to support Taiwan independence in an effort to avoid becoming the center of an irredentist controversy. It is hard to conceive of a circumstance in which an American leader would adopt a different position unless the entire relationship with China were in turmoil, in which case Taiwan would be but one aspect of a dramatically deteriorated strategic picture, and unification would not likely be an active issue.

12. No one could draw up a new constitution in Taiwan today that included references to the theoretical links that tie the island to the mainland as the current constitution does. Amending the constitution in some way would allow the drafters to finesse that issue by simply ignoring those provisions. But drafting a totally new document, as Chen proposed in late September 2003, would eliminate that possibility.

13. This narrower focus was most clearly seen in the May 17, 2004 "authorized statement" of the State Council and Communist Party Taiwan Affairs Offices as well as in the March 2005 "Anti-Secession Law." It has also been pointedly referred to since then by senior PRC officials. Indeed, the scope of highest concern has been even further narrowed. It has moved from the broad concept of "independence" to the rather loose term "*de jure* independence" and finally to the highly focused issue of "*de jure* independence through constitutional change." Moreover, whereas Beijing used to object to any change in the 1947 "Republic of China" constitution on the grounds that amendment inevitably moved Taiwan further in the direction of a new national identity, in fact the PRC's "red lines" no longer relate to all constitutional changes, but only to those that would be seen as touching on sovereignty or questions of independence versus unification.

14. David Shambaugh looks in some detail at the issue of the "de facto encirclement" of China. See David Shambaugh, "China's Military Modernization" in Tellis and Wills, *op. cit.,* p. 73ff.

15. Zhang Yunling and Tang Shiping, "China's Regional Strategy," *op. cit.*, p. 55.

16. This transformation is explored in depth by Benjamin L. Self, *The Dragon's Shadow: The Rise of China and Japan's New Nationalism* (Washington, D.C.: The Henry L. Stimson Center, November 2006).

17. The Japan Defense Agency (since transformed into the Ministry of Defense) reported in late 2006 that PLA naval vessels spotted in the East China Sea and sea areas near Japan numbered six in 2004, four in 2005, but none in 2006. Maritime exploration ship activity in the Japanese Exclusive Economic Zone (EEZ) had also dropped

off sharply, from eighteen occasions in 2004 to none in 2006. Moreover, the Air Self-Defense Force had scrambled to guard against Chinese intrusions into Japanese airspace thirteen times in 2004, 107 times in 2005, but only once in 2006. ("PRC Military Vessel Activities Slow Down in East China Sea; Anti-Japanese Moves Suppressed?" *Sankei Shimbun*, 4 November 2006 (translated by Open Source Center, JPP20061106026001).

18. "China-IEA Joint Workshop on Oil Security, 30 and 31 October 2006, Beijing," statement available at http://www.iea.org/Textbase/work/2006/Jointchina/jointstatement. pdf. Other information on IEA's outreach to China can be found at http://www.iea. org/Textbase/subjectqueries/nmc/china.asp.

19. Jonathan D. Pollack, "Sino-American Relations in the Early Twenty-first Century" in Pollack, ed., *Strategic Surprise? op. cit.*, p. 19.

13

Assessing the Threat

Michael D. Swaine and Oriana Skylar Mastro

THE CHAPTERS IN THIS VOLUME examine three sets of variables that are critical to any accurate understanding of the nature and extent of the PLA threat to Taiwan's security: relevant PLA capabilities (particularly compared with those of the United States and Taiwan), the dynamics of escalation and crisis instability in a Taiwan confrontation, and the overall influence of the regional security environment. The most important questions relating to these variables include the following: Is the PLA acquiring capabilities that are currently altering—or will soon threaten to alter—the balance of forces across the Taiwan Strait in its favor, thus potentially increasing the likelihood of a Chinese use of force? Also, are improving PLA capabilities increasing the likelihood that China will deter or defeat a possible U.S. attempt to assist Taiwan in the event of such a conflict across the strait? Under which types of conflict scenarios would such potential dangers be most likely? What is needed to reduce such threats? Would a crisis or potential conflict between the United States and China over Taiwan prove especially difficult to manage or control, thus increasing the likelihood of inadvertent and highly dangerous escalation? What factors or features of such a conflict would generate the greatest degree of escalation or overall instability and why? What can be done to reduce such instabilities? Finally, to what extent and in what manner does the larger Asian security environment influence the threat posed to Taiwan by China's growing military capabilities? What can the United States do to shape the regional environment in ways that lower the propensity for crisis or conflict?

This volume addresses in various ways most, if not all, of these questions. In some instances, it reinforces (and hence makes even more credible) existing assessments and views already present in other scholarly and policy-related studies. In other instances, the chapters in this volume offer analyses that are somewhat at odds with assessments found in the existing literature. The remainder of this chapter assesses the significance of those points in light of views found in the existing literature; identifies the most important points made in the preceding chapters that are of greatest relevance to the above questions; and examines the possible implications of the preceding analyses for future policies in the United States and Taiwan.

PLA CAPABILITIES

According to the 2006 Department of Defense (DoD) report on China's military modernization, China's military options with respect to Taiwan are: (1) persuasion and coercion, (2) limited force operations (information operations [IO], special operations forces [SOF], short-range ballistic missiles [SRBMs], or limited air strikes), (3) an air and missile campaign, (4) a blockade, and (5) amphibious invasion.[1] Since at least late 2002, many close observers of China's ongoing military buildup (including both the Pentagon and nongovernmental PLA specialists) have increasingly argued that past PLA efforts to acquire, develop, deploy, train, and operationalize a range of capabilities specific to these five options are beginning to bear significant fruit. Such developments include:

- The deployment of significant numbers of more capable ballistic missiles, air defense missiles, submarines, destroyers/frigates, strike and multi-role aircraft, as well as efforts to attain the capability to attack carriers with ballistic missiles;[2]
- Improvements in long-range tracking and targeting and in command, computers, control, communications, intelligence, surveillance, and reconnaissance (C4ISR), including likely space-based assets;[3]
- Enhanced amphibious capabilities and improvements in SOF and reconnaissance, including new SOF units and amphibious *divisions;*
- The likely near-term operational deployment of Airborne Warning and Control Systems (AWACs), in-flight refueling, and cruise missiles;

- Much more realistic training exercises;[4]
- Growth in the size and importance of a noncommissioned officers (NCO) corps;
- Adoption of appropriate new doctrine, strategy, and tactics (largely from 1999);
- Significantly improved defense-industrial capabilities.[5]

At the same time, many observers assert that Taiwan is not improving its own military capabilities in many areas to a level and at a pace sufficient to ensure the maintenance of a credible deterrent against Chinese coercion or a PLA attack. Some observers focus on the continued inability (or unwillingness) of Taiwan's political leaders to approve the acquisition of a range of significant weapons systems approved by the United States in April 2001; others, such as Ashton B. Carter and William J. Perry, point to declining levels of Taiwanese defense spending[6] (Taiwan's defense spending has decreased from almost half of government outlays in the 1950s to 25 percent by 1995, to 16 percent in the early 2000s[7]). Stephen M. Young, director of the American Institute in Taiwan, expressed this view, stating "We [the U.S. government] believe that Taiwan is not responding appropriately to this steady buildup of the military across the Taiwan Strait." He comments further that he is disappointed in the inability of the Taiwan Legislative Yuan to pass an appropriate defense budget that provides funds for the weapons systems that President Bush offered Taipei in 2001.[8] Expressing what is perhaps an even more extreme view, Shirley Kan writes, "In Taipei, domestic politics dominate. Strategic thought is lacking. There is no sense of urgency when it comes to Taiwan's self-defense."[9] The Taiwan military is also showing concern. Lieutenant General Hsu Tai-sheng notes, "The Chinese People's Liberation Army poses a severe threat to our naval vessels with their superior submarines, and as their jet fighters far outnumber ours, we would suffer great damage to our air force."[10]

As a result of these developments, some observers have become increasingly concerned that Beijing is steadily shifting the balance of power across the Taiwan Strait in its favor by acquiring capabilities that will permit it to rapidly weaken or destroy Taiwan's capacity to resist, despite Taipei's efforts to prevent this, and severely complicate (or in some cases prevent) U.S. efforts to come to the assistance of Taiwan in a timely and effective manner. For example, according to *Jane's Defence Weekly*, by 2010, China should have a military edge over Taiwan given current military buildup and modernization trends.[11] Mark Stokes agreed with this assessment as early as 1999, asserting "...emphasis on information dominance, missile forces, and air defense could decisively tip the cross-Strait military balance in Beijing's favor."[12] According to an article in *The Far Eastern Economic Review*, the Chinese are focusing on anti-access measures aimed at keeping the United States out of any conflict over Taiwan. Ronald O'Rourke stated in a report to Congress that "some analysts speculate that China may attain (or believe that it has attained) a capable maritime anti-access force, or elements of it, by about 2010."[13]

However, not all analysts agree that, in former CIA Director Porter Goss' words, "Beijing's military modernization and military buildup is tilting the balance of power in the Taiwan Strait."[14] According to the former commander of U.S. Pacific forces and Admiral (retired) Dennis Blair, Chinese efforts at military modernization "have not significantly altered the balance of power" across the strait and will not do so in the foreseeable future. The recent 18 percent increase in Beijing's budget, Blair argues, "largely go[es] for personnel expenses, maintenance and then a certain amount of acquisitions" and therefore should not be interpreted in terms of potential weapons systems acquired.[15] In addition, according to a very recent statement by Blair, China's deployment of SRBMs along the Taiwan Strait has not reached a level where it could have a decisive political effect on Taiwan. He stresses that it is very difficult to bomb a country into submission, and China only has approximately 800 missiles. Moreover, Taiwan is "hardening and dispersing" its forces to reduce the efficacy of any PLA missile attack.[16]

Blair adds that China is not on the verge of rivaling the United States in the Western Pacific because many key U.S. maritime and air capabilities are improving at a much faster rate than are those of China. For example, the highly advanced F/A-22 fighter aircraft just finished its operational testing and evaluation; combat exchange ratios between F/A-22s and any other fighter in the world will almost certainly be in double digits in favor of the F/A-22. Moreover, according to Blair, U.S. naval battle groups will soon be equipped with an enormously complex command and control system that provides very high clarity to the battle picture, can handle stealth targets, and makes every anti-air weapon count. He observes that the Chinese are years from being able to field and maintain such a system.[17]

Others add that Taiwan retains a qualitative advantage while China has only a quantitative edge that is not enough to overcome the Taiwan Air Force (TAF) and significant geographical challenges. Ronald O'Rourke, for example, argues that in spite of naval modernization efforts, the PLA Navy (PLAN) has significant areas of weakness, including "capabilities for operating in waters more distant from China, joint operations, C4ISR . . . long-range surveillance and targeting systems, anti-air warfare (AAW), antisubmarine warfare (ASW), mine countermeasures (MCM), and logistics."[18] Finally, Admiral Timothy Keating, incoming commander of the U.S. forces in the Pacific, dismisses reports of recent Chinese gains in submarine development, stating "they are well behind us technologically. We enjoy significant advantages across the spectrum of defensive and offensive systems, in particular undersea warfare."[19]

As indicated in the Introduction, the chapters in this volume largely reinforce the image of a much more capable PLA that poses clear implications for Taiwan's security. For example, Kenneth Allen comments that although it is unclear whether PLA Air Force (PLAAF) pilots are better than those of the TAF, PLAAF aircraft have been conducting more sophisticated air-to-air combat than they were five years ago. In addition, the TAF is at a disadvantage because its runways are likely to be the first targets of PLA missile strikes.[20] In naval capabilities, Bernard Cole notes that, as of 2007, the two sides are roughly equal in surface combatant capability; however, he also points out that the PLAN submarine and aviation forces are far superior to those of Taiwan. Cole observes that the PLAN regards its submarine force as "pos[ing] the most serious naval threat to foreign forces, especially U.S. aircraft carriers." In addition, Cole argues that basic geography severely limits the viability of any Taiwanese defense against a Chinese seaborne assault supported by air operations.

In addition to such rather straightforward assessments of specific armed services and combat conditions, other authors in this volume address less frequently examined aspects of the PLA's improving capabilities. Dean Cheng's analysis of China's efforts to conduct joint operations, focused on a single, intense campaign, is of particular relevance in this regard. As Cheng indicates, China's ability to conduct joint operations is a highly significant factor in the cross-strait balance, especially because amphibious operations as well as the seaborne delivery of ground forces against a hostile shore both require the ability to operate jointly. He points out that if the Chinese were able to coordinate and execute a joint campaign in a Taiwan contingency, this would allow them to take advantage of the strengths and counterbalance the weaknesses of all of their armed services, thus improving their chances of operational success; the less the Chinese rely on one service, the fewer opportunities for the United States to exploit Chinese military weaknesses. Therefore, Chinese military doctrine has evolved to include joint operations as a major objective. Moreover, as Cheng points out, the Chinese are learning about joint operations from other militaries directly though their participation in multilateral military efforts, such as combating floods, and indirectly through studying the doctrines and war experiences of other militaries. Roy D. Kamphausen and Justin Liang agree, and describe in detail how China's expanding military-to-military relations with many nations as well as its participation in UN peacekeeping operations and other multilateral exercises are enabling China to learn from other militaries to better prepare its own military for a Taiwan contingency.

A second underexamined area in which the PLA is adding significantly to its capabilities is information operations (IO). As James Mulvenon states, the Chinese believe that computer network operations (CNO) could be used to delay or deter a U.S. intervention in a Taiwan crisis, giving Beijing enough time to force Taiwan's capitulation before U.S. reinforcements arrive. Hence, the Chinese have developed the ability to attack U.S. civilian networks (NIPRNET) in order to disrupt its coordination of transportation, communications, and logistics, while maintaining deniability. Moreover, Mulvenon states that Taiwan possesses a highly informationalized society and economy, making its critical infrastructure especially vulnerable to IO attacks. He observes that Taiwan's current capabilities and readiness level are much lower than other states under such a direct threat, such as South Korea (ROK) and Israel.

The chapter by Andrew Yang provides a qualified acknowledgment of some of the deficiencies of Taiwan's military in handling the growing Chinese threat to the island. Yang observes that the Taiwanese government has recognized, to a certain degree, the weaknesses of its defenses against a mainland attack if deterrence were to fail. However, he also stresses that Taiwanese defense modernization has been focused for some time on improving its abilities to deter long-range precision air strikes, a naval blockade, an amphibious landing, and SOF, despite funding problems. If Taiwan is able to protect critical military and strategic targets from precision strike and prevent China from disrupting its command and control systems early in a conflict, Yang believes that it may be possible for Taiwan to hold off the Chinese until the United States can intervene. To this end, he notes that the Taiwanese are building up a range of defensive capabilities. However, they are also acquiring what he defines as limited offensive capabilities, to strengthen deterrence against a rapid PLA strike. On the other hand, Yang also acknowledges that Taiwan's defense modernization efforts remain significantly constrained by the inability of the legislative and executive branches of government to come to a consensus about the appropriate amount of funding to dedicate and the type of force structure desired.

Finally, Roger Cliff offers a rather pessimistic overall assessment of the implications of improving PLA capabilities for the ability of the United States to come to Taiwan's assistance in a crisis. He argues that China is steadily acquiring a wide range of increasingly sophisticated weaponry and support systems—many comparable to those in the U.S. inventory—that greatly enhance its capacity to conduct "anti-access" operations against U.S. forces operating near Taiwan, despite current and planned advances in U.S. capabilities in the region. Most notably, these include, by 2015, a dozen modern destroyers with air defense capabilities comparable to the U.S. Aegis system, several dozen modern diesel-electric attack submarines, possibly a dozen nuclear-powered type 093-class attack submarines, and perhaps the missile technology and C4ISR necessary to hit a moving ship at sea. Cliff asserts that the combination of these PLA advances, China's close proximity to Taiwan, and existing limits on U.S. forward-deployed forces in the Western Pacific will give Chinese forces a growing advantage over time, especially if China were to undertake preemptive or surprise attacks on U.S. forces in a Taiwan contingency.

Should one conclude from the above that the volume's authors endorse, on balance, the notion that the combination of the PLA's growing capabilities and the limitations of both U.S. and Taiwan forces is resulting in a shift in the balance of power across the Taiwan Strait? As noted in the Introduction, Roger Cliff certainly thinks so. He concludes that the balance of military power is shifting in China's favor not only with regard to Taiwan, but across the Western Pacific as a whole. He adds that "...by 2015 China is likely to enjoy a significant quantitative advantage in a conflict with the United States [over Taiwan], particularly in its early stages."

None of the other authors in this volume explicitly echo Cliff's conclusion, although some draw rather troubling implications from their analysis. For example, Cole states that largely because Taiwan is "greatly outnumbered [by China] in terms of manpower and number of aircraft and submarines, [it] would be able to survive in an all-out war scenario [with China] only for a limited period of time." Cole also contends that if an initial Chinese assault on Taiwan were not successful, it is possible that Beijing would retreat, regroup, and launch another attack. The number of times that the United States might be willing to intervene in a cross-strait crisis thus becomes a key variable in China's deterrent strategy. Mulvenon notes that Taiwan's defense structure has remained highly vulnerable to SOF and fifth-column attacks which, Yang points out, could disrupt the military command and control, decapitate the national command authority, and provide intelligence for follow-up attacks.

On the other hand, several authors note significant limitations on Chinese capabilities that cast doubt on the notion that the balance of power is shifting in Beijing's favor, especially regarding any attempt to seize the island outright. The analyses by Cole and Allen suggest that China still faces many operational challenges to conducting any major amphibious assault on Taiwan, which requires air superiority and the ability to coordinate and deploy assets to a specific location. Allen explains that China's ability to maintain air superiority would depend greatly on the rules of engagement (ROE) in any conflict. If the United States were to bomb Chinese airfields, thus forcing China to move its aircraft farther away from the location of engagement, the Chinese would not be able to fly enough sorties to maintain air superiority in a Taiwan conflict. Even with air superiority, Cole cautions that the PLAN's ability to conduct an amphibious assault is still limited by factors both within and outside of Beijing's control. For example, the physical geography of the strait means that there are very few suitable landing areas for beaching craft. Current PLAN plans probably include the use of merchant ships in an amphibious lift, because of the insufficient number of PLAN amphibious ships; however, their lack of proper equipment and training greatly diminish their operational usefulness. In addition, Andrew Yang suggests that China would need to successfully sustain a naval blockade before it could launch an amphibious assault—a problematic undertaking at best.

It must also be pointed out that Cliff's analysis does not take into consideration Taiwan's ability to hold off a Chinese attack for the approximately ten days that it would take the United States to transfer critical additional forces from outside the Western Pacific to the theater. Cliff acknowledges that, once on the scene, such forces would likely prove decisive in a Taiwan conflict. One cannot assume that, despite their deficiencies, Taiwan's forces would be unable to resist Chinese coercion or an outright assault for these crucial ten days. Andrew Yang does not draw that conclusion, despite his recognition of Taiwan's shortcomings. Furthermore, as Yang points out, any attempt by Beijing to resolve the Taiwan situation once and for all through the use of force requires far more than the ability to seize the island. Once Taiwan's defenses are overcome, Beijing needs to replace the Taiwanese government with one that is pro-China, eliminate all of Taiwan's defense capabilities and defense links with the United States, and restore order by forcing or enticing the Taiwanese populace to accept the new arrangements. Taiwan, on the other hand, only needs to survive the attack. Such requirements on Beijing's part further complicate any assessment of a shift in the balance of power toward China.

The analysis presented in this volume also highlights limitations in PLA capabilities that apply to a variety of conflict scenarios other than an all-out invasion. For example, Dean Cheng notes that even though China has dedicated much time and effort to formulating an approach to joint campaigns, it is currently in the very early stages of implementing any true jointness capability. If China were to conduct joint operations in an attack on Taiwan, it would be its first experience with this new doctrine and therefore it is difficult to assess whether the PLA would be able to actualize its goal of achieving jointness. James Mulvenon suggests that China's information warfare operations could prove to be more limited than many expect by pointing out that the Chinese overestimate the U.S. reliance on computers in military deployments. According to Mulvenon, even though the potential damage of Chinese IO on U.S. abilities to coordinate and deploy to the Taiwan theater in a conflict might increase in the future, the United States could nonetheless coordinate its logistics systems without the use of its computer networks.

Thus, on balance, the analysis of PLA capabilities contained in this volume offers a decidedly mixed picture of the military situation across the Taiwan Strait. On the one hand, it does not unequivocally confirm a shift in the balance of power in Beijing's favor; China will continue for a long time to face daunting challenges, especially to any attempt to seize Taiwan via an all-out invasion. In particular, it cannot be assured of air superiority or the success of a naval blockade of the island in any foreseeable time frame. The former is essential to the success of a wide range of contingencies. For the moment, and probably for several years to come, the relatively superior TAF—which is in the process of integrating into its force structure aircraft such as the F-16, the Mirage 2000, and the Indigenous Defense Fighter in tandem with airborne warning and control platforms such as the E-2T—can probably blunt the worst threats that could be mounted by the PLAAF. Moreover, China does not currently possess the amphibious and airborne forces required for a major attack and it does not appear to be focusing its efforts on acquiring such capabilities in the future.[21] Finally, none of the analyses presented herein would lead one to conclude that China has achieved or is about to achieve the capability to overcome Taiwanese resistance before U.S. forces could intervene.

That said, this volume certainly reinforces the concern among many observers that China is acquiring new and enlarged military capabilities in specific areas (and thus perhaps even "narrowing the gap" vis-à-vis both Taiwan and the United States) in ways that could, over time, weaken deterrence and thereby destabilize the cross-strait military balance. In particular, increases in specific PLA air and naval capabilities (e.g., those most applicable to anti-access and area denial operations, such as long-range cruise missiles and submarines), integration of a joint warfare doctrine that maximizes available assets, growing asymmetrical options in areas such as IO, as well as an expanding arsenal of SRBMs, might together lead the Chinese leadership to regard certain "lesser" military options—such as panic-inducing air and missile attacks or a rapid, decapitation strike involving preemptive attacks and a variety of SOF and fifth-column actions—as possibly worth undertaking under extreme circumstances. Such an option would gain credibility if Chinese leaders were to believe that they could quickly establish a military *fait accompli* that the United States would find difficult to reverse without a major escalation of the conflict. Under such circumstances, China's leaders might conclude that they would enjoy a distinct advantage over the United States, given their apparent belief that Washington would have less resolve than Beijing in a major crisis over Taiwan and thus would seek to avoid a prolonged or intense conflict. Such beliefs are discussed in the next section.

ESCALATORY DYNAMICS OF A TAIWAN CRISIS

In recent years, informed observers have focused in greater detail on the complexities of Sino-American crisis management and the instabilities of a political-military crisis over Taiwan in particular. The majority of these studies conclude that many American and Chinese views as well as the past behavior of both parties in relevant crises could produce significant levels of instability, perhaps resulting in unwanted escalation and highly dangerous levels of military conflict. For example, such studies point out that both countries:

- Hold dangerous images and assumptions that undermine crisis management;
- Emphasize showing resolve and acting decisively in a crisis more than making efforts to reassure the adversary;
- Have engaged in sudden, rapid, asymmetrical escalation in past crises;
- Remain subject to significant bilateral communication problems; and
- Are adversely influenced by features of the decision-making process, domestic politics, and the actions of third parties (such as Taiwan).[22]

Moreover, studies also point out that a serious Sino-American crisis over Taiwan could prove *particularly* difficult to control. In such a major[23] crisis, U.S. and Chinese leaders would likely have a very strong incentive to communicate enormous resolve in ways that could make it difficult to set or sustain limited objectives, exercise self-restraint, and maintain flexibility. According to Admiral (retired) Dennis Blair,

There is a good possibility that China would not accept de-escalation and a negotiated settlement following the initial phases of a conflict over Taiwan . . . . Sacrifices will have been made, prestige will have been spent, and victory must be declared and justified. The real wildcards are Chinese actions with their nuclear weapons and Chinese attacks on U.S. allies in the region. Current Chinese thinking and actions seem conservative, but there could be changes under heavy political pressure. Should China escalate in any of these directions, then new dynamics come to the fore that turn "teaching Taiwan (and the United States) a lesson" into a show-down on the future of Asia.[24]

In short, once in a major crisis over Taiwan, China and the United States might have great difficulty controlling escalation into an even larger conflict.

Several of the authors in this volume validate this general assessment, and add significantly to our level of understanding regarding the potentially destabilizing dynamics of a Taiwan crisis. Allen and Cole examine this issue primarily from the perspective of the deployment patterns and operating features of the Chinese (and Taiwan) air force and navy, respectively. Roberts assesses the potential crisis instabilities inherent in the nuclear postures and general crisis views of both China and the United States, while Henley looks at the instabilities that might derive from China's overall military doctrine. Mulvenon and Romberg discuss Chinese assumptions (some would say misperceptions) regarding the relative level of resolve that Beijing and Washington would likely display in a major crisis. In most of these cases, the presence of Taiwan as a third actor in a Sino-American crisis is recognized as a serious potential catalyst for instability or unwanted escalation.

Allen points out that specific encounters, such as an inadvertent collision of aircraft (for example, due to pilot error or engine malfunction) followed by miscalculations on one or both sides, could serve as a catalyst for a conflict to break out and escalate. The increasing number of Chinese and Taiwanese aircraft that routinely fly to the small airspace of the center line increases this threat to crisis stability across the strait. Allen points out that both sides have historically accused each other of crossing the line and subsequently used the media to escalate the situation and gain public support. In addition, according to Allen, certain activities, such as the forward deployment of China's aircraft, could be seen as deterrence by China, escalation by the United States, and outright preparation for an offensive attack by Taiwan. If signs of deterrence from any of the three parties are unclear and misinterpreted as a sign of preemptive action, a superficially stable situation could rapidly deteriorate into a conflict. Beijing might view a crisis as an opportunity to implement its preexisting operations plans, and Taiwan, viewing the buildup, may decide to preemptively strike mainland targets while its forces are still capable, thus drastically escalating the crisis. Finally, from a broader perspective, Allen notes that the offensive military doctrines of all three militaries and belief that escalation, not concession, is the best way to achieve favorable war termination conditions make escalation in the Taiwan Strait even more likely.

The potential for escalation in a maritime scenario is also high, according to Cole. The geography, hydrography, and climate of the Taiwan Strait would make it difficult for commanders to correctly assess a crisis situation involving naval actions, thereby increasing the potential for escalation due to the unintended consequences of their misinformed decisions. Moreover, Cole argues that the level of mutual suspicion discussed by Allen could also produce crisis instability in a maritime context; for example, if a submarine is lost due to mechanical failure, it is possible that the country involved might conclude it was the result of hostile actions and retaliate.

Brad Roberts contends that U.S. and Chinese misperceptions about each other's nuclear doctrines and how they might threaten the use of nuclear weapons in a Taiwan contingency also create an environment of instability. Roberts agrees with the above-mentioned view that strong levels of confidence and a fundamental belief by both sides that "strong action will induce the enemy to exercise restraint" could cause escalation in a Taiwan scenario because "actions taken to demonstrate resolve and credibility may induce not restraint by the enemy but an intensification of conflict." Furthermore, Roberts contends that some U.S. and Chinese experts see "nuclear wars as potentially manageable in the sense that they can be fought in a way that secures vital interests and inflicts decisive defeat on the enemy." In short, both sides "seem generally confident of their nation's ability to identify and manage nuclear risks in war." Such misplaced confidence can lead to serious miscalculations and unintended escalation of disastrous proportions.

Unfortunately, as Roberts points out, both countries have focused their efforts on deterrence, but have not devoted adequate time to preparing for the failure of deterrence. Moreover, because of a lack of transparency, it is unclear whether Chinese nuclear doctrine would stress seizing the initiative as its conventional missile doctrine does. The Chinese position that "once armed conflict is inevitable, no effort should be spared to strive for strategic initiative" therefore can be highly destabilizing. Though China is concerned about U.S. long-range precision strike systems and wishes to ensure a strong enough deterrent to eliminate the possibility of U.S. preemption against China, it has not yet formally weakened its "No First Use" (NFU) position. Roberts states that attention needs to be paid to future developments in this area because such a shift might have serious implications for escalation control.

Henley's chapter on Chinese military doctrine reinforces the concerns regarding unintended escalation expressed by Roberts in the nuclear area. According to Henley, Beijing has historically overestimated its abilities to manipulate both its opponent's perceptions and reactions as well as the scale, scope, intensity, and duration of a crisis. Assessments of the PLA's views on war control show that Beijing does not believe that good crisis management precludes the use of military force; instead, visible military deployments could be used to gain the initiative and deter opponents by signaling resolve. This arguably increases the chance that the opponent might misinterpret a deterrence signal as a major threat. Furthermore, in Henley's view, Chinese doctrine regards a deliberate intensification of the conflict as a tactic to increase bargaining power. This means that whether China plans to take aggressive military action or is just posturing in an effort to gain the political initiative could be unclear to outsiders. These positions, coupled with Beijing's emphasis on seizing and holding the initiative, could be seen by others as a major threat, creating further instability. Finally, Andrew Yang's chapter reinforces Henley's argument. Yang argues that, in a major crisis over Taiwan, the need for Beijing to achieve its objectives before the United States can intervene militarily will compel it to focus on preemptive strike and "quick strike" capabilities, thus decreasing the chances of gradual escalation.

Mulvenon argues that Beijing also appears to remain confident of its assessments of U.S. casualty aversion, will to fight, and commitment to Taiwan. He argues that this is the case despite the apparent fact that

Beijing has demonstrated on numerous occasions its inability to correctly predict U.S. responses to its military initiatives (the most recent case being the 1996 crisis). Romberg adds that China sees Taiwan as a core national issue, but perceives it as only a marginal one for the United States. Again, such assessments obviously create problems for the U.S. deterrent against China and could lead to grave miscalculations on the part of Beijing that result in unintended escalation.

Finally, we should note that, in contrast to such pessimistic assessments, Kamphausen and Liang argue that some of China's military actions might arguably contribute to crisis stability by enhancing deterrence without necessarily provoking the other side. They cite certain operations such as air surveillance and amphibious training exercises designed to show China's resolve regarding Taiwan. Kenneth Allen adds that Beijing controls the number of PLAAF flights to the center line as a tool for deterrence and to show displeasure about particular developments. The extent to which such PLA actions actually serve to reassure and deter, rather than provoke, is of course extremely difficult to determine.

INFLUENCE OF THE ASIAN SECURITY ENVIRONMENT

The overall power structure, political views, and core relationships that constitute the Asian security environment can exert an important, albeit largely indirect, influence over the current and future threat situation in the Taiwan Strait. Most observers of the regional security environment do not make such an explicit linkage, or they do so largely in passing. Others clearly offer analyses that pose implications for Taiwan without directly stating it. In general, the recent literature suggests that Asia's security environment affects Taiwan's security in two important ways, as a result of (a) likely enhancements in the U.S.-Japan security alliance and changes in the larger U.S. military posture in maritime Asia and (b) possible changes in the broader bilateral or multilateral political and military relationships that Beijing and Washington have with other countries throughout the Western Pacific, including most notably South Korea, Australia, and some key Southeast Asian states.[25]

The former could produce contrasting consequences for Taiwan's security. On the one hand, if properly handled, a strengthening and expanding U.S.-Japan security alliance could enhance the ability of the United States to deter a possible Chinese use of force over Taiwan, despite considerable improvements in PLA capabilities. The United States and Japan are clearly attempting to send such deterrence signals regarding Taiwan. The agreement originally drafted in 1999 and revised in 2004 (which addressed provisions of logistic support, supplies, and services between the Self-Defense Forces of Japan and the Armed Forces of the United States of America) includes "operations in response to situations in areas surrounding Japan," which is defined as areas that have "an important influence on Japan's peace and security.[26]" More specifically,

> Under Article 6 of the Japan-U.S. Security Treaty, U.S. forces are granted the use of facilities and areas in Japan for the purpose of contributing to Japan's security, as well as international peace and security in the Far East. The United States has stationed its armed forces in Japan in accordance with this article.[27]

In a joint statement, Japan and the United States listed a common strategic objective in the region: "Encourage the peaceful resolution of issues concerning the Taiwan Strait through dialogue."[28] Whether such signals are having the desired effect is not generally discussed. They certainly do not seem to have diminished China's commitment to building a stronger military posture of direct relevance to the Taiwan Strait. Some might even argue that such statements contributed to the Chinese passage of the Anti-Secession Law, one month after the above-mentioned joint U.S.-Japan statement of February 2005. This law arguably escalates the intensity of the deterrence signaling over Taiwan that is occurring between China and the U.S./Taiwan.[29]

If mismanaged, a strengthened U.S.-Japan alliance could greatly exacerbate overall Sino-American strategic tensions and deepen Chinese fears that Taiwan might seek *de jure* independence with American and/or Japanese support or acquiescence. And, should deterrence fail in the Taiwan Strait, an enhanced U.S.-Japan alliance would almost certainly ensure Japan's significant, early involvement in a serious conflict, thus no doubt exacerbating the adverse consequences that such a conflict would pose for the region. Under its recently elected, strongly nationalistic Prime Minister Shinzo Abe, Japan is arguably moving ever closer to the United States, increasingly acquiring many of the military and diplomatic attributes of a "normal" power, and perhaps strengthening its capacity to intervene in a Taiwan conflict in support of the United States. To some observers, Tokyo is also becoming more pro-Taiwan.[30] Some Diet members have even proposed that Taiwan participate in search-and-rescue exercises with the Japanese Maritime Self-Defense Forces.[31] The Chinese are no doubt concerned by such moves, which is arguably one reason why they are attempting to improve relations with Tokyo after a period of significant tension over history issues and resource disputes.[32] The danger in this situation is that Washington and Tokyo might pursue ever closer security ties regarding Taiwan on the assumption that Beijing—and perhaps other countries in the region—has little choice but to accept them. This could precipitate Chinese (over)reactions that result in greater political-military tension and notable movement toward a divided region.[33]

The impact of the latter factor of bilateral and multilateral relationships could also vary enormously, depending largely on how Beijing and Washington manage their overall relationship with other key Asian states. Beijing's relations with Asia could serve to not only further constrain Taiwan's strategic support in the region, but also perhaps limit U.S. diplomatic and military options in an escalating crisis or conflict with China over the island. The success of such a strategy (which is without a doubt an important element of China's current Asia policy) would of course depend on how the United States reacts to such moves over time and the overall nature of Washington's relations with key countries. If mismanaged, Chinese and U.S. actions and reactions could adversely affect Sino-American relations and force countries to choose sides in a deepening dispute over Taiwan. On the other hand, if properly handled, regional relations with both Beijing and Washington could act as a mutual deterrent and brake on possible provocations originating from Beijing, Washington, and/or Taipei.

Some observers believe that U.S. influence in East Asia is already declining relative to that of China. Such a trend, if true, could contribute to a reduction in U.S. options in a Taiwan crisis. Of particular importance in this regard are U.S.-South Korean relations, given Seoul's proximity to both Japan and Taiwan and the presence of U.S. forces on the peninsula that could prove invaluable in a crisis over Taiwan. According to some analysts, "the U.S-South Korea alliance has been deeply shaken by the North Korean nuclear crisis,"[34] partly because South Korea seeks reconciliation with the North while the United States has by and large resisted dealing with the North bilaterally. Despite recent attempts to strengthen the alliance, some observers believe that anti-Americanism among South Koreans has become a major political issue for ROK leaders, who in turn cannot seem subservient to the United States. In terms of U.S. forces in South Korea, major issues have emerged in recent years over operational control of the combined command in wartime,[35] which could be of significant relevance to a Taiwan conflict that involved U.S. forces. Moreover, some observers point out that South Korea has many positive economic and political reasons to pursue closer, more cooperative ties with Beijing, largely regardless of the state of U.S.-South Korean relations. For example, Sunhyuk Kim and Wonhyuk Lim state that "South Korea aims to support China's peaceful development and to prevent a U.S.-Chinese confrontation, which would likely have a very negative effect on the Korean peninsula."[36] Finally, many analysts decry what they see as a major decline in U.S. influence relative to China in Southeast Asia and the region in general, with adverse consequences for Washington.[37] According to David I. Steinberg, "Any significant diminution of U.S. attention, concern and commitment in the area, and specifically to South Korea, could result in a South Korean-Chinese relationship (already China has become the South's largest trading partner) detrimental to stability of Northeast Asia."[38] In contrast, other observers such as Robert G. Sutter think that assessments of declining U.S. influence in both Northeast and Southeast Asia are vastly overstated.[39]

In this volume, Alan Romberg and Alex Liebman also emphasize the relevance of the larger regional security environment to the Taiwan situation. Romberg points out that many regional dynamics, such as whether Japan decides to develop extensive conventional offensive capabilities or nuclear weapons, affect China's assessment of its threat environment and therefore its calculations about the cross-strait balance. For example, he notes, "Japan's deepening role as an alliance partner, not just in terms of logistical support but potentially as a more active participant in a Taiwan contingency as well, is of great concern to PLA military planners." In contrast, China is much calmer about South Korea because bilateral political, economic, cultural, and security relations have improved substantially over the past few years. Romberg adds that, because a Taiwan crisis itself would significantly contribute to regional instability by potentially involving U.S. allies—Japan and/or South Korea—or even by compelling other regional actors to choose sides, the Chinese are making a deliberate effort to eliminate regional involvement in a Taiwan contingency. He states: "it is clear that Beijing is wasting no time in seeking to develop relationships that will help ensure that the United States would have fewer opportunities to launch attacks on China," including ensuring that countries do not allow the United States to use their bases for such purposes.

Liebman's analysis points out the challenges facing China in its attempts to shape the regional environment to support its interests vis-à-vis Taiwan through the use of multilateral fora and relations. He argues that, on the one hand, even though the results of China's strategy toward multilateral interactions have been mixed, it has been "quite effective in its vital goal of marginalizing Taiwan." On the other hand, China is aware that its military modernization is provoking concern among its neighbors. Chinese efforts at reassurance and deterrence "have not allowed China to escape from the fundamental dilemma: efforts at deterrence make signals of reassurance less credible (and vice versa)." According to Liebman, Beijing realizes that its ability to reassure other countries in the region that its rise will be peaceful would only be weakened if China were to engage in a military confrontation over Taiwan, especially if it were perceived to have taken aggressive action toward the island. In such an instance, countries may react by balancing against China, which would change the Asian security dynamic considerably and undermine China's strategy of using "multilateral institutions to shape the strategic environment in a way which makes countervailing coalitions unlikely to form."

IMPLICATIONS AND RECOMMENDATIONS

The analysis and assessments in this volume regarding PLA capabilities, the dynamics of a Taiwan crisis, and the effects of the regional environment together pose some notable implications for Taiwan's future security environment and suggest some possible military-political actions that should be taken to reduce the potential for crisis and conflict.

Although the balance of power across the Taiwan Strait is not unequivocally shifting in China's favor, the combination of growing Chinese military capabilities in key areas, the high stakes involved for China (and the United States and Taiwan), and Beijing's apparent propensity to (a) signal strong resolve through both military and diplomatic means; (b) emphasize seizing and maintaining the initiative in a serious crisis; and (c) assume that it would possess greater resolve than the United States in a crisis over Taiwan could together increase the likelihood that China's leaders might employ force under extreme circumstances. Moreover, U.S. and Taiwanese views toward military deterrence and crisis management could contribute to such a dangerous situation—largely via the continuation of Taiwan's arguably inadequate military response to the growing threat and America's tendency to assume that it will continue to enjoy escalation dominance in a crisis with China, while also prizing military initiative and resolve.

Several of the authors in this volume offer specific suggestions for the United States and/or Taiwan that address these concerns. James Mulvenon recommends that the United States reduce some of its operational vulnerabilities by strengthening computer network defenses and by conducting exercises in which it is forced to process information in different ways, such as deploying forces in the event of a computer network attack. This is especially vital since the U.S. system is becoming more automated and, therefore, more vulnerable. Most notably, Roger Cliff outlines in detail a wide range of adjustments that the United States must make to its force posture in order to reverse what he believes to be a steady shift in the balance of power in the Western Pacific in China's favor. These adjustments are also needed to fend off a large-scale Chinese preemptive attack on U.S. and Taiwanese forces and to intervene in the Taiwan Strait with overwhelming force on very short notice. They include: (a) major increases in the size and sophistication of U.S. forward-deployed air and naval forces (in many cases, well beyond currently planned levels); (b) the deployment to the Pacific theater of the most capable new air and naval weapons systems that the United States has to offer over the next decade or so; (c) a major strengthening of both passive and active air defenses at key bases and facilities across the region; (d) improvements in defenses against covert attacks on U.S. facilities and in the ability to detect surprise attacks from China; and (e) major increases in the readiness level of U.S. forces in the Western Pacific, to the point where they are able to transition to a wartime footing and deploy significant numbers of air and naval units almost immediately, even when indications of a possible Chinese attack are weak or ambiguous.

Given the analysis and evidence presented in this volume, there is no question that many measures can and should be undertaken to reduce the threat of conflict between China and the United States and Taiwan and to minimize the chances of inadvertent escalation in a crisis or armed clash. On the broadest level, the United States needs to continue to improve its ability to react swiftly and with sufficient force to deter or shut down a Chinese attack—preferably without escalating the confrontation greatly by striking the Chinese mainland early on. This means that U.S. forces must, on the one hand, maintain effective countermeasures against any significant attempt by Beijing to delay U.S. deployments to the vicinity and, on the other hand, sustain an unambiguous ability to interdict Chinese forces without attacking a wide range of targets on the mainland. In support of this objective, we agree with the above assessment that the United States should undoubtedly strengthen the defenses of its regional bases and military assets against Chinese attack and forward-deploy some additional forces. The United States should also improve its early warning systems and intelligence in order to detect any Chinese preparations for a preemptive attack, and reduce its vulnerabilities to computer attacks.

However, the precise level and type of U.S. forces, readiness levels, warning systems, and defensive structures required cannot be determined in any detail without knowing exactly which measures Washington currently is undertaking and its specific plans for the future. That said, it seems that the extensive and ambitious improvements called for by Roger Cliff might be excessive and unnecessary, especially if one believes that it is, at the very least, premature—and perhaps even inaccurate—to conclude that the balance of forces in the Western Pacific is shifting in China's favor.

In general, the improvements suggested by Cliff would have the effect of placing the United States on a continuous "near-war" footing in the Western Pacific, responding repeatedly in major ways to the slightest suspicion of Chinese aggression. From a purely financial perspective, this would be extremely costly. More importantly, as David Shambaugh argues, "modern weapons alone do not make for a modern military."[40] Romberg agrees, stating that "the 'problem' is not so much one of a simple capabilities match-up; the issue is whether each side develops reliable capacities, including asymmetric ones, to cope successfully with the strengths of the other side." Moreover, even if called for and desired, it is unlikely that the United States will have the capacity to augment its forces in the Pacific theater in the foreseeable future to the levels that Cliff recommends. As Bud Cole states, "the war on terrorism has severely impacted U.S. military resources worldwide, including the Pacific theater, as units from all the services redeploy in normal cycles to the Middle East and Southwest Asia." Equally important, the kind of massive buildup and hair-trigger readiness of U.S. forces in Asia called for by Cliff could also be counterproductive, promoting more aggressive Chinese military and political policies vis-à-vis Taiwan and other issues than currently exist. This could result in greater, not lesser, instability for Taiwan. Finally, as indicated above, Cliff's analysis does not take into account the possibility that Taiwan could resist a Chinese attack long enough to permit the United States to bring overwhelming forces to bear from outside the Pacific theater. Such a Taiwan capacity would reduce considerably the need to undertake the extensive improvements in regional U.S. forces that Cliff recommends. [41]

In addition to undertaking further improvements in U.S. capabilities, Washington should also actively seek to discourage or, in some cases prevent, Beijing's acquisition of military capabilities or related technologies that could directly challenge U.S. military superiority in critical areas relevant to Taiwan, such as long-range, real-time surveillance and electronic intelligence; precision strike; command, control, and communications; and battle management. As David Shambaugh states, "the pace and scope of PLA modernization has been negatively affected" by its lack of access to Western sources of supply.[42] To maintain advantages in these areas, the United States should maintain its arms embargo and encourage the European Union (EU) to do the same. Moreover, as Admiral Timothy Keating argues, the U.S. military should also increase its military-to-military interactions and exercises with China at various levels and in various fields to promote mutual trust and understanding and because, on balance, such demonstrations of U.S. military power will serve as a deterrent against the Chinese.[43]

There is also no doubt that Taiwan needs to overcome its domestic political problems and devote more resources to defense. Taipei's continued paralysis over the defense budget, along with its ongoing and seemingly intractable debate over the level and type of capabilities that Taiwan needs, highlights the inability of the Taiwanese leadership and military to develop a clear, agreed-upon, and convincing defense strategy; it also suggests that Washington has failed to assist Taipei in developing a more realistic, attainable set of capabilities. Such capabilities should be grounded on the assumption that: (1) Taiwan cannot defend itself unaided by the United States; and (2) Taiwan's primary strategic objective is to resist an initial PRC attack (militarily, politically, and socially) until the United States can deploy forces sufficient to repel further attacks and prevent escalation, if necessary by bringing forces in from outside the Pacific theater.

In short, Taipei needs to focus such defense efforts primarily on enhancing its capacity over the near to medium term to fend off Chinese military coercion (or an outright attack) for at least two weeks without, however, resorting to actions that could dramatically escalate the crisis or conflict, such as preemptive strikes against mainland targets. This implies a sharper focus on acquiring capabilities oriented toward early detection; mobility and rapid response; more effective ASW; more expansive air and missile defense; stronger passive defenses; the protection of key political, military, and economic sites; the strengthening of the security of Taiwan's entire intelligence infrastructure; a more survivable, integrated national and operational-level command and control system; improvements in training and morale; a more expansive, better trained and committed NCO corps; and a reduction in army dominance over many reform and development decisions.[44]

Some observers argue that, given the costs and political obstacles involved in significantly enhancing its defensive capabilities, Taiwan should acquire a potent offensive strike capability as a deterrent, largely via the acquisition of ballistic missiles with either conventional or (some argue) nonconventional (i.e., nuclear or chemical) warheads. They argue that such a deterrent would be cheaper, less complex, and more effective and could be acquired more rapidly than defensive capabilities, and unlike defensive capabilities, would be obtainable through largely indigenous means (i.e., without reliance on the United States or other powers). Some types of conventionally armed, offensive-oriented weapons (such as the conventional precision-guided bombs and missiles discussed by Andrew Yang) might be useful in limited numbers (e.g., to suppress PLA ship-based weapons systems and coastal, land-based air defenses). Yet any discussion of the potential benefits of such weapons assumes that a doctrine can be developed that avoids their use in ways that might produce inadvertent escalation in a crisis or conflict.

Furthermore, in spite of these potential benefits, we agree with Mike McDevitt that the notion of Taiwan deploying an extensive offensive capability designed to deter China through the threat of punishment is "absurd."[45] First, no agreement exists in Taipei regarding what type of offensive capability and doctrine could serve as a credible deterrent (counterforce? countervalue? preemptive use?). Second, the acquisition of a credible counterforce deterrent capability against PLA targets would require enormous resources and effort (e.g., to field an adequate counterforce arsenal and to acquire a reliable surveillance, tracking, targeting, and bomb damage assessment capability). Third, such a force would be vulnerable to a Chinese first strike, especially because Beijing most likely has greater resources and capabilities than Taipei to engage in a "defense-offense" missile competition. Fourth, a countervalue deterrent would almost certainly require long-range, weapons of mass destruction strike capabilities, which could provoke a PRC preemptive attack and the United States would oppose. Fifth, as McDevitt points out, attempts to build such a deterrent force would be a waste of resources and dangerous because it could cause Taiwan to neglect its real defense and give the leadership excessive confidence that could lead to miscalculation.[46]

In addition to the above improvements in U.S. and Taiwan military capabilities and relations with the PLA, Washington should also remain attentive to the potential impact on the Taiwan situation of events in the larger regional security context. Regarding U.S. alliances, Romberg argues that "the implications of the failure to rectify the weaknesses in U.S.-ROK and U.S.-Japan ties could be substantial" and therefore "the weakening of the U.S. alliance system . . . ought to be a matter of considerable concern to Washington policy makers." Liebman's focus on China's regional strategy highlights the influence of multilateral institutions and the perceptions of other regional actors on regional security in general and on China's evolving position and its implications for a Taiwan contingency in particular. Liebman's chapter suggests that because of its central role, the United States should pay more attention to the regional environment and its institutions, perhaps even devising its own strategy to shape it to favor U.S. interests.

There is little doubt that the United States should strive to enhance its involvement in regional multilateral security interactions, improve relations with South Korea, and continue to deepen its security alliance with Japan in order to maintain a strong and credible deterrent toward China over Taiwan, as Romberg and Liebman suggest. However, Washington also needs to give serious thought to the possible negative medium- and long-term consequences of a continued expansion in Japanese military capabilities and roles, in particular, for the larger U.S.-China relationship and Taiwan's security. At what point might such an expansion become counterproductive by provoking stronger Chinese reactions than might otherwise occur and perhaps raising concerns among other states in the region? In the absence of a more open and inclusive security architecture in the Asia-Pacific, such actions could contribute significantly to regional bipolarization and perhaps even encourage pro-independence groups on Taiwan to undertake destabilizing unilateral actions. In general, the United States needs to couple any advances in its military posture and relationships with regional states that have clear implications for China and Taiwan with reassuring political initiatives designed to improve security relations and build confidence among *all* major regional powers, including China. We agree with a recent CSIS report that the United States needs to work with China and other states to develop a more inclusive Asian architecture while strengthening the U.S. bilateral strategic dialogue with China, in order to "discourage more narrow Chinese initiatives in multilateral institutions that aim to minimize the positive regional influence of the United States."[47]

Finally, some of the authors in this volume, as well as other studies on crisis management cited above, identify several actions that the United States and China could undertake to reduce the chances of inadvertent escalation in a Taiwan crisis. These include efforts to:

- Expand mutual understanding of each side's hostile images and assumptions through a scholarly dialogue and related elite surveys;
- Raise awareness and understanding within both governments of the dangers of Sino-American political-military crises and develop new tools for managing them through "track-two" dialogues and bilateral crisis simulations;
- Enhance crisis communication through the creation of a joint governmental political-military working group designed to develop a set of procedures and mechanisms for improving crisis signaling and

each side's understanding about how the other side makes decisions in a crisis; and

- Establish clear ROE for naval and air forces that could reduce the propensity for escalation.[48]

Taken together, the above recommendations regarding improvements in the U.S. and Taiwanese force posture and doctrine, defense infrastructure, and crisis management capability could contribute significantly to reducing the threat of crisis and conflict in the Taiwan Strait. However, military-centered actions of whatever type do not constitute the ultimate key to stability in the Taiwan Strait. The Taiwan problem is essentially political and the solution must therefore be political. As the United States and Taiwan develop countermeasures to China's military buildup, they must also repeatedly convey a strong, consistent, and credible message of reassurance to the Chinese that they will not allow improved U.S. and Taiwan military capabilities to provide a shield for Taiwan's continued movement toward independence. If the Taiwan government is unwilling to do this, Washington must do so unambiguously. For its part, the Chinese government must also maintain *the credibility* of its assurance to the United States—and to Taiwan—that it will continue to seek a peaceful solution to the cross-strait imbroglio as a first priority. In the military arena, this implies the avoidance of any actions (e.g., sudden deployments, exercises, etc.) that might signal a preparation for the use of force against the island. The threat of military conflict over Taiwan cannot be entirely eliminated as long as the present-day political impasse remains between Taipei and Beijing. However, much more can, and should, be done to reduce that threat.

NOTES

1. U.S. Department of Defense, *Annual Report to Congress, Military Power of the People's Republic of China 2006*.
2. For more on the weapons systems that the PLA has acquired, see David Shambaugh, "China's Military Modernization: Making Steady and Surprising Progress," in Ashley J. Tellis and Michael Wills, eds., *Strategic Asia 2005–2006: Military Modernization in an Era of Uncertainty* (Washington, D.C.: The National Bureau of Asian Research, 2005).

3. For more on China's space-based assets, see Michael P. Pillsbury, "As Assessment of China's Anti-satellite and Space Warfare Programs, Policies and Doctrines," prepared for the U.S.-China economic and Security Review Commission, January 19, 2007.

4. For more information about PLA training, see Susan M. Puska, "Rough but Ready Force Projection: An Assessment of Recent PLA Training," in Andrew Scobell and Larry M. Wortzel, eds., *China's Growing Military Power: Perspectives on Security, Ballistic Missiles, and Conventional Capabilities* (Carlisle, Penn.: Strategic Studies Institute, 2002).

5. For more information on China's defense industry, see Evan S. Medeiros, Roger Cliff, Keith Crane, and James C. Mulvenon, *A New Direction for China's Defense Industry,"* (Santa Monica, Calif.: Rand Corporation, 2005).

6. Ashton B. Carter and William J. Perry, "China on the March," *The National Interest,* March/April 2007.

7. Jonathan Adams, "Taiwan Lowers its Defenses," *Far Eastern Economic Review,* April 2007.

8. *Taipei Times,* May 4, 2007, p. 1.

9. Shirley Kan, "Frog in the Well and Chicken Little," *PacNet,* no. 9A, February 28, 2007.

10. "Simulation Shows Taiwan Weak Against PRC Attack, MND Says," *Taiwan News,* April 25, 2007.

11. "China Could Have Military Edge by 2010," *Agence France Presse,* April 25, 2007.

12. Mark A. Stokes, "China's Strategic Modernization: Implications for the United States," *Strategic Studies Institute,* September 1999, p. 140.

13. See the summary of Ronald O'Rourke, "China Naval Modernization: Implications for U.S. Navy Capabilities—Background and Issues for Congress," *CRS Report for Congress,* November 18, 2005.

14. Porter Goss, "Current and Projected National Security Threats to the United States," Hearing before the Senate Select Committee on Intelligence, February 16, 2005, p. 17, http://intelligence.senate.gov/threats.pdf (last accessed May 2, 2007).

15. "Cross-strait Military Balance 'Stable': US Pacific Commander," *AsiaPulse News,* March 29, 2001.

16. Interview with Admiral Dennis Blair," US-Asia Pacific Council's March newsletter, March 2007.

17. Personal correspondence with Denny Blair, 2006.

18. See the summary of Ronald O'Rourke, "China Naval Modernization: Implications for U.S. Navy Capabilities—Background and Issues for Congress."

19. Charles Snyder, "New Pacific Commander Vows Commitment to Taiwan," *Taipei Times,* March 10, 2007.

20. The TAF also faces the issues of pilot scarcity and inadequately trained maintenance technicians; these are important factors that need to be considered. For

more on Taiwan's problems with maintaining its air force, see "Low Availability of Mirage Jet Fighters 'Unacceptable': KMT Lawmaker," CNA, May 14, 2007.

21. This can also be inferred from the fact that China is not prioritizing investments in capabilities necessary to take Taiwan by force (amphibious shipping, mine clearance capabilities, naval gunfire support, and close air support). Instead, according to Dennis Blair, China's military improvements that affect Taiwan are dominated by increasing the physical or economic damage it can do to the island (missiles, air strikes, submarines).

22. For more on escalation dynamics and crisis management, see Michael D. Swaine and Zhang Tuosheng, eds., *Managing Sino-American Crises: Case Studies and Analysis* (Washington, D.C.: Carnegie Endowment, 2006); Andrew Scobell and Larry M. Wortzel, eds., *Chinese National Security: Decisionmaking under Stress* (Carlisle, Penn.: Strategic Studies Institute, 2005).

23. A major crisis over Taiwan would presumably involve actions by any side that were perceived by China or the United States as altering, or potentially altering, the status quo in unacceptable directions (that is, the crossing of one or more of the so-called "red lines"), thus requiring a vigorous reaction.

24. Personal correspondence, May 2007.

25. For more on the U.S.-Japan security alliance and U.S. military posture, see Richard L. Armitage and Joseph S. Nye, "The U.S.-Japan Alliance: Getting Asia Right through 2020," *CSIS Report,* February 2007; Jonathan D. Pollack, "The United States and Asia in 2004: Unfinished Business," *Asian Survey XLV,* no. 1, January/February 2005. For more on bilateral or multilateral relationships, see "Building an Open and Inclusive Regional Architecture for Asia," *CSIS Policy Dialogue Brief,* November 2006; Robert A. Scalapino, "The State of International Relations in Northeast Asia," *Asia Policy* 3, January 2007.

26. Agreement between the Government of Japan and the Government of the United States of America concerning reciprocal provision of logistic support, supplies, and services between the self-defense forces of Japan and the armed forces of the United States of America, http://www.mofa.go.jp/region/n-america/us/security/agreement.pdf. (last accessed May 8, 2007).

27. Ministry of Defense (Japan), "Significance of the Japan-U.S. Security Arrangement," http://www.mod.go.jp/e/defense_policy/japans_defense_policy/3/2.htm (last accessed May 8, 2007).

28. "Joint Statement U.S.-Japan Consultative Committee," February 19, 2005. http://www.mod.go.jp/e/defense_policy/japans_defense_policy/3/7.htm (last accessed May 8, 2007).

29. Chen Yali and Eric Hagt, "Anti-Secession Law: Provocation or Compromise?" *China Brief* 5, no. 1, January 4, 2005; Dan Blumenthal and Randy Scheunemann, "Tense Straits: Washington Signals Timidity toward Chinese Bellicosity," *National Review,*

January 27, 2005; John J. Tkacik, Jr., "China's New "Anti-Succession Law" Escalates Tensions in the Taiwan Strait," *Heritage WebMemo #629*, December 21, 2004.

30. Hiroyasu Akutsu, "Tokyo and Taipei Try to Tango," *The Far Eastern Economic Review* 170, no. 1 (January/February 2007): 32.

31. Ibid.

32. For more on the historical issue, see Minxin Pei and Michael D. Swaine, "Simmering Fire in Asia: Averting Sino-Japanese strategic Conflict," *Carnegie Policy Brief*, no. 44, November 2005; Nobuhiro Hiwatari, "Japan in 2005: Koizumi's Finest Hour," *Asian Survey XLVI*, no. 1, January/February 2006. For more on the East China Sea dispute, see Mark J. Valencia, "The East China Sea Dispute: Prognosis and Ways Forward," *PacNet*, no. 47A, September 15, 2006; Scott Snyder "The South China Sea Dispute: Prospects for Preventive Diplomacy," *United States Institute of Peace, Special Report No. 18*, August 1996.

33. That said, we should note that some observers also point out that the U.S.-Japan relationship is not free of difficulties. For example, Romberg argues in this volume that even though recent public opinion polls in Japan have shown substantial and growing support for the alliance, there is greater tension and fragility to the relationship than is obvious—or healthy. He states that both countries will need to be alert to the implications of this situation and to rectify it as best they can.

34. David I. Steinberg, "Repairing Seoul's Tattered Alliance," *The Far Eastern Economic Review*, May 2007.

35. Ibid.

36. Sunhyuk Kim and Wonhyuk Lim, "How to Deal with South Korea," *The Washington Quarterly*, Spring 2007, p. 79.

37. For more on China in Southeast Asia, see Joshua Kurlantzick, *Charm Offensive: How China's Soft Power Is Transforming the World* (New Haven, Conn.: Yale University Press, 2007); Dana Dillion and John J. Tkacik, Jr., "China's Quest for Asia," *Policy Review* 134, December 2005/January 2006; Larry M. Wortzel, "China and Southeast Asia: Building Influence, Addressing Fears," in Andrew Scobell and Larry M. Wortzel, eds., *Shaping China's Security Environment: The Role of the People's Liberation Army* (Carlisle, Penn.: Strategic Studies Institute, 2006).

38. David I. Steinberg, "Repairing Seoul's Tattered Alliance."

39. Robert G. Sutter, *China's Rise: Implications for U.S. Leadership in Asia* (Washington, D.C.: East-West Center, 2006); Robert G. Sutter, "United States-East Asian Relations: An Optimistic Outlook," *American Asian Review* 20, no. 4, Winter 2002; Robert G. Sutter, *China's Rise in Asia* (Oxford, UK: Rowman & Littlefield Publishers, Inc., 2005).

40. David Shambaugh, "China's Military Modernization: Making Steady and Surprising Progress," pp. 98–99.

41. This is not to say that Cliff's argument and recommendations have no merit. They certainly should be discussed and examined in detail, including a closer examination of the role of Taiwan's military capabilities, as we suggest.

42. David Shambaugh, "China's Military Modernization: Making Steady and Surprising Progress," p. 98.

43. Charles Snyder, "New Pacific Commander Vows Commitment to Taiwan."

44. Michael D. Swaine, "Deterring Conflict in the Taiwan Strait: The Success and Failures of Taiwan's Defense Reform and Modernization Program," *Carnegie Paper*, no. 47, July 2004.

45. Michael McDevitt, "For Taiwan, the Best Defense Is Not a Good Offense," *PacNet*, no. 9, February 22, 2007, http://www.csis.org/media/csis/pubs/pac0709.pdf (last accessed May 8, 2007).

46. Ibid.

47. "Building an Open and Inclusive Regional Architecture for Asia," *CSIS Policy Dialogue Brief*, November 2006.

48. For a fuller discussion and explanation of these recommendations, see Michael D. Swaine, "Conclusion: Implications, Questions, and Recommendations," in Michael D. Swaine and Zhang Tuosheng, eds., *Managing Sino-American Crises: Case Studies and Analyses* (Washington, D.C.: Carnegie Endowment, 2006).

Bibliography

8th United States Army, Korea, http://8tharmy.korea.army.mil/ (accessed November 4, 2006).

ABC Radio Australia. "Military Agreements Signed in Philippines China Defense Talks." May 23, 2005, http://www.abc.net.au.

Acharya, Amitav, and Richard Stubbs. "Theorizing Southeast Asian Relations: An Introduction." *The Pacific Review* 19, no. 2 (2006): 125–134.

Adams, Jonathan. "Taiwan Lowers Its Defenses." *Far Eastern Economic Review,* April 2007.

Agence France-Presse. "China Could Have Military Edge by 2010." April 25, 2007.

———. "China Detains Two More Taiwanese Suspected of Espionage." February 13, 2004.

———. "Taiwan Attempts Damage-Control After Alleged Chinese Spy Ring." August 7, 2003.

Akutsu, Hiroyasu. "Tokyo and Taipei Try to Tango." *The Far Eastern Economic Review* 170, no. 1 (January/February 2007): 32.

Albright, David, and Corey Gay. "Taiwan: Nuclear Nightmare Avoided." *Bulletin of the Atomic Scientists* 54, no. 1 (January/February 1998): 54–60.

Allen, Kenneth W., and Eric A. McVadon. *China's Foreign Military Relations.* Washington, D.C.: Henry L. Stimson Center, 1999.

Allen, Kenneth W., and John F. Corbett, Jr. "Predicting PLA Leader Promotions," in *Civil-Military Change in China: Elites, Institutes, and Ideas After the 16th Party Congress,* ed. Andrew Scobell and Larry W. Wortzel, pp. 257–78. Carlisle, Pa.: Strategic Studies Institute of the US Army War College, 2004.

Armitage, Richard L., and Joseph S. Nye. *The U.S.-Japan Alliance: Getting Asia Right through 2020.* Washington, D.C.: Center for Strategic and International Studies, February 2007.

ASEAN. *ASEAN Statistical Yearbook*. Jakarta: ASEAN Secretariat, 1993–2004.

Asian Tribune. "Pakistan, China Multifaceted Ties Irreversible." February 17, 2006, www.asiantribune.com/show_news.php?id=17146 (accessed February 20, 2006).

AsiaPulse News. "Cross-Strait Military Balance 'Stable': US Pacific Commander." March 29, 2001.

Associated Press. "U.S. to Deploy Intercept Missiles in Japan." June 26, 2006.

Ba, Alice. "Who's Socializing Whom? Complex Engagement in Sino-ASEAN Relations." *The Pacific Review* 19, no. 2 (2006): 157–79.

Bao Guojun and Zhang Xiaoqi. "Junshi Kexueyuan Gai Jin Zuo Zhan Lilun Yanjiu Gugan Peiyang Moshi" (Academy of Military Science [AMS] is the Backbone and Model for Operational Doctrine Research). *Jiefangjun Bao* (*PLA Daily*) (Beijing), June 3, 2005, http://www.chinamil.com.cn/site1/ztpd/2005-06/03/content_220696.htm (accessed April 19, 2007).

Batschelet, Allen W. "Effects-Based Operations for Joint Warfighters." *Field Artillery Journal* (May-June 2003), http://www.army.mil/professionalwriting/volumes/volume1/june_2003/6_03_3.html (accessed April 19, 2007).

BBC Monitoring International Reports. "Espionage, Corruption Cases in China, Dec 03–Feb 04." February 14, 2004.

BBC News. "China Gives Cambodia $600m in Aid." April 8, 2006, http://news.bbc.co.uk/2/hi/asia-pacific/4890400.stm (accessed March 29, 2007).

Bergsten, Fred. "Towards a Tripartite World." *The Economist*, July 15, 2000, p. 23.

Bi Xinglin, ed. *Zhanlüe Lilun Xuexi Zhinan* (*Guide to the Study of Campaign Theory*). Beijing: National Defense University Press, 2002.

Blair, Bruce. "Chinese Nuclear Preemption." *China Security* 1 (Autumn 2005): 12–22.

Blank, Stephen. "Islam Karimov and the Heirs of Tiananmen." *Eurasia Daily Monitor* 2, no. 115 (June 14, 2005), http://www.jamestown.org/publications_details.php?volume_id=407&issue_id=3365&article_id=2369877 (accessed March 29, 2007).

Blasko, Dennis J. *The Chinese Army Today: Tradition and Transformation for the 21st Century*. New York: Routledge, 2006.

Blumenthal, Dan, and Randy Scheunemann. "Tense Straits: Washington Signals Timidity Toward Chinese Bellicosity." *National Review*, January 27, 2005.

Burles, Mark, and Abram N. Shulsky. *Patterns in China's Use of Force: Evidence from History and Doctrinal Writings*. Santa Monica, Calif.: RAND Corporation, 1999.

Burns, Robert. "Air Force Wants to Put Fighters and Bombers Back on Guam in Pacific." *Associated Press*, January 13, 2004.

Bush, Richard C. *Untying the Knot: Making Peace in the Taiwan Strait*. Washington, D.C.: Brookings Institution Press, 2005.

Cao Zhi and Li Xuanliang. "Hu Jintao Qiangdiao Tuidong Guofang he Jundui Jianshe You Kuai You Hao de Fazhan" (Hu Jintao Stresses the Need for Rapid Development of National Defense and Armed Forces). *Xinhua News Service*, March 11, 2006, http://www.pladaily.com.cn/site1/big5/database/2006-03/11/content_432416.htm (accessed April 23, 2007). Translation at OSC CPP20060311001006.

Capaccio, Tony. "Navy Lacks Plan to Defend Against 'Carrier-Destroying' Missile." *Bloomberg.com*, March 23, 2007.

———. "Pentagon to Shift Navy Forces to Counter Rising China." *Bloomberg.com*, January 25, 2006.

Cha, Victor D. "Shaping Change in the Alliance." *East Asia* 21, no. 2 (Summer 2004): 42–48.

Chang Yihong. "Is China Building a Carrier?" *Jane's Defence Weekly*, August 17, 2005.

Chen Yali and Eric Hagt. "Anti-Secession Law: Provocation or Compromise?" *China Brief* 5, no. 1, January 4, 2005.

Chin Chien-li. "Profile of Communist China's First Deputy Chief of General Staff Ge Zhenfeng." *Chien Shao* (Hong Kong), no. 171, May 1, 2005, in FBIS-CHI.

China News Agency. "Taiwan Bought US$1.1B. Worth of Conventional Arms Last Year." August 30, 2005, in U.S-Taiwan Business Council *Taiwan Defense and Security Bulletin.* August 31–September 6, 2005.

China Post. "Beijing Arrests Military Officers on Spy Charges." April 17, 2004.

Christensen, Thomas J. "China, the U.S.-Japan Alliance, and the Security Dilemma in East Asia," *International Security*, 23, no. 4 (Spring 1999): 49–80.

Cliff, Roger, et al. *Entering the Dragon's Lair: Chinese Antiaccess Strategies and Their Implications for the United* States. Santa Monica, Calif.: RAND Corporation, 2007.

The Commission on the Intelligence Capabilities of the United States Regarding Weapons of Mass Destruction. *Report to the President of the United States.* March 31, 2005.

Congressional Budget Office. *Long-Term Implications of Current Defense Plans: Detailed Update for Fiscal Year 2005.* September 2004, http://www.cbo.gov/showdoc. cfm?index=5864&sequence=0 (accessed September 30, 2005).

Cortes, Lorenzo. "Surface Warfare Chief Identifies Primary Anti-Access Threats." *Defense Daily*, July 9, 2004.

Crane, Keith, et al. *Modernizing China's Military: Opportunities and Constraints.* Santa Monica, Calif.: Rand Corporation, 2005.

CSIS Policy Dialogue Brief. "Building an Open and Inclusive Regional Architecture for Asia." November 2006.

Cui Shizeng and Wang Junyi. "Advancing Military Transformation with Chinese Characteristics, Strengthening 'Integrated-Style Joint Operations.'" *Jiefangjun Bao* (*PLA Daily*) (Beijing), July 7, 2004.

Dai Qingmin. *Introduction to Information Operations.* Beijing: People's Liberation Army Press, 1999, *Junnei Faxing*.

Dai Zhixin, Feng Weihua, and Yang Xiaogang. "Making a Comeback after 'Defeat'— Account of How a Certain Water Transport Group Drills Hard on Support Capabilities

Aiming at Actual Battles." *Jiefangjun Bao* (*PLA Daily*) (Beijing), February 6, 2002. FBIS-CPP20020206000059.

Dan Xiufa. "Shenhua Mao Zedong Junshi Sixiang Yanjiu de Xin Shiye" (A New Perspective on Deepening Study of Mao Zedong's Military Thought). http://www.pladaily.com.cn/item/mzd/jn/048.htm (accessed April 23, 2007).

Dangdai Zhongguo Kongjun (China Today: Air Force). Beijing: China Social Sciences Press, 1989.

De Castro, Renato Cruz. "Philippine Defense Policy in the 21st Century: Autonomous Defense or Back to the Alliance?" *Pacific Affairs* 78, no. 3 (2005): 403–22.

Defense Minister Tang Yao-ming's report at the Legislative Yuan. *Legislative Gazette* 91, no. 62 (2) (November 2, 2002), 198–203.

Dent, Christopher M. "Taiwan and the New Regional Political Economy of East Asia." *The China Quarterly* 182, no. 1 (June 2005): 385–406.

Dillion, Dana, and John J. Tkacik, Jr. "China's Quest for Asia." *Policy Review* 134, December 2005/January 2006.

Ding Jianjun, and Zhang Kunping. "A Certain Technical Unit of the Beijing MR Develops Joint Repair Bases on the 'Battlefield.'" *Jiefangjun Bao* (*PLA Daily*) (Beijing), June 26, 2004.

Dobson, Wendy. "Deeper Integration in East Asia: Regional Institutions and the International Economic System." *The World Economy* 24, no. 8 (2001): 995–1018.

Downs, Erica Strecker, and Phillip C. Saunders. "Legitimacy and the Limits of Nationalism: China and the Diaoyu Islands." *International Security* 23, no. 3 (Winter 1998): 114–46.

Du Houyin, et al. "Implementing the Integration of Campaign Systems." *Jiefangjun Bao* (*PLA Daily*) (Beijing), November 23, 2004.

Dutton, Peter A. "International Law and the November 2004 'Han Incident.'" *Asian Security* 2, no. 2 (June 2006): 87–101.

The Economist. "We're Just Good Friends, Honest." March 17, 2007, p. 45.

Editor. "Joint Operations: Everyday but Still Remarkable." *Signal* 4, no. 6 (March 15, 2007), http://www.imakenews.com/signal/e_article000771254.cfm?x=b11,0,w (accessed April 23, 2007).

Eielson Air Force Base, http://www.eielson.af.mil/ (accessed November 24, 2006).

Ellings, Richard J., and Aaron L. Friedberg, eds. *Strategic Asia 2003–04: Fragility and Crisis.* Seattle: National Bureau of Asian Research, 2003.

Evans, M.H.H. *Amphibious Operations: The Projection of Sea Power Ashore.* New York: Brassey's, 1990.

"Facts." Kadena Air Base, http://www.kadena.af.mil/facts.htm (accessed November 24, 2006).

Feng Changsong. "Tigao Dayin Zhanlüe he Ezhi Zhanlüe de Nengli" (Raise Abilities to Win and Contain Wars). *Jiefangjun Bao* (*PLA Daily*) (Beijing), August 27, 2003. Translation at OSC CPP20030827000124.

Ferguson, Charles, Evan S. Medeiros, and Phillip G. Saunders. "Chinese Tactical Nuclear Weapons," in *Tactical Nuclear Weapons: Emergent Threats in an Evolving Security Environment*, ed. Alistair Millar and Brian Miller, pp. 110–28. London: Brassey's, 2003.

Finkelstein, David M. "U.S.-China Military Relations: The Time Is Right to Deepen the Dialogue." *CSIS Freeman Report*, October 2005.

Foreman, William. "Taiwan Arrests Military Officer on Spy Charges—The Third Such Case in Month." *Associated Press*, December 3, 2003.

Fravel, M. Taylor. "Regime Insecurity and International Cooperation: Explaining China's Compromises in Territorial Disputes." *International Security* 30, no. 2 (Fall 2005): 46–83.

Friedberg, Aaron. "'Going Out': China's Pursuit of Natural Resources and Implications for the PRC's Grand Strategy." *NBR Analysis* 17, no. 3 (September 2006).

Fullilove, Michael. "Angel or Dragon? China and the United Nations." *The National Interest*, no. 85 (September/October 2006): 67–75.

Gao Rui, ed. *Zhanlüe Xue* (*The Science of Military Strategy*). Beijing: Junshi Kexue Chubanshe, 1987.

Gao Yubiao, ed. *Lianhe Zhanyi Jiaocheng* (*Joint Campaigns Textbook*). Beijing: Junshi Kexue Chubanshe, August 2001.

"Garrison Hawaii." U.S. Army Garrison Hawaii, http://www.25idl.army.mil/usaghi/sites/about/facts.asp (accessed November 24, 2006).

Gertz, Bill, and Rowan Scarborough. "Inside the Ring." *Washington Times*, May 20, 2006.

GlobalSecurity.org. "Andersen AFB." http://www.globalsecurity.org/military/facility/andersen.htm (accessed November 24, 2006).

———. "Kunsan Air Base." http://www.globalsecurity.org/military/facility/kunsan.htm (accessed November 24, 2006).

———. Osan Air Base. http://www.globalsecurity.org/military/facility/osan.htm (accessed November 24, 2006).

Glosny, Michael A. "Heading Toward a Win-Win Future? Recent Developments in China's Policy Towards Southeast Asia." *Asian Security* 2, no. 1 (2006): 24–57.

Goldstein, Lyle, and William Murray. "Undersea Dragons: China's Maturing Submarine Force." *International Security* 28, no. 4 (Spring 2004): 161–96.

Gordon, Michael. "Secret U.S. Study Concludes Taiwan Needs New Arms." *New York Times*, April 1, 2001.

Goss, Porter. "Current and Projected National Security Threats to the United States," *Hearing Before the Senate Select Committee on Intelligence*, February 16, 2005, p. 17, http://intelligence.senate.gov/threats.pdf (accessed May 2, 2007).

Green, Michael. "Executive Decisions: Natural Allies?" *The Indian Express*, March 1, 2006, http://www.indianexpress.com/res/web/pIe/full_story.php?content_id=88748 (accessed March 29, 2007).

Guangming Daily. "Zhongguo Junshi Zhuanjia Tichu Xiandai Zhanzheng Moqiu 'Gao Kongzhi'" (Chinese Military Specialists Address the Quest for 'High Control' in

Modern Warfare). April 28, 2004, http://news.xinhuanet.com/mil/2004-04/28/content_1444426.htm (accessed April 23, 2007).

Halloran, Richard. "Submarines Focus on Terrorism." *Honolulu Advertiser*, November 26, 2006.

Han Jiahe and Xiong Chunbao. "Qiantan Junshi Weiji Kongzhi" (A Brief Discussion of Military Crisis Control). *Zhongguo Guofang Bao* (*China's National Defense*) (Beijing), October 22, 2001, p. 3, http://www.pladaily.com.cn/gb/defence/2001/10/22/20011022017053_zhxw.html (accessed April 23, 2007). Translation at OSC CPP20040218000058.

Handel, Michael I. "Corbett, Clausewitz, and Sun Tzu." *Naval War College Review* 53, no. 4 (Autumn 2000): 106–23.

Henley, Lonnie. "The Legal and Regulatory Basis for Defense Mobilization in China." Paper presented at CNAC/RAND conference on mobilization and the PLA. Warrenton, Va., February 2005.

Hiwatari, Nobuhiro. "Japan in 2005: Koizumi's Finest Hour." *Asian Survey XLVI*, no. 1, January/February 2006.

Holmes, James R., and Toshi Yoshihara. "The Influence of Mahan upon China's Maritime Strategy." *Comparative Strategy* 24, no. 1 (January-March 2005): 53–71.

Hong Bin. "Discussing the Six 'Forms' of New Military Transformation." *Jiefangjun Bao* (*PLA Daily*) (Beijing), July 23, 2003.

Hsu, Brian. "Taiwan Naval Officer Gets Life for Espionage." *Taipei Times*, December 18, 2002.

Hu Angang, and Men Honghua. "The Rising of Modern China: Comprehensive National Power and Grand Strategy." Paper presented at the KIEP international conference on "Rising China and the East Asian Economy," Seoul, South Korea, March 19–20, 2004, www.kiep.go.kr/common/board_file_down.asp?74518|1 (accessed April 13, 2007).

Hund, Markus. "ASEAN Plus Three: Towards a New Age of Pan-East Asian Regionalism? A Skeptic's Appraisal." *The Pacific Review* 16, no. 3 (2003): 383–417.

Information Office of the State Council of the People's Republic of China. *China's National Defense in 2000*. Beijing: October 2000.

———. *China's National Defense in 2004*. Beijing: December 2004.

———. *China's National Defense in 2006*. Beijing: December 2006, http://english.people.com.cn/whitepaper/defense2006/defense2006.html (accessed April 23, 2007).

International Institute for Strategic Studies. *The Military Balance 2006*. London: Oxford University Press, 2006.

———. *The Military Balance, 2007*. London: Oxford University Press, 2007.

Jane's All the World's Aircraft. "Sukoi Su-30 (Su-27PU)." December 19, 2005.

———. "XAC JH-7." June 16, 2006.

Jane's Defence Weekly. "China Country Briefing." April 13, 2005, pp. 22–28.

Jane's Fighting Ships. "Los Angeles Class (SSN)." May 2, 2006.

————. "Luyang II (Type 052C) Class (DDGHM)." January 29, 2007.

————. "Ohio Class (SSGN)." May 2, 2006.

————. "Virginia Class (SSN)." August 3, 2005.

Jane's Fighting Ships, 2006-2007. London: Jane's Information Group, 2006.

Jane's Land-Based Air Defence. "Lockheed Martin Missiles & Fire Control Theater High-Altitude Area Defense (THAAD) Missile System." August 11, 2006.

Jane's Strategic Weapon Systems. "PAC-3 (ERINT)." March 19, 2007.

Jiefangjun Bao (PLA Daily) (Beijing). "20 Shiji Zhanzheng Liugei Women de Sikao Heshi" (Reflections and Insights on 20th Century Warfare). December 25, 2000. Translation at OSC CPP20001225000027.

————. "The Chinese Nation Is Invincible. "September 3, 2005, http://english.chinamil.com.cn/site2/news-channels/2005-09/03/content_286714.htm (accessed April 25, 2007).

————. "Guofangbu Juxing Shengda Zhaodai Hui Relie Qingzhu Jian Jun 79 Zhounian Chen Bingde Chuxi" (Ministry of National Defense Holds Magnificent Reception to Warmly Celebrate the 79th Anniversary of the Founding of the PLA; Chen Bingde Presides.). August 1, 2006, http://www.pladaily.com.cn/site1/database/2006-08/01/content_542314.htm (accessed April 23, 2007).

————. "Officers from 24 Countries to Observe Military Drill." September 27, 2005, http://english.chinamil.com.cn/site2/news-channels/2005-09/27/content_303718.htm (accessed April 23, 2007).

————. "PLA General Staff Department Issues New All-Army Military Training Work Regulations." January 15, 2005.

————. "President Hu Meets with Rumsfeld." October 20, 2005, www.chinamil.com.cn.

Johnston, Alastair Iain. "Is China a Status Quo Power?" *International Security* 27, no. 4 (Spring 2003): 5–56.

————. "Socialization in International Institutions: The ASEAN Way and International Relations Theory," in *International Relations Theory and the Asia Pacific,* ed. G. John Ikenberry and Michael Mastanduno, pp. 107–62. New York: Columbia University Press, 2003.

Kan, Shirley. "China and Proliferation of Weapons of Mass Destruction and Missiles." *CRS Report for Congress,* October 2, 2006.

————. "China/Taiwan: Evolution of the 'One China' Policy—Key Statements from Washington, Beijing, and Taipei." *CRS Report for Congress,* June 1, 2004.

————. "Frog in the Well and Chicken Little," *PacNet,* no. 9A, February 28, 2007.

————. "U.S.-China Military Contacts: Issues for Congress." *CRS Report for Congress,* July 28, 2004.

Kao, Chieh-chien. "What Limits Has 'Unrestricted Warfare' Exceeded—Also Discussing the Phenomenon Where 'Readers and Experts Stick to Their Own Views,'" *Ta Kung Pao* (Hong Kong), June 21, 2000.

Katzenstein, Peter J. "Regionalism and Asia." *New Political Economy* 5, no. 3 (November 2000): 353.

Kawasaki, Tsuyoshi. "Neither Skepticism nor Romanticism: The ASEAN Regional Forum as a Solution for the Asia-Pacific Assurance Game." *The Pacific Review* 19, no. 2 (2006): 219–37.

Keefe, John. "Anatomy of the EP-3 Incident, April 2001." CNA Corporation *Project Asia* Report, January 2002.

Kemmer, John. "An Uncertain Future: The Politics of U.S.-China Military Relations— From Nixon, to George W. Bush, and Beyond." *Issues & Studies* 41, no. 2 (June 2005): 171–215.

Kim, Samuel S., ed. *The International Relations of Northeast Asia*. Lanham, Md.: Rowman & Littlefield Publishers, Inc., 2004.

Kim, Sunhyuk, and Wonhyuk Lim. "How to Deal with South Korea." *The Washington Quarterly*, Spring 2007: 79.

Kristensen, Hans M., Robert S. Norris, and Matthew McKinzie. *Chinese Nuclear Forces and U.S. Nuclear War Planning*. Washington, D.C.: Natural Resources Defense Council and the Federation of American Scientists, 2006.

Kuo Nai-jih. "Percentage of Hits of Ship-Carried Artillery of the Communist Troops Reaches 90 Percent." *Lieh-Ho Pao* (Taipei), August 23, 2001. FBIS-CPP20010823000121.

Kurlantzick, Joshua. *Charm Offensive: How China's Soft Power is Transforming the World*. New Haven, Conn.: Yale University Press, 2007.

Lam, Willie. "Hu Jintao's Driving Influence on Chinese Military Modernization." Jamestown Foundation's *China Brief* 5, no. 17 (August 2, 2005).

Lampton, David M. "China's Rise in Asia Need Not Be at America's Expense," in *Power Shift: China and Asia's New Dynamics*, ed. David L. Shambaugh, pp. 306–26. Berkeley: University of California Press, 2006.

Laur, Timothy L., and Steven L. Llanso. *Encyclopedia of Modern U.S. Military Weapons*. New York: Berkley Books, 1995.

Legislative Gazette 93, no. 30 (June 6, 2004): 278.

Legislative Gazette 96, no. 17 (March 17, 2006): 135.

Lennox, Duncan. "Terminal High-Altitude Area Defense." *Jane's Strategic Weapon Systems*, February 21, 2005.

Lewis, Jeffrey G. *The Minimum Means of Reprisal: China's Search for Security in the Nuclear Age*. Cambridge, Mass.: MIT Press, 2007.

Lewis, John Wilson, and Xue Litai. *China Builds the Bomb*. Stanford, Calif.: Stanford University Press, 1988.

Li Bin, Zhao Baogen, and Liu Zhiwei. "China Will Have to Respond." *Bulletin of Atomic Scientists* 57, no. 6 (2001): 25–28.

Li Daguang. "Space Dominance: The Basis for Victory in Information War." *Zhongguo Guofang Bao* (*China's National Defense*) (Beijing), January 6, 2004.

Li Jian and Liu Guichou. "Development and Changes in Integrated Joint Operations Command." *Zhongguo Guofang Bao* (*China's National Defense*) (Beijing), April 21, 2005.

Li Xiaobing. "PLA Attacks and Amphibious Operations During the Taiwan Straits Crises of 1954–1955 and 1958," in *Chinese Warfighting*, ed. Mark A. Ryan, et al. New York: ME Sharpe Press, 2003.

Li Yingming and Liu Xiaoli. "An Analysis of Integrated Joint Operations." *Jiefangjun Bao* (*PLA Daily*) (Beijing), April 12, 2005.

Lieber, Keir A., and Daryl G. Press. "U.S. Nuclear Primary and the Future of the Chinese Deterrent." *China Security* (Winter 2007): 66–89.

Lieggi, Stephanie. "Going Beyond the Stir: The Strategic Realities of China's No-First-Use Policy." *Nuclear Threat Initiative*, December 2005, http://www.nti.org/e_research/e3_70.html (accessed March 29, 2007).

Lilley, James R., and Chuck Downs. *Crisis in the Taiwan Strait*. Washington, D.C.: National Defense University Press in cooperation with the American Enterprise Institute for Public Policy Research, 1997.

Lin Hu, ed. *Kongjun Shi* (*History of the Air Force*). Beijing: PLA Press, PLAAF Headquarters Education and Research.

Ling Peixiong and Li Xucheng. "New Efforts at Teaching Joint Operations Command at National Defense University." *Jiefangjun Bao* (*PLA Daily*) (Beijing), June 5, 2005.

Lu Daohai. *Xinxi Zuozhan* (*Operations Information*). Beijing: PLA Arts and Literature Press, 1999, *neibu faxing*.

Lu Linzhi. "Preemptive Strikes Crucial in Limited High-Tech Wars." *Jiefangjun Bao* (*PLA Daily*) (Beijing), February 14, 1996.

Lu Ning. *The Dynamics of Foreign-Policy Decisionmaking in China*, 2nd ed. Oxford: Westview Press, 1997.

Ma Ping. "Shuli Kexue de Zhanlue Guan" (Foster a Scientific Strategic Outlook). *Jiefangjun Bao* (*PLA Daily*) (Beijing), May 1, 2001, p. 3, http://www.pladaily.com.cn/gb/pladaily/2001/05/01/20010501001038_gdyl.html (accessed April 23, 2007). Translation at OSC CPP20010501000034.

Mahan, Alfred Thayer. *The Influence of Sea Power upon History, 1660–1783*. New York: Dover, 1987.

Mao Zedong. "On Protracted War, May 1938" in *Selected Works of Mao Zedong*, Vol. II. Beijing: Foreign Languages Press, 1961, paragraph 83.

Marine Aircraft Group 12, http://www.1maw.usmc.mil/index.asp?unit='MARG-12' (accessed April 9, 2007).

"Marine Links." III Marine Expeditionary Force, http://www.iiimef.usmc.mil/marinelinks.htm (accessed November 24, 2006).

McCready, Douglas. *Crisis Deterrence in the Taiwan Strait*. Carlisle, Pa: Strategic Studies Institute of the US Army War College, 2003.

McDevitt, Michael. "Beijing's Bind." *The Washington Quarterly* 23, no. 3 (2000): 177–86.

————. "For Taiwan, the Best Defense Is Not a Good Offense," *PacNet*, no. 9, February 22, 2007.

McDonald, Joe. "China Parades Accused Taiwanese Spies in front of Cameras amid Tensions with Island." *Associated Press*, January 16, 2004.

McVadon, Eric. "China's Maturing Navy." *Naval War College Review* 59, no. 2 (Spring 2006): 90–107.

Medeiros, Evan S. *Chasing the Dragon: Assessing China's System of Export Controls for WMD-Related Goods and Technologies*. Santa Monica, Calif.: RAND Corporation, 2005.

Medeiros, Evan S., et al. *A New Direction for China's Defense Industry*. Santa Monica, Calif.: RAND Corporation, 2005.

Medeiros, Evan S., and M. Taylor Fravel. "China's New Diplomacy." *Foreign Affairs* 82, no. 6 (November/December 2003): 22–35.

Mei Ling. "PLA's Amphibious Landing Capability Development." *Studies on Chinese Communism* 35, no. 4 (April 15, 2001): 55–64.

Miles, Donna. "Pace Visits Guam to Assess Infrastructure Growth Plans." *American Forces Information Service News Articles*, June 2, 2006, http://www.defenselink.mil/news/Jun2006/20060602_5311.html (accessed December 1, 2006).

Ministry of Defense, Japan. "Joint Statement U.S.-Japan Consultative Committee," February 19, 2005. http://www.mod.go.jp/e/defense_policy/japans_defense_policy/3/7.htm (accessed May 8, 2007).

————. "Significance of the Japan-U.S. Security Arrangement." http://www.mod.go.jp/e/defense_policy/japans_defense_policy/3/2.htm (accessed May 9, 2007).

Ministry of Foreign Affairs, Japan. "Agreement Between the Government of Japan and the Government of the United States of America Concerning Reciprocal Provision of Logistic Support, Supplies, and Services Between the Self-Defense Forces of Japan and the Armed Forces of the United States of America." http://www.mofa.go.jp/region/n-america/us/security/agreement.pdf (accessed, May 8, 2007).

Ministry of National Defense, Taiwan. "National Defence Policy and Military Strategy," in Ministry of National Defence *National Defence Report 2006, Rep. of China*. Taipei, 2006, pp. 92–93.

————. *Republic of China: 2006 National Defense Report*. Taipei: Ministry of National Defense, August 2004.

Minnick, Wendell. "Challenge to Update Taiwan's SIGINT." *Jane's Intelligence Review*, February 1, 2004.

————. "Spook Mountain: How US Spies on China." *Asia Times Online*, March 6, 2003, http://www.atimes.com/atimes/China/EC06Ad03.html (accessed April 25, 2007).

————. "Taiwan-USA Link Up on SIGINT." *Jane's Defence Review*, January 23, 2001.

Misawa Air Base, http://www.misawa.af.mil/ (accessed November 24, 2006).

Missile Defense Agency. "Aegis Ballistic Missile Defense." Missile Defense Agency Fact Sheet, www.mda.mil (accessed July 2006).

BIBLIOGRAPHY 377

Mohan, C. Raja. "SAARC Reality Check: China Just Tore up India's Monroe Doctrine."
The Indian Express, November 14, 2005, http://www.indianexpress.com/res/web/
ple/full_story.php?content_id=81928# (accessed March 29, 2007).

Morrison, Wayne M. "China's Economic Conditions." *CRS Report for Congress,* July 12,
2006.

Mulvenon, James. "The PLA and the 16th Party Congress: Jiang Controls the Gun?"
China Leadership Monitor no. 5 (Winter 2003).

———. "PLA Divestiture and Civil-Military Relations: Implications for the Sixteenth Party
Congress Leadership." *China Leadership Monitor,* no. 1, part 2 (December 2001).

Mulvenon, James, and David M. Finkelstein, eds. *China's Revolution in Doctrinal Affairs:
Emerging Trends in the Operational Art of the Chinese People's Liberation Army.* Alexandria, Va.: CNA Corporation, 2005.

Mulvenon, James C., and Andrew N. D. Yang. *The People's Liberation Army as Organization.* Santa Monica, Calif.: RAND Corporation, 2002.

National Statistics Bureau (China). *China Statistical Yearbook.* Hong Kong: *Xianggang
Jingji Daobao She,* 1994–2004.

"Navy to Field Terminal Phase, Sea-Based Missile Defense Capability." *Inside the Navy,*
June 5, 2006.

Nobuyoshi, Sakajiri. "China Offers Gas Field Proposal." *Asahi Shimbun,* March 7, 2006,
http://www.asahi.com/english/Herald-asahi/TKY200603070421.html (accessed March
29, 2007).

Nolan, Janne E., and Douglas MacEachin. *Discourse, Dissent, and Strategic Surprise:
Formulating U.S. Security Policy in an Age of Uncertainty.* Washington, D.C.: Institute
for the Study of Diplomacy, Georgetown University, 2006.

Nu Li, Li Jiangzhou, and Xu Dehui. "Strategies in Information Operations: A Preliminary Discussion." *Military Science,* April 2000.

Office of the Secretary of Defense. *Annual Report to Congress: The Military Power of the
People's Republic of China.* Washington, D.C.: Department of Defense, July 2005.

———. *Annual Report to Congress: The Military Power of the People's Republic of China.*
Washington, D.C.: Department of Defense, 2006.

O'Rourke, Ronald. "China Naval Modernization: Implications for U.S. Navy Capabilities-
Background and Issues for Congress." *CRS Report for Congress,* November 18, 2005.

Pan, Philip. "China Arrests 43 Alleged Spies; Move Increases Effort to Undermine Taiwanese President." *Washington Post,* December 24, 2003.

Pan Zhenqiang. "China Insistence on No-First-Use of Nuclear Weapons." *China Security*
1 (Autumn 2005): 5–9.

Parson, Ted. "China Develops Anti-Ship Missile." *Jane's Defence Weekly,* January 25, 2006.

Pehrson, Christopher J. "String of Pearls: Meeting the Challenge of China's Rising Power
Across the Asian Littoral." *Carlisle Papers in Security Strategy.* Carlisle, Pa.: Strategic
Studies Institute of the US Army War College, July 2006.

Pei Fang. "Major Operation to Be Performed on Military Logistic System." *Kuang Chiao Ching* (Hong Kong), March 16, 1999, 50-52. Translation at OSC FTS19990402000398.

Pei, Minxin, and Michael D. Swaine. "Simmering Fire in Asia: Averting Sino-Japanese Strategic Conflict." *Carnegie Policy Brief*, no. 44, November 2005.

Peng Guangqian. "The Historical Declining of Absolute War and Sun Tzu's Thinking of War Control." *Journal of Binzhou University* 22, no.5 (2006): 107–12, http://www.wanfangdata.com.cn/qikan/periodical.Articles/bzszxb/bzsz2006/0605/060520.htm (accessed April 23, 2007).

———. "Shijie Junshi Biangai You San Da Yingxiang Zhongguo Tuijin San Chuang Xin" (Three Major Influences of the Worldwide Revolution in Military Affairs on Chinese Advancement). *Liaowang Xinwen Zhoukan* (*Outlook Weekly*), June 10, 2003, http://www.chinanews.com.cn/n/2003-06-10/26/312572.html (accessed April 23, 2007).

Peng Guangqian, and Yao Youzhi, eds. *Zhanlüe Xue* (The Science of Military Strategy) Beijing: Junshi Kexue Chubanshe, 2005.

People's Daily (Beijing). "Zhongyang Junwei Zhuxi Jiang Zemin Qianshu Mingling Wo Jun Xin Yi Dai Zuozhan Tiao Ling Banfa" (CMC Chairman Jiang Zemin Signs Order Implementing Our Army's New Generation of Operational Regulations), January 25, 1999, http://www.people.com.cn/item/ldhd/Jiangzm/1999/mingling/ml0003.html (accessed April 23, 2007).

People's Liberation Army. *Chinese Military Encyclopedia*. Beijing: Junshi Kexue Chubanshe, July 1997.

Pi Mingyong and Wang Jianfei. "Zhichi Ezhi Zhanzheng yu Dayin Zhanzhengde Tongyi" (Uphold the Unity of Containing War and Fighting and Winning War). *Jiefangjun Bao* (*PLA Daily*) (Beijing), April 6, 2006, http://theory.people.com.cn/GB/49150/49152/4275658.html (accessed April 25, 2007).

"PLA Deputy Chief of Staff Xiong Guangjie Discusses the New Military Transformation." http://jczs.sina.com.cn (accessed September 17, 2003).

Pollack, Jonathan D., ed. *Strategic Surprise? U.S.-China Relations in the Early Twenty-First Century*. Newport, RI: Naval War College Press, 2004.

———. "The United States and Asia in 2004: Unfinished Business." *Asian Survey XLV*, no. 1, January/February 2005.

Pomfret, John. "China Ponders New Rules of 'Unrestricted Warfare.'" *Washington Post*, August 8, 1999, A01.

———. "Taiwanese Mistake Led to 3 Spies' Executions." *Washington Post*, February 20, 2000.

Powell, Colin, and Joseph Persico. *My American Journey*. New York: Ballantine Books, 1995.

Puska, Susan M. "Rough but Ready Force Projection: An Assessment of Recent PLA Training," in *China's Growing Military Power: Perspectives on Security, Ballistic Missiles, and Conventional Capabilities*, ed. Andrew Scobell and Larry M. Wortzel. Carlisle, Pa: Strategic Studies Institute of the US Army War College, 2002.

Roberts, Brad. "China and Ballistic Missile Defense: 1955 to 2002 and Beyond." IDA Paper P-3826, Alexandria, Va.: Institute for Defense Analyses, 2003.

Ross, Robert S. "The Geography of the Peace: East Asia in the Twenty-First Century." *International Security* 23, no. 4 (Spring, 1999): 81–118.

Scalapino, Robert A. "The State of International Relations in Northeast Asia." *Asia Policy* 3, January 2007.

Scobell, Andrew, and Larry W. Wortzel, eds. *Chinese National Decisionmaking under Stress.* Carlisle, Pa: Strategic Studies Institute of the US Army War College, 2005.

Scott, Richard. "Boosting the Staying Power of the Non-Nuclear Submarine." *Jane's International Defence Review* 32, November 1999: 41–50.

Self, Benjamin. *The Dragon's Shadow: The Rise of China and Japan's New Nationalism.* Washington, D.C.: Henry L. Stimson Center, November 2006.

Sha Lin. "Two Senior Colonels and 'No-Limit Warfare.'" *Zhongguo Qingnian Bao* 28 (June 1999): 5.

Shambaugh, David. "China Engages Asia: Reshaping the Regional Order." *International Security* 29, no. 3 (Winter 2004/2005): 64–99.

———. "China's Military Modernization: Making Steady and Surprising Progress," in *Strategic Asia 2005–06: Military Modernization in an Era of Uncertainty,* ed. Ashley J. Tellis and Michael Wills. Seattle: National Bureau of Asian Research, 2005.

———. *Modernizing China's Military: Progress, Problems, and Prospects.* Berkeley, Calif.: University of California Press, 2002.

———, ed. *Power Shift: China and Asia's New Dynamics.* Berkeley, Calif.: University of California Press, 2005.

———. "Rumsfeld Ventures into the Middle Kingdom." *International Herald Tribune,* October 17, 2005.

Sharpe, Samuel. "An ASEAN Way to Security Cooperation in Southeast Asia?" *Pacific Review* 16, no. 2 (2003): 231–50.

Shen Dingli. "Nuclear Deterrence in the 21st Century." *China Security* 1 (Autumn 2005): 10–14.

Shen Weiguang. "*2010* Xinxi Zaihai: Fazhan Guojia Shengcun Zhanlüe" (2010 Information Disaster: a Developing Country's Survival Strategy). *Xinhua* (Beijing), 2005.

———. *Fulai Shijie Zhanzheng (Future World War).* Zhejiang: Zhejiang Daxue Chubanshe, 2000.

———. *Lun Zhongguo Junshi Geming (On the Chinese Revolution in Military Affairs).* Beijing: Xinhua Chubanshe, 2004.

———. *Xin Zhangzheng Lun (On New War).* Zhejiang: Zhejiang Daxue Chubanshe, 2000.

———. *Xinxizhan (Information War).* Zhejiang: Zhejiang Daxue Chubanshe, 2000.

Shulsky, Abram N. *Deterrence Theory and Chinese Behavior.* Santa Monica, Calif.: RAND Corporation, 2000.

Snyder, Scott. "The South China Sea Dispute: Prospects for Preventive Diplomacy." *United States Institute of Peace, Special Report no. 18,* August 1996.

Sokolski, Henry, and Andrew J. Grotto. "Is the North Korea Deal Worth Celebrating?" *Council on Foreign Relations Online Debate,* March 16, 2007, http://www.cfr.org/ publication/12791/ (accessed March 28, 2007).

South China Morning Post. "Taiwan Detains Woman over Alleged Spying." January 30, 2004.

"Statement of Admiral Jay L. Johnson Chief of Naval Operations United States Navy and General James L. Jones Commandant of the Marine Corps United States Marine Corps before the Senate Armed Services Committee on 19 October 1999 Concerning Vieques." October 19, 1999.

Steinberg, David I. "Repairing Seoul's Tattered Alliance." *The Far Eastern Economic Review,* May 2007.

Stokes, Mark A. *China's Strategic Modernization: Implications for the United States.* Carlisle, Pa.: Strategic Studies Institute of the US Army War College, September 1999, p. 140.

Storey, Ian James. "Living with the Colossus: How Southeast Asian Countries Cope with China." *Parameters: US Army War College* 29, no. 4 (Winter 1999/2000, 1999): 111.

Straits Times. "Top PLA Officers Accused of Spying for Taiwan." April 16, 2004.

Stubbs, Richard. "ASEAN Plus Three: Emerging East Asian Regionalism?" *Asian Survey* 42, no. 3 (May-June, 2002): 440–55.

Sun Xi'an and Wang Xiongli. "PLA Nanjing MR Conducted Tri-Service Communications Exercise in July." *Renmin Qianxian,* July 15, 2004, in FBIS-CHI.

Sun Xiangli. "China's Nuclear Strategy." *China Security* 1 (Autumn 2005): 23–27.

Sutter, Robert G. "China's Regional Strategy and Why It May Not Be Good for America," in *Power Shift: China and Asia's New Dynamics,* ed. David L. Shambaugh, pp. 289–305. Berkeley: University of California Press, 2006.

——. *China's Rise: Implications for U.S. Leadership in Asia.* Washington, D.C.: East-West Center, 2006.

——. *China's Rise in Asia.* Oxford, UK: Rowman & Littlefield Publishers, Inc., 2005.

——. "United States-East Asian Relations: An Optimistic Outlook." *American Asian Review* 20, no. 4, Winter 2002.

Suttmeier, Richard P., Xiangkui Yao, and Alex Zixiang Tan. "Standards of Power? Technology, Institutions, and Politics in the Development of China's National Standards Strategy." *NBR Special Report,* June 2006.

Swaine, Michael D. "Conclusion: Implications, Questions, and Recommendations," in *Managing Sino-American Crises: Case Studies and Analyses,* ed. Michael D. Swaine and Zhang Tuosheng. Washington, D.C.: Carnegie Endowment for International Peace, 2006.

——. "Deterring Conflict in the Taiwan Strait: The Success and Failures of Taiwan's Defense Reform and Modernization Program." *Carnegie Paper,* no. 47, July 2004.

———. *The Role of the Chinese Military in National Security Policymaking*, revised edition. Santa Monica, Calif.: RAND Corporation, 1998.

Swaine, Michael D., and Ashley J. Tellis. *Interpreting China's Grand Strategy: Past, Present, and Future*. Santa Monica, Calif.: RAND Corporation, 2000.

Swaine, Michael D., and Roy D. Kamphausen. "Military Modernization in Taiwan," in *Strategic Asia 2005–06: Military Modernization in an Era of Uncertainty*, ed. Ashley J. Tellis and Michael Wills. Seattle: National Bureau of Asian Research, 2005.

Swaine, Michael D., and Zhang Tuosheng, with Danielle F. S. Cohen, eds. *Managing Sino-American Crises: Case Studies and Analyses*. Washington, D.C.: Carnegie Endowment for International Peace, 2006.

Taiwan News. "Former Taiwan Spy Chief Denies Leaking Secrets During His Four Years in China." April 14, 2004.

———. "Simulation Shows Taiwan Weak Against PRC Attack, MND says." April 25, 2007.

Tao Shelan. "Defense Ministry's Foreign Affairs Office: In Developing China-US Military Relations, It Is Necessary to Seek Common Ground While Reserving Differences." Open Source Center CPP20051020057061. Beijing: *Zhongguo Xinwen She* [in Chinese], October 20, 2005.

Technology and Information Committee, Legislative Yuan. "The Report on C⁴ISR Capability and Evaluation of National Military Science and Technology Policies." *Legislative Gazette* 88, no. 28 (May 29, 1999): 182–83.

Tellis, Ashley J., and Michael Wills, eds. *Strategic Asia 2005–06: Military Modernization in an Era of Uncertainty*. Seattle: National Bureau of Asian Research, 2005.

Terada, Takashi. "Constructing an 'East Asian' Concept and Growing Regional Identity: From EAEC to ASEAN+3." *Pacific Review* 16, no. 2 (2003): 251–77.

Thomas, Timothy. "Chinese and American Network Warfare." *Joint Forces Quarterly*, August 2005: 76–83.

Tian Jingmei. "The Bush Administration's Nuclear Strategy and Its Implications for China's Security." A working paper of the Center for International Security and Cooperation, Stanford University, March 2003.

Tkacik, John J., Jr. "China's New 'Anti-Succession Law' Escalates Tensions in the Taiwan Strait." *Heritage WebMemo #629*, December 21, 2004.

Under Secretary of Defense (AT&L). *Selected Acquisition Reports* (electronic database). Washington D.C.: U.S. Department of Defense, various years from 1964 to 2005.

United States Army. *2005 Army Modernization Plan*. February 2005, http://www.army.mil/features/MODPlan/2005/ (accessed September 20, 2005).

United States Department of the Army. "Missile Procurement, Army, Department of the Army Procurement Programs, Committee Staff Procurement Backup Book, Fiscal Year (FY) 2007 President's Budget." http://www.asafm.army.mil/budget/fybm/FY07/pforms/missiles.pdf (as of September 18, 2006).

United States Forces Korea Command, http://www.usfk.mil/USFK/index.html (accessed November 4, 2006).

The United States and Japan: Advancing Toward a Mature Partnership. Washington, D.C.: Institute for National Strategic Studies, National Defense University, October 2000.

United States Navy. "Aircraft Carriers – CV, CVN." *United States Navy Fact File,* http://www.navy.mil/navydata/fact_display.asp?cid=4200&tid=200&ct=4 (accessed November 29, 2006).

———. "Attack Submarines – SSN." *United States Navy Fact File,* http://www.navy.mil/navydata/fact_display.asp?cid=4100&tid=100&ct=4 (accessed November 29, 2006).

———. "Cruisers – CG." *United States Navy Fact File,* http://www.navy.mil/navydata/fact_display.asp?cid=4200&tid=800&ct=4 (accessed November 29, 2006).

———. "Destroyers – DDG." *United States Navy Fact File,* http://www.navy.mil/navydata/fact_display.asp?cid=4200&tid=900&ct=4 (accessed November 29, 2006).

———. "Ships in the Seventh Fleet." *Commander, Seventh Fleet,* http://www.c7f.navy.mil/Pages/shippage.htm (accessed November 24, 2006).

———. "Ships, Submarines, and Aircraft." *Commander Navy Region Hawaii,* http://www.hawaii.navy.mil/ (accessed November 24, 2006).

———. *Vision/Presence/Power: 2005 Guide to U.S. Navy Programs.* http://www.navy.mil/palib/policy/vision/vis05/top-v05.html (accessed October 5, 2005).

"Units." Elmendorf Air Force Base, http://www.elmendorf.af.mil/units/ (accessed November 24, 2006).

"Unrestricted War —New Concept of War Presented by Non-Military Experts." *Liaowang,* no.11, March 13, 2000: 55–56.

U.S. Army 2nd Infantry Division, http://www-2id.korea.army.mil/units/ (as of November 4, 2006).

US-Asia Pacific Council Newsletter. Interview with Admiral Dennis Blair. March 2007.

U.S. Department of Defense. *Annual Report to Congress: Military Power of the People's Republic of China 2006.* Washington, D.C.: U.S. Department of Defense, 2006.

———. "FY04 Report to Congress on PRC Military Power." July 2004.

———. "FY06 Report to Congress on PRC Military Power." June 2006.

———. "Joint Media Availability with Secretary Donald Rumsfeld and General Cao Gangchuan." News Transcript, October 19, 2005, http://www.Defenselink.Mil/Transcripts/2005/Tr20051019-Secdef4121.Html (accessed April 23, 2007).

———. *Program Acquisition Costs by Weapon System.* Washington D.C., February 2005, http://www.defenselink.mil/pubs/pdfs/QDR20060203.pdf (accessed September 26, 2006).

U.S. Department of State. "U.S.-Japan Alliance: Transformation and Realignment for the Future." http://www.state.gov/documents/organization/55886.pdf (accessed November 22, 2006).

U.S. Joint Chiefs of Staff. *Joint Doctrine for Amphibious Operations*, JP 3-02, September 19, 2001, http://www.dtic.mil/doctrine/jel/new_pubs/jp3_02.pdf (accessed April 25, 2007).

———. *Joint Warfare of the US Armed Forces*, JP 1, 1991.

———. "USS George Washington to Replace USS Kitty Hawk as U.S. Navy's Forward Deployed Carrier." http://www.defenselink.mil/releases/2005/nr20051202-5177.html (accessed November 28, 2006).

Vagts, Alfred. *Landing Operations*. Washington, D.C.: Military Service Publishing Company, 1946.

Valencia, Mark J. "The East China Sea Dispute: Prognosis and Ways Forward." *PacNet*, no. 47A, September 15, 2006.

Vaughn, Bruce, and Wayne Morrison. *China-Southeast Asia Relations: Trends, Issues, and Implications for the United States*. Congressional Research Service: The Library of Congress, April 4, 2006, http://www.fas.org/sgp/crs/row/RL32688.pdf (accessed March 29, 2007).

VanNierop, Deborah. "PACAF Unveils First F-22." U.S. Pacific Air Forces, August 3, 2006, http://www.pacaf.af.mil/news/story_print.asp?id=123024586 (as of April 14, 2007).

Wang Congbiao. "Shishi Keji Qiang Jun Zhanlüe: Tigao Wo Jun Xiandai Fangwei Zuozhan Nengli—Xuexi Jiang Zemin "Lun Kexue Jishu" (Implement the Strategy of Strengthening the Military Through Science and Technology to Improve the Defensive Combat Capabilities of China's Military —Studying Jiang Zemin's 'On Science and Technology'). *Jiefangjun Bao* (*PLA Daily*) (Beijing), February 13, 2001. Translation at OSC CPP20010213000086.

Wang Houqing and Zhang Xingye, eds. *Zhanyi Xue* (*The Science of Campaigns*). Beijing: Guofang Daxue Chubanshe (National Defense University Press), May 2000.

Wang Jisi. *China's Changing Role in Asia*. Washington, D.C.: Atlantic Council of the United States, January, 2004, http://www.isn.ethz.ch/pubs/ph/details.cfm?q51=wang+jisi&id=10617 (accessed March 29, 2007).

Wang Wenrong, ed. *Zhanlüexue* (The Science of Military Strategy). Beijing: Guofang Daxue Chubanshe, 1999.

Wang Zhiyuan et al., eds. *Lianhe Xinxi Zzuozhan* (*Joint Information Operations*). Beijing: PLA Arts and Literature Press, 1999.

Wang Zhongchun. "Nuclear Challenges and China's Choices." *China Security* (Winter 2007): 52–65.

Watanabe, Chisaki. "Japan, U.S. Announce Plan to Deploy Patriots in Okinawa." *Associated Press*, June 20, 2006.

Wei Jincheng. "New Form of People's War." *Jiefangjun Bao* (*PLA Daily*) (Beijing), June 25, 1996, p. 6.

Wen Tao. "China to Speed up Military Transformation with Chinese Characteristics, Push for Informationization of Armed Forces." *Ching Pao* (Hong Kong), June 1, 2003, pp. 40–42. Translation at OSC CPP20030609000087.

Wenweipo News (Hong Kong). "PLA Fujian Military District to Conduct Maritime Logistic Replenishment Drill." July 23, 2004.

Windybank, Susan. "The China Syndrome." *Policy* 21, no. 2 (Winter 2005): 28–33.

Wortzel, Larry M. "China and Southeast Asia: Building Influence, Addressing Fears," in *Shaping China's Security Environment: The Role of the People's Liberation Army*, ed. Andrew Scobell and Larry M. Wortzel. Carlisle, Pa.: Strategic Studies Institute of the US Army War College, 2006.

Wu Yung-ch'iang. "PRC Military Comments on Hu Jintao's 'New Four Points' on Military Administration." Open Source Center CPP20050922510005. *Ta Kung Pao* (Hong Kong) [in Chinese], September 22, 2005.

Xiao Tianliang. *On War Control*. Beijing: National Defense University Press, 2002.

Xinhua (Beijing). "China, Senegal Resume Diplomatic Ties." Open Source Center CPP20051025079027 [in English], 25 October 2005.

———. "Chinese Mainland Smashes Taiwan Spy Ring." December 24, 2003.

———. "Taiwan Spies Visited by Families." January 20, 2004.

———. "Text of Communiqué Issued by Fifth Plenum of 16th CPC Central Committee 11 Oct." Open Source Center CPP20051011062054 [in Chinese], October 11, 2005.

Xu Wen. "Xiandai Jubu Zhanzheng dui Wo Guo Wuqi Zhuangbei Dong Yuan Zhunbei de Qishi" (The Inspiration of Modern Local War for China's Weapons and Equipment Mobilization Preparation). *Zhongguo Kongtian* (Aerospace China) (Beijing), no. 3, 2004, http://www.space.cetin.net.cn/docs/ht0403/ht0403htzc03.htm (accessed April 30, 2007).

Xue Xinglin, ed. *Zhanyi Lilun Xuexi Zhinan* (*Campaign Theory Learning Guide*). Beijing: National Defense University Publishing House, November 2001.

Yahuda, Michael. "The Evolving Asian Order: The Accommodation of Rising Chinese Power," in *Power Shift: China and Asia's New Dynamics*, ed. David L. Shambaugh, pp. 347–62. Berkeley: University of California Press, 2006.

Yang Zhiyuan, and Peng Yanmei, eds. *Zhanshu Xue* (*The Science of Tactics*). Beijing: Junshi Kexue Chubanshe, 2002.

Yao Youzhi and Zhao Dexi. "The Generalization, Conservation, and Development of Strategy." *China's Military Science* (Beijing), September 30, 2001, pp. 120–27. Translation at OSC CPP20011126000199.

Yao Yunzhu. "The Evolution of Military Doctrine of the Chinese PLA from 1985 to 1995." *Korea Journal of Defense Analyses* (Winter 1995).

Yu Jiang. "Zhanzheng Kongzhi: Zouchu Lisuo bu Ji de Wegu" (War Control: Getting Out of an Exhausting Difficult Situation). *Jiefangjun Bao* (*PLA Daily*) (Beijing), March 25, 2004, http://www.pladaily.com.cn/gb/defence/2004/03/25/200403250 17054.html (accessed April 26, 2007).

Yu Shifu and Yin Xinjian. "Mao Zedong Ezhi Zhanzheng Sixiang Chutan" (An Initial Exploration of Mao Zedong's Thought on Containing War). *Junshi Lishi* (Military

History) (Beijing) 2000, no. 1, http://www.cass.net.cn/zhuanti/y_kmyc/zhuanjia/ a00130.html (accessed April 26, 2007).

Yuan Wenxian. "Strengthening Communications and Training in Joint Operations." *Jiefangjun Bao* (*PLA Daily*) (Beijing), April 9, 2002, in FBIS.

Yuan Zhengling. "Jiji Fangyu Zhanlüe Hanwei Guojia Liyi—Jiedu '2002 Nian Zhongguo de Guofang'" (An Active Defense Strategy to Protect National Interests— Understanding the 'National Defense of China 2002'). *Jiefangjun Bao* (*PLA Daily*) (Beijing), December 24, 2002, http://www.pladaily.com/gb/defence/2002/12/24/ 20021224017143_zhxw.html. Translation at OSC CPP20021224000044.

Zhang Peigao, ed. *Lianhe Zhanyi Zhihui Jiaocheng* (*Joint Campaign Command Course Materials*). Beijing: Junshi Kexue Chubanshe, May 2001.

Zhang Xingye. "The Important Aspects of the Conduct of Joint Campaign." *Zhongguo Junshi Kexue* 2, 2001.

Zhang Yiyu. "General's Discussion: Informationalized Warfare Will Change Future Battlefields." *Jiefangjun Bao* (*PLA Daily*) (Beijing), March 2, 2005.

Zhang Zhaozhong. *Shei Neng Daying Xia Yiyang Zhanzheng?* (*Who is Able to Win a War?*). Beijing: Zhongguo Qingnian Chubanshe, 1999.

———. *Shuizai Zhizao Zhanzheng?* (*Who Makes War?*). Beijing: Dangdai Zhongguo Chubanshe, 2001.

———. *Wangluo Zhanzheng* (*Network Warfare*). Beijing: Jiefangjun Wenyi Chubanshe, 2001.

———. *Zhanzheng Likai Women Youduoyuan?* (*How Far Away Is War?*). Beijing, Jiefangjun Chubanshe, 1999.

———. *Zhongguo Rangzhan Zoukai* (*China Allows Warfare to Get Away*). Beijing: Dangdai Zhongguo Chubanshe, 2001.

Zhao Quansheng. "Beijing's Dilemma with Taiwan: War or Peace?" *The Pacific Review* 18, no. 2 (2005): 217–42.

Zheng Bijian. *China's Peaceful Rise: Speeches of Zheng Bijian, 1997–2005*. Washington, D.C.: Brookings Institution Press, 2005.

Zhong Songlai. "The Military Reform of the United States in the Post-Vietnam War Era." *Zhongguo Junshi Kexue*, January 2002.

Index

Page numbers followed by an *f* or *t* indicate figures and tables.

A

Abe, Shinzo
  in normalization of Japanese
      power, 352–353
  on nuclear weapon development,
      35
  on "one China" policy, 314
  rapprochement attempts by, 124
  visit to China by, 324
Academy of Military Science, 87,
      97, 244
Access points, 8, 135. *See also* Basing
      facilities
Aegis system, 292
Afghanistan, border closure with, 132
Africa peacekeeping missions,
      120–121
Air assets
  comparison of, 9–10, 341
  helicopter capability develop-
      ment, 135

PLAAF
  planned, 287
  in Taiwan scenario, 155–157,
      269
PLAN, 191–192, 211*t*
rules of engagement for
  impact on conflict outcome,
      10–11, 344
  PLAAF, 175–177
  Taiwanese, 278, 279*f*
Taiwanese, 158, 193
U.S.
  forward basing of, 299–300
  planned, 293
  in preemptive strike preven-
      tion, 297
  in Taiwan scenario, 157–158
Air attack option
  assets in support of, 269
  countermeasures to, 270–272,
      280–281
Air-blockage scenario, 171–172
Air collision
  of EP-3/J-8 aircraft, 164, 322

U.S.
  with Japan, 21, 313–314,
    327–328
  role in Taiwan deterrence sce-
    nario, 351–355
  with South Korea, 317, 328
  weakening of, 316–317
Amphibious assault
  capability of, in power projection,
    126
  counterattack to, 274–275
  physical impediments to, in
    Taiwan Strait, 188,
    344–345
  in Taiwan scenario, 79–80, 274
Amphibious assets
  PLAN, 191, 210t
  Taiwanese, 193, 211t
Andersen Air Force Base, 298
Anti-access operations, 17, 340, 343
Anti-satellite tests, 72–73
Anti-Secession Law
  in deterrence strategy, 31
  military option in, 267
  U.S. statements in provoking,
    352
Anti-ship cruise missiles, 288
Anti-submarine warfare (ASW)
  Taiwan capability in, 16,
    273–274
  in Taiwan Strait, 188
  U.S. capability in, 196–197
APT. See Association of Southeast
    Asian Nations Plus Three
Armenia, combined exercise with,
    129
Arms embargo, 358
Arms sales, U.S., 16, 280
Army (U.S.), 286

Art of War (Sun Tzu), 87
ASEAN. See Association of
    Southeast Asian Nations
Asia-Pacific Economic Cooperative
    (APEC), 37
Asia policy. See Hub and spokes
    multilateralism strategy;
    National security issues
Asian Bond Market Initiative
    (AMBI), 44
Asian Common Market, 43
Asian financial crisis of 1997-1998,
    economic integration fol-
    lowing, 42, 43–44
Asian Monetary Fund, 44
Asian Network, 43
Asian security environment,
    351–355. See also
    National security issues
Association of Southeast Asian
    Nations (ASEAN)
  foreign direct investment and,
    44–46, 45f
  percentage of trade with, 47f
  regional integration and, 41–44
  in South China Sea territorial dis-
    putes, 29
  Taiwanese trade with, 45, 46f
  world trade by region, 46f
Association of Southeast Asian
    Nations Plus Three (APT)
  gerrymandering in, 37–39, 38f
  in hub and spokes multilateralist
    strategy, 4, 33–34
  percentage of trade with, 47f
  world trade percentages, 46f
Association of Southeast Asian
    Nations Regional Forum
    (ARF), 37

H

Hacker wars, 257–259
Haiti peacekeeping mission,
119–120
Han Guang Exercise (Taiwan), 282
18th exercise, 281
Hawaii, U.S. forces in, 286
Helicopter capability development,
135
Henley, Lonnie D., 6, 7, 85, 348,
350
High-speed anti-radiation missile
(HARM), 16, 280–281
Horizontal escalation, 12, 89,
196
Hsu Tai-sheng, 339
Hu Jintao, 39, 87
Hub and spokes multilateralism
strategy
ASEAN Plus Three in, 33–34
defined, 32–33
effectiveness of, 39–40
gerrymandering in, 37–39, 38f
objectives of, 4, 39
other institutions in, 37
Shanghai Cooperative
Organization in, 34–35
Six-Party Talks in, 35–36
South Asian Association for
Regional Cooperation in,
36–37
Taiwan marginalization by, 40
vs. bilateral alliances, 39
Hwa Wei Satellite project, 270

I

India
attempts to marginalize, 34, 39

in multilateral system balance-of-
power, 36–37
Indonesia, 42
Information operations, 73. *See
also* Computer network
operations
patriotic hacking in, 14, 257–259
potential effectiveness of, 255–
259, 345–346
reliability of sources on, 243–245
in Taiwan scenario
effectiveness of, 14
focus on Taiwan, 246–249
focus on U.S., 250–255
unclassified network disruption
in, 245–246
Information Operations, 252
Information technology, in joint
campaign doctrine, 57
Initiative. *See* Preemptive attack
Intelligence operations. *See also*
Information operations
China, 248–249
Taiwanese, 270, 276
U.S., 296, 297, 302
International Institute for Strategic
Studies, 37
International security environment,
war control in shaping, 88
Intimidation, in war control, 7,
92–93
Ivanov, Sergei, 129

J

Jane's Defence Weekly, 340
Japan
air defense systems in, 300–301
air surveillance of, 123–124

Contributors

Michael D. Swaine is a senior associate in the Carnegie Endowment for International Peace's China Program. He has produced several seminal studies, which have expanded American and Chinese governmental officials' understanding of the Chinese military and its role in national security decision making, and Taiwan's national security decision-making process. Dr. Swaine spearheaded and currently co-directs a multi-year collaborative project on key aspects of Sino-American crisis management with a Beijing-based think tank. Dr. Swaine was named the first holder of the RAND Center for Asia Pacific Policy Chair, and also served as research director for the center. His most recent book is *Managing Sino-American Crises: Case Studies and Analysis* (Carnegie Endowment, 2006). He received a Ph.D. in government from Harvard University.

Andrew N. D. Yang has been on faculty at National Sun Yat-sen University since 1986, and is the Secretary General of the Chinese Council of Advanced Policy Studies (CAPS). He has trained as a security studies specialist particularly in the area of military competition and military balance in East Asia as well as PLA modernization and its impact on East Asia security.

Evan S. Medeiros is currently a senior political scientist at the RAND Corporation in the Washington, D.C. office. He specializes in research on Asian security affairs, China's foreign and national security policies,

U.S.-China relations, and Chinese military affairs. Prior to joining RAND, Dr. Medeiros was a senior research associate for East Asia at the Center for Nonproliferation Studies at the Monterey Institute of International Studies, in Monterey, California. He has recently published a book chapter titled "China's Evolving Nuclear Doctrine," as well as three RAND studies: *A New Direction for China's Defense Industry* (MG-334-AF); *Chasing the Dragon: Assessing China's System of Export Controls on WMD-Related Goods and Technologies* (MG-353), and *Modernizing China's Military: Opportunities and Constraints* (MG-260-AF). He holds a Ph.D. in international relations from the London School of Economics and Political Science, an M.Phil in international relations from the University of Cambridge, and an M.A. in China studies from the University of London.

Oriana Skylar Mastro was a junior fellow with the China Program at the Carnegie Endowment for International Peace during 2006–2007. She holds a B.A. from Stanford University in East Asian Studies with honors in International Security. Fluent in Mandarin Chinese, she will pursue a Ph.D. in politics at Princeton University beginning fall 2007.

* * * *

Kenneth W. Allen is a senior analyst at the CNA Corporation, where he deals with Chinese military issues. Prior to this, he was a senior associate at the Henry L. Stimson Center, executive vice president of the U.S.-Taiwan Business Council, and served twenty-one years in the U.S. Air Force (1971–1992), including assignments in Taiwan, Berlin, Japan, Hq Pacific Air Forces, and Washington, D.C. He also served as the Assistant Air Force Attaché in China from 1987 to 1989. He has written several books and articles on China's military. He received a B.A. from the University of California at Davis, a B.A. from the University of Maryland in Asian studies, and an M.A. from Boston University in international relations.

Dean Cheng is a senior Asia analyst at the CNA Corporation. He specializes in Chinese military and technology issues and has written extensively on Chinese military doctrine, China's space program, and China's military-industrial base. Prior to joining CNA, he worked for Science Applications International Corporation and the U.S. Congress Office of Technology Assessment.

Roger Cliff is a senior political scientist at the RAND Corporation specializing in East Asian security issues. His areas of recent research at RAND have included China's future military capabilities, Chinese perceptions of Taiwan, future U.S.-China security relations, Chinese antiaccess strategies, and China's aerospace industry. He is currently engaged in a study of Chinese air power. Dr. Cliff received his Ph.D. in international relations from Princeton University's Woodrow Wilson School of Public and International Affairs. He holds an M.A. in Chinese studies from the University of California, San Diego, and a B.S. in physics from Harvey Mudd College.

Bernard D. Cole (Captain, USN, Ret.) is a professor of international history at the National War College in Washington, D.C., where he concentrates on the Chinese military and Asian energy issues. He previously served thirty years as a Surface Warfare Officer in the Navy in the Pacific. He commanded USS *Rathburne* (FF 1057) and Destroyer Squadron 35 and served as a Naval Gunfire Liaison Officer with the Third Marine Division in Vietnam, Plans Officers for Commander-in-Chief Pacific Fleet, and special assistant to the Chief of Naval Operations for Expeditionary Warfare. Dr. Cole's latest books are *"Oil for the Lamps of China": Beijing's 21st Century Search for Energy* (Washington, D.C.: Institute for National Strategic Studies, National Defense University, 2003) and *Taiwan's Security: History and Prospects* (New York: Routledge, 2006). Dr. Cole earned an M.P.A. in national security affairs from the University of Washington and a Ph.D. in history from Auburn University.

Lonnie D. Henley is the Deputy National Intelligence Officer for East Asia in the Office of the Director of National Intelligence. He served twenty-two years as a U.S. Army China Foreign Area Officer and military intelligence officer in Korea, at DIA, on Army Staff, and in the History Department at West Point. After retirement from the army, he was Defense Intelligence Officer for East Asia and then senior intelligence expert for Strategic Warning at DIA. Leaving DIA in 2004, he worked for two years with CENTRA Technology, Inc., and rejoined government in 2006. He also teaches Chinese security issues at Georgetown University. He was educated at West Point; at Oxford University, as a Rhodes Scholar; at Columbia University; and at the Joint Military Intelligence College.

Roy D. Kamphausen is vice president of National Security Affairs and director of the Washington, D.C. office of the National Bureau of Asian Research. He is a retired U.S. Army China Foreign Area Officer and previously served as a military attaché in Beijing, intelligence analyst, strategic plans officer on the Joint Staff, and as the China Country Director in the Office of the Secretary of Defense.

Justin Liang is a program associate with the National Bureau of Asian Research, focusing on national security affairs and East Asian policy issues. He has worked in a research capacity at the East-West Center in Honolulu, Hawaii and the Asia-Pacific School of Economics and Government at Australian National University (ANU) in Canberra, Australia. A graduate of Princeton University, Liang earned an M.A. in international affairs (specializing in Asian security) from ANU, where he was a Rotary Ambassadorial Scholar and Hedley Bull Fellow.

Alex Liebman is a Ph.D. candidate in Harvard University's Department of Government. A 2001 graduate of Yale University, he spent two years studying, teaching, and traveling in China on a Yale-China fellowship. His work has been published in *The Chinese Journal of International Politics, Contemporary Southeast Asia,* and the *South China Morning Post.* His dissertation evaluates whether states rising in power cause conflict in the international system.

James Mulvenon is acting director of DGI's Center for Intelligence Research and Analysis, where he runs a team of more than a dozen Chinese linguist-analysts performing contract research for the U.S. government. Previously, Dr. Mulvenon was a political scientist at the RAND Corporation in Washington, D.C. and deputy director of RAND's Center for Asia-Pacific Policy. A specialist on the Chinese military, his current research focuses on Chinese C4ISR, defense research/development/acquisition organizations and policy, strategic weapons doctrines (computer network attack and nuclear warfare), patriotic hackers, military leadership and corruption, and the military and civilian implications of the information revolution in China. His book *Soldiers of Fortune* (Armonk, NY: M.E. Sharpe, 2001) examines the Chinese military's multi-billion dollar business empire. Dr. Mulvenon received his Ph.D. in political science from the University of California, Los Angeles.

Brad Roberts is a member of the research staff at the Institute for Defense Analyses in Alexandria, Virginia, with expertise on the proliferation and control of weapons of mass destruction. Dr. Roberts also serves as an adjunct professor at George Washington University and as a member of the board of directors of the United States Committee of the Council for Security Cooperation in the Asia Pacific. He has a B.A. from Stanford University, an M.Sc. from the London School of Economics and Political Science, and a Ph.D. from Erasmus University, Rotterdam.

Alan D. Romberg is a senior associate and director of the East Asia Program at the Henry L. Stimson Center in Washington, D.C. Among his government posts, he served as Principal Deputy Director of the State Department's Policy Planning Staff (1994–1998) and Principal Deputy Assistant Secretary of State and Deputy Spokesman of the Department (1981–1985). He was a C.V. Starr Senior Fellow for Asian Studies at the Council on Foreign Relations (1985–1994). He has written extensively on U.S. policy toward the People's Republic of China, Taiwan, Korea, and Japan. He is author of *Rein in at the Brink of the Precipice: American Policy Toward Taiwan and U.S.-PRC Relations* (Washington, D.C.: The Henry L. Stimson Center, 2003).

CARNEGIE ENDOWMENT FOR INTERNATIONAL PEACE

The Carnegie Endowment for International Peace is a private, nonprofit organization dedicated to advancing cooperation between nations and promoting active international engagement by the United States. Founded in 1910, Carnegie is nonpartisan and dedicated to achieving practical results. Through research, publishing, convening and, on occasion, creating new institutions and international networks, Endowment associates shape fresh policy approaches. Their interests span geographic regions and the relations between governments, business, international organizations, and civil society, focusing on the economic, political, and technological forces driving global change.

Building on the successful establishment of the Carnegie Moscow Center, the Endowment has added operations in Beijing, Beirut, and Brussels to its existing offices in Washington and Moscow, pioneering the idea that a think tank whose mission is to contribute to global security, stability, and prosperity requires a permanent international presence and a multinational outlook at the core of its operations.

The Endowment publishes FOREIGN POLICY, one of the world's leading journals of international politics and economics, which reaches readers in more than 120 countries and in several languages.

9 780870 032387